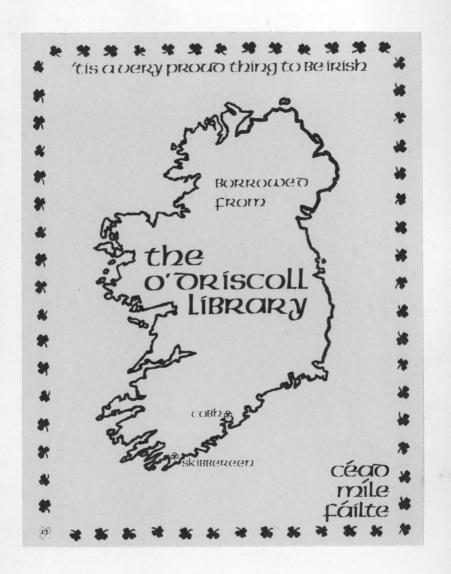

'tis a very proud thing to be irish

BORROWED
FROM

the
O'DRISCOLL
LIBRARY

COBH
SKIBBEREEN

céad
míle
fáilte

PARNELL

Chas. S Parnell

PARNELL

A Biography

By

JOAN HASLIP

Frederick A. Stokes Company

New York   1937

FOREWORD

In writing this book, I wish to express the deep debt of gratitude I owe first and foremost to Mr. Barry O'Brien's standard life of Parnell, and to Captain Henry Harrison's *Parnell Vindicated,* which is particularly valuable in showing up the inaccuracies of some of the later biographies, while in a more slender compass both T. P. O'Connor's *Parnell* and William O'Brien's *Parnell, the Real Man* supply a fund of personal anecdotes. I also wish to thank Dr. Best, of the National Library, Dublin, who has given me so much help and encouragement; to Mr. Basset of the British Museum for giving me permission to study the Gladstone papers, and the Hon. Charles Russell for putting at my disposal the uncorrected proofs of the Parnell Commission reports. My grateful thanks are also due to the dowager Marchioness of Aberdeen; to Mr. Joseph Hone; to Mr. Michael Macdonagh (who, as a correspondent of the *Freeman's Journal,* assisted at the meetings in Committee Room 15); to Mr. Shane Leslie; and to the staff of the London Library. And chiefly I want to pay a personal tribute to the memory of the late Robert Cunninghame Graham, who, with his human insight and kindly tolerance, helped me to understand the character of Parnell.

I have deliberately avoided footnotes, as I find they impede the reader's progress, but at the end of the book there is a full bibliography giving all the sources from which the text is drawn.

June 1936.   JOAN HASLIP

"In the opinion of an English Statesman, no man is good for Ireland, until he is dead and buried. Perhaps the day may come when I may get a good word from English Statesmen as being a moderate man after I am dead and buried."

PARNELL at Wexford, October 9th, 1881

CHAPTER ONE

PLANTED on the crest of the Wicklow hills, the square stone house looked out over the wide valley through which the river Avonmore threaded its way past groves of birches and silver firs. To the left was the little town of Rathdrum; beyond lay Avoca and Glendalough, bare gorse-scented moors and heather-tufted boglands and mountains scarred by the mark of quarries. The gardens stretched down towards the river with smooth lawns shadowed by giant beech-trees and azaleas blazing amidst the larches. With its kennels and stables, its summer-house and cricket pavilion, Avondale was the typical domain of the well-to-do Irish landlord, unpretentious and comfortable, dignified without laying any claims to architectural beauty. It was the home of the Parnells, who, in spite of their English descent, were as much a part of the country of their adoption as the granite house built from the stone of their local quarries.

Dublin had known Parnells ever since the days when Dean Swift and Tom Parnell, the Archdeacon of Clogher, exchanged their letters from Addison and Pope in the gray courtyards of Trinity. But there had only been Parnells at Avondale for two generations. Their ancestral estates lay in Armagh and Queen's County, and this Wicklow property was but a legacy bequeathed to the younger members of the family by a friend and admirer of Sir John Parnell, the incorruptible minister, who fought against the hated Union in the old Parliament on College Green. In latter days, Sir John and his sons had always been the first to support Ireland's claims in the hostile atmosphere of Westminster. Though belonging to the Protestant ascendency, they had taken part in the struggle for Catholic emancipation; though landlords, they had advocated Agrarian reform.

But the minister's grandson, John Henry Parnell, the present squire of Avondale, had no wish to mix himself up in the political dissensions of the day. He was content to lead the care-free life of the country gentleman, to be a magistrate and Deputy-Lieutenant for his county, to be Master of the local hounds and captain of his own cricket club. Agriculture was his dominating hobby, and he was far too much interested in the science of forestry and the reclaiming of his lands to pay much attention to the stormy meetings in Conciliation Hall, where O'Connell's fading glory was being challenged by the passionate youth of the Young Irelanders. Fastidious, cultured and utterly without ambition, he was content to drift peacefully through life, and his charm was such as to induce a spoilt little American belle to prefer his suit to that of his cousin Powerscourt.

At the age of twenty-one the two young men had set out on a grand tour through Mexico and the States, and in Washington they had both fallen to the charms of the lovely daughter of Commodore Stewart, the famous old "Ironsides" of the American Navy. Delia Tudor Stewart had been so spoilt and adulated that she could afford to reject the eligible peer and please her own fancy by marrying his cousin. This was the most adventurous deed of Mr. Parnell's life. She was barely eighteen when he brought her back to Avondale, and with her superabundant vitality, her hysterical enthusiasms and inordinate vanity, she was hardly likely to be a peaceful wife. The Parnells were proud of their lineage, but John Henry's American bride, sprung from the stock of sturdy Ulster emigrants, had a pride that was almost insane. Her grandfather, Tudor, had fought against the English in the War of Independence. During the Anglo-American hostilities of 1812, her father had earned the title of "the Yankee Nelson." According to popular hearsay, her mother's wedding gift had been two captured British frigates, and she hated England with the inbred, inherited hatred of the Irish exile. She was used to spectacular deeds and dramatic gestures, for ever since childhood she had lived in the glaring limelight of public approbation. It speaks for her strength of character that during the first twelve years of her married life she was willing to lead a calm settled existence at Avondale, where she gave vent to her excessive energy by producing eight children during this comparatively short period. But even the labors of child-bearing could not damp her exuberant spirits, and in the summer of 1846, as she sat nursing her eighth baby, she was still a lovely young woman, whom unfortunately her husband was beginning to find as tiresome as she was unmanageable.

In the brief intervals between her various confinements, she had discovered that she was politically minded, and her politics were of the kind most prone to irritate the local Wicklow gentry. The Howards, Powerscourts and Carysforts were horrified when their charming young friend professed herself to be a rebel, a "repealer," a "Tenant Righter." The flags of Grattan's Volunteers, which hung above the fireplace in the hall of Avondale, inspired her to wild, treasonable speeches. She devoured the inflammatory literature of Mitchell and Gavan Duffy; she sobbed over the poetry of Davies and Mangan, and her blue eyes flamed with anger when she held forth at Unionist dinner-parties on the cruelty of England's rule. Still, she had never been known to refuse any of the Lord Lieutenant's invitations. Her children's nurses were English, and when she planned their futures, there were always to be English schools and universities for the boys, and the glories of the London season for the girls. Dublin was considered far too provincial to be a proper setting for her offspring. In fact, Mrs. Parnell's patriotism was very theoretical, and when the dark clouds of the coming famine gathered on the horizon there was no landlord's wife in Ireland more *insouciante* than she.

Already, in the late autumn of 1845, English ministers in Whitehall were aware that, through a mysterious blight, one half of the potato crop in Ireland had failed. Sir Robert Peel's Government, conscientious but dilatory, badgered in turn by Protectionists and Manchester economists, hampered by all the complicated machinery of a red-taped bureaucracy, wasted precious months in appointing a scientific commission to enquire into the causes of Irish distress. In Downing Street they lacked the imagination to visualize peasants starving in

Connaught. Seized in the throes of a ministerial crisis, the coming Irish famine was nothing more than an election cry for the Free Traders. Sir Robert declared himself as a partizan of Cobden, and the Corn Laws were repealed. Still ships laden with wheat and oats sailed out of Irish ports while the Irish people died of hunger. With the exception of the potato, all the produce grown on the land belonged to the landlord. Estates heavily mortgaged by absentee proprietors, managed by ruthless agents, were rented in small holdings at exorbitant prices. The crops of corn and barley went to pay the rent; the potato fields represented the tenants' means of livelihood, and during the early spring of 1846 men had to stake their last pennies to buy foreign seed with which to strengthen their new crop. It was a fierce summer, with hot sultry days broken by wild storms of rain and thunder, and throughout the countryside the potato fields flowered green and luxuriant. Food was at famine prices, but the hungry people hoped for an ample harvest.

Disaster came in a single night. Towards evening on the first day of August a white, evil-smelling fog enveloped the country. In every province of Ireland, men saw this strange, thick mist floating over the fields. It was the same putrefying fog that had first heralded the blight the year before on the coast of Wexford. The potato harvest was doomed. By the 3rd of August the flowering fields were black, rotting wastes, and the entire cottier population of the country was faced with starvation. All during the winter the farmers had struggled, half naked and underfed, so as to save their precious crops. Now they were too weak even to protect their wheat and barley from the rapacious agents. Their wives and children died when in their own haggards stood stacks of corn, marked with the landlord's cross. Ignorant and unquestioning, they listened to the priests, who preached that the landlords must be paid their dues, while they put their trust in God. They had no leader, for, though there were the poets and dreamers of the *Nation* to inspire them with noble sentiments, there was no Robert Emmet to bid them take their pikes and fight for their families' lives. O'Connell was now a pathetic old man, who, while pleading his country's cause, still clung to the tail of the English Whigs.

Political economists reigned supreme at Westminster, for the Peelites had been defeated at the hustings and Lord John Russell, author of the most blundering Relief Act which ever passed into British legislation, propounded the doctrines of Free Trade to a starving nation. In Ireland, the public relief works, started by the previous Government, were suspended, and ninety-eight thousand persons were thrown out of employment, while Lord John, aided by a group of blue-stocking economists, drew up a Labour Rate Act, which remains to this day a monument to the crassness of officialdom. When the news of the total failure of the potato crop reached England, he met Parliament with a speech which, though full of good intentions, signed the death warrant for one million of Queen Victoria's Irish subjects. There was to be no interference of any kind with grain merchants and retailers, who were to be allowed to indulge in the wildest speculations at the expense of a famine-stricken population. According to the Reverend O'Rourke, corn representing the landlords' rent was sold to British merchants and sometimes crossed St. George's Channel as much as four times while English and Irish retailers speculated on the daily increasing prices. Relief works were to be started for which the Government was prepared to advance a considerable sum, but, in order to justify his principles, Lord John insisted that these works were to be strictly unproductive, so as not to compete with private enterprise. In a country where there were miles of bogland to be reclaimed and where there were whole districts without a single railway, the people were employed making roads leading to nowhere. The relief officers paid by task work, and the dire necessity of earning enough money with which to buy a handful of Indian corn forced the peasants to leave their own fields untilled, while those who were already too weak from starvation very often lacked the strength to complete their labors and died in hundreds on the roadside.

It was an artificial famine, for the crops of corn and oats and barley had never been more plentiful, and had the ports been closed to the export of food, and had profiteering been forbidden, black '47 need never have made such a dark blot on the history of British rule in Ireland. The hinged carts of Bantry and Skibbereen, from which loads of shroudless corpses were dropped into pits dug in the country churchyards; the pestilence raging in Irish workhouses; the coffin ships of the Atlantic filled with starving emigrants, many of whom never lived to see the American shores, were all the result of Lord John Russell's well-meaning but theoretical economics.

Two generations had passed since a Parliament of Irish landlords had legislated for their own country, and in those two generations the landlords had forgotten their obligations to their people. In many cases they were powerless to help; years of thriftless extravagance had landed them in the hands of moneylenders, and they were too busy keeping their heads above water to waste many tears over their famine-stricken tenants. The rents went to pay their debts, to enable them to live as gentlemen for a little longer before the Encumbered Estates Act swept them into penury. The great absentee proprietors were the curse of Ireland, for, in spite of deriving large incomes from their lands, they were still exempt from taxation, and it was only a few of the resident landlords who did their duty towards their tenants by renouncing their rents at a time when the daily increasing poor rates came out of their own pockets.

When one glances through the social chronicles of the times, one is amazed to read of the aristocracy going hunting and shooting, dancing and picnicking, all during the summer and winter of 1846. The Parnells followed their neighbors' example, but their tenants never went hungry. The failure of the potato crop, which spelt disaster in the stony plains of Connaught, did not have the same effect in the rich valleys of Leinster. There was want and poverty all over Ireland, but the ghastly scenes of death and pestilence were never witnessed in the Wicklow hills. Mr. Parnell gave up his rents, and his wife sent money to various charitable enterprises. But, though Delia cried with emotion when she read of the peasant women feeding their children with seaweed, it never entered her head to emulate those young English Quakers who, fearless of contagion, were nursing the sick in the workhouses of Cork and Mayo. Among them was a certain Mr. Forster, destined to become a minister of the Crown and Chief Secretary for Ireland; destined also by a cruel stroke of fate to become anathematized by the people he had served with such a selfless love, destined to put Charles Stewart Parnell into Kilmainham Jail.

Mrs. Parnell was not of the stuff of philanthropists and saints, and she would dry her lovely eyes in time to prepare herself for a picnic in the Arklow quarries or a garden party at Powerscourt, where she would exasperate the English officers by asserting in her slow, soft American voice that it was British misrule which had caused the people's sufferings. But never for a moment did she dream of altering the trend of her easy, pleasant life. Avondale was always full of guests for cricket matches and shooting-parties, and in that warm happy house, with the model dairies and well-stocked farms, her children never even knew of the existence of the famine. While Mrs. Parnell nursed her eighth baby, whom she called Charles Stewart after his famous grandfather, there were women in the south and west of Ireland with children starving at their shriveled breasts. Over thirty years were to pass before Charles Stewart Parnell heard the full tale of these horrors from the lips of Michael Davitt, born during the same year in a humble cabin in pestilence-ridden Mayo.

CHAPTER TWO

BLACK '47 passed, leaving the country as a giant graveyard. A new year dawned with a revolution born from despair. The leaders were poets and idealists, high-minded patriots, impractical dreamers; but not all the eloquence of John Mitchell nor the heroism of Smith O'Brien could rekindle the flame of rebellion in a disease-ridden, starving people. It was a pathetic revolution nipped in the very bud, and after all the inflammatory writings of the *Nation,* the long months of planning and secret meetings, there were just a few passionate days of insurrection and everything was over. The flower of the Young Irelanders were on their way to Australian convict settlements; the hills were scoured for fugitives, and informers thrived in the towns: '48 failed, as so many risings in Ireland have failed, owing to dissension among the leaders and hostility from the priests.

Then came the Encumbered Estates Act and the great clearances; landlords feverishly evicting their tenants in order to sell their properties as grazing land; a new class of proprietor coming into being—hard, sharp business men, who rack-rented the peasants ten times more than any thriftless, debt-ridden landlord; the steady flow of emigrants to America; Keogh and Sadleir posing as the people's champions in favor of Tenant Right, then betraying them at Westminster by currying favor with the Whigs; a gloomy, hopeless period, with Cardinal Cullen and his bishops ruling Dublin with rigid dogmatism, killing the united Nationalist sentiment which for a brief period had inspired Catholic and Protestant alike.

But under the beech-trees of Avondale life went on undisturbed by any event other than the birth or death of a young Parnell. Two children died in infancy and the eldest son was killed in the hunting-field. But the others thrived and prospered, and a band of gay, mischievous little creatures could

be seen running harum-scarum through the gardens, racing
donkeys across the lawns, and paddling for gold in the river.
They graduated in every age and size from Delia, who was
already a lovely young lady of fashion, to Theodosia, who was
little more than a baby. There were Emily, John, Sophy and
Charles, Fanny, Anna and Henry, and, though they all loved
one another with a fierce, loyal affection, they were incapable
of being together without having violent quarrels and scenes
of jealousy.

The most spoilt of them was Charles Stewart, who, with four
brothers and sisters older than himself and four younger, allowed himself all the vagaries of an only child. At first, he
was so small that he was nicknamed "Tom Thumb," so nervous
and highly strung that he could never be punished severely.
He once very nearly died as a baby owing to his mother having
thoughtlessly shut him up in the drawer of a large press when
an unexpected visitor came to call during his feeding-time. It
was only several hours later that his muffled yells brought his
nurse to the rescue.

Small wonder that the country people called Mrs. Parnell
a flighty woman, for, though she was devoted to her children,
she was quite incapable of looking after them. Bored by the
social amenities of the neighborhood and still more bored by
the domesticity of her home, there was little for her to do
except to pick quarrels with her husband. The children grew
up in an atmosphere of family rows and political discussions,
until their father declared once and for all that politics were
taboo at Avondale. A warm-hearted English nurse, called Mrs.
Twopenny, took charge of Charles Stewart when he was little
more than a baby, and she was the first person on whom he
lavished all the concentrated, possessive love of his shy, passionate nature. Clutching tightly to her hand, he would ex-
plore the beauties of his home, searching for birds' eggs among
the clumps of wild rhododendrons, watching the fish rise in
the river where the great flat stones took on silvery glints in
the sun. Ensconced on her knee, he would drive to the slate

quarries and watch the men striking fire into the hillside, and sometimes they would go as far as Aughavanagh to gather heather on the moors and drink bowls of buttermilk at the keeper's cottage.

Mrs. Twopenny taught him to love his own familiar surroundings. "There's no place like home," she told him, and his deep-rooted affection for Avondale was one of the dominant traits of his childhood.

As he grew older he developed into a despotic and self-willed little tyrant bent on outrivaling his brothers and sisters in any game or feat of daring. With his high spirits and mocking humor he could be an enchanting companion, and his elder brother John allowed himself to be completely dominated. Mrs. Twopenny fondly asserted that Charles was born to rule, and at the age of six he was so spoilt as to be utterly unmanageable. But there was another side to his character, an abnormal sensitiveness and reticence, which left him solitary and aloof in the midst of a large family. This intense reserve was coupled with a suspicious jealousy which made him ready to take offense at the slightest rebuff. There was something frightening and unbalanced about his sudden black rages, when he would threaten to smash a housemaid's head because she had clumsily broken half his collection of birds' eggs. At such moments his face would twitch with passion, strange lights would flame in his dark eyes, his voice would go shrill and harsh and his small hands would clench in rage. He never knew remorse or regret, and even as a child he could never be brought to apologize for any of his actions.

In 1852 his parents made the first of their desultory attempts to send him to school. He was still far too young and too delicate to go to the ordinary English boys' school, so they had the somewhat curious idea of sending him to a select academy for girls at Yeovil in Somerset. Though he was only a child of six, he bitterly resented the fact of having only girls to compete with, and he complained to his brother John that they bothered him out of his life by making up to him. At the end of his second term he fell ill with an attack of typhoid fever, which affected his brain, and from that time onwards, all during his life, he was subject to sudden attacks of somnam-bulism and periods of nervous prostration when he was liable to suffer from mental aberrations. The famous doctor who prescribed a peaceful life at home had no intimate knowledge of the Parnell family. He had no idea that the beautiful, pale-faced woman, who seemed so concerned over her son's health, was herself a victim to superstitious fears and fits of hysteria, nor that way back in the Parnell ancestry there lurked the shadows of inherited melancholia. Even Tom, "the sweet-mannered" poet beloved of Pope, had been affected with the malady, and the eldest son of Sir John Parnell had passed his life behind heavy grilles. In every generation there had been some harmless eccentric, some gloomy valetudinarian leading a solitary existence, but when John Henry, who himself pos-sessed an iron constitution, married the daughter of a hardy American commodore, the skeleton seemed safely buried. Ap-pearances were misleading, for Delia Parnell, who was capable of exhausting even her large, healthy husband, and who had given birth to twelve babies without losing her looks, and who thought nothing of traveling to and fro across the Atlantic, was by no means a strong woman. It was her taut nerves which gave her that over-abundant vitality, that inherent restlessness, which in later life made it impossible for her to remain in the same place for longer than a few weeks.

This nervous vitality, coupled with the Parnell temperament, was a dangerous heritage for the children growing up in the woods of Avondale. It would have been far better for Charles to lead an ordered, regulated life away from his mother's in-fluence, away from her dangerous, contradictory doctrines, which were so hard for a child to understand. She taught him to hate England, yet she had banished him there at the age of six, and when he was nine years old he was sent there again, this time to a proper boys' school at Kirk Langley in Derby-shire, where he was very happy for a few terms until ill health forced him to return to Avondale, where a series of inefficient governesses and tutors was put in charge of his education. The vicar of Rathdrum, who gave him Scripture lessons, found him impossible to teach, but his father's agent was amazed at the aptitude he showed for practical science. He would spend hours watching the men at work in the quarries, interested in every mechanical device for the cutting of the stone, and he was never so happy as when he was allowed to make some ingenious experiment of his own, whether it was draining out a pond or building a boat, making grapeshot out of molten lead or launching out on a dangerous display of fireworks. He had a clear constructive brain which was mainly interested in material things. Only his little sister Fanny knew how to touch the imaginative chord in his nature. With her ardent, enthusiastic temperament, she was the first to be influenced by her mother's political sentiments, and she would tell her brother stirring tales of Wolfe Tone and Napper Tandy, of Lord Edward Fitzgerald bleeding to death in prison and Dwyer fighting for his life on the boglands of Aughavanagh. The tin soldiers of their mimic battles, which took place in the old hay-loft, were always led by rebel heroes. These heroes were still alive for children who were allowed to run wild in the Wicklow hills, the birthplace of so many risings.

The great rebellion of 1641, the revolt of 1798, the last desperate attempt of Robert Emmet, had left hallowed places up on the gorse-scented moors, where many an old fort or roofless cabin was a place of pilgrimage. There was not a farmhand on the estate of Avondale who had not heard at his mother's knee of the massacres of '98, and there were certain stories which Fanny could not bear to hear, but which Charles would insist on being told a hundred times. Hugh Gaffney, the old gate-keeper, had been an eye-witness of some of the most terrible scenes of the rebellion, and he never tired of telling of how a poor wretch had been flogged at the end of a cart, with the flogging inflicted on his stomach instead of his back, so that his bowels protruded long before he was dead. Then he would point a withered finger to the sentry-box at Rathdrum, which was said to be haunted by the rebel's spirit. The boy, who listened to old Gaffney's tale with a curious detached air, as if he was not really interested, treasured every word so carefully that over twenty years later he told the story to a colleague without omitting a single detail of the narrative.

During the years to come there were to be counter-influences at work. There were his companions at Cambridge and in the Wicklow militia, who made him ashamed of his mother's Fenian friends; and, above all, there was his father, who, true to the traditions of his class, upheld the rule of Dublin Castle. Charles was a great favorite with his father, with whom he shared an enthusiasm for cricket and shooting, and when Mrs. Parnell found life at home so uncongenial that she decided to spend most of the year in Paris, it was Charles who remained in Ireland, while the rest of the family were transplanted to French schools and London drawing-rooms, where Delia and Emily created a sensation with their beauty.

After two brilliant seasons, Delia married an American millionaire living in Paris. She was a strange girl, with melancholy depths in her great dark eyes and a cold remote manner which enhanced her tragic beauty. Chaperoned by a worldly, calculating aunt, she accepted Mr. Livingstone Thompson's proposal merely because he was so much in love with her and had so much more money than anyone she had met before. Unfortunately, Emily had none of her social ambitions, and at the age of fifteen she had already formed a disastrous attachment for young Arthur Dickinson, the son of their nearest neighbor. He was the typical hard-drinking, hard-living good-for-nothing who has been immortalized in so many Irish novels, but he was sufficiently fascinating for Emily to remain faithful to his memory when, chaperoned by Lady Howard, she made the tour of the London ballrooms.

None of the younger Parnell children had any interest in Delia. To them she was a lovely, inanimate stranger who gave them expensive presents but never even wanted to kiss them;

and there is evidence to show that her adoring, jealous husband found her an equally unsatisfactory wife. Emily, on the contrary, was warm and loving, an ethereal little sprite, who was never too grown-up to join in their games or to inspire their most daredevil escapades, and who, though she was accounted one of the best dancers among the débutantes of her year, would take any amount of trouble in teaching her shy little brothers how to waltz.

In spite of his affection for his brothers and sisters, Charles did not regret their departure, and he was probably never so happy as during the few months he spent alone with his father. With his jealous, reserved nature, he was not made to lead a communal life, and, given a gun or a rod, he was perfectly content to spend the whole day by himself.

Then, one summer afternoon in 1859, John Henry Parnell suddenly fell ill while playing in a cricket match at Phœnix Park. He had been suffering from internal rheumatism (perhaps appendicitis), and had been warned by his doctor not to indulge in violent exercise. The advice was ignored, and by the time Charles reached the Shelbourne Hotel his father was dead. Charles was only thirteen at the time, a shy, reserved, undemonstrative boy, who had learned to love his father during the last months, and who was old enough to realize that the one steadying influence in his life had gone.

CHAPTER THREE

AFTER Mr. Parnell's death, all was confusion. His widow hurried back from Paris, to find that he had left her completely unprovided for and dependent on the liberality of her sons. The guardians quarreled among themselves, while an efficient Dublin solicitor took advantage of the situation to make surreptitious love to the fifteen-year-old Sophy. Finances were in a muddle, for, following the custom of his class, Mr. Parnell had always lived beyond his means, and his will was both complicated and unfair. Emily, his favorite daughter, was disinherited on account of her unfortunate love-affair. His eldest son, John, who was supposed to be heir-presumptive to a rich uncle, was saddled with the unproductive Armagh estate, additionally burdened by a head rent payable to Trinity College and by annuities for his younger sisters. By leaving Charles the family home, Mr. Parnell adhered to the tradition which decreed that Avondale should always pass to the second son.

The guardians declined to accept the responsibility of looking after their charges, and the young Parnells were made wards in Chancery, a conscientious uncle finding the necessary sum of money which would entitle Emily to the same privileges as her brothers and sisters. Avondale was let, the livestock was sold and the court granted Mrs. Parnell an allowance for the education of her children. The hardest condition enforced was that she was forbidden to take them out of the country, so for the next few years they lived in furnished houses on the Wicklow coast, where they came into closer contact with one another than they had ever been before. For the first time in their lives they were forced to practise economy—a noble effort on their mother's part, which lasted for a very short time. John and Charles became inseparable companions, and the injustice of their father's will made not the slightest difference to their relationship. Emily pined away for her worthless young captain, and Sophy, availing herself of one of Mrs. Parnell's rare illnesses, eloped to Scotland with the ardent solicitor. After being married at Gretna Green, she promptly returned to her mother's home, where she led a virginal life for the next five years, until she was dismissed as a ward of Chancery at the age of twenty-one. Her husband, Mr. MacDermott, had achieved his aim by marrying into the family, and he was far too careful a lawyer to run the risk of being punished by the courts for running off with their ward; so Mrs. Parnell still remained in happy ignorance of the misalliance of the loveliest of her daughters. Fanny spent her time writing precocious poetry, full of treasonable sentiments, which her mother recited with pride to her horrified relations.

It was while they were living at Kingstown that the news of the American Civil War broke over Europe. The fortunes of Ireland were closely interlinked both with North and South; among the soldiers of the Federal and Confederate armies were the survivors of black '47 and the revolutionists who had fought under the banner of Smith O'Brien at the ill-fated battle of Ballingary. Led by generals like Meagher and Sheridan, they began to realize their power as a fighting force, and it was among them that James Stephens spread the first germs of the Fenian movement, a political organization which aimed at separating Ireland from England and at establishing an Irish republic.

Old Mrs. Stewart was at this time visiting the Parnells, and the family divided themselves into violent partizanship either for the North or South, Charles supporting his mother in upholding the Federal States. Both mother and children would become so heated in these political arguments that on many an occasion physical force would be resorted to, with considerable damage both to crockery and furniture. It was characteristic of the Parnells to ignore the horrors of civil war, when brothers fought against brothers, for, in spite of their intense emotionalism, there was something slightly callous about them, a certain ruthlessness, which made them, however beautiful, however charming, curiously inhuman. Charles Stewart had the family trait to a marked degree. In his violent championship of the

North, he refused to conceive the possibility that there might be some justification for the other side. This inability to see anyone else's point of view was his strength and in a way his weakness. He was slow to form a decision, but, once he had made up his mind, he was inexorable, and it was only many years later, when he himself was a witness to the sufferings of the South, that he admitted the injustice of the reconstruction plan.

It was his grandmother who first made him aware of his American parentage, and, in the opinion of one of his colleagues, "Charles Stewart Parnell, both in physique and in character, was more of an American than of any other nationality. That slight frame, inspired by inflexible resolution and dauntless courage, was the type of the strange and picturesque and daring race which combines such extraordinary strength and enterprise of character with a physique more delicate in form and appearance than that of any other nationality in the Aryan world." Physically he resembled his grandfather, Stewart. He had the same aquiline features, well-shaped head and slim supple body, but his face was prouder, more finely bred, and there were strange, unquiet lights in the dark eyes. Already the young women, strolling along the piers at Kingstown, turned to look at him in appraisal and admiration, but at sixteen his attitude towards women was the same as when, as a child of six, he had complained that the little girls bothered him out of his life.

At last Mrs. Parnell realized that her sons were lamentably uneducated, and she received permission from the court to send them to an English crammer, where they could be prepared for Cambridge. Charles never felt at home in the peaceful rectory of Chipping Norton, where the cultured parson painted elegant water-colors, while his wife mothered all the young men under her roof. He was already a prey to nervous superstitions, and he made up his mind to dislike the place on the very day of his arrival, when he slipped in the doorway and almost fell through a pane of glass, then looked round to find a graveyard on the opposite side of the road. This trivial incident filled him with the gloomiest forebodings. John was popular with both masters and pupils, but Charles inspired the same sentiments as his mother, who, on her first appearance, had horrified the Reverend Mr. Wishaw by breaking out into invective against the British Government. The poor parson had never heard such treason in his life, and her son had the same gift for disturbing the peace of his surroundings. He was rude and obstinate and before he had been there a month he had managed to quarrel with most of his masters. He refused to take any interest in anything except science and mathematics, and when he was bored he was capable of sitting through a meal in complete silence. The mocking humor which delighted his family, the simplicity and charm of manner which made him so popular with his tenants, were never displayed either to his masters or his colleagues. When John remonstrated with him on his churlish behavior, he would reply, "My idea is to mind my own affairs and leave other people's alone." He was a difficult pupil to teach, as he would never admit a mistake, and once he went so far as to contradict Mr. Wishaw when he was construing a Greek play. The gentle-mannered parson tried to convince him by showing him the right words in the lexicon, but he calmly replied, "Yes, the lexicon says you are right, but I expect the lexicon is wrong." [1]

With all this dogged obstinacy, he had a strong inferiority complex; he always felt that every Englishman considered himself his superior, and he would say to John, "These English despise us just because we are Irish. We must stand up to them. That's the only way to treat them." As a young man he was obsessed by the idea that people looked down on him because he was Irish. This feeling prevented him from making any friends either at school or at Cambridge, and it is a curious coincidence that during the sixteen years he spent in the House

[1] In later years, when he misquoted some lines of Moore in one of his speeches, he assured Tim Healy that he thought his rendering of the verse was better than the original.

of Commons the only member outside his own party with whom he became at all friendly happened to be a Scotsman.[1]

He was always on the defensive, and his icy reserve got him the name of being arrogant and aggressive, but though his school-fellows disliked him they admired his skill at cricket and his readiness to fight boys much stronger than himself. His physical courage was one of his salient characteristics, and few people realized his constant struggle against nerves and ill health. There was something very brave and pathetic about the way in which he tried to cure himself of his attacks of somnambulism by tying his legs to the bed, and he once fell into a towering rage when he discovered that his mother had requested his valet to sleep in a neighboring room.

He spent two years at Chipping Norton and four at Cambridge, where he became a student of Magdalene College in the summer of 1865. But whether he was at school or at a university, he managed to spend most of the year in Ireland. Financial affairs were now settled, and Avondale was no longer let, but Mrs. Parnell still preferred to live in Dublin, and at his mother's house in Upper Temple Street, Charles Stewart heard the first warnings of the Fenian movement. The air was thick with conspiracy and mystery, and hard-faced desperadoes, engaged in secret missions, were constantly passing in and out of the door. In her passion for sensational excitement, Mrs. Parnell allowed her house to become one of the chief meeting-places for the rough-and-ready Irish-American officers, who slouched into her drawing-room smelling of whiskey and wet tweeds.

Fenianism was rampant in Dublin. Stephens and O'Mahoney were swearing in batches of disaffected Irish soldiers in every quayside tavern, and, as every secret movement in Ireland has to voice its sentiments through the organs of the Press, *The Irish People,* edited by John O'Leary, preached the doctrines of revolution under the very walls of Dublin Castle. Charles took an intense dislike to these revolutionary activities; the aristocratic

[1] The late R. B. Cunninghame Graham.

young Tory was unable to appreciate the nobility and heroism
of these men, who "weighed so lightly what they gave," and
who were willing to sacrifice their lives in an attempt to stir
the country out of the apathy and despair into which it had
fallen ever since the betrayal of the Tenant Right movement.
He chiefly resented the fact that his little sister, Fanny, should
prostrate herself at the feet of men like O'Donovan Rossa and
John O'Leary. Already, in 1863, she was writing impassioned,
patriotic verse in the columns of *The Irish People,* and even
John was afflicted with the general madness to the extent of
accompanying her on her visits to the newspaper offices. Not
that John was much of a Fenian, for, in reaction to their mother's
politics, both the brothers had enlisted as volunteers in the
Queen's militia. Curiously enough, Mrs. Parnell approved of
their joining the army; in spite of her revolutionary leanings,
she was still in assiduous attendance at every viceregal party.
Lord Carlisle, the Viceroy, was one of her most intimate friends;
and that cold-blooded cynic, who encouraged the evictions by
saying that "the more people who left Ireland, the more prosperous the country," must have been highly amused to hear Mrs.
Parnell expatiate on her loyalty to the Queen and her hatred
of the Government.

After a few weeks of Dublin, Charles was always ready to
get away to Avondale, his own home, of which he was now the
undisputed master. Fanny and John would accompany him,
and they would seek out the old places and the old faces they
had loved as children. Mrs. Twopenny was still there to take
them for long walks in the woods, and Hugh Gaffney's family
was now large enough to supply most of the servants in the
house. There were grouse to be shot on the moors at Aughavanagh and fish to be caught in the rivers, and on fine days there
were picnics among the ferns and moss-grown ruins of Glendalough. Neighbors came to call, and they re-found many old
friends, though none of the young Wicklow squires could make
Fanny forget the romantic beauty of John O'Leary. What a
relief it was for the shy, nervous boy to find himself back among

the people who had known him all his life and who accepted him as one of themselves. Nowhere in the world was he so happy as in his own home. Only then did he realize how much he hated England.

No wonder his career at Cambridge was undistinguished, considering he only spent a few weeks there in every term, and it is typical of the defensive, belligerent attitude which he always adopted in England that his career should have ended in a brawl. His years at the university left no mark on him. He hunted and played cricket and picked up acquaintances among the pretty girls in the neighborhood. Like most shy young men, he found it easier to get on with women of a lower class, and there were tea-shop girls and daughters of local farmers with whom he had passing affairs which he invested with a certain romantic quality. His sister, Mrs. Dickinson, in her very inaccurate biography, has tried to elaborate one of these flirtations into a grim and sordid tragedy for which there is absolutely no foundation. Curiously enough, several of Parnell's biographers have painted him as a sensuous libertine, whereas, in reality, he was singularly austere and pure in his relationships with women. Sex did not play a prominent part in his life, but he needed affection, and, even at the very height of his career, affection was a sentiment he rarely inspired. His family was devoted to him, but he lacked the most precious of all gifts, the art of making friends, and when Emily and Sophy married and John settled in America and Fanny became immersed in Fenianism, he found he was a very lonely man.

CHAPTER FOUR

THE Fenian movement had failed. In a crowded Dublin court-house, O'Donovan Rossa was being tried for high treason, and near the dock sat Fanny Parnell, with her great gray eyes over-brimming with tears, while a bunch of flowers faded in her hands. All day she had tried to summon up the courage to throw them at the prisoner, but she had been overwhelmed by his tragic bravery and the solemnity of the court. A raw young man from Skibbereen, he stood faced with years of penal servi-tude which would gradually transform him into a callous brute whose name was destined to strike terror into the hearts of every law-abiding citizen. The judge read out the terrible sentence and the court had the edifying spectacle of the lovely Miss Parnell bursting into tears because one of the Fenian murderers had been convicted. With her overheated imagination, Fanny already saw herself as the next occupant of the dock, with the prison doors clanking behind her. Her nerves were on edge; for weeks she had sat in the stifling court-houses, while heroes like John O'Leary were being marshaled to their trial. When she re-turned home in the evenings, she found that she was always followed by detectives, while her mother's house was under surveillance. Dublin was full of spies and informers; people mistrusted their nearest neighbors, and when members of the Protestant ascendancy took to dabbling in treasonous politics, even their friendship in high quarters did not protect them from the rigors of police espionage.

It was the winter of 1865. For the last year Fenianism had taken hold of the country. Even the army was disaffected, and in every village able-bodied young men enrolled themselves as members of the Irish Republican Brotherhood. At the end of the Civil War, hundreds of disbanded Irish-American officers landed in Ireland, and through their spies the officials of Dublin Castle heard rumors of an impending rising. But the movement, which seemed so strong, was doomed to failure. The Fenians had no arms; there was one rifle for every five hundred men and James Stephens had to placate his followers with promises of ammunition to be contributed by American sympathizers. A gun-running ship was sighted off the Irish coast; the British Government took alarm, and in the month of September the offices of *The Irish People* were seized by the police, the leaders were arrested and the Habeas Corpus Act was suspended. Then began the mockery of the Fenian trials, with packed juries, presided over by Judge Keogh, the most corrupt of all the judges on the Irish Bench.

Isaac Butt, the brilliant barrister and politician, who had started life as a scholar of Trinity and a champion of Conservatism, who as a young man had been singled out to confront O'Connell in the three days' debate on Repeal and whose Tory politics had not prevented him from espousing the national cause in defending the Young Ireland leaders in 1848, now undertook to be counsel for the Fenian prisoners. It was an open secret that a considerable part of his fees came out of the purse of Mrs. Parnell, and it was at his mother's house that Charles Stewart first met the future "Father of Home Rule." He was then at the very height of his profession, a genial, lovable man, popular in every stratum of society, generous to the point of foolishness, a noble-hearted patriot with a rare tolerance and understanding for human weakness, and Charles was just a handsome Cambridge undergraduate with an English accent and an undisguised disapproval of his mother's Fenian friends. He often complained that half the so-called patriots who called at Temple Street were nothing more than tramps and impostors, and on certain occasions he even went so far as to throw them out of the house.

It is curious that it should have been the Fenian cause which brought Isaac Butt and Parnell into their first personal contact; that it should have been the influence of Fenianism which made the Tory barrister declare himself the advocate of Home Rule, and that in the end it should have been the Fenians who deposed him in favor of the young Wicklow squire.

Of all the men who dedicated their lives to Irish Nationalism, one of the most selfless was Isaac Butt. When he undertook to defend the rebel prisoners, he gave up all his other briefs, and the very hopelessness of the cause inspired him to some of his most brilliant flights of rhetoric. He gives, himself, a touching testimony to the prisoners' high sense of honor:

"I was placed towards most of them in a relation which gave me some opportunity of observing them in circumstances that try men's souls. Both I and those that were associated with me in that relation have often been struck by their high-mindedness and truthfulness, that shrunk with sensitiveness from subterfuges, which few men in their position would have thought wrong. No mean or selfish instruction ever reached us. Many, many messages were conveyed to us, which were marked by a punctilious and almost overstrained anxiety to avoid even a semblance of departure from the strictest line of honor. There was not one of them who would have purchased safety by a falsehood, by a concession, that would have brought dishonor on the cause, or by a disclosure that would have compromised the safety of a companion. They were enthusiasts of great heart and lofty minds, and in the bold and unwavering courage with which one and all they met the doom, which the law pronounced upon their crime against its authority, there was a startling proof that their cause and their principles had power to inspire in them the faith and the endurance which elevated suffering into martyrdom."

The trials dragged on. There was a panic at the Castle when James Stephens escaped from captivity, and the abortive rising of 1867 brought fresh prisoners to the dock. Mrs. Parnell, no longer content merely to finance the Fenians, now became actively involved by sheltering suspects in her house. She even helped one man to escape to America by disguising him in her own clothes, and one night Fanny Parnell came home to find the police clamoring at the door. She and her mother were living alone at this time, and, in spite of their indignant protests, the detectives insisted on searching the house. Fanny's answer was to pack her clothes and spend the night at a neighboring hotel. Dublin gossips found plenty to say on the subject of Mrs. Parnell spending the night with police in the house while her eighteen-year-old daughter went unchaperoned to an hotel. All that the detectives discovered was a sword belonging to Charles's militia uniform, which they carried off in the fond belief that it was a Fenian weapon. In spite of her indignation at their behavior, Fanny had enough sense of humor to enjoy writing to her brother that the police had walked off with part of his uniform. Charles was at Cambridge when he heard the news, but he hurried back to Ireland, furious with the Castle authorities, not only for their impudence in taking his sword but for daring to search his mother's bedroom and turning his little sister out of the house. In his rage, he said, "I will give the police something better to do than turning my sister into the street."

Those words of wounded pride were strangely prophetic. Actually, both Fanny and her mother rather enjoyed being raided by the police. It was Fanny's highest ambition to be labeled as a Fenian, and she even went so far as to write poetry describing her titled relations as "coroneted ghouls, trampling on the liberties of the people."

In spite of being thoroughly irritated by the whole business, Charles found that the only way to deal with her hysterical patriotism was to treat it all as if it were a joke. He resented the chaffing he had to endure from his brother officers on the subject of his missing sword. And chiefly he resented the fact that any member of his family should be mixed up with a gang of revolutionaries. Luckily, his mother began to be slightly disheartened by Irish politics. She may also have realized that her pretty daughter would be better employed in gracing a Parisian ballroom than in conspiring in a Dublin back street; so, with the benediction of the courts, Mrs. Parnell and the younger members of her family took up their residence in Paris.

In the year 1867, while revolutionary centers were being raided all over Ireland and Fenian organizers were being arrested in the streets of Manchester and Liverpool, Charles Stewart Parnell celebrated his coming-of-age in his Wicklow home. It was all done in the proper traditional spirit, and during the three days' festivities there was not a farm-hand or guest who did not go reeling to bed at night. The entertainment was organized by Arthur Dickinson, who, since he had married into the family, showed a real flair for spending their money. He had given up his commission in the army and was now living comfortably on his brother-in-law, hunting his horses and making free with his cellar. Ostensibly, he was supposed to be a land agent and to look after John Howard's property in Armagh, but he displayed more talent for organizing a party than for collecting rents. Charles was delighted to have the Dickinsons living with him, for they brought life and gaiety to Avondale. Emily was an enchanting hostess and Arthur was the best of companions. Between them they filled the house with hard-drinking officers and pretty women, and no squeamish morals prevented Emily from having what she called a "real spree." During the three days' cricket match held in his honor, the young host was the only member of the house-party who went to bed sober. Naturally, most of his female guests tried to make love to him. His romantic good looks were very appealing: that beautiful mouth, with just a touch of weakness; those piercing red-brown eyes, which gave such frank looks of appraisal and then suddenly softened in a charming smile. Even his voice was hard to resist —that low, clear monotone, hesitant, questioning, but never really waiting for the answer, as if he were merely questioning himself and slowly forming his own decision. He was very ready to flirt with his pretty visitors when he took them for moonlight walks by the river, but the next morning at breakfast they would find him curiously unapproachable, wrapped up in his own interests and utterly indifferent to them. During the daytime he concentrated on cricket, and, though he was a firm and somewhat tyrannical captain, he had the greatest difficulty in disciplining a team which showed much more inclination for philandering under shady trees than for running about in the hot sun.

The fame of this party spread through the country. There were stories told of officers breaking into a widow's bedroom and of drunken orgies in which flirting was carried beyond the accustomed limits. The neighbors were shocked, but the more indulgent said that Charles was only sowing his wild oats and mothers with marriageable daughters looked benignly on the owner of Avondale with a rent roll of four thousand a year.

Meanwhile in the village of Haslingden, in Lancashire, a one-armed Irish workman called Michael Davitt celebrated his coming-of-age by offering himself as a volunteer in the Fenian raid on Chester Castle.

CHAPTER FIVE

In September 1867 the prison van which was conveying two Fenian leaders from the police courts to Salford Jail was attacked in the streets of Manchester. The prisoners were rescued, but the shot which fired the lock and set them free accidentally shot a police sergeant, and for this unpremeditated crime three men, Allen, Larkin and O'Brien, were tried and sentenced to death. Political feeling ran high at the time; there were rumors of dynamite plots and of secret stores of ammunition. The whole of the north of England was in a panic of fear and loathing of the Irish Fenians. Years later, John Bright said: "I believe that the three men were hanged because it was a political offense and not because it was an ordinary murder of one man committed by one man and by one shot. I believe it was a great mistake."

There is no doubt that the injustice of the execution of the Manchester Martyrs helped to cement the foundations of the great Nationalist movement, in which men of every class and of every creed united in their struggle for independence.

On a November dawn, Allen, Larkin and O'Brien were hanged in the yard of Salford Jail. All night long a howling mob had danced and jubilated outside the prison, singing "Rule, Britannia!" There was no pity for the prisoners, though they had all solemnly sworn at their trial that they had no intent to kill. It was enough that they had gloried in their treason, that on hearing their sentence they had all cried out: "God save Ireland!" In the eyes of the English people, they were murderers and traitors.

The news of their death filled Ireland with bitterness and sorrow. The courage with which they had met their fate inspired T. D. Sullivan to write the lines with the refrain of "God save Ireland"—lines which, to this day, are sung at every Irish gathering throughout the world. Commemorative funeral processions were held all over the country in which constitutional

Nationalists and revolutionists walked side by side. Professors of Trinity College and Catholic bishops joined in the cause of justice. The leaders were in prison, but Fenianism was more prevalent than ever. A member of the Irish Republican Brotherhood told Mr. Barry O'Brien that they had a stronger hold on the country after the rising than they had ever had before, for they had thousands of new sympathizers, who would never have touched them in 1865.

Among their new sympathizers was Charles Stewart Parnell. The courage and chivalry of the men, who in broad daylight had rescued their comrades in the crowded streets of a hostile town, filled him with admiration. He was at Cambridge when he read of the executions, and his natural dislike of the English became intensified by this travesty of justice. The hanging of three men for one accidental murder struck him as both cowardly and brutal; it was the act of a panic-stricken Government, pandering to the people's thirst for blood. He knew nothing of Irish politics and of Irish history, for in those days he hardly ever read a book, but the Parnells had always been Nationalists and he remembered the stories which his mother used to recount of his great-grandfather, Sir John, who had fought against the Union to the very last, uncorrupted by the wiles and bribes of Pitt and Castlereagh. When he heard old Gaffney's tales of the rebellion, he felt himself to be a Wicklow man first and an Irishman afterwards, and his English ancestry was buried in the annals of time.

There were many things for Charles to brood over during those months at Cambridge: the humiliation of having had his mother's house searched by the police and of having his sister treated as a suspect. Where was the renowned English justice, when untried prisoners were kept in solitary confinement and young boys were sent to penal servitude on the perjured evidence of some paid informer? Half involuntarily he found his sympathies veering towards the Fenians, but then came the dynamite explosion at Clerkenwell, in which innocent people were killed and maimed, and he was far too sensitive and fastidious to feel anything but horror for the men who had planned such a desperate outrage.

It was Fenianism which taught Mr. Gladstone the depths of Irish disaffection, which forced the disestablishment of the Irish Church in 1868 and the Land Bill of 1870. He himself declared in the House of Commons: "In my opinion and in the opinion of many, with whom I communicated, the Fenian conspiracy has had an important influence with respect to Irish policy. The influence of Fenianism was that when the Habeas Corpus Act was suspended, when all the consequent proceedings occurred, when the overflow of mischief came into England itself, when the tranquillity of the great city of Manchester was disturbed, when the metropolis itself was shocked and horrified by an in-human outrage, when a sense of insecurity went abroad far and wide—then it was when these phenomena came home to the popular mind and produced that attitude of attention and pre-paredness on the part of the whole of the population of this country, which qualified them to embrace in a manner foreign to their habits in other times the vast importance of the Irish controversy."

The horrors of the dynamite explosion, which finally led the English to lend a listening ear to the Irish claims which they had ignored year after year, deterred Charles Parnell from tak-ing any further interest in politics. Occasionally, while riding through the countryside with his sister, Emily, he would make some remark about the Manchester executions, but as Emily, apart from being a whole-hearted Unionist, had very little in-terest in politics, she was hardly a sympathetic audience.

In 1869 Charles was sent down from Magdalene College on a charge of misconduct. A case had come up before the County Court in which a local merchant, named Hamilton, claimed damages against him for alleged assault. Hamilton asserted that, while driving home one evening, he came across two drunken men sitting on the roadside. When he stopped to offer assistance, one of them said: "We want none of your damned help," while the other one sprang up and knocked him down. Parnell's version was that he and the other undergraduate were perfectly sober and were merely waiting for some other members of their party who had gone off in search of a fly. Mr. Hamilton had accused him in the grossest language of being drunk, and the only answer to his impertinence was to knock him down. A police constable gave evidence that Parnell was sober at the time, but the assault was admitted and he had to pay considerable damages.

The college authorities decided to send him down for the remainder of the term, and, had he wished it, he could have returned to take his degree, but academic honors held no charms for him. There was far more important business to be seen to at Avondale, where there were slate quarries to be developed and land to be reclaimed and new saw-mills to be built, out of which he hoped to make a profitable income. Four thousand a year did not go very far when, apart from the claims of a big estate, he had not only an extravagant mother to support, but also his sisters, whose small annuities hardly covered their dressmakers' bills.

None of the Parnell girls had any idea of money; it just drifted through their fingers, whether it went to pay for a creation of Worth or a pension for some Fenian widow. They were living with their uncle in Paris, where Fanny was being fêted as *la belle Americaine*. Poets and artists paid tribute to her wit and beauty, and the little conspirator of Temple Street now graced the balls of the British Embassy. Her brother thought nothing of coming over from Ireland for one of these parties, and in the last days of the Second Empire, when the Napoleonic eagles still flaunted above the Tuileries, before the Prussian cannon shattered the last of the courts immortalized by Winterhalter, the young Parnells took their place among the fashionable crowds who rode in the Bois in lemon kid gloves and trailed their taffeta petticoats across the parterres of Auteuil.

In Ireland the great amnesty movement was on foot. Isaac Butt had not forsaken his clients in their prison cells, and had inspired the country to unite in protesting against the injustice of their confinement. In England the raid on Chester Castle had failed, and the evidence of a vile informer, named Corydon, was sending young Fenian idealists, like Michael Davitt, to years of hell in Dartmoor Prison.

Amongst his Wicklow neighbors and in his uncle's house in the Champs-Élysées, Charles Parnell heard little talk of politics. Occasionally Fanny still found the time to pay surreptitious visits to the dubious Irish revolutionaries who plotted fantastic conspiracies in the cafés of Montparnasse, and she would come home and tell her brother of the growing strength of the American Fenian Society, the "Clan-na-Gael."

The rich Americans who frequented Charles's uncle's house in Paris and his sister's palace at St. Germain had very little sympathy with revolutionary movements. They were railroad pioneers and lumber kings in search of European culture, with wives and daughters whose greatest ambition was to curtsey to the Empress Eugénie. Among the lovely heiresses who drifted through the Paris drawing-rooms was a Miss Woods, with whom Charles fell in love at first sight. She was radiant, vivacious and self-assured, and her metallic brilliance fascinated the diffident young man who, in spite of his sophisticated appearance and frigid manner, still treasured all the dreams and doubts of adolescence; but perhaps her greatest charm lay in her spontaneous vitality and boisterous health, which made her such a glowing contrast to his delicate, nerve-ridden sisters. She was supremely normal, and, like so many of her class and kind, she was a theoretical idealist and a practical materialist at heart. She was idealist enough to allow herself to fall in love with the handsome young Irishman, who attracted every woman's attention when they rode together in the Bois. The fact that he was the grandson of Admiral Stewart appealed to her romantic sense, but at the same time she worshiped at the altar of success. In the America of 1870 men set out to conquer new tracts of territory and returned to lay their spoils before their brides. It was all very primitive but very reassuring for a woman's pride, and in Charles Parnell the spoilt little heiress found none of the driving-force which would inspire him to be anything more than a simple country gentleman. In her egotism she resented the fact that he showed no wish to make a career for her sake. Still, he was sufficiently ardent and sufficiently fascinating to conquer all her doubts, and by the end of the summer they were engaged. He loved her with the passionate, exclusive love of which the Parnells were capable. He was moody, jealous and possessive, and she was flirtatious, cold and virginal. There were quarrels and reconciliations and there must have been moments when she was frightened by the strength of his passion, moments when those strange red lights in his eyes made her doubt his sanity.

Maybe it was in a sudden panic of fear that Mary Woods decided to accompany her parents to Rome, without so much as bidding Charles good-by. Owing to the force of his physical infatuation, this temporary separation left him utterly despondent. He returned to Ireland but was unable to concentrate on any business. He ignored his neighbors and roamed the hills like any love-sick boy. After a month he could stand the separation no longer and pursued his *fiancée* to Rome. Flattered and touched by his ardor and genuinely pleased to see him again, the capricious beauty gave him a warm welcome, and after an idyllic winter he returned to Avondale to prepare his home for the arrival of his bride. In Rome she had convinced him that she loved him, his doubts and jealousies had vanished, and he was a normal, happy young man, ready to take up his position in the county, to beget a family, and to settle down to a quiet peaceful existence. Then one day he received a letter from his *fiancée* telling him that she was going back to America, expressing no wish to see him and no regrets at her departure, and never once mentioning the fact of their engagement.

CHAPTER SIX

In the spring of 1872, John Howard Parnell, of Westpoint, Alabama, received a telegram from his brother announcing his arrival. It was sent from Newport, Rhode Island, for with dogged obstinacy Charles had pursued his *fiancée* across the Atlantic. In the alien atmosphere of a fashionable resort he managed to make her understand some of the misery and heartache she had made him suffer and for a short while she let him believe that she still cared for him. She was as charming and as affectionate as ever. Then one evening she told him quite bluntly that their engagement was canceled, as she could never bring herself to marry an obscure Irish country gentleman, who had no higher ambitions than the running of his estate. She added that she needed a brilliant and famous husband whom she could respect as well as love.

This is the story told by all Parnell's biographers and verified by members of his family. Still, it is hard to believe that even the most mercenary and materialistic young woman would deliberately hurt her lover's pride to this extent unless she had been actuated by some deeper motive. It is doubly hard to believe in view of the fact that a few years later Miss Woods was content to settle down with a drab, unromantic young man with no claim to either position or fame.

There may have been other reasons which prevented her from marrying Parnell—the instinctive fear of a very normal person towards someone who is unbalanced. His unreasoning fits of jealousy and rage must have been hard to forget for a girl who had been idolized and spoilt since her childhood and who had never been contradicted in her life. There must have been moments when she dreaded the idea of living with him in a strange country far from her relations and friends. She had seen his lovely sister, Delia, fretting herself into a state of melancholia in her palace at St. Germain, embittering her husband's life by her brooding silences, and she knew that Anna was afflicted with

34

sudden fits. There was something odd about the Parnells, something that made her feel slightly uneasy, and her lover's morbid
suspicions and strange moods may have given her an unpleasant
foretaste of what her life would be. Still, there is no excuse for
the way in which she dismissed him without even a word of
tenderness or apology. In all the months that she had known
him, she had never learnt to understand or appreciate the quality
of his love. She was a cold-blooded materialist, trying to delude
herself that she was a romantic idealist, and in her unconscious
cruelty she ruined Parnell's youth.

It was nine years before he ever looked at another woman
with anything but suspicion and mistrust. In a way Mary
Woods can be held responsible for those nine years of loneliness,
for those casual, promiscuous affairs out of which Parnell never
got any satisfaction, and those long periods of unnatural auster-
ity; the empty rooms of Avondale, the dreary Bloomsbury lodgings, the sordid little adventures in railway hotels. When he
finally met a woman whom he not only loved but trusted, all
his natural craving for affection, all the starved passion in his
nature, made that love develop into an obsession which swept
aside every scruple and regret.

Charles arrived in Alabama in a gloomy, despairing mood,
bringing a restless, disturbing element into his brother's peaceful
life. John was perfectly contented, growing his peaches and
cotton, superintending negro labor and fraternizing with the
kind of Irishmen whom he would never have met in his own
country. Charles did nothing but complain of the greasy Southern food, the insolent familiarity of the newly enfranchized
negroes and the discomfort of the hotel where he had been forced
to stay the first night and where he had to share a room with
half a dozen of his not very cleanly compatriots. This primitive
life was not fit for a Parnell, and it was galling to think that
the Americans who had never seen an Irish gentleman in their
lives might class him together with the emigrants who were
crowding into Alabama to seek their fortunes in the newly discovered coal-mines.

The inferiority complex from which he had suffered in his schooldays was now stronger than ever; an American girl had jilted him because he was a mere Irish country squire. He was so abnormally sensitive on this subject that when he and his brother visited the pioneer of the Alabama collieries, he was convinced that they would have been treated with more respect if the man had not known their nationality. He told John, "You see, that fellow despises us because we are Irish, but the Irish can make themselves felt everywhere if they are self-reliant and stick to each other. Just think of that fellow, where he has come from, and yet he despises the Irish!" His feeling for Irish unity did not prevent him from having a stand-up fight with an Ulster man who dared to criticize the house which John was building for him on his estate. In later years the man was proud to remember that he had once been knocked down by the great Irish leader, who, white with fury, had told him that his house was far too good for him.

The heartache and humiliation which Charles had suffered during the past months had had a bad effect on his whole nervous system. On his first arrival in the South he suffered from acute indigestion and insomnia, and he would spend hours shut up in his room, sunk in a state of apathy; then gradually he began to take a new interest in life, and, together with John, he visited cotton-mills and factories, coal-fields and lumber depots. The hard, primitive country, which at first he had disliked and despised, began to take a hold on him. He felt the urge to work, spurred on by that underlying driving-force he had inherited from his American ancestors. He was obsessed by the longing to justify himself in his own eyes, to rid himself of the stigma of being a mere Irish country squire. With his practical mind and taciturn speech he found it easier to get on with the hard American business men than with the young gentlemen of leisure he had met at Cambridge and in Paris, and soon he was involved in speculations on Wall Street and in signing contracts to supply Irish-made goods for the American markets—

goods that could be manufactured on his own estate at Avondale.

The South was still suffering from the after-effects of the Civil
War. The famous Fourteenth Amendment, enforced at the
point of the bayonet, had paralyzed private industry and enterprise. A Government under the control of negroes and poor
whites in States where the colored population outnumbered the
whites had been nothing short of disastrous. The country was
recovering, but there had been much unnecessary bitterness and
humiliation which could never be forgotten. Charles Parnell,
who had grown up as a staunch adherent of the Federal cause,
now saw the injustice with which men like Stevens and Sum-
mers had hounded down their former enemies. He saw the
Southern States reduced to the position which Ireland occupied
in the British Empire, and, as his sympathies veered round to
the defranchized leaders of the Confederate armies, his thoughts
turned back to politics. It was in America that he first realized
the dormant strength of the Irish people. All over the continent,
through their industry and enterprise, the victims of the Great
Clearances and the survivors of the famine had proved themselves to be first-class colonizers. They were to be found in every
stratum of society. He met millionaires and State governors
who had landed on the shores of Hudson Bay as starving Connaught peasants. Given a fair chance, the Irishman was capable
of holding his own with any race in Europe. It was the iniquitous injustice of the land system which destroyed him in his
own country.

"If Irishmen were self-reliant and stuck to each other, they
could make themselves felt everywhere"—this idea had been
slowly maturing in Parnell's mind ever since his schooldays. He
was to prove it in the British House of Commons, when he and
his seven lieutenants defied Disraeli's ministry; he was to prove
it by prevailing on Irish-American sympathizers to supply the
exchequer of the Land League.

But all his political ideas were still in a hazy, unformed state.
He was very slow at making up his mind or taking any deci-

sion, but, once he had adopted a certain course, he never turned back. An old retainer of the family told Mr. Barry O'Brien, "If it was only the picking up of a piece of stick on the ground, Master Charles would take about half an hour thinking of it. He never would do anything at once, and when he grew up it was just the same. I would sometimes ask him to make some alterations about the place. 'I will think of that, Jim,' he would say. Then he would come back maybe in two days' time and say, 'I have considered it all,' and would do what I asked or not, just as he liked."

In the new year of 1872, Charles returned to Ireland, suffering from a severe nervous shock following a railway accident in the Alabama coal-fields, in which he and his brother narrowly escaped being killed. Shortly beforehand, on the river-front of New Orleans, an old negro had prophesied to him that he was about to die. On the morning of the accident he met John at the junction of Montgomery and changed from his sleeping-car into a day carriage. When the train became derailed, the sleeping-car was burnt to cinders. This escape increased his superstitious fears, and for months afterwards he was a prey to gloomy presentiments.

John was severely injured in the accident, and the two brothers were forced to stay in a primitive hotel in the center of the mining district, where not only were they made to share the same bed and feed on pieces of half-cooked bacon, but where they had no nursing or attendance other than the occasional visit of an Irish priest. John gives a touching account of how Charles, in spite of his own injuries, nursed him as tenderly as any woman, never leaving him for a moment. During the past months the two brothers had recaptured the old intimacy of their childhood. With painful difficulty Charles had confided the bare outline of his unfortunate love-affair, and John had respected the confidences and never questioned any further. It was pathetic to see how much Charles depended on him in his loneliness, so that finally John let himself be persuaded to return with him to Ireland.

The year 1872 brought wealth to the Parnells. Sir Ralph Howard died, leaving John as one of his principal heirs. Mr. Stewart had a fatal attack of Roman fever and Mrs. Parnell, instead of being dependent on her sons, now came into a large fortune, so that her daughters were able to indulge in their wildest extravagances. Fanny, looking frail and lovely in her expensive furs, stood waiting for her brothers on the snow-bound pier at Queenstown. They had hardly stepped inside the hotel at Cork before she told them all about her latest love-affair with a penniless painter. In Dublin, Emily Dickinson gave a series of rowdy parties in their honor, where, with hysterical gaiety, she made a brave attempt to conceal the fact that she was miserably married to a hopeless drunkard. Sophy was the only sister who showed no ability for spending her mother's money, and she was losing her ethereal beauty in a life of dreary domesticity, while Anna was following in Fanny's footsteps by bearing banners at amnesty meetings and indulging in romantic attachments for republican leaders.

A new movement was on foot. The amnesty meetings, in which constitutionalists and revolutionists had joined in demanding the release of the Fenian prisoners, had inspired a strong national sentiment all over the country. The disestablishment of the Irish Church and the Land Act of 1870 had come too late to stem the tide of political discontent. It was in vain that Mr. Gladstone hoped to settle the Agrarian question with a Land Bill mangled by the House of Lords.

Before 1870 a tenant held his farm under a yearly tenancy, and was liable to eviction at six months' notice, while he was not entitled to any compensation for the improvements he had made on his holding. Only in Ulster was there a custom entitling the farmer to claim the value of his improvements from the landlord or incoming tenant; and this same custom, unsanctioned by the law but enforced by the strong combinations of farmers and agreed to by the landlords, admitted that a tenant should be allowed to remain in possession as long as he paid his rent, which should not be put up excessively.

Mr. Gladstone's scheme was to enforce the Ulster Tenant Right system all over Ireland. There was to be compensation for improvements as well as a payment for the tenant's "goodwill," which was not to be paid in the case of his having been evicted for refusal to pay rent, unless the judge authorizing the eviction said it was due to exorbitant rent or failure of crops.

But the English Parliament was not prepared for such a sweeping measure of land reform, and the Bill was mutilated by amendments and subsidiary clauses. The landlords still kept the power to raise their rents, and though on such occasions the tenants could renounce their holdings, there was no fixity of tenure or right of sale, nor were they entitled to any compensation unless they had paid up to the latest gale day. Evictions were still as numerous as ever and the emigration ships as crowded.

Isaac Butt, the genial, expansive barrister who had pleaded the Fenian cause so eloquently in the criminal courts of Green Street and who had discoursed on Tenant Rights to indifferent audiences at Westminster, now realized that the only salvation for his country lay in a Federal Parliament with the right of managing her own internal affairs. To revive the old repeal agitation of the 'forties would frighten the moderate Nationalists from joining the movement. The term "Home Rule," invented by a Trinity professor, satisfied the aspirations of the Whig gentry and Tory patriots while it held out hopes to the Fenians of a future Irish Republic.

In the spring of 1876 the first Home Rule Association of Ireland, a remarkable gathering of men of every faith and of every political creed, met at the Bilton Hotel in Dublin to protest against legislative union with Great Britain.

CHAPTER SEVEN

It was John Parnell who first broached the subject of politics on a summer morning in 1873, while the two brothers were enjoying a hearty breakfast. At Avondale, breakfast took place at noon and was combined with lunch, for Charles had a habit of staying up half the night and not coming down till late in the morning. It was an incongruous meal, with porridge and cream, and eggs, and mutton chops, and every variety of home-made bread baked by Mrs. Gaffney. There was never much conversation over the breakfast-table, for Charles disliked talking while eating; and the brothers sat in silence, until John remarked over the sheets of the *Freeman's Journal,* "Charles, why don't you go into Parliament? You are living all alone here; you represent the family and you ought to take an interest in public affairs. Our family were always mixed up with politics, and you ought to take your place. Go in and help the tenants and join the Home Rulers."

For a moment there was no answer. Charles went on eating in his slow, methodical way, slicing off the tip of his egg, frowning slightly as if he doubted its freshness, then looking across at his brother with a slow, thoughtful glance, and saying: "I do not see my way. I am in favor of the tenants and Home Rule, but I do not know any of the men who are working in the movement."

John replied: "It's easy to know the men—go and see them."

"Ah, that's what I don't quite see. I must look more around for myself first. I must see a little more how things are going. I must make out my own way. The whole question is English dominion; that is what is to be dealt with, and I do not know what the men in this movement intend."

Charles laughed, and added: "But, John, why don't you go into Parliament? Why shouldn't we make a start with you? You are the head of the family."

Shy, unassuming John, who, like his father, wanted nothing more than a quiet, untroubled existence, and who was already

41

beginning to regret the loss of his Alabama peach-farm, relapsed into horrified silence at the very idea of entering into public life.

The subject was dropped, and it was many months before John realized that his brother was taking a serious interest in Irish politics. The National movement was growing in strength, the most notable by-elections in the last two years had been won by Home Rulers, and, as member for Limerick, Isaac Butt had assumed the leadership of the new party. Manchester business men like Mitchell Henry, Protestant landlords like Blennerhassett, Young Ireland veterans like John Martin, all took the Home Rule pledge, and were elected to Parliament in spite of the opposition of the clergy and the *Freeman's Journal*. By the end of the year 1873 the Home Rule Association had become the Home Rule League, and both the Catholic Church and the country's most powerful newspaper had been won over to the new cause.

Yet still Parnell was content to lead the quiet life of a country gentleman, to be a member of the Synod of the disestablished Church and High Sheriff for his county, to superintend the working of his new saw-mills and to search for mineral wealth in the Wicklow hills and rivers. His neighbors advised him to marry and to take up his position in the country, but he felt restless and unsettled. He occasionally made a trip to Paris to visit his family, but it was a somber, republican Paris, with all the glitter and exuberance of the Second Empire departed from her streets, with the statue of Strasbourg draped in mourning and the shadow of Bismarck still heavy over the town. Miss Woods had taught him to resent and mistrust the beautiful American women who pursued him with such relentless energy, and he was no longer in the mood to flirt with capricious girls in the by-ways of the Bois.

He knew that his future lay in politics, but he could not bring himself to make the first step towards getting to know the men, many of whom did not belong to his own class and with whom he would have so little in common. When the Ballot Act was extended to Ireland, emancipating voters from the tyranny of the landlords, he perceived that here at last was a chance for an independent Irish party—a strong, united party elected by the people, uninfluenced by English opinion. But it was only during the General Election of 1874 that he finally decided to stand as member for his county and to enlist himself in the National cause. When he broke the news to John and the Dickinsons in the middle of a convivial family party, they were all delighted. Only Emily was somewhat incredulous. Politics and Tenant Right bored her to tears, and she could not believe that her handsome, lackadaisical brother, who up till now had had nothing better to do than to pay her debts, was going to champion the Irish cause on the back benches of Westminster.

Parnell had made up his mind, and once he had decided to take a certain course he was impatient of the slightest delay. The next morning found him at the offices of the *Freeman's Journal* interviewing the proprietor, Mr. Gray, a recent convert to Home Rule. Gray was rather impressed by the tall, slight, nervous young man, with the long, pale fingers ornamented by a sapphire signet ring, for, in spite of his slow, painful delivery and foppish dress, he seemed to know his own mind, and there was something arresting about those piercing brown eyes, with their peculiar, wondering look. He was young and inexperienced, but he bore an historic name. A great-grandson of Sir John Parnell, who was willing to pay his own electioneering expenses, was an asset to the party. Being a High Sheriff, he was not entitled to be put up for election until he had been relieved of his office by the Lord Lieutenant. So Gray sent him round to Dublin Castle, where that rigid disciplinarian, Lord Spencer, refused to relieve him of his duties until he had complied with certain formalities. The other candidates were already in the field and there was no time to lose. Charles, who had worked himself up to the excitement of an electioneering campaign, was not going to be hampered by red tape. If he couldn't stand for Wicklow, John should represent the family, and John, who had never had the courage to refuse his brother's whims, found himself being hustled down to Rathdrum, where an election address composed by Charles was placed into his trembling hands. In this address he promised to fight for the repeal of the Union, for the Ulster Tenant Right system and fixity of tenure, for denominational education and the speedy release of the remaining political prisoners.

With the support of the local clergy he was nominated as a National candidate, though there was already another Home Ruler standing. But all Charles's enthusiasm could not get John elected for Wicklow. In the eyes of the peasants he was an Armagh landlord, who on one occasion had been accused of rack-renting his tenants; in the eyes of the local farmers he had committed the unforgivable sin of farming in America, for at the time there was a growing fear among the agricultural classes that the American market would ultimately ruin their trade. No man was more relieved than John Howard when he found himself at the bottom of the poll. And no one was more disappointed than his brother, who in his capacity of High Sheriff was the first to see the results. During the campaign, Charles had violated every rule by which a sheriff was entitled to retain office; he had toured the county, canvassing in every cottage, and in the excitement of the moment he had once climbed on to a cart in the midst of a cattle fair and made a spirited though somewhat stuttering speech to a crowd of suspicious farmers and recalcitrant sheep. Curiously enough, the local people were not enthusiastic when one of the gentry whom they had always looked upon as a staunch Conservative suddenly came forward to champion their rights. And it was only through the loyal support of the parish priest that the Protestant landlord escaped some rough handling.

The elections of 1874 resulted in an overwhelming Conservative victory. Mr. Gladstone retired to Hawarden, to his theological treatises and the hewing down of superfluous oak-trees. Mr. Disraeli reigned at Downing Street, weaving his far-flung imperialistic dreams—Disraeli, who in his ardent youth had been a staunch supporter of Ireland's claims, and who in the House of Commons of 1844 had stated:

"A dense population in extreme distress inhabit an island

where there is an Established Church, which is not their Church, and a territorial aristocracy, the richest of whom live in a distant capital. Thus they have a starving population, an absentee aristocracy, an alien Church, and in addition, the weakest executive in the world. Well, what then would honorable gentlemen say if they were reading of a country in that position? They would say at once—'The remedy is revolution.' But the Irish could not have a revolution. And why? Because Ireland is connected with another and more powerful country. Then what is the consequence? The connection with England became the cause of the present state of Ireland. If the connection with England prevented a revolution and a revolution was the only remedy, England logically is in the odious position of being the cause of all the misery in Ireland. What then is the duty of an English minister? To effect by his policy all those changes which a revolution would do by force. That is the Irish question in its integrity."

Now Disraeli regarded the demand for Home Rule with cynical contempt. Before he had been a year in power he was responsible for a stringent Coercion Act, and he wound up his ministry in 1880 by a letter to the Viceroy, the Duke of Marlborough, rousing hatred against Ireland purely for party purposes.

In the Government of 1874, Colonel Taylor, member for County Dublin, became Chancellor of the Duchy of Lancaster, and on seeking re-election he found that the Home Rule League had decided to contest the seat. Fifty-nine Home Rulers, ranging from Catholic Whigs to Fenians, had been returned at the General Election, but now the exchequer was empty and the League had to search for a candidate who was willing to pay his own expenses. It was not a tempting proposition for any aspiring politician, as Colonel Taylor was very popular in his constituency and there was not the slightest hope of a Home Ruler being returned for Dublin.

The members of the League were surprised when young Parnell offered his services. He was no longer a Sheriff and was entitled to stand, but he was such a nervous, delicate fellow, so hopelessly ignorant of current affairs and utterly deficient of any political faculty, that it seemed absurd to put him up as a candidate for one of the most important constituencies in Ireland. His historical knowledge was limited to the story of the Manchester Martyrs. He did not know the rudiments of Home Rule but he was interested in Fenianism, and, oddly enough, it was with the Fenian members of the party rather than with the men of his own faith and class that Parnell chose to identify himself.

The man who warmly supported his candidature was Isaac Butt. He was delighted to have made a convert of the haughty young aristocrat who had remained so disdainfully aloof when his sister recited her stirring verses at the feet of John O'Leary. Under the reticence and hesitant, nervous manner, Butt divined the iron purpose and inflexible will of a man who, once he had made up his mind, would never stand aside, whatever obstacle was in his path. And with his infectious enthusiasm he convinced his colleagues that they had a splendid recruit—an historic name—young Parnell of Wicklow, who, unless he was mistaken, the Saxon would find a nasty customer, though he was such a good-looking fellow.

There were certain members of the League on whom the dandified Wicklow squire made an unfavorable impression. They disliked his English accent, his monotonous drawl and cold, distant manner. He struck T. W. Russell, the future Liberal minister, "as one who knows nothing and will never do anything." And O'Connor Power described him as a nice, gentlemanly fellow who was hopelessly ignorant and quite unable to speak. "Will he go straight?" was the question of most of the members, and John Martin, the rugged veteran of '48, said in his hard Northern accents, "If he gives his word, I will trust him. I would trust any of the Parnells."

Owing to his being the great-grandson of the "incorruptible" minister and son of the woman who had helped to finance the Fenian cause, Parnell was nominated to stand for County Dublin.

He made his first public appearance at a meeting in the
Rotunda, where he was supported by A. M. Sullivan, who has
left us a description of the scene. The excitement and fighting
spirit which inspired him during his brother's electioneering
campaign deserted him now that he stood confronted by a sea
of faces in the historic hall of the Rotunda. Mr. Sullivan writes:
"To our dismay he broke down utterly, he faltered, he paused,
went on, got confused, and, pale with intense but subdued nervous anxiety, caused everyone to feel deep sympathy for him.
The audience saw it all and cheered him kindly and heartily,
but many on the platform shook their heads, safely prophesying
that if ever he got to Westminster, no matter how long he stayed
there, he would either be a silent member or be known as 'single-
speech Parnell.'"

He made such a pathetic exhibition of himself that his supporters were really relieved when he sat down. The more kindly
minded thought that he was nothing more than a respectable
mediocrity, the more cynical dismissed him as "a bloody fool."
When he made his first appearance on the platform, he adopted
the attitude with which in later days he was to face the House
of Commons, standing very erect, with one arm held behind his
back, his fingers clenched in his palm, while the other hand
clutched the lapel of his jacket. Few people noticed that when
he came down from the platform his hands were covered in
blood. In his nervousness he had dug his nails deep into his
palms.

In the Dublin elections Colonel Taylor was returned by an
overwhelming majority, but Parnell was not a man to be discouraged by defeat. It acted on him as a stimulant and Peter
Gaffney described him coming home after the elections, striding
up the beech avenue at Avondale, "looking so handsome and
grand and devil-may-care," greeting his retainers with a smile.
"Well, boys, I am beaten, but they are not done with me yet."

His chance came a year later when John Martin, who had been
the first to vouch for his integrity, died suddenly, leaving a vacancy in the representation of Meath. Parnell was adopted as

candidate, and in April 1875 he was placed at the head of the poll. Bonfires blazed all over the county, there were scenes of wild rejoicing, and he was carried in triumph through the streets of Trim. The end of the evening saw the future Irish leader addressing his electors from the perilous platform of a large barrel of porter.

He took his seat in the House of Commons on April 22nd, 1875, the very day that Joseph Gilles Biggar, that little "hump-backed leprechaun," tried his first experiment in obstruction.

CHAPTER EIGHT

On the night of June 30th, 1876, Sir Michael Hicks-Beach, Chief Secretary for Ireland, was addressing a bored and indifferent House. Mr. Butt's annual motion for an enquiry into the Home Rule demand was receiving its usual summary treatment from the hands of the Tories. During the session of 1874, Mr. Disraeli had made one of his most brilliant and cynical speeches on the same subject. With gentle banter he had protested against "the absurd insistence of the Irish in proclaiming to the world that they are a subjugated and conquered race. England has been subjugated quite as much, but has never boasted of it"; and he added that he was opposed to Home Rule in the interests of the Irish themselves, he was opposed to it because he wished to see a united people welded in one great nationality. Mr. Disraeli set the tone for his followers, and from then onwards the Irish were laughed at and despised. Home Rule was treated as a joke, while Isaac Butt was looked upon as an amiable, good-hearted fellow, who, except for his misguided politics, was an excellent dinner companion and first-class wit.

There was an air of apathy about the House when Sir Michael stood up to speak; members in evening dress strolled in on their way from a dinner-party to a reception; Mr. Disraeli rested one thin, elegant foot against the Speaker's table, his silk hat shading his tired, glazed eyes, and Sir Michael spoke in the slightly humorous, supercilious accents which Conservative members adopted when discussing Irish affairs. He dismissed the demand for Home Rule as absurd and irrelevant and he said, "Of all the extraordinary delusions which are connected with the subject, the most strange to me appears the idea that Home Rule can have the effect of liberating the Fenian prisoners, the Manchester murderers." "No! No!" A low, vehement voice interrupted him. Sir Michael dropped his glasses and stared in stupefaction at the slight young man with the white face and dark, blazing eyes who confronted him on the Irish benches.

49

Both Tories and Whigs were profoundly shocked by the member for Meath who dared to uphold a murder, and cries of "Withdraw" rang out from every quarter. The Chief Secretary, looking straight in the face of the offender, said in his most crushing tones, "I regret to hear that there is an honorable member in this House who will apologize for murder." His words were greeted with wild cheers.

Mr. Parnell rose slowly and deliberately, and in a cold, clear voice he answered, "The right honorable gentleman looked at me so directly when he said that he regretted that any member of the House should apologize for murder that I wish to say as publicly as I can that I do not believe, and never shall believe, that any murder was committed at Manchester."

There were cries of enthusiasm from the Irish benches, and a sensation of discomfort permeated the Government quarters. Sir Michael fumbled with his papers and passed hastily on to another subject.

For over a year Parnell had been content to remain little more than a spectator in the House of Commons. His maiden speech had been far from brilliant, but it had included one sentence containing the essence of his political *credo:* "Ireland is not a geographical fragment of England, she is a nation." During the session of 1875 he would sometimes sit in one of the side galleries, observing the performers below with cold detachment, as if he had nothing to do with that band of rhetorical, gesticulating Irishmen who brought up bill after bill, only to have them ignominiously dismissed. Occasionally he entered into the fray by speaking a few words delivered modestly in a thin, nervous voice, but his lack of knowledge of political affairs, and his ignorance of the rules of debate, kept him in the background. He would wander through the passages and lobbies, stopping his colleagues to ask them some simple question on parliamentary procedure. He was never ashamed to ask for information, though in later years he confessed to a young member that "the only way to learn the rules of the House is by breaking them." During those early days he watched and criticized and learned, and his natural hatred of England became intensified when he saw the way in which Irish claims were treated in the House of Commons. Isaac Butt was far too gentlemanly and conciliatory in his methods. He was humiliating the cause by his courteous deference to British opinion, and the majority of his followers were respectable constitutional agitators who would only fight in accordance with the polite code of an assembly of gentlemen. Joseph Biggar was the only one who distinguished himself from his colleagues by his total disregard for etiquette and rules; it was the grotesque little Belfast pork butcher who gave Parnell his first lessons in parliamentary tactics. Biggar's one idea was to make himself as disagreeable as possible. He was a Fenian and a member of the supreme council of the I.R.B.,[1] and he had entered the Imperial Parliament merely to see how much mischief he could do there. If English members refused to take an interest in Irish affairs, Irish members should retaliate by holding up Government bills. By interfering in British legislation they could show that, even if they were not strong enough to get their own bills passed, they were still able to obstruct the business of the House. So long ago as the 'fifties, John Henry Moore, a Mayo landlord and a champion of Tenant Right, had used obstruction as an effective weapon, and it was Joseph Ronayne, a Young Ireland veteran and witness of Moore's successful tactics, who taught Biggar how to proceed on the same lines.

In 1872 Ronayne had been elected member for Cork, but he had participated in the failure of so many Irish movements, both constitutional and revolutionary, that he was too disillusioned to take any active part in parliamentary debate. He knew that Butt's methods of conciliation and friendly moderation would never win Home Rule. Cynically he said, "There's nothing for an Irishman to do in that House of Commons except angle for a place and turn drunkard."

On the very day that Parnell took his seat in the House,

[1] Irish Republican Brotherhood.

Joseph Gilles Biggar, the honorable member for Cavan, had held up Mr. Disraeli's Coercion Bill for four hours, while he waded through statutes, blue-books and newspapers, occasionally digressing on some totally irrelevant subject, exasperating the House by his croaking voice and benevolent smile. This was his first experiment in obstruction, and Parliament was powerless in his hands. Then there was the historic occasion when he took advantage of an almost obsolete privilege, by which any member was entitled to have the galleries cleared on objecting to the presence of strangers. Mr. Biggar chose to "espy strangers" at the moment when the Prince of Wales was listening to a debate. The standing orders had to be hastily suspended, and no man in England was more cordially disliked than the honorable member for Cavan, who was delighted at the confusion he had caused.

From the very first, Parnell focused his attention on the strange, uncouth little man who refused to be intimidated either by the sneers of the English or the pained disapproval of Isaac Butt. A curious friendship developed between the Ulster tradesman and the fastidious young landlord. This friendship was based on their mutual dislike of England and their resentment of the way in which Butt was conducting the constitutional agitation. It was Biggar who introduced Parnell into Fenian circles, and who brought him to the notice of John Barry, a member of the I.R.B. and founder of the Home Rule Confederation of Great Britain. The Fenians were tired of parliamentary agitation, and it was only their personal gratitude towards Isaac Butt which kept them from open opposition. Already, in 1875, Parnell had attracted their attention by his brave behavior at the time of the O'Connell centenary celebrations in Dublin. The Home Rule Confederation over which the Fenians had a predominating influence had been started to further the cause in England by organizing the Irish vote. In certain Northern constituencies the Irish population was large enough to force a prospective candidate to take the Home Rule pledge, and it was from towns such as Liverpool and Manchester that delegations were sent to Dublin to assist at the demonstrations in honor of O'Connell. They came with flags and banners and a great "amnesty car" bearing the words *Freedom for the Political Prisoners*. And all would have passed off quietly if the organizers of the celebrations had not refused to give a place in the procession to Fenians or Fenian sympathizers. There was a free fight; the traces of the "amnesty car" were cut and the horses driven off; but the situation was saved by a band of young men, who dashed to the front, seizing the traces of the car and dragging it forward themselves. Parnell was their leader. The daredevil spirit which had come over him during the Wicklow election, and his resentment of any form of injustice, gave him the courage to break through an excited mob. When the celebrations were over and the delegates foregathered in the lounge of the Imperial Hotel, no one would have thought that the silent young man with the curling chestnut whiskers and pale, effeminate hands would have been capable of such pluck and determination.

It was then that he first attracted the notice of the Fenians, but it was only after his defiance of the Chief Secretary and his public vindication of the Manchester Martyrs that they gave him active support. In later years John Barry used to boast, "We got Parnell a platform; we made him"; but, though it may be true that he mounted to power on their shoulders, he never made them the slightest concession. He never consented to join their organization, though they could be useful to him in helping him to wipe out the Whigs and nominal Home Rulers who formed the majority of the Irish party. In one of his speeches to his constituents he said, "The Irish people should watch the conduct of their representatives in the House of Commons," for he was convinced that the average Nationalist member was too secure and comfortable in his seat to adopt an aggressive policy, and only when the public of Ireland learnt to criticize their delegates could one hope for a strong Home Rule party. Fenian agitation would help to stimulate public opinion, not only in Ireland but in the north of England.

The I.R.B. might talk of physical force, but there was no hope of a revolution. Ireland was too small a country for a rebellion; there was not room enough to run away. It was one of Parnell's favorite assertions that Washington saved America by running away and that if he had been in Ireland he would have had to surrender in six weeks. He was essentially a practical man, and there was nothing idealistic about his political outlook. He believed in the principles of his great-grandfather, Sir John Parnell, who, when Grattan declared that the nation would yet recover its liberty, and Castlereagh shouted, "Rebellion! Treason!" answered, "No, for we shall recover our rights by constitutional means." And he resolved to fight the battle along constitutional lines, but by violating every rule of the constitution.

At the meetings of the Home Rule Confederation of Great Britain, Parnell met men of the most varied types, holding widely divergent views. There was the vice-president, Frank Hugh O'Donnell, a brilliant, embittered journalist, who had been elected for Galway, and unseated owing to his having libeled his opponent. More cultured and more cosmopolitan than the majority of his colleagues, inordinately vain and ambitious, he hoped to play a leading rôle in politics, but he had neither money nor position and he was forced to make his living as a leader-writer. He had spent many years in Paris, where he had been one of Fanny Parnell's worshiping and unknown admirers, and it was his rapturous enthusiasm for her beauty and her brains which gained him her brother's friendship.

Charles was leading a very lonely life in dreary Bloomsbury lodgings, eating solitary meals in City restaurants. He was a natural ascetic, and the pleasures of the table and luxuriant surroundings meant nothing to him, but all his life he hated solitude and on many an evening he could be found at a music-hall, vague and self-absorbed, paying not the slightest attention to the performance, merely having gone there for the sake of the warm, happy crowds. Apart from his colleagues, he was utterly friendless, and he made a point of avoiding his Anglo-Irish connections and Unionist relations when he saw how Butt was ruining his position by fraternizing with English members and Whig landlords.

He was grateful for O'Donnell's friendship, and, in the days when he was still learning the methods of obstruction, the journalist's smooth, subtle mind devised tactics which the rugged, blundering Biggar would never have thought of. At first O'Donnell was flattered to have Parnell listening to him with attention, taking his advice and following up his methods, but then he began to be jealous. He knew that though he was the better educated and the more brilliant of the two, Parnell, with the prestige of his famous name and his handsome and commanding presence, would always outrival him, and it was this insane jealousy which led to irreparable quarrels. In later years he wrote of his former friend with cruel spite and venom, describing him as "one of those *ci-devants* in the train of Mirabeau who had quarreled with their order and thirsted to humiliate it, a *grand seigneur manqué*, which explains both his indiscriminate hatred of the Irish landlords amongst whom he is almost a *déclassé*, as well as his petty arrogance to his own followers." It was a mean, paltry attack. Far from being a *déclassé*, Parnell was on friendly if not intimate terms with his Wicklow neighbors up to the day that he became nominated as a Nationalist candidate. His political principles not only alienated him from his class but made him incur severe financial losses, for his unsuccessful candidature for Dublin and his election expenses at Meath had momentarily drained his bank balance.

It was Parnell's fate to come across men who in the meanness of their natures fawned on him at first, then turned on him in spite: O'Donnell, O'Shea and finally Tim Healy, the greatest and meanest of them all.

At the meetings of the Home Rule Confederation, Parnell met a man of a very different caliber: Justin McCarthy, that kindly, gentle scholar who offered him the warm-hearted hospitality of a cultured Irish household. In one of the volumes of his reminiscences McCarthy gives us a description of Parnell in the 'seventies:

"He was very tall, very handsome, with finely-molded, delicate features. His eyes were especially remarkable. I have not seen others like them. Their light was peculiar, penetrating and, to use aptly a somewhat hackneyed term, magnetic. His manners in private life were singularly sweet and winning, and in the company of his friends he was both humorous and witty."

This is the description of one who knew him well, and the picture it conveys is singularly different from the frigid, arrogant Parnell of popular hearsay.

The McCarthys lived in Gower Street, only a stone's throw away from Parnell's lodgings in Keppel Street, and it was with them that he spent the happiest hours. Surrounded by a group of high-spirited children, the cold, reserved politician became again the mischievous boy who had dropped lumps of molten lead from the ruined tower at Avondale. All young people adored him, for he had a simple, direct way of addressing them, as if they were his intellectual equals.

From the genial friendliness of the McCarthy home he would return to the alien atmosphere of the House of Commons, where he was still content to be a silent member.

It was during the recess, in Ireland, that he voiced his views and aspirations on public platforms. Feared by the moderate Home Rulers and cheered by the Fenians, he began to command large audiences; from a thin-voiced, stuttering novice he developed into a clear, incisive speaker. There was no rhetoric about his speeches, no fine flow of language; they were cold, short and direct, and they inspired confidence in his public.

In the autumn a meeting of advanced Nationalists voted an address to President Grant congratulating the American people on the centenary of their independence, and they appointed O'Connor Power and Parnell to be their deputies.

Only five years had passed since Parnell had crossed the Atlantic, an irresponsible young Irishman pursuing a capricious heiress. Now he came entrusted with a mission from the Irish

Fenians, accompanied by O'Connor Power, the most extreme of the Home Rule members, an ex-political prisoner, and an adherent of the I.R.B. Three years later he was to come again as the acknowledged leader of his people, "the uncrowned King of Ireland."

CHAPTER NINE

On the 12th of April, 1877, Mr. Butt was peacefully enjoying a post-prandial cigar in the smoking-room of the House of Commons when a disheveled and irate member burst into the room to say that Parnell and Biggar were holding up the Mutiny Bill by blatant obstruction. Close on his heels came Sir Michael Hicks-Beach, now sadly fallen from his heights of Olympian superiority, imploring Mr. Butt to administer a public reprimand to his unruly lieutenants. The dignity of the House of Commons was at stake; they were making a farce of all the recognized laws of parliamentary procedure, reporting progress when many of the clauses were unopposed and suggesting amendments when there was nothing which needed serious discussion. All through the evening they had deliberately blocked the Bill, disturbing members at their dinners and keeping them at their posts, while hostesses like Lady Bradford were infuriated to hear that their guests were being detained by the antics of some rascally Irishmen. Parnell and Biggar had no social engagements; they would eat a chop in five minutes, either at the Westminster Palace Hotel or in the dining-room of the House, and they would be back again in their seats refreshed, alert and disarmingly calm, as if they raised their objections in a sincere endeavor to help the Government with their work.

The House could afford to laugh at Biggar, whom Disraeli had nicknamed the "leprechaun," and aristocratic Tories could sneer at the little provision merchant "who exudes the odor of bacon fat." But Parnell was one of themselves. His English origin betrayed itself in his icy, penetrating accents, his impassive face and authoritative manner. Here was no malleable, excitable Celt, to be bullied, bribed or coaxed into submission. The founder of the Parnell family had been a stubborn Cheshire merchant, Lord Mayor of his native town of Congleton, and his stubborn will had come down through the generations to a descendant who was a more inveterate enemy of England than any Gaelic peasant. In Wolfe Tone's autobiography, he confesses that "hatred of England is so deep-rooted in my nature that it is an instinct rather than a principle." So it was with Parnell.

At the very outset of his career he had declared to his brother that the root of the Irish trouble lay in British dominion. On his mission to America, he was indignant to find that President Grant refused to accept an address from the Irish people unless it was presented through the English ambassador, and he looked upon every injustice and humiliation inflicted on Ireland as a personal affront.

With all his kindly moderation Butt was merely exposing his party to ridicule and contempt. Home Rule could be won only by fighting, not by negotiating. Smooth speeches would not get anything done. There was need of rougher work. The Irish must show that they meant business, for the House of Commons was far too comfortable a place, and the English were far too comfortable everywhere.

The Mutiny Bill gave him his first big opportunity. Supported by Biggar and Major O'Gorman, the rollicking, Rabelaisian member for Waterford, whose gigantic girth gave an air of opulence and importance to the Irish benches, Parnell pursued his relentless and uncompromising tactics. "To work only in Government time, to aid anybody to spend Government time. Whenever you see a bill, block it; whenever you see a raw, rub it." Such were the methods of the obstructionists as expressed by Dwyer Gray, who joined their ranks in the middle of the session, and with a smile Parnell would allude to what he called "Biggar's four gospels."

Sunk in the depths of a comfortable armchair, Isaac Butt was rudely awakened from the pleasant after-effects of his bottle of port. It was distressing for him to think that a man of Parnell's class and breeding should intentionally set out to degrade one of the finest institutions in the world, and, though he was the mildest and most tolerant of men, he felt it incumbent on him to repudiate Parnell for damaging his country's cause by his aggressive policy.

When he rose, amidst the cheers of the English members, to denounce one of his own countrymen, he might have realized that he was sealing his political doom in Ireland. But his reverential attitude towards the traditions of St. Stephen's had always been his weakness and now it was to be his downfall.

He regretted that the time of the House had been wasted in such a miserable and wretched discussion, and he expressed his disapproval of the course taken by the honorable member for Meath. It was a course of obstruction, and one against which he had to enter a protest. He was not responsible for the member for Meath and could not control him. But he had a duty to discharge to the great nation of Ireland and he thought he would discharge it best by saying that he disapproved entirely of the conduct of the honorable member for Meath. Then he sat down, flushed with embarrassment and indignation, his large round face gleaming with sweat, while enthusiastic cheers rang out from both Whigs and Tories.

Parnell remained calm and impassive, a cold, cynical smile on his face, his dark, inscrutable eyes staring straight in front of him—the eyes which someone once described as those of a "self-centered sphinx," and all he said was, "The honorable and learned gentleman was not in the House when I attempted to explain why I had not put down notice of my amendments." In his deference to English public opinion, Isaac Butt had accused him on third-hand evidence, and to repudiate a colleague meant losing the sympathy of every Nationalist organization.

A voluminous correspondence between Butt and Parnell appeared in the *Freeman's Journal,* in which both stated their own view in direct opposition to the other. Butt wrote: "I feel that I am in a position in which I can judge of the effect that is likely to be produced by any 'policy of obstruction.' It must tend to alienate from us our truest and our best English friends. It must waste in aimless and objectless obstruction the time which we might in some form or other obtain for the discussion of Irish grievances. It must expose us to the taunts of being unfit to administer even the forms of representative Government, and even of discrediting and damaging every movement we make. . . . We have the duty of maintaining before the civilized world the dignity of the Irish nation and the Irish cause. That will only be done while we respect ourselves and our duties to the assembly of which we are members—an assembly to degrade which is to strike a blow at representative institutions all over the world, a blow that will recoil with terrible severity on the very claims we make for our own country, but which, whatever be its effects, would be unworthy of ourselves and our cause."

In Parnell's reply, he stated: "I cannot sympathize with your conclusions as to my duty towards the House of Commons. If Englishmen insist on the artificial maintenance of an antiquated institution which can only perform a portion of its functions by the 'connivances' of those interested with its working, in the imperfect and defective performance of much of even that portion—if the continued working of this institution is constantly attended with much wrong and hardship to my country, as frequently it has been the source of gross cruelty and tyranny, I cannot consider it my duty to connive in the imperfect performance of these functions, while I should certainly not think of obstructing any useful, solid or well-performed work."

From now onwards Parnell declared himself in open enmity to Isaac Butt and the moderate Home Rulers. He had a small following of his own—seven able and daring lieutenants, who delighted in incurring the displeasure of the House. There were Captain Nolan, an officer in Her Majesty's army and member for Galway, and Dwyer Gray, son of the proprietor of the Catholic newspaper which supported Isaac Butt. There were Harley Kirk, a monosyllabic tenant farmer, and Frank Hugh O'Donnell, who, after winning a recent by-election at Dungarvan, was rapidly proving himself to be the most daring of the obstructionists. The Fenians were represented by Biggar and O'Connor Power, one of the ablest orators in the House of Commons, and Major O'Gorman lent an air of inconsequential joviality to the bitterest battles. Behind this handful of men was the tremendous force of the Home Rule Confederation of Great Britain. In his bland, authoritative manner, Parnell told John Barry, "You must get me a platform. You must arrange meetings in England, for I must show that I have something at my back." But when Barry had arranged the meetings and submitted the list to him, instead of showing any gratitude, Parnell relapsed into the deepest gloom when he found that he was to speak at thirteen meetings. Did not Barry realize that thirteen was the most unlucky number, and that the whole cause was doomed to failure unless one meeting was put off or another one added? And the president of the Home Rule Confederation, who had been instrumental in the raising to power of Isaac Butt, was forced to humor his superstitious fears.

Parnell was such a contrast to the loquacious agitators and demagogues who belonged to what was a so-called secret society. His silence itself was extraordinary, and he would listen quite patiently, never contradicting or offering the slightest suggestion. In all practical matters he was quick and clear-headed, full of energy and resource, going straight to the point without wasting any time over side-issues. A business talk in his rooms at Keppel Street was never interrupted by the pleasant amenities of a whiskey and soda or a cup of tea. Being himself abstemious, it did not strike him that his guest might need some refreshment in working hours. And because of his silence and reserve, because he withheld himself from his colleagues so that not one of them could boast of his intimacy, he gradually gained an ascendency over the Confederation.

During his tour of the north of England, at the meetings in Liverpool and Manchester, he came for the first time into contact with the great crowds of a manufacturing town. He was too nervous and self-conscious either to appreciate or to be inspired by the frenzied enthusiasm of the Irish exiles, but he deliberately set himself out to make wild and incendiary speeches. In the sweltering summer heat, under the dust-laden skies of the Black Country, he assured his audiences that as it was in the past, so would it be in the future, and that only through violence could the British Parliament be brought to listen to Irish demands. Catholic emancipation had been granted when an English king had been frightened of revolutionary action, and it had been fear of the Fenians which had caused the Irish Church to be disestablished and the Land Bill of 1870 to be passed.

After the meetings came the long, dreary banquets, the endless speeches and effusive handshakes from men who never began to exist for him as human beings, who were just part of the machinery which would help him to destroy British pride and prejudice. Then followed the sleepless nights in railway hotels, with trains shunting under the windows, with screaming whistles punctuating snatches of to-morrow's speeches. And at times the loneliness would be so unbearable that he would listen to Biggar's counsels—kindly, lecherous Biggar, with his engaging, elf-like grin. In later years many a barmaid in Liverpool and Manchester could boast of her friendship with the Irish leaders.

At Westminster, obstruction was more rampant than ever. In the decorous gloom of the Upper House, Lord Beaconsfield mourned the departed dignity of what was once an assembly of gentlemen. When the Mutiny and Prison Bills came up for discussion, Parnell obstructed not only for the mere sake of blocking the Bills but also in a genuine desire to mitigate their severity. One of his amendments to the prison code was that political prisoners should not be subjected to the same treatment as common felons, and he was one of the first to advocate that flogging should be abolished in the army and navy.

In these fights with the Government it was natural for him to assume the leadership of his small party, though both O'Donnell and O'Connor Power were not only more accomplished tacticians, but also far more brilliant orators. He was a superb fighter and for sheer tenacity he had no equal. It was Sexton who once said of him, "You find on top a little dust that you can blow hither and thither as you please, and then you come on granite." Not only was he a superb fighter but he knew just how far he could go without running the risk of being suspended. Every move was calculated, and many a time an impulsive colleague was ordered to slow down at the very moment when the Speaker was about to call him to order.

Never were the obstructionists so formidable as during the fight over the South Africa Bill. Actuated by the sincerest motives, Parnell bitterly opposed the annexation of the Transvaal, and for once he gave the impression of having lost his habitual poise and aloofness. Even his voice had changed. Hoarse and guttural with passion, at times rising to a thin shriek, at times little more than a hiss between clenched teeth, his short, contemptuous speeches struck hard at the Government benches, while Sir Stafford Northcote, the Leader of the House, waited for him to commit himself by some injudicious remark. With the exception of a few Liberal members, the House gave the Government its united support, and the atmosphere was tense when Parnell cried out, "As it was with Ireland, so it is with the South African colonies, yet Irish members are asked to assist the Government in carrying out their selfish and inconsiderate policy. Therefore as an Irishman, coming from a country that has experienced to its fullest extent the results of English interference in its affairs and the consequences of English cruelty and tyranny, I feel a special satisfaction in preventing and thwarting the intentions of the Government in respect of this Bill."

He had barely finished his sentence before the place was in a turmoil of excitement. In the confusion of the moment he was understood to have asserted that he would thwart the business of the House of Commons. Sir Stafford moved that the words of the honorable member be taken down. The Speaker was sent for and the Conservatives were jubilant, for it really looked as if Parnell had played into their hands. He was called upon to explain, and in his explanation he again emphasized his condemnation of the Government. His words were declared to be out of order and he retired to the gallery, where he looked down as a detached spectator on to the heated scene below. It was a

Liberal member who first drew the attention of the House to Sir Stafford Northcote's deplorable blunder by saying: "Surely the Chancellor of the Exchequer would not contend that the member for Meath should be punished because he wished to thwart the intentions of the Government?" And the Chancellor was forced to admit his mistake, while Parnell, accompanied by Biggar, returned to his place and resumed his speech at the point where he had been interrupted.

The fight over the South Africa Bill reached its climax on the night of July 31st. The front benches of both the Government and the Opposition had agreed to carry the Bill through the committee stage at a single sitting, and Parnell and his small band set themselves out to prevent what they described as an "act of rash legislation." The House met at four o'clock in the afternoon and remained in committee until six o'clock the following evening. For twenty-six hours, seven Irishmen held up the Bill until they were threatened with the penal powers of Parliament. Feeling ran high as the night dragged on, while members fumed in impotent rage at the unwritten laws of custom and tradition which prevented them from suppressing an insufferable minority. Sir Stafford Northcote and Sir William Harcourt joined forces in an impassioned attack on the Irish obstructionists; four successive chairmen were called in; Isaac Butt was once more prevailed upon to denounce his colleagues, and from the Peers' Gallery Lord Beaconsfield looked down upon the wreck of his Parliament. Batches of members relieved each other at set intervals, others snatched a few moments' sleep in the library and smoking-room, and crowds gathered round the refreshment bars, keeping up their strength with cups of strong coffee.

As the morning sunlight poured through the Gothic windows on to crumpled shirts, unshaven chins and heavy-lidded eyes, a solitary figure was to be seen sitting in the Ladies' Gallery. It was Fanny Parnell, just arrived from Paris and glorying in the discomfiture of the English. Dressed in exquisite evening clothes, with her frail little face framed in its dark curls, she introduced a curiously incongruous element. That night Parnell was the most hated man in England. Yet when they saw him, together with his lovely sister, strolling down the passages, looking so handsome and debonair, even the most die-hard of Tories turned to look in admiration. He remained all night at his post, and it was only late on the following morning that he retired for a few hours' rest to the Westminster Palace Hotel. In his book on the Home Rule movement Michael Macdonagh describes the seven obstructionists:

"Parnell so cold and disdainful, that his speeches imparted an icy chill; Biggar more elf-like than ever, with an expression on his face of unholy delight in the prevailing confusion; O'Connor Power massively severe and argumentative; Captain Nolan lecturing the members and wagging his head at them for a body of stupid subalterns, with whom as a commanding officer he was more sorrowful than angry; Dwyer Gray conducting himself like a schoolboy, as if it were all excellent fun, and in keeping with the rôle adopting a light and bantering tone; Harley Kirk, the tenant farmer who, having no gift of speech, contented himself with moving that progress be reported, or that the chairman do leave the chair; and O'Donnell, perhaps the most provocative and challenging of all the group."

It was adding insult to injury when Biggar retired to sleep in the library, stretching himself out on three chairs, so that many a tired Tory could not even find a place to rest, but O'Donnell recounts a delightful anecdote of parliamentary chivalry, of how, when he was waiting in the queue at the refreshment bar, the Honorable James Lowther, Under-Secretary of State for Colonial Affairs, offered him his cup of coffee, saying, "I am sure you are tired. You ought to be, for you have a hundred of our fellows dead-beat."

It was during Parnell's absence that Sir William Harcourt threatened the obstructionists with the penal powers of the House. In O'Donnell's words: "The venue had been changed from a contest of physical endurance to a menace of expulsion, and in the circumstances the committee might proceed with the regular discussion of the Bill."

When Parnell returned the crisis was over, and it was one of the few occasions when he lost control of himself. White with annoyance, he turned to O'Donnell, muttering, "Why the devil did you haul down the flag?" and O'Donnell replied imperturbably, "My dear Parnell, go to the devil and enquire."

The fight over the South Africa Bill established Parnell's position in Ireland. He had flouted the Government and wrecked the prestige of the House of Commons. For defying British public opinion he was acclaimed as a hero by his own people. Isaac Butt was sacrificed, as so many Irish patriots had been sacrificed before him, and Parnell was mainly responsible for deposing his old leader. Personal considerations did not enter into the question—he was the last man to be influenced either by personal affection or animosity. He was only aware that there was work to be done and that Butt was unfit for the task. On September 1st, at a meeting of the Home Rule Confederation of Great Britain, the old leader was deposed and Charles Stewart Parnell was elected as president. An eyewitness describing the scene in the conference-room tells us how Parnell sat "looking like a bit of granite," never giving a friendly look or smile to anyone, never betraying the slightest emotion when Isaac Butt left the room—a broken old man with tears in his eyes.

CHAPTER TEN

THE gray dawn was rising beyond the Wicklow mountains and a driving rain was sweeping over St. George's Channel when, lunging and plunging through a heavy sea, the mail boat fought its way into Dublin Bay, to where a small group of men, wrapped in heavy ulsters, stood waiting on Kingstown Pier. Four Fenian prisoners discharged on tickets of leave were returning to Ireland, and three members of Her Majesty's Parliament had braved the wind and rain of a winter night to welcome them back to their country. There was the jovial, stout Major O'Gorman, cracking jokes with every porter and harbor official, as at home in the stationmaster's private room as if he were back in the officers' mess of the Connaught Rangers. And there was O'Connor Power, the only one of the three who had any real knowledge of the sufferings and privations which the prisoners had endured. He was a Connaught man, sprung from peasant stock, who at the age of fifteen had left his native country to work in the Lancashire cotton mills, where he had become involved in the Fenian conspiracy of '67 by taking part in the desperate attempt at raiding Chester Castle. It was then that he first met Michael Davitt, the one-armed Mayo workman who was returning to Ireland that morning from seven years of penal servitude. After the failure of the rising, he himself had been arrested and imprisoned for six months without a trial, and on his release he had thrown himself heart and soul into the great amnesty meetings. He had been one of the chief workers and organizers of the new movement, and he had helped John Barry to promote the Home Rule Confederation of Great Britain. Through sheer will-power and perseverance the ill-educated mill-hand had become a cultured and delightful speaker who was capable of lecturing on the most varied subjects, but, in spite of all his energy and eloquence, the members of the very Confederation of which he had been the chief organizer chose to pass him over in favor of Parnell. When the latter was elected president, O'Donnell remarked to him, "You and I don't stand a chance. They want their little bit of a county gentleman." Already he was assumed to be a mere follower of the man whom not so long ago he had regarded "as hopelessly ignorant, with no political capacity whatsoever."

It was with bitterness that he saw Parnell stepping out of the Marine Hotel, striding up to the windswept pier, and noticed how all the Press reporters and Fenian representatives, who had assembled to welcome the remanded prisoners, gathered round him, and how he never turned to address a word to any of them, but went straight ahead to the very end of the pier where the coal-barges were moored. There he stood watching the high, black waves dashing against the lighthouse, his clothes blown by the wind, the rain dropping from his beard, a rigid, immovable figure.

The cells of Dartmoor, a Lancashire mill and the woods of Avondale. Was patriotism strong enough to make these men forget their backgrounds? It was one of the first days of the new year, and the Yuletide log was still burning in the hall of Avondale. Christmas had been gay and joyous. Fanny and Anna and Theodosia had been at home and had insisted on converting the new barn into a ballroom. Even Mrs. Parnell had consented to spend a few quiet weeks in her old home, in view of the fact that she had lost almost her entire fortune in a Wall Street panic and was once more dependent on her sons. John had returned to Alabama, so Charles was saddled with the whole burden of his absurd, irresponsible family. It never occurred to him to resent the calm way in which his mother took it for granted that he would be willing to indulge her whims and fancies, nor did he attempt to put the slightest check on his sisters' extravagances. Soon they would be moving to America to settle down in Admiral Stewart's old home at Bordentown, New Jersey, and Avondale would once more be empty except for Emily and her drunken husband. Fanny would no longer be curled up in her fur rug, the sofa strewn with scraps of verse; Fanny, who wished to be a martyr for Ireland and yet could not stand the slightest discomfort. "How cold your house is, Charlie!" she would complain, coughing into a scented handkerchief. The place would look so empty without Anna's easel standing in the hall and her paints and brushes littering every room. Slipshod, untidy Anna, more vehement and more fanatical than Fanny, yet charming and delightful in the very illogicality of her opinions and the intensity of her enthusiasms.

Over the laden tea-table at Avondale there had been such heated political discussions, with Anna all on fire to meet Michael Davitt, who had been sent to prison in 1870, and who had been utterly forgotten until Isaac Butt asked someone to search the papers for the trial of a poor young fellow whose case had been overlooked. Her one wish was to accompany her brother to Kingstown, to meet her hero on his arrival, while Emily said, in her high, frivolous little voice, that it was "so boring of Charlie to insist on meeting those convicts" when he could have hunted with her instead; and Theodosia, the youngest and most beautiful of the Parnells, who had all the local gentry trailing at her heels, quoted what one of her beaux had said about those "Fenian Murderers." These diverging political views had no effect on the family's personal relationships. Emily called her favorite hunter "Royal" and Charles called his "Home Rule," and when they hacked home along the wet roads after a day's hunting, Emily would imitate the die-hard Tory squires who had been so angry at finding a Nationalist in the hunting-field. Avondale with the family at home was still the warm, happy house which Charles loved more than any other place in the world.

The mail boat had arrived and the crowds were descending the gangway, but it was only when the last of the passengers had left the pier that four haggard men came out on deck. Slowly they moved down the gangway, as if every step were an effort to their tired, emaciated bodies. One of them was taller than the rest, with an empty coat-sleeve flapping in the wind, his face gaunt and ascetic, his eyes the dark fanatic eyes of a Socialist dreamer. The Press reporters and Fenian representatives gathered round. Parnell stepped forward to shake hands with Michael Davitt, his long, white, aristocratic fingers clasping a hand worn and rough with oakum picking.[1]

There were crowds standing in the rain at Westland Row to cheer Michael Davitt, Sergeant McCarthy, Corporal Chambers and John P. O'Brien, English convicts and Irish heroes, and when they recognized Parnell they cheered still more for the man who had trampled on the rules and regulations of the British Parliament.

From Westland Row they drove to Morrison's Hotel, Parnell's Dublin headquarters, and, just as they were sitting down to breakfast, Sergeant McCarthy staggered, fainted and never recovered consciousness. Worn out by his prison sufferings, he was dead before his wife could reach him. This tragic incident made a tremendous impression on the suave young host who had invited his guests more out of duty than enthusiasm. Now he came into direct contact with men who were willing to risk all, and lose all, out of devotion to their country. As he helped McCarthy to a sofa and leant over to hear his last words, he felt irresistibly drawn to an organization which could inspire men to such sacrifices. If he had not been essentially practical he might have been persuaded to join the Fenian Society, but they were against the Catholic Church and Parnell refused to fight the Church. His aim was to bring all Irish forces into line, and he would no more fight with the Church than with the Fenians. His one *credo* was "Irish unity," and he would go to any lengths to prevent quarrels or dissensions among his own people.

Even in his relationship with Isaac Butt he had only defended himself when his leader had repudiated him. At the Home Rule conference, held in Dublin at the beginning of the year 1878, a few members such as A. M. Sullivan still cherished the hope of closing the breach between them, but the old man was as strong as ever in his condemnation of obstruction and Parnell

[1] Davitt was not exempted from oakum picking in spite of his one hand. He also did it with his teeth.

had no choice but to stand up for his policy. Butt was now a broken man, and it was pathetic to see him dragging himself round the House of Commons. Not so long before, one of his friends and followers had warned him that "young Parnell will be the death of you," and he had laughed the idea to scorn, answering, "Nonsense! I can drive him out of public life with a word." Now, ruined in health, on the verge of bankruptcy, disillusioned in all that he held most dear, he was no match for Parnell, backed by the extremists, even though he was still the nominal leader of his party, supported by the moderate Home Rulers with entire control of the funds and the backing of the whole Irish Press.

Dwyer Gray had succeeded to the proprietorship of the *Freeman's Journal,* and after a brief appearance as an obstructionist he quarreled with Parnell, so that his paper preserved its old allegiance to Isaac Butt, in opposition to his colleagues of the past session. There was not an important newspaper in England or Ireland that spoke in favor of the new policy, until T. D. Sullivan of the *Nation* commissioned a young relative to write a weekly parliamentary letter in his paper. Timothy Healy, a twenty-three-year-old shorthand clerk in the offices of the North-Eastern Railway at Newcastle-on-Tyne, and a native of Bantry, County Cork, came to London with the salary of a pound a week to write in glowing terms of the man who had inspired him with a hero-worship from the moment he heard him speak at a political meeting in Leeds. John Barry had been the first to recognize the boy's talents, and he had given valuable help in organizing the great demonstrations in the north of England. At Leeds, Healy had shaken hands with Parnell and fallen under the spell of those strange red-brown eyes, that soft, courteous voice. From then onwards he was his willing slave, till jealousy, wounded vanity and offended pride inflamed his raw peasant's susceptibilities.

He came to London in the spring of 1878, a small boyish figure, with enquiring brown eyes, who could be seen loitering round the lobbies while Parnell procured him orders of admission. In triumph he would write to his brother at Newcastle-on-Tyne saying, "Parnell, in the matter of getting admission to the House, has stood by me like a brick, putting down my name whenever there was an opportunity and apologizing if he missed it." Mr. Healy was very useful, but it is doubtful whether Parnell ever felt any affection for the rather common, bumptious little man who week after week wrote him up with such passionate admiration, annihilating his enemies with his brilliant, corrosive wit. Occasionally Tim would be allowed to join the small party of Irish members who dined at Gatti's in the Strand, meals where everyone talked except Parnell, who was usually content to listen, smiling appreciatively at a witty story, rarely contributing one of his own, but always charming and affable with that slightly aloof manner which forbade any attempt at intimacy.

There was another young journalist in whom Parnell inspired a devotion far more solid and reliable than Healy's hysterical hero-worship. In T. P. O'Connor he found a friend, who, after all the mud-flinging of the divorce court and the cruel faction of "the split," could still write a fair and unbiased judgment of a once beloved leader. In those early days T. P. was a parliamentary reporter for the Central News Agency, and he first met Parnell on a summer evening on the terrace of the House of Commons, when the young leader stopped to talk to him about his policy of obstruction. He describes the charm of his appearance and of his manners, the way in which he insisted on giving him dinner when he found he had detained him beyond the usual hour for a meal, and how he gave the impression of one who had no home, no place to go. The House was not sitting, and yet he lingered round Westminster as if he had nothing else to do.

The amusements of a great capital, the theater and the night life held no attraction for Parnell, and when he indulged in them it was out of sheer loneliness. By nature he was thoroughly domestic. He loved children and animals and was one of the few men who was a true monogamist. Many a time he declared that marriage would have given him a distaste for political life, for it made a man too comfortable. He found amusement in curious, unexpected places. One of the few occasions on which he really enjoyed himself was when he and a colleague went to the Agricultural Hall to watch a walking match between an Irishman and an American. The Irishman won, and Parnell handed the German bandmaster two sovereigns to strike up "God Save Ireland" instead of "God Save the Queen." The German compromised by playing "Tramp, Tramp, Tramp, the Boys are Marching," which has the same tune, until the member for Islington, who happened to be present, lodged a complaint.

The bonfires which blazed on the hills of Connaught to celebrate the release of Michael Davitt reflected the dawn of a new era. The very day he was discharged, the ex-Fenian rejoined the I.R.B. and was elected a member of the supreme council, but he was obsessed by one subject alone—the Agrarian question. He followed in the steps of Henry George, and his mind was that of a Utopian dreamer. In Parnell he met one possessed of a fanaticism as great as his own, but whereas his fanaticism was that of a visionary, Parnell's was that of a hard, practical politician inspired by pride and loathing for England and a ruthlessness ready to accept any sacrifices. Davitt was struck by the power and directness of his personality, "by the proud, resolute bearing of a man of conscious strength, with a mission, wearing no affectations, but without a hint of Celtic character or a trait of its racial enthusiasm. An Englishman of the strongest type molded for an Irish purpose."

Born in the famine year of 1846, Michael Davitt and Charles Stewart Parnell were the two great forces in the new movement. One deliberately allowed himself to be influenced by the other. Davitt proved to Parnell that the root of the trouble was not so much "British dominion" as Irish landlordism. The eviction scene of his childhood, when his family was thrown out on to the roadside and their home destroyed in front of their eyes, the overcrowded emigrant ship, his mother begging in the streets of Manchester, were memories which influenced the whole course of his life, and the stories of the Great Hunger, a famine caused by the landlords' neglect, were the only stories he ever heard in his dreary, hopeless childhood. Working in a factory and losing his arm, the long years in Dartmoor and Portland, where he had been thrown together with the vilest criminals, had left him singularly free of bitterness. The nobility of his nature and the selflessness of his aims impressed Parnell, who was far too fastidious even to envisage the nameless indignities and privations of prison life. It was not through lack of strength or courage that he confessed to Michael Davitt that "I could never face penal servitude." For a man of his temperament, with his family's mental history, it was the solitude and silence which were too horrible to think of. In his opinion it was far better to kill a warder and get hanged than have to endure years of agony and of possible insanity. When Davitt recounted his experiences, Parnell said very quietly: "It would drive me mad." Then he added, with that queer, uneasy look in his eyes: "Madness is a word we don't use lightly in our family."

Davitt influenced Parnell, but it was the constitutionalist who inspired the Fenian to relinquish the irreconcilable attitude adopted by the supreme council of the Irish Republican Brotherhood by making him believe that a handful of men fighting the British Government on its own ground could do more for the Irish farmer than any of those hard, desperate revolutionaries who were determined to adhere to their old policy of open warfare. Parnell stressed the necessity of united action by declaring that "if the Land question is to be the vital question, every true Nationalist must join in the agitation." But though he was perfectly willing that men like Davitt should drive the ship, he insisted on steering it himself.

CHAPTER ELEVEN

"No, I will never join any political secret society, oathbound or otherwise. It would hinder and not assist me in my work for Ireland. Others can act as seems best to themselves."

Parnell dismissed the subject, and looked out at the dreary landscape of the English Midlands. He and Davitt were traveling up to Lancashire, to speak at a political meeting, and the ardent Fenian was trying to persuade him to join a revolutionary movement, in which conspiracy and arms should play only a subsidiary part. Davitt still clung to the Utopian schemes he had evolved in the solitude of his cell. There was to be a war against the landlords and better housing for the laborers, and he had worked out a fantastic plan by which the Irish parliamentary party should make a reasoned demand for Home Rule, and, in the case of the demand being refused, they were all to leave the House of Commons in a body, return to Ireland, summon a National Convention and go into session as an informal legislative assembly. His eyes were shining with enthusiasm as he propounded his scheme, and Parnell smiled his quiet, slightly deprecatory smile, for really there were times when one couldn't take Davitt seriously. Still, the day was approaching when the Fenians would try and force his hand and Michael Davitt was the only member of the supreme council on whom he could rely as an ally. The governing body of the Irish Republican Brotherhood consisted of eleven members, but the power lay chiefly in the hands of two men—Charles Kickham and John O'Leary, and these leaders of '65 who had undergone years of imprisonment and exile were utterly irreconcilable. Scholars, idealists and hopeless romantics, they still insisted on keeping alive the separatist spirit, they still dreamed of open revolution and still believed that the anglicizing influence of parliamentarianism was demoralizing to their cause. At the beginning of the year 1878, Kickham brought forward a resolution pledging the council to sever all connection with the parliamentary party.

The resolution was carried, and John Barry was forced to resign, while Joseph Biggar and Pat Egan, a Dublin baker and prominent Fenian who had given his support to Parnell, were expelled from the council. The Fenian Society included men of every type, from the high-minded and intransigent leaders to the murderous Invincibles; from Home Rulers to the Ribbon men of West Meath. And it was only the governing body which had declared against Parnell and his constitutional policy. Had he been foolhardy he would have taken up the challenge by attempting to smash their society; but he merely waited his turn and in his speeches there was just enough of treason to convince the average Fenian that his methods should be given a trial. Many of the rank and file were in favor of united action, and in their eyes Parnell was the very man to fight the English, "for he is so like themselves, cool, callous, inexorable, always going straight to the point and not caring much how he gets there."

Meanwhile, on the other side of the Atlantic, the leaders of the Clan-na-Gael were watching Parnell's movements with interest, men of a very different caliber from the poets and romantics who led the Irish Republican Brotherhood. Whether gunmen or dynamiters or members of respectable professions, the Irish-American survivors of the famine combined a sentimental love for their mother country with an unreasoning and relentless hatred of England. The woes of Ireland fetched a good premium in the popular Press. In the columns of the *Irish World,* Patrick Ford lashed to a frenzy all the useless bitterness and passion of the famine days by writing up week after week hair-raising memories of political convicts and sensational stories of young Irish girls who had been forced to go on the streets of New York. How different were the principles of John O'Leary when he asserted, "There is one thing one must never do to save a nation; one must never cry in public!" With Spartan spirit he would refuse to discuss his prison experiences, saying, "There was nothing to complain of. I was in the hands of my enemy." If one joined the Clan it was no good being squeamish about methods or principles; one contributed to Patrick Ford's skirmishing fund without enquiring too deeply what use was being made of one's dollars, for they might help to finance a lecture tour by Michael Davitt or another Clerkenwell explosion. There were black sheep in the society as there are in every secret society, and if, on the whole, they were guilty of greater excesses than the members of the I.R.B., it can be argued that, being citizens of the United States, they could hate England with equal severity and safety. The men who launched the dynamite campaign never heard the echoes of the explosions on the other side of the Atlantic.

From the day that Parnell came into direct contact with the Fenians and the Clan-na-Gael he rarely ventured out without a revolver in his coat pocket, and he was well aware of the danger of the forces which were helping him to power.

Matters came to a head in the spring of 1878, when Dr. Carroll, a chief of the Clan-na-Gael, arrived in London and invited Parnell and O'Donnell to meet the Fenian leaders in his rooms at the Surrey Hotel. It was not so much a meeting as a conference, where one party was determined to be as intractable as ever, while the other one refused to commit itself. In the anteroom sat a Fenian official on duty to prevent any spying or interruption, and there was the usual atmosphere of conspiracy and mystery. Dr. Carroll was tough and direct in his methods, and he was interested to know whether the doctrines of physical force and the active policy of obstructive parliamentarianism could ever cooperate. It was soon obvious that John O'Leary refused to be convinced by any arguments put forward by the constitutionalists. The session had hardly begun before he said in his cold, courteous manner, "I ought to forewarn you, gentlemen, that I have not yet been able to see how Ireland is to be freed by keeping the Speaker of the English House of Commons out of bed." Parnell spoke very little. He was never in favor of giving explanations, and as he glanced round at the hard, vigilant faces, he knew that the wisest tactic was to remain silent. Over thirteen years had passed since he had met John O'Leary in his mother's Dublin drawing-room. Then the Fenian leader was a tall, proud young man who held himself like a conqueror, so confident of success, but who already in those days had that detached, unworldly quality which had become accentuated by years of privation and misery. Fanny had loved him and he had never even been aware of it, and her brother had resented his sister's passion. In those days he was indifferent and contemptuous of all that O'Leary upheld and fought for. Now his spontaneous sympathies were with the Fenians, only his cold, logical reasoning held him back, and the Fenians respected him because he was faithful to the opinions he always professed. It was men like John Barry and O'Connor Power whom they resented, men who had joined their organization and then deserted them in order to win laurels on popular platforms.

O'Leary and O'Donnell did most of the talking. The latter declared that if any Irishman really loved his country, he should assist the Irish cause in every walk of life and on every occasion. Surely a Fenian should try and promote the election of honest, capable Nationalist candidates in preference to place-hunters and time-savers. If a hundred of their voters could elect an honest man, had they the right to stand by and wait for their insurrection, while a rotten member got the place? But the Fenian leader stuck to his hidebound principles. "No true member of the I.R.B. can take the parliamentary oath of allegiance. Every Irishman who enters the British Parliament becomes corrupted, and the only way to save one's honor is to keep aloof from everything English." Whereupon O'Donnell stuck his aggressive monocle into his eye and enquired in his most ironic manner, "Even from English literature, Mr. O'Leary?" for everyone knew the Fenian chief to be an ardent student of Shakespeare.

Dr. Carroll soon realized that his meeting was doomed to failure. As one of the most extreme members of the Clan-na-Gael, he favored the physical force doctrine. He was so obsessed by his hatred for England and his desire for revenge that his wish to injure England was far greater than his love for Ireland, but at the same time he was a hard-headed business man and he had very little use for O'Leary's lofty idealism. If he could convert Parnell to more extreme methods, the vast exchequers of the Clan-na-Gael, the whole of Patrick Ford's skirmishing fund, would be at his disposal, but Parnell refused to be converted. When they came out of the hotel, he turned to O'Donnell with a laugh, saying: "The Fenians want to catch us, but they are not going to." There was something very infectious about his laughter, for his whole face would light up in merriment and his eyes would sparkle with fun. No, the Fenians weren't going to catch him. Still, he considered that O'Donnell had declared himself too much in open opposition to their principles, and unknown to his colleague he arranged another interview with Carroll and O'Leary, in which he went so far as to say: "Purely physical force movements have always failed in Ireland, but I do not want to break up your movement; on the contrary, I wish it to go on. Collect arms, do everything that you are doing, but let the open movement have a chance too. We can both help each other." He refused to discuss his own plans and tactics for the simple reason that he had no formulated ideas with regard to his future actions.

The Agrarian question was assuming formidable proportions. All over Ireland the people were clamoring against the iniquitous rents. Evictions were augmenting year by year; every clause of Mr. Gladstone's Land Bill had been violated and misinterpreted by the landlords without the slightest interference from the law. There was no freedom of contract between owner and tenant, and in County Galway, where rack-renting was more frequent than in any other part of Ireland, a remarkable old man named Matthew Harris had started the Tenants' Defence Association of Ballinasloe. The farmers who joined this society demanded what were known as the "three f's"—free sale, fair rents and fixity of tenure; but how could a little local society wage war against the powerful landlords backed by armed forces?

After proving himself a complete failure at the Colonial Office, James Lowther succeeded Sir Michael Hicks-Beach as Chief Secretary for Ireland. With Russia at the gates of Constantinople and a British army marching on Kabul, with the fleet in Besika Bay and the Indian troops at Malta, Lord Beaconsfield had very little time to spare for Irish affairs, so, in a moment of careless cynicism, he sent a sporting country gentleman, who called the Land Bill of 1870 "an act of undiluted Communism," to grapple with a country which the bad harvests caused by excessive rainfall had brought to the verge of famine.

Ever since James Stephens had started the I.R.B., the Fenians and the farmers had been at daggers drawn. Occasionally an outraged tenant had joined a Ribbon lodge in order to revenge himself on a tyrannical landlord, but the Fenian leaders had never taken any interest in the Agrarian question. Kickham and O'Leary only believed in military insurrection, and Michael Davitt was the first member of the supreme council to advocate a Land war. He received little encouragement in revolutionary circles, and gradually he drifted towards the advanced constitutional Nationalists, who, led by Parnell, were willing to make the "three f's" and "peasant proprietary" a plank in their parliamentary platform.

Parnell had no distinct convictions on the Land question. His views were still in a process of formation, and he had many a talk with Michael Davitt expressing himself in favor of a form of State tenantry. According to Davitt, he was never really in favor of peasant proprietary, though he advocated it as a party proposal. "He knew the economic danger which existed in absolute class ownership of land in a country with little or no alternative industry for the masses except agriculture, and how prone the Irish peasant would be to mortgage his interest to banks, when once he possessed a proprietary right in his farm. If there was Home Rule, what did it matter whether they were proprietors or tenants with fixity of tenure and low rents?" And when Michael Davitt talked of the ultimate nationalization of land, Parnell treated him with the patronizing affection which one accords to a somewhat unreasonable child.

The Clan-na-Gael still waited for Parnell to declare himself, and, though Dr. Carroll had ranged himself on the side of the physical force party, there were other men in the movement who favored combined action between the parliamentary and revolutionary forces. Their leader was John Devoy, an ex-soldier in the foreign legion, who had been a Fenian agent in the rebellion of '65. He had spent five years in prison before he was liberated, and after his release he had settled in the United States, where he had become a prominent member of the Clan. He was linked up with extremists like Patrick Ford and O'Donovan Rossa, but, unlike those fire-eating apostles of vengeance, he was both cool-headed and far-seeing, and he advocated the policy which became known as "the New Departure—combined action of constitutionalists and revolutionists for the common purpose of national independence." Unlike the majority of the Irish exiles, he realized the vital importance of the Land question, and that the only solution was for the Fenians and the farmers to cooperate in an open movement for the destruction of landlordism. The revolutionaries should mingle in the public life of the country, they should interest themselves in whatever interested the bulk of the people, and by joining in the popular agitation they would further their own cause.

In Michael Davitt he found what he considered to be an ideal leader for an Agrarian revolt, a Fenian who was a Socialist, who accepted the English workman as a brother and who cared more for the rights of the Connaught peasants than for the perilous glories of a military insurrection; a martyr who could command the sympathies of Irish and American audiences by the record of his prison sufferings. What Devoy ignored was the curious trait in the Irish peasantry which made them unwilling to accept as leader anyone springing from their own class or creed. Daniel O'Connell had been the one great Catholic leader and he had been a Kerry landlord, while all the Emmets and Wolfe Tones, the Edward Fitzgeralds and the Smith O'Briens, had been neither Catholics nor peasants. For hundreds of years it had been a tradition for members of the Protestant ascendency to be the popular champions of Irish Nationalism. As a Mayo peasant, Michael Davitt was fully aware of this inherited prejudice, and one of the reasons why he was so anxious to secure Parnell's cooperation in the Agrarian movement was that he saw in the young Wicklow landlord the very man whom the small farmers in the west of Ireland would be willing to accept as leader. His handsome face and personal charm, his commanding manners and popularity as the hero of the obstruction scenes, had already raised him to a position which enabled him to dictate to men of far wider political experience. But whereas Michael Davitt regarded Parnell merely as a nominal leader, Parnell himself was determined to secure absolute power, and in his eyes the Land movement was yet another weapon with which to fight the British Government.

Davitt crossed over to America in August 1878. Officially he went to visit his mother, who had settled in Pennsylvania, but he was also bound on a secret mission to discuss the political situation with the leaders of the Clan-na-Gael. Parnell knew of this mission, but he never gave him a single instruction or message to the American Nationalists. They would have to declare themselves openly on his side before he would show them his hand, and even when Devoy cabled to him the terms on which they would be willing to support him, he never bothered to answer the cablegram.

The terms were:

(1) Abandonment of the federal demand and substitution of a general declaration in favor of self-government.
(2) Vigorous agitation of the Land question on the basis of peasant proprietary, while accepting concessions tending to abolish arbitrary evictions.
(3) Exclusion of all sectarian issues from the platform.
(4) Irish members to vote together in all Imperial and home questions, to adopt an aggressive policy and energetically resist coercive legislation.

Devoy refused to be discouraged by Parnell's silence, and, together with Davitt, he traveled across the States attending vast meetings of the Clan, in which they advocated that all American

Nationalists should openly participate in public movements in Ireland. The majority of the Clan-na-Gael were converted to their views. The telegram to Parnell was published in the *New York Herald* and Devoy addressed a letter to the *Freeman's Journal* declaring his views, regardless of the fact that the Catholic newspaper still adhered to Isaac Butt's policy and regarded even Parnell as a dangerous extremist. Irish-American feelings were stirred from New York to Chicago, from San Francisco to the Canadian frontier. After a hundred years, Grattan's prophetic words were being fulfilled. A hundred years before he had begged England not to refuse to the loyalty of Ireland the privilege she had offered to the arms of America, and he had added: "Do you see nothing in that America but the grave and prison of your armies? Do you not see in her range of territory, cheapness of living, variety of climate and simplicity of life, the drain of Europe? Whatever is bold and disconsolate to that point will precipitate, and what you trample on in Europe will sting you in America."

CHAPTER TWELVE

JOHN DEVOY described the Agrarian question as "the engine with which to drag Home Rule," and the Land agitation began to take shape from the time when Parnell addressed a great meeting at Tralee, when Michael Davitt returned from America and Devoy broke the terms of his amnesty by paying a secret visit to the west of Ireland. The country was in a desperate condition, for the potato crop had failed and dark memories of the "Hungry 'Forties" clouded the horizon. In the last year of his life, suffering constant pain and harassed by his creditors, Isaac Butt still reverted to his old methods of persuasion and conciliation in the hopes of obtaining some measure of Land reform from the blindest and most inefficient of all Chief Secretaries. But the Home Rule League of his creation was already a thing of the past, and, though his followers refused to accept his resignation, any new member who attached himself to the party declared himself a Parnellite. His last public appearance was at a Dublin meeting, where he defended his policy with a vigor and eloquence worthy of his prime. The next day he fell ill, and three months later, in May 1879, he was buried in the small churchyard of his native village in Donegal.

The tragedy of his gradual decline and death was engulfed in the sweeping tide of the Agrarian revolt. T. P. O'Connor accuses Parnell of having given him the details of the sad story "with a frigidity which chilled and almost shocked me," but it was his very ruthlessness which made Parnell into a great leader. There was not the slightest trace of sentimentality in his nature, and he never bothered to affect an emotion he did not feel. Butt's day was over, and it was pointless to regret what was really a timely relief.

During the winter of 1878-79, Parnell was leading a life which would have exhausted men of a far stronger physique—a life of constant journeying between Ireland and Westminster. Every porter at Holyhead, every steward on the mail boat, was familiar with the tall, bearded man, who never tipped less than a sovereign and who seemed quite indifferent to the roughest crossing. On many an occasion, when the Irish members kept the House of Commons sitting all night, Parnell would suddenly appear in the early morning still dressed in his traveling clothes, having just got off the train. And there is a story told of how he once changed his suit in a hansom cab on his way from Euston to Westminster. The Conservatives would be filled with uneasy apprehension when they saw him quietly taking his place below the gangway, for they knew that it would be several hours before they would get to bed. He always disliked the House of Commons and he really enjoyed upsetting the Tory squires. His maxim was: "Punish and worry them, for an ounce of parliamentary fear is worth a ton of parliamentary love."

In the session of 1878 the Government took up the question of obstruction, and appointed a committee to enquire into the subject of public business. Closure, that effective and paralyzing gag on the liberties of the House, had not yet been invented, but it was a happy moment for the Lobby humorists and caricaturists when Mr. Parnell was placed on the committee. The arch-obstructionist must have found himself in a somewhat curious situation cross-examining the Speaker, the Chairman of Committees and all the other high authorities, on parliamentary procedure, and he took great pains to enquire into the exact definition of "obstruction." But when he drafted a report written from his own point of view the other members of the committee refused to accept it.

The Land question was the dominating question of the moment, and it was not to be solved on the back benches of Westminster. Concessions had been begged for too often. "Reduced rents" had been a party cry ever since the days of Tenant Right, and the Government refused to admit that there was any distress in the country. The parliamentarian turned his back on the scenes of his triumph and launched out on a campaign in towns where he was little more than a name and where the people were downtrodden and apathetic from sheer want and misery.

William O'Brien, working as a reporter on the *Freeman's Journal,* a paper still running in opposition to the Parnellite party, has left us a description of that first Land meeting at Tralee, when Parnell addressed "a rough and tumble meeting, half farmers, half Fenians, with several tipsy interrupters." This speech was delivered under cruel difficulties, but it fired his audience, and O'Brien himself was "captured heart and soul" by his peculiar personal charm.

Traveling in an unheated Irish railway carriage from Mallow to Tralee, the two young men had what O'Brien describes as an "astonishingly confidential chat," in which Parnell showed himself to be as romantic as Lord Edward Fitzgerald, with a "sweet seriousness *au fond,* any amount of nervous courage, a delicate reserve without the smallest suspicion of *hauteur;* strangest of all, humor, and above everything else, simplicity."

One can picture so well the gloom of a November evening in Tralee, with the Atlantic mists enveloping the gray mud flats, the straight, dreary street leading to the public hall, with the damp exuding from the walls and the air stuffy with the smell of gas and stale porter; the apathetic audience strolling in from the shebeens to hear a Wicklow landlord tell them that nothing short of a revolution would bring about a change in the Land laws, advocating the establishment of a tribunal for fixing rents and the creation of a peasant proprietary; the people cheering in a dispirited fashion, knowing in their hearts that there was only one way out—to summon the forces of "Captain Moonlight" [1] and light the flames of Agrarian crime.

Revolution to Parnell meant an open organized revolt. To the ignorant Kerry peasant it meant reverting to the old "whiteboy" methods of marauding the hills at night, maiming and houghing the landlord's cattle and murdering the hated agent.

When Parnell became the tenants' champion, the moderate Home Rulers scoffed that "it was Michael Davitt who had him by the ear," but the Land meeting at Tralee took place before

---

[1] "Captain Moonlight" was the popular nickname for the outrage-mongers.

Davitt's return from America and it was Parnell who sowed the first seeds of agitation in an apathetic and disheartened people. After the meeting O'Brien accompanied him to his hotel, and was amazed to find him quite hopeful and confident about the future. "The public has not been encouraging to start with, but they have a far worse audience in the House of Commons," and later in the evening, when a convivial group of local Nationalists sat drinking punch in the hotel-keeper's private parlor, a sturdy farmer said: "Mr. Parnell, it will take an earthquake to settle the Land question," and he replied in his quiet, drawling voice, "Then we must have the earthquake."

Michael Davitt was the "Father of the Land League," but it was Parnell who destroyed the last remnant of feudalism in Ireland, and if you stay to-day in one of those old stone country houses, where the grazing fields are under the watchful eye of a Dublin land commissioner, you will still hear your host inveighing against the man who betrayed his own class and drove them to ruin. The constant society of semi-revolutionaries, whose youth had been one continual struggle against poverty and privation, influenced Parnell in his attitude towards the landlords. He disliked them with a fanaticism which was very near hatred, yet when he visited his own constituency he still went out with the Meath hounds, in spite of the fact that he was barely on speaking terms with any other member of the hunt. The drawing-rooms of Viceregal Lodge and the Kildare Street Club saw him no more, but he never traveled otherwise than first class, and he preferred staying at a small select hotel to staying at the Imperial, which was the favorite haunt of every Dublin Nationalist. He despised the landlords of his own generation. "The only good things they have to show for themselves are their hounds and, perhaps, in the Roscommon County, their horses," but he still lived in the traditions of his class. Grattan's Parliament had been won by the gentlemen of Ireland, the volunteers had been raised by the Earl of Charlemont, and when Parnell dreamt of bringing back a National Assembly to College Green, he did not intend corner-boys and farmers to sit in the seats of his ancestors.

In January 1879, John Devoy arrived in Ireland, and his visit seems to have been public property for everyone except the authorities. He came to Dublin, and could be met walking down Sackville Street in broad daylight. He was to be found almost every evening at a social semi-revolutionary club in Nassau Street, or sharing a beefsteak with Michael Davitt at Bailey's restaurant. Before he had been there a week, every paper in Ireland published the policy of the "New Departure." This policy included the terms Devoy had dictated in his cablegram to Parnell, but it also laid stress on special legislation for the "encouragement of Irish industries, the development of Ireland's natural resources, substitution as much as possible of cultivation for grazing, reclamation of waste lands, protection of Irish fisheries and improvement of peasant dwellings; assimilation of the county to the borough franchise and reform of the grand jury laws and also those penalizing the right of convention in Ireland. Vigorous efforts were to be made to improve and nationalize popular education and to obtain once more for the Irish people the right to carry arms." By sheer coincidence, the law penalizing the rights of convention was repealed this very year which saw the birth of the Land League.

Devoy had not been very long in Dublin before Davitt arranged a meeting between him and Parnell—a meeting in which the conversation was general and where Parnell's part was chiefly that of a listener. He kept up an attitude of friendly neutrality towards the revolutionary movement, nothing more. There was no necessity for him to form an alliance with John Devoy. By his presence at Tralee and his vigorous speeches at Land meetings throughout the country, he had already shown Michael Davitt that he was willing to take a part in an Agrarian movement. It was for Devoy to make the concessions, not for him, and he listened attentively to everything that was said about the Clan-na-Gael. However important it might be for him to gain the support of those vast Irish-American forces, he was not going to run the risk of binding himself to any definite terms or to identify himself publicly with men such as O'Donovan Rossa and Patrick Ford, whose names were anathema to all right-thinking people. He had taken up the Agrarian movement from the day when he asked Charles Kickham if he thought that the people felt keenly on the Land question, and the veteran Fenian leader, who took very little interest in the failure of crops and agricultural distress, answered: "Feel keenly on the Land question! I am only sorry to say that I think they would go to hell for it."

It was Charles Kickham who offered the most vehement opposition to the "New Departure," when Devoy and Davitt went over to Paris to assist at a meeting of the supreme council of the I.R.B. He regarded the whole policy as dishonest and immoral, and, owing to his being deaf and refusing to listen through an ear-trumpet, it was impossible to argue with him. He had the support of the whole council, but John O'Leary, scrupulously honest and invariably courteous whether in friendship or in war, decreed "that while no alliance should be entered into between the supreme council and the parliamentarians, the officers of the organization should be left free to take part in the open movement if they felt so disposed, such officers were only to be held responsible for any acts or words deemed to be injurious to the revolutionary cause." It was a sentiment worthy of the man who, during a Fenian riot in Limerick, had declared "that the claim to close one's opponent's mouth, whether it comes from the Pope of Rome or a Limerick workman, is a foul tyranny."

Devoy returned to America, where he defied the supreme council by spreading the doctrines of the "New Departure," and Davitt started out on his crusade through Connaught, organizing tenant defense associations in every town. Isaac Butt died, and Mr. Shaw, the President of the Munster Bank, was elected as sessional chairman of the Home Rule League. "Sensible Shaw," as he was known, was a cool, unemotional business man without very much personal ambition, and it was highly unlikely that he would oppose any independent action on the part of his colleagues. Parnell voted for him, knowing very well that his leadership would be purely nominal and that he himself would be left as complete master of the situation.

In the spring of 1879 the question of flogging in the army came up again before the House of Commons, and Biggar and Parnell still showed themselves determined to fight to the very last for the abolition of the "cat." They were influenced partly by humane reasons, partly by the fact that the Army Regulation Bill gave them a splendid opportunity for obstruction, and now many of the advanced Liberals began to think that an alliance with "those rascally Irishmen" might be quite useful. A General Election was impending, and the "abolition of the cat" was a very good cry for catching the voters. It was a subject that was bound to raise a certain amount of popular feeling, and Mr. Chamberlain, the "Robespierre" of Birmingham, who brought the spirit of a new age into Disraeli's Parliament, associated himself with Parnell over the Army Regulation Bill. During the past years he had resented the Irish Nationalists, "who are bound to give a good deal of trouble by forcing on the English Parliament that iron-hand system of *clôture* which has been found necessary in almost every other deliberative assembly." Now he stifled his scruples for party purposes, and, when some of his colleagues refused to support him in the fight, because they did not wish to take up a question which Parnell had begun, he said: "What does it matter who has begun it, if it is the right thing to do? Let us go in and take the question out of his hands"; and Parnell was shrewd enough to let the Radicals lead in the attack, knowing full well that a man like John Bright would join with Chamberlain and yet would refuse to associate himself with an obstructionist. Whenever they flagged, he and Biggar and their followers were always ready to come into the field. The battle raged all through the session. Orthodox Liberals such as Sir William Harcourt and Lord Hartington united with the Conservatives, and it was only when one of the Irish members forced the Minister of War to produce a "cat" in the library of the House that the members fully realized the iniquity of the punishment which was being meted out to Her Majesty's soldiers. The exhibition of the "cat" forced the Government to abolish flogging in the army except in extreme cases where death was the alternative.

Unscrupulous in their methods and ruthless in their pride, Chamberlain and Parnell were both born leaders of men, true fighters who never stood up in the House of Commons without their opponents feeling extremely uncomfortable. Parnell was the more unscrupulous and the greater of the two, for Chamberlain allowed himself to be influenced by his personal feelings and Parnell never did. Neither friendship nor enmity played the slightest part in his political calculations. He was out to make the best bargain he could, and he stopped at nothing. If a man opposed him, he flung him aside and he was quite indifferent as to what means he used to gain his object.

In 1879 the relations between the two men were friendly and pleasant, but they were strictly business relations and when they met they usually talked "shop." Parnell's conversational powers were limited and he had no small talk.

One evening Chamberlain invited him to dine at Richmond with Sir Charles Dilke and John Morley, who was then editing the *Fortnightly Review,* and the brilliant politician and cultured man of letters were amazed at the young Irishman's astounding ignorance. John Morley was fond of describing his first meeting with Parnell, who at that time was so romantically handsome—"like a George Meredith hero"—and who seemed so indifferent to the fact that he was detested by the vast majority of Englishmen. In reality Parnell was acutely sensitive, and, according to Justin McCarthy, one of the reasons why he went out so little was because he felt that most Englishmen disliked him, and, even though his hosts might like him, some of their guests might not want to meet him. He said often, "I am nervous about being disliked. I hate to be hated." In his apparent indifference to public opinion, in his open contempt of British politicians, lay the secret of his success. Sir Charles Dilke attributed his power to his aloofness, and he once told Mr. Barry O'Brien that "Parnell hated England, English ways, English modes of thought. He would have nothing to do with us. He acted like a foreigner. We could not get at him as at any other member in English public life. He was not one of us in any sense. Dealing with him was like dealing with a foreign Power."

As they sat over their whitebait and hock in the dining-room of the Star and Garter, the four men discussed the possibilities of Home Rule, and Parnell showed himself to be frank and clear and essentially practical. The non-committal tactics which he used with the Fenian leaders were the very opposite to those which he used with the English Radicals. Charles Dilke and John Morley were on his side, for they were both convinced that Irish Home Rule was desirable for the good of the two countries; only Chamberlain was more moderate in his views. He wanted to satisfy Ireland by giving her a full and fair share of all the advantages which England had. In case that did not succeed, he said that he was prepared to go the full length of Home Rule. But he never seriously contemplated anything more than local self-government. His ideal was an Ireland imprisoned in the giant tentacles of "the Caucus."

While he fraternized with the Radical leaders at Richmond, at the Westminster Palace Hotel and on the terrace of the House of Commons, Parnell accepted Davitt's invitation to speak at a Land meeting at Westport, County Mayo, on June 8th, 1879. As a native of Mayo, Davitt was organizing the first great Land meetings in his own county. These meetings were primarily held as demonstrations in favor of reduced rents. When Parnell accepted the invitation to speak at Westport, he came up for the first time against the prelates of the Catholic Church. Dr. McHale, the archbishop of Tuam, condemned the meeting in an open letter to the Press and warned him not to participate in the movement; but he did not hesitate for a moment. The people were starving, the landlords were refusing to abate their rents, Dublin Castle was strangling the country with coercive legislation, and foreign competition, especially that of America, was ruining Irish trade. After the launching of the archbishop's thunderbolt, Davitt called on Parnell in Morrison's Hotel, and expected to be told what he had already heard from the other men he had invited to speak at Westport. They declared themselves in sympathy with the movement, but declined to go against the decree of the local bishop. Parnell was quite unmoved. He said, "Will I attend? Certainly. Why not? I have promised to be there, and you can count on my keeping that promise."

CHAPTER THIRTEEN

WESTPORT lies in the heart of feudal Ireland, with the walls of Lord Sligo's demesne encircling the town, and every tradesman and farmer, every cottier and fisherman, looks for his living to the big house whose wooded park slopes down to the edge of Clew Bay. Lord Sligo's cattle browse under the shadow of Croagh Patrick and his ghillies guard the waters of the Mayo lakes; but in the spring of 1879, when Connaught was threatened with famine by the recurrence of the potato blight, his agent refused the smallest abatement of rent. A few weeks later Michael Davitt summoned his giant meeting in the square of Westport, not a stone's throw away from Lord Sligo's estate agency, and Mr. Parnell, as elegant and as immaculate as any of his lordship's guests, stood up to address thousands of sullen farmers.

His speech was vigorous and defiant. A fair rent was a rent a tenant could reasonably pay according to the times. God only helped him who helped himself, and if they were not going to be dispossessed, as they were dispossessed in 1847, they must show the landlords—and here he used his famous phrase which traveled the length and breadth of Ireland—"You must show the landlords that you intend to hold a firm grip on your homesteads and lands."

Parnell dwelt on this phrase at an uproarious Land meeting at Limerick, where the Fenians cheered for an Irish republic in the hearing of the parish priest. He stood above the surging crowds, one hand clutched in the lapel of his jacket, the other arm held behind his back with the fist tightly clenched, and he waited quite calmly for the uproar to subside before he delivered one of those short, cold-blooded speeches which seemed to stir the public more than any rhetorical effort. "Stand to your guns," he said, "and there is no power on earth which can prevail against the hundreds of thousands of tenant farmers in this country." He repeated this advice at Tipperary, where the broad-minded, large-hearted Dr. Croke, archbishop of Cashel, defied his fellow-dignitaries of the Catholic Church by favoring the new movement.

Formerly, in the days of Tenant Right, this fearless and war-like priest had opposed the edicts of Cardinal Cullen by publishing a letter advocating the policy which long afterwards became the policy of the Land League: "That there should be established in each parish a tenants' society, including if possible every tenant farmer in the parish, whose members would take a pledge in the terms of promising God, their country and each other, never to bid for any farm or land from which any industrious farmer in his district had been ejected. Should any person violate the pledge, his name should be struck off the register as unworthy to associate with honest men. To sustain the tenantry there should be established at the same time, in the chief town of every district, a tenant protection society, consisting of shop-keepers, professional men and artisans, which would collect a fund for the sustenance of tenants unjustly evicted. If any member bid for land from which a tenant farmer had been ejected, he should forfeit his membership and at the same time the call and patronage of his townsfolk and the district."

The man who had the courage to propound these doctrines in the 'fifties now gave his warm and active support to the grim, sturdy Tipperary farmers who were being slowly ruined by foreign competition undermining their butter and cattle trade, but he did not openly identify himself with the new movement until the following year, when he gave his public benediction to the Land League.

"Keep a firm grip on your homesteads" became the popular slogan of the Agrarian agitation, which was beginning to alarm the rack-renters of Connaught, though it was deliberately ignored by the Press. The *Freeman's Journal* gave only the most meager reports of the speeches held at the Land meetings, for the quarrels between the proprietor and Parnell had been accentuated by a controversy over the Irish University Bill which had come up before the House of Commons. Parnell, regardless of the fact that he was still a member of the synod of the disestablished Church, supported the extreme Catholics in their demand for a Catholic university. And Dwyer Gray, who was not only a convert but the owner of the great Apostolic newspaper, joined with the majority of the Irish members in compromising with the Government. At a committee meeting in the House, where feelings and words ran high, Parnell was reported to have referred to Mr. Gray and his followers as "papist rats," for having deserted him over a bill which was to benefit members of their own creed. Parnell never said these words, for he had far too great a control over his tongue to damage his position with his Catholic countrymen by using that "Orange epithet," and he was content to call Gray a "damned coward" in front of his colleagues. Still there were many people present who believed that he had spoken in this offensive manner, and, in the columns of the *Freeman's Journal,* Gray made a great deal of capital out of the unfortunate episode until a group of Catholic members, who had assisted at the meeting, wrote an open letter to the newspaper emphatically denying that Parnell had ever spoken in those terms. The whole of Ireland resounded with the "papist rats" episode, and people said that "Dwyer Gray's ambition is to put Parnell aside and make himself a sort of dictator worthy of high consideration from the Liberals when they come into power."

During these days Parnell was so overworked in the House of Commons that Tim Healy wrote to his brother, "He will ultimately go mad if no relief comes to him from Ireland, or break down under the strain." And it was Tim Healy who gradually became so indispensable to Parnell that when the House adjourned he would get him to accompany him back to his lodgings, where the brilliant and indefatigable little journalist would deal with a vast unsorted pile of drafted reports and newspaper cuttings. Healy's advice was usually good, and he had a clear, legal brain, with a genius for organizing. In fact, he was invaluable, and whether or not he was personally sympathetic was quite immaterial. Parnell appreciated his talents, and when there was a by-election at Ennis, and the Parnellites decided to put up one of their own candidates against Mr. O'Brien, Q.C., a whole-hearted Whig who had only taken the Home Rule pledge in exchange for the backing of the *Freeman's Journal,* the chief's first choice fell on Healy. If Tim stood, Parnell offered to pay his electioneering expenses out of his private purse, but the young journalist was in no hurry to win his parliamentary laurels, and when T. D. Sullivan wired from Ennis that the election would be a walk-over for O'Brien, Healy said that he would only stand "if all Ireland is so pumped out that a candidate cannot be got to save the seat." At the very last moment one of his journalistic friends on the *Chronicle* offered to take his place, and Parnell went down to Ennis to support a handsome but utterly unknown candidate.

His descent on the town roused the people, and, in spite of the violent opposition of the *Freeman's Journal* and the antagonism of the bishops, an adventurous journalist who had fought in the Franco-Prussian War was returned in preference to Crown Prosecutor O'Brien.

Tim Healy tells the story of how he dragged Parnell away from the House of Commons just in time to have a few hours' sleep before catching the morning mail to Ireland, and how the chief slept in his clothes, while he watched by his bedside to make sure that he did not miss his train. But the most touching of all is the description of how he grilled a steak for breakfast, his first and last essay at cookery, and how Parnell ate the steak without reproach.

The by-election at Ennis was a great Nationalist victory, and the circulation of the *Freeman's Journal* suffered in consequence. Mr. Gray, who, according to William O'Brien, one of the most indulgent and admiring members of his staff, was "somewhat over-ready to accept the blind decree of destiny with an indulgent skepticism," resolved to have no more open quarrels with Parnell, and, by way of retrieving the fortunes of his paper, he identified himself with the Nationalist movement by despatching O'Brien to the west of Ireland to give a detailed and accurate account both on the Land agitation and on the prevalent distress in the country. All along the Atlantic coastline, from Sligo down to Bantry Bay, O'Brien traveled through the rotting wastes of potato fields, and in front of every estate office he found a mob of starving wretches begging for reduced rents. The four richest landlords of Connaught had combined against the Land agitation by refusing even an abatement of ten per cent. In Dublin, James Lowther still cracked his jokes at the expense of the starving population, while the police officials were ordered by the Government to discredit O'Brien's reports. The Gombeen men grew fat on the rich fields from which the rightful owners had been evicted, and sheer despair was driving the people to miserable Agrarian outrages and murder.

Such was the state of the country in the autumn of 1879, when Michael Davitt came to Parnell with the proposal of sweeping the various tenants' defense societies into one great organization, with a central committee in Dublin and local branches throughout the country. It was a dangerous proposal, for the law penalizing conventions had only just been repealed and a central office which would be held responsible for every act committed by a local branch would have enormous difficulties to overcome. The moderate members of the parliamentary party, who identified themselves with Tenant Right, refused to have anything to do with an organization which was the direct outcome of the "New Departure," but every ardent young Nationalist was being swept into the Agrarian agitation—men like John Dillon, son of John Blake Dillon of the '48 movement, and Thomas Sexton, who grew to be one of the greatest orators in the House of Commons; Fenians like Pat Egan and John Brennan, who in 1878 had supported the constitutionalists against the orders of the supreme council. Parnell recognized the Land League as a dynamic force which would make him independent of all the nominal Home Rulers. The risks would be great, but to hold himself apart meant political suicide. Here was the one great opportunity for uniting farmers, Fenians, Home Rulers and priests, and in a united Ireland lay the salvation of the country.

To discipline the forces of "Captain Moonlight" to suit his own purposes, and to convert the bishops from their rigid Tory convictions, seemed impossible tasks for one man to perform, but these were Parnell's two great aims, and at a meeting of the Home Rule League he said, "Unless we unite all shades of political opinions of the country, I fail to see how we can expect ever to attain national independence." This speech dealt a heavy blow at the Home Rule League, which had sadly degenerated since the day when men of every faith and of every political creed had met at the Bilton Hotel to protest against the union with England. Like the "repealers" of the 'forties, the majority had degenerated into Whigs and place-hunters, and there were a number of men in the party whom Parnell meant to fight at the next election.

On October 21st, 1879, the first conference of the Irish National Land League was held at the Imperial Hotel in Dublin. Mr. Parnell was elected as president, with Messrs. Biggar and Egan as honorary treasurers and Messrs. Davitt, Kettle and Brennan as honorary secretaries. The League was formed for the purpose of forcing a reduction of rents and of facilitating the creation of a peasant proprietary, and from the very day of its foundation it launched out on its campaign against the Government. The usually admiring Mr. Healy criticized what he considered to be rash policy on the part of Mr. Parnell. According to him, "no sensible or sagacious politician would have gone at that convention with a rush as he did, without rhyme or reason." He was yet to learn that Parnell was the least impetuous of men, and that he never took a decision without looking at the question from every angle, and that his seemingly most reckless actions were usually those which were the most carefully calculated.

Violent speeches were delivered all over the country, and on November 19th the Government, which up till now had ignored the existence of the Land movement, committed the fatal mistake of arresting Michael Davitt, Daly, a Mayo journalist, and Killen, a barrister, on the charge of making treasonous speeches at a meeting near Sligo. Parnell's answer to this drastic act was to assist, the following Saturday, at the first eviction which had taken place since the formation of the Land League. In a Mayo village he found eight thousand desperate men, who had come from every corner of the county, armed with their blackthorns and ready to fight the squadrons of mounted police sent down by the orders of Dublin Castle. There would have been an ugly riot if he had not commanded the people "to be dignified, orderly and peaceful in your conduct, for the future of our movement depends on our attitude this day, and if we give no excuse for violence our great cause is won."

He controlled the proceedings from the very beginning, and he and Brennan climbed on to a rath and addressed the crowds in the presence of the police, who had been instructed to fire at the first sign of trouble. Brennan spoke first, thrilling his audience by a wild and passionate speech, then Parnell stood up and said, in his calm, imperturbable manner, that he was very much afraid that as a result of that speech Mr. Brennan would be sent to share Mr. Davitt's fate, and he exhorted the people to remain within the law and constitution. "Let us stand, even though we have to stand on the last plank of the constitution." These were cool, judicious words to address to a seething mass of uneducated peasants, but his quiet, definite sentences inspired them with confidence, while his limitless courage and complete belief in himself gave them a feeling of security.

Whenever Davitt spoke on the nationalization of land, expounding his Utopian dreams, the majority of the tenant farmers did not know what he was talking about; it was all above their heads and, as Parnell once said, "Davitt would get stoned by the farmers only he talks Greek to them." But the Wicklow landlord spoke to them in a language they could understand. To keep a firm grip on their homesteads and to hold the harvests were orders which every peasant was ready to obey. In the face of Parnell's determined opposition and the menacing appearance of the crowds, the sheriff decided to call off the eviction, and the people dispersed without a single shot being fired. There had been a dangerous moment when the crowd had begun to surround the constabulary, and Parnell had been forced to strike at one of the leaders with the head of his umbrella. It was his coolness and pluck which won the day, and a police officer said afterwards, "If it hadn't been for you, Mr. Parnell, there would have been murder." "Yes," he answered, with a smile, "and suicide."

A few days later the Government retaliated by arresting Mr. Brennan, and then started the grotesque farce of the Sligo prosecutions. Davitt, Daly, Killen and Brennan were the traversers, and in the middle of the trial the Irish executive, realizing that no jury could be got to convict the Leaguers, and not daring to run the risk of their being found "Not guilty," dropped the prosecution and discharged the prisoners.

Every man in Ireland, from the Unionist landlord to the humble cottier, laughed at the ineffectual activities of the Government. But the Land League was still in infancy, and if the Chief Secretary had adopted strong measures it could easily have been crushed. The Leaguers had no funds and it was to collect money for their starving countrymen that Parnell and Dillon set out for New York on December 21st, 1879.

CHAPTER FOURTEEN

THE crossing had been rough, so rough that even a hardened sailor like Parnell was rarely to be seen walking the decks, and when the *Scythia* dropped anchor in New York harbor on January 2nd, 1880, the irrepressible American reporters, who boarded the ship at eight o'clock in the morning, got a very bleak reception from most of the passengers. Parnell was peacefully eating his breakfast when he was surrounded by a dozen eager faces, each one bent on having an exclusive interview, and for once he had to conquer his aversion to answering direct questions or stating a definite opinion on a subject. The success of his mission depended largely on publicity, and in order to beg money for the Irish farmers the most modest and most independent of men had to sink to the level of a showman. Parnell always admitted that he hated public assemblies, for he was nervous and disliked crowds, but during the next two months he was to visit sixty-two cities, addressing vast audiences, who expected to hear some golden-voiced Daniel O'Connell instead of a shy young man who spoke with an embarrassingly English accent. He was to take part in public processions and preside at endless banquets, with deputations waiting on him at every hour of the day, and the reporters who besieged him at quarantine were only a foretaste of what was in store for him. He told them, "I am a delegate from the Nationalist League. I do not come to America as a private gentleman or as a member of Parliament." And when they asked if he thought that the change he proposed could be brought about without violence, he answered, "It should be so, and it is to this end we are striving. There is force enough in moral power when it is brought to the support of a just cause. We propose only that the tiller of the soil shall be its owner. Then, and then only, will he have a permanent interest in it and become a good citizen. We are in no way 'Communists' as you know the word here or as we know it from the French models." These words, reported by

103

the American Press, were addressed to the hundreds of thousands of Irish-Americans who distrusted the methods of the Clan-na-Gael and who had to be persuaded that the Irish Land League favored a moderate and law-abiding policy. On the other hand, there was the Clan, whose extreme members had warned their colleagues not to trust Parnell, who would use them for his own purposes and make their movement subservient to his own. These men had to be convinced that to settle the Anglo-Irish question by open warfare was an impossibility. If they were hostile to the parliamentary movement, let them at least desist from attacking it. All he asked for was to be given a fair trial.

On the eve of his departure for America, a Home Rule member said to Barry O'Brien, "Well, Parnell has his work cut out for him now at all events. If he can hold his ground with the Clan-na-Gael and afterwards hold it in the House of Commons, he will win Home Rule. The Clan-na-Gael are the open and avowed enemies of England. Their policy is to strike her anywhere and anyhow. What is Parnell going to say to them? If he speaks with an eye to the House of Commons, his speeches won't go down with the Clan. If he speaks with an eye to the Clan, his speeches will be used with tremendous effect against him in the House. It is all very well for men who are not members of Parliament to go among revolutionists, but the member of Parliament has to face the music at St. Stephen's, and how Parnell is going to face it after his visit to the Clan-na-Gael, I don't know."

What the Home Rule member did not realize was that Parnell was quite indifferent to British opinion. Ireland could only become a nation when Irishmen all over the world were united in their aims, and from the moment he landed in New York harbor he ignored the fact that he was a member of Her Majesty's Parliament.

A reception committee consisting of two hundred prominent Irish-Americans, including his own sisters, came out in a revenue cutter to greet him on board, while deputations from the chief

American cities presented him with beautifully printed addresses. There were numberless speeches and toasts to be endured before he was allowed to be a few moments alone with his family, who had been waiting in the harbor since dawn.

The Parnell girls were already public characters. Fanny's poems were published in every American magazine, Anna worked at the Irish Central Relief Bureau in New York and neglected her painting in her efforts to raise funds for the Land League, while Theodosia was known through her beauty alone, for she was the only one of the three who refused to be involved in Nationalist politics. Unknown to her family, she was engaged to an English naval officer. All the sisters led their own lives, and not one of them took the slightest interest in the other's private affairs. Mrs. Parnell was waiting for her son at the Fifth Avenue Hotel, and she at once took matters into her own hands. The indomitable old lady proved herself to be a most efficient impresario, and as the daughter of one of America's popular heroes she added to the glory of her already famous son.

When Parnell addressed his first meeting in Madison Square Garden, his mother sat in the front row, with her strange, blue eyes fixed on his face, "those large, staring, expressionless, weird eyes" which many years later haunted T. P. O'Connor when he declared against her son at a public gathering in Chicago.

Some of Parnell's biographers assume him to have been indifferent towards his sisters and to have treated his mother in a niggardly fashion. These are the very basest of calumnies. The Parnells were devoted to one another, but each one was too much of an individualist to stand the restraining influence of family ties. Even as children they had never really fitted into the communal atmosphere of Irish country life, but they were passionately loyal to one another, and now Charles's mother and sisters advised and instructed him as to the right attitude to adopt towards the different Irish circles in New York. When he was commissioned to write an article on the political situation in his country, it was Fanny who wrote it under his name, and he admitted ruefully that it was much too good and that everyone would know he had never written it. There was very little intimacy between Charles Parnell and his favorite sister. Many years had passed since he had dissuaded her from marrying a penniless painter whom she adored, and from that day Fanny never made any confidences. She was still beautiful in an unquiet, disturbing fashion, with her sad gray eyes which seemed too large for her frail, sculptured face, and her passionate nature now found its chief outlet in her fanatically patriotic poems. She suffered from insomnia and she was playing havoc with an already delicate heart by swallowing every kind of sleeping-draught. But there were moments when she could still behave like a delightful, irresponsible child—as when she commanded John Devoy to steal a black cat from the *New York Herald* office which she insisted brought Gordon Bennett all his luck. Any man who ever had any personal contact with her, from the rugged John Devoy to the emotional Tim Healy, fell under her charm, for "she was gay and feminine without a trace of the poetess or blue stocking."

Eight thousand Americans of Irish extraction gathered in Madison Square Garden to hear Parnell and Dillon define the objects of the Land League. An admission fee was charged for the benefit of the Irish relief funds, and the Fenian element was predominant, for when Parnell disclaimed that the money raised in America would be used for organizing resistance in Ireland, the news was coldly received. He realized that he was disappointing the majority of the audience when he said, "I must in truth and honesty tell you, however unpopular such a statement may be, that not one cent of the money contributed and handed to us will go towards organizing an armed rebellion in Ireland." These words struck only a momentary chill. By the end of his speech he had fascinated his American audience in the same way as he fascinated the Connaught peasants, and even the Mayor of New York promised his cooperation by calling a mass meeting with a view to raising funds.

Speaking at Brooklyn on January 24th, the Irish leader disarmed the revolutionary element in the crowd by saying, "I do not ask you to send armed expeditions over to Ireland," and when a hot-head cried out, "That's what we would like to do," he took up the challenge. "I think I know what you are going to say, and what you would like to do, and what you are willing to do, and how willing you will be to help us all, but we ask you to help us in preventing the people who have taken our advice and who are exhibiting an attitude of devotion which has never been surpassed—what we ask you to do is to help us in preventing these people from being starved to death."

Parnell's path in America was full of pitfalls. He quarreled with Dr. Carroll, who resented his making enquiries about the Clan-na-Gael as if he were already master of the situation. The *New York Herald* was against him from the very beginning, in spite of having John Devoy on its staff, and a considerable part of the Eastern Press echoed the opinions of Gordon Bennett. Socially Parnell was not a success. While he was in New York he accepted an invitation to dine with some prominent members of the Catholic clergy and turned up two hours late for dinner. His apology was not calculated to soothe the offended hierarchy: a notorious agitator from San Francisco had called to see him and had stayed too long. In his eyes the gunman and the clergyman were on an equal footing; they were both indispensable to his cause.

In spite of the numerous difficulties, Parnell and Dillon made a triumphal progress across the continent. Dogged by spies, anathematized by the *Herald* reporters and menaced by the extremists, they never deviated from their original program, and it was only many years later, in the gloom of the London Law Courts, when England's most respectable newspaper summoned as witnesses the lowest class of paid informer, that the whole drama of Parnell's American tour was unfolded to the public. It was nothing short of a miracle how he passed scatheless through the plots and counter-plots that were woven round

him.   British Government spies shadowed him when he fraternized with Patrick Ford and the instigators of the Clerkenwell explosion, and agents of the Clan-na-Gael followed him
from city to city.   Parnell was not an imaginative man, and his
lack of imagination now stood him in good stead.   When he
addressed the people, he spoke with the direct simplicity and
self-confidence of one who had nothing to fear.   At Cincinnati
he made his famous "last link speech."   He said: "I feel confident that we shall kill the Irish landlord system, and when we
have given Ireland to the people of Ireland we shall have laid
the foundation upon which to build up our Irish nation.   The
feudal tenure and the rule of the minority have been the
corner-stone of English misrule.   Pull out that corner-stone,
break it up, destroy it, and you undermine English misgovernment.   When we have undermined English misgovernment we
have paved the way for Ireland to take her place among the
nations of the earth.   And let us not forget that that is the ultimate goal at which all we Irishmen aim.   None of us, whether
we be in America or in Ireland or wherever we may be, will be
satisfied until we have destroyed the last link which keeps Ireland bound to England."   In the eyes of the English this speech
was rank treason, but it won over to his side the most recalcitrant
members of the Clan-na-Gael.

When Parnell spoke at Boston, Wendell Phillips was in the
chair and told his audience, "I come here, as you have done,
from a keen desire to see the man that has forced John Bull to
listen."   At Troy, New York, a hardened old Irish patriot
stepped on to the platform and handed him twenty-five dollars,
saying, "Here's five dollars for bread and twenty for lead."

At Washington he was accorded the privilege of addressing
Congress.   This honor had previously been granted to only two
foreigners, Kossuth and Lafayette.   But to the Americans Parnell
was not a foreigner, and it was his ability to understand their
mentality which made his tour a success.   He understood their
weaknesses and took advantage of them.   The majority of the

people who attended his meetings came out of curiosity. They wanted not so much to hear him speak as to see him in the flesh. Therefore he avoided the public processions and the places where they could see him without paying admission fees. When they had parted with their money, he was willing to gratify their love of personal contact, and he and Dillon took turns in handing round the collection plate at the end of the meeting. In his modest, self-depreciatory way, he said afterwards to one of his colleagues, "When John Dillon and I had sufficiently depressed the meeting, we went round with our hats and collected money." And very often the haggard features of the "Irish Christ" made a far greater impression on the audience than Parnell's cold, aristocratic appearance. There is an amusing anecdote told of a State governor who, after presiding at one of the numerous banquets, confessed to a friend, "Somehow Parnell did not impress me a bit. When I saw this sleek young dude, as well fed as you or I and a darned sight better groomed, I said to myself, 'The *Herald* knows what it's about. The idea of sending out a man like that, to tell us they are all starving!' But when the other man, poor Dillon, came along with hunger written on every line of his face, I said, 'Ah, that's a different thing. There's the Irish famine right enough,' and I guess my five hundred dollar bill would not wait in my pocket any longer."

It was an exhausting, nerve-racking life for two men who were far from strong, and Dillon was unable to cope with the vast pile of correspondence which kept pouring in from all parts of the country. Parnell never even opened a telegram, and, as they traveled from place to place, their business affairs got into such a state of chaos that a secretary had to be summoned from Ireland. Tim Healy was the inevitable choice, and he threw up his job the moment he received his orders. Two days later he was on a boat steaming out of Queenstown harbor. In New York he was welcomed by John Devoy and the Parnell girls, who lost no time in telling him just what they thought of John Dillon. Charles was a thousand miles away in the West, and many people were offended because they could not get replies to their letters and invitations. No one knew definitely where he was or what he was going to do, and, according to his sisters, it was John Dillon's business to act as his secretary, as well as speaking and lecturing all over the country. With childish inconsistency they regarded the most trivial matters as if they were of vital importance. Dillon's carelessness about his personal belongings, the way he would leave his slippers in one hotel and his night-shirt in another, so got on their nerves that they treated it as if it were a serious offense. Much to his amusement, Tim Healy found that he was regarded as a "heaven-sent genius," though he was shrewd enough to see that he would be the next victim if anything went wrong. Meanwhile he basked in the sunshine of their favors, ate the delicious oyster soup they had specially ordered for him, and toured the newspaper offices with John Devoy, who was Parnell's indefatigable ally. He found that the *Herald* was deliberately suppressing the reports of the Land Leaguers' magnificent receptions in the West, while Gordon Bennett, in the hopes of ousting Parnell, had started a rival Irish famine fund.

There were now four separate relief funds for the benefit of the starving Irish. The stark reality of an approaching famine had at last penetrated to Dublin Castle, and the Duchess of Marlborough had issued an appeal to collect money for the distressed areas. Dwyer Gray, who was now Lord Mayor of Dublin, had refused to cooperate with the Castle, and had started a Mansion House fund on what he considered to be a wide national basis. This independent action on his part put an end to social intercourse between the Mansion House and the Castle and eventually led him to give Parnell the support of the *Freeman's Journal*. But in the early months of 1880 his policy was still to belittle the efforts of the Land Leaguers, and not a penny of the money collected by the Mansion House went to help an evicted tenant.

When Healy joined Parnell at Davenport, Iowa, he was able

to enlighten him as to the situation at home. The peasants were beginning to offer serious resistance to their landlords, the distress in the country could no longer be denied, and, with his usual incompetence, Mr. Lowther was trying to solve the problem by loaning money to the landlords for the purpose of starting relief works. There were so many charitable organizations on foot that Healy suggested that Parnell's future efforts should be directed entirely towards raising money for the Land League. His advice was acted on, and from now onwards it was Healy who directed and advised a nervous, irritable man, who had exhausted both his health and patience. It was Healy who gave the interviews and entertained the Press, and on many occasions even wrote the speeches as their Pullman car rumbled through the frozen Northern States. There was so much work to do that Parnell and Dillon had been forced to separate after the tremendous demonstrations in Chicago. In their enthusiasm the Irish population of the great commercial city had made them endure the most embarrassing ordeal. They had to stand on a platform facing ten thousand people, while a muscular young giantess recited a long, eulogistic poem in their honor. On their way back to the hotel, Parnell gave vent to his real feelings, and this was one of the few occasions when Dillon heard him use bad language. He loathed the continual publicity, the way he was never allowed to be five minutes alone; even when he traveled there were deputations waiting in the snow at every station, and every man had to be shaken by the hand and listened to with smiling patience. Cards and circulars had to be handed out as if he were nothing but a bagman, and, as soon as he reached an hotel, a crowd gathered in his sitting-room. But they all subscribed to his fund; even the sleeping-car attendant on the train to Canada, who was so attentive to his needs, had parted with a hundred-dollar bill at his meeting in St. Louis, and he wrote to Pat Egan: "The enthusiasm increases in volume as we proceed from place to place. Military guards and salvoes of artillery salute our coming, and the meetings which we address, although a high admission charge is made, are packed from floor to roof. State governors, members of Congress, local representatives, judges, clergymen, continually appear on the platform."

In Canada he received a tremendous ovation, though the archbishop of Toronto had warned him not to come, as the "Orangemen" threatened to make trouble. Only a few weeks previously, O'Donovan Rossa had been assaulted by the mob, but Parnell ignored the advice, and both in Toronto and Montreal he was greeted by thousands of cheering Irish and French citizens. In the latter place every house was illuminated in his honor, and he received such a royal welcome that Tim Healy wound up the meeting by referring to him as the "Uncrowned King of Ireland." This epithet clung to him during the ten years of his meteoric career. Popular enthusiasm was roused, the whole town went mad about him, and, as Healy said, "everyone was affected but himself." But this man, who outwardly gave the impression of having no heart or nerves, had rushed to a telegraph office the minute he arrived in Montreal in order to telegraph to his mother that he was quite safe from the fear of "Orange" riots, for poor Mrs. Parnell was in constant fear that his steps were dogged by enemies.

After the triumphant reception in Montreal, Parnell returned to the hotel to find a cablegram from Joseph Biggar saying, "Parliament dissolved. Return at once." And early next morning he and Tim Healy started homewards via New York, while Dillon was ordered to remain behind and keep the movement going. Forty thousand pounds had been collected in the space of two months, but the Fenian secretaries of the Land League stipulated that none of the money was to be expended in the interests of parliamentarianism. In spite of his triumphs, Parnell was depressed and moody. The last two months had overtaxed his physical strength, and before him was the prospect of fighting an election with an empty exchequer. He was fatigued in mind and body, and, as their train sped southwards to New

York, Healy found it impossible to rouse him from his gloom. He was obsessed by doubts and fears, and as they passed over the St. Lawrence River he looked out at the frozen landscape and said half to himself, "I wonder, would any man pay to hear me speak a second time?"

His last evening in New York was spent with his family, and Healy was profoundly shocked at the Parnells' outward indifference to one another. There were no demonstrations of affection or loving words, and when, in the middle of dinner, Theodosia suddenly announced that she had booked a passage on the same boat as her brother, as she was going to Paris to be married to Lieutenant Paget, "the others did not seem to be in the least surprised or to care a damn, though none of them had ever heard of the project before." Charles never even said that he was pleased to have her company, but, when she appeared on board, no lover could have been more attentive. Every morning they could be seen arm-in-arm pacing the decks, and in the middle of the ocean the Irish agitator and the prospective bride of an English naval officer celebrated St. Patrick's Day by opening a bottle of champagne to the glory of Ireland.

Before leaving New York, Parnell summoned a meeting at the Fifth Avenue Hotel for the purpose of forming an American Land League. A committee of seven was appointed, and out of those seven, four were members of the Clan, with John Devoy as chief secretary. Parnell disliked the Clan, for he knew that it would be impossible to dictate to them once he was back in Ireland, but he could not ignore them. The constitutionalists who joined the American Land League did so at his request, but the Fenian element was still predominant, and the binding together of such divergent parties was due to his tact and genius. In two months he had succeeded in uniting the Irish-American forces, but they were forces capable of committing excesses over which he would have no control.

On March 10th, Parnell left New York in a blinding snowstorm. The 69th regiment, which at one time was composed entirely of Fenians, escorted him to the harbor, and as the ship passed the pier out into the river the military band played, and an immense crowd cheered him as he stood bareheaded in the storm, bowing his acknowledgments and "looking like a king."

CHAPTER FIFTEEN

THE first Midlothian campaign gave the death-blow to the Tory Government. To quote Morley, "Gladstone's tremendous projectiles pounded the ministerial citadel to the ground. He had a nation at his back. What had been vague misgiving about Lord Beaconsfield grew into sharp certainty; shadows of doubt upon policy at Constantinople or Kabul or the Cape became substantive condemnation; uneasiness as to the national finances turned to active resentment." Gladstone had emerged from the "temple of peace" at Hawarden to launch the most powerful personal attack that had ever struck a rival minister, and Lord Beaconsfield had ignored the issues on which he was accused, the blunders of Sir Henry Layard at Constantinople and of Sir Bartle Frere in the Transvaal, by dissolving Parliament on a completely unexpected issue. His manifesto to the country took the form of an open letter to the Duke of Marlborough, Viceroy of Ireland, in which he attempted to make Home Rule the storm-center of the coming election.

"A danger in its ultimate results scarcely less disastrous than pestilence or famine, which now engages your Excellency's anxious attention, distracts Ireland. A portion of the population is attempting to sever the constitutional tie which unites it to Great Britain in that bond which has favored the power and prosperity of both. It is to be hoped that all men of light and learning will resist this destructive doctrine. The strength of the nation depends on the unity of feeling which should pervade the United Kingdom and its widespread dependencies. The first duty of an English minister should be to consolidate the cooperation which renders irresistible a community educated as our own in an equal love of liberty and law." Then came his counter-attack on Mr. Gladstone: "And yet there are some who challenge the expediency of the Imperial character of the realm. Having attempted and failed to enfeeble our colonies by their policy of decomposition, they may perhaps now recognize in the disintegration of the United Kingdom a mode which will not only accomplish but precipitate their purpose." This attack was ineffective, for at this period Gladstone had not yet concentrated on the problem of Home Rule, and in an address to the electors of Midlothian he said, "If you ask me what I think of Home Rule, I must tell you that I will only answer when you tell me how Home Rule is related to local government. . . . We have got an overweighted Parliament, and if Ireland or any other portion of the country is desirous and able so to arrange its affairs that, by taking the local part or some local part of its transactions off the hands of the Parliament, it can liberate and strengthen Parliament for Imperial concerns, I say I will not only accord a reluctant assent, but I will give a zealous support to any such scheme. One limit, gentlemen, one limit I know to the extension of local government. It is this, nothing can be done, in my opinion, by any wise statesman or right-minded Briton, to weaken or compromise the authority of the Imperial Parliament," and he accused the Tories of having endangered the Union by maintaining in Ireland "an alien Church, an unjust Land law and franchises inferior to our own"—the very points on which Mr. Disraeli had accused the Opposition in 1844.

In Parnell's absence the Home Rule Confederation of Great Britain published an election manifesto saying, "Lord Beaconsfield has issued in the guise of a letter to the Viceroy of Ireland a declaration of war upon your country and your friends. The ministry is seeking to obtain a renewed term of office by sowing dissensions and hatred between Englishmen and Irishmen, and Lord Beaconsfield's vicious manifesto directly appeals to the worst passions and prejudices for the purpose of stirring up Englishmen against Irish Nationalists." Mr. Shaw, the moderate Home Rule leader, in a reply to Lord Beaconsfield, declared that "the Prime Minister has not thought it beneath his position to issue an electioneering manifesto placing false issues before the electors of the Empire and tending to excite the worst passions of the ignorant."

The country was already in the throes of the General Election when Parnell and Healy landed at Queenstown on March 21st. As they approached the coast, Parnell looked in vain for a tender full of welcoming friends, and for once he dropped his mask of studied indifference and complained bitterly that not one of his colleagues had thought it worth while to meet him. It was a revelation for Healy to see the true character of one who outwardly was a man of bronze. "His disappointment contrasted with his usual calm was tragic. . . . He enlarged on the work he had done in America and said it deserved better reward than indifference. In an instant he bared his soul and let me know that his ordinary reserve was merely a mask."

But when, rounding the bend of Cork harbor, there came a tender full of cheering men, Parnell became the superman once more. His whole body stiffened, his eyes hardened, and not by a look or a sign did he show how glad he was to see them. There was Biggar in his shabby sealskin waistcoat, welcoming them in his harsh, Belfast accents, and Davitt with his gaunt face wreathed in smiles, waving a handkerchief in his one hand, and Sexton and T. D. Sullivan singing a joyous refrain. Parnell received them as if they had parted only half an hour ago, and Healy watched and noted that his acting was superb.

He had adopted that frigid mask from the early days of 1874, when he stepped down from the platform in the Rotunda with his hands covered in blood where the tightly clenched nails had torn the skin, and this attitude of Olympian calm and sublime detachment put him on a plane above his followers. The Irish people, who had loved O'Connell for his personal characteristics and human frailties, worshiped Parnell as one who, to quote Mr. William O'Brien, "had the divine right of genius to govern." He was the unapproachable leader who never stepped down from his pedestal to parade the intimacies of his private life in the cottages of his constituents, for he was far too sensitive to expose himself to the curiosity of the masses. He was never a demonstrative man, and in moments of emotion he was apt to be inarticulate. His early upbringing in a family in which no member ever questioned the others on their private affairs made him resent the slightest interference from his colleagues, and such was the awe in which he was held that not one of them dared to criticize him behind his back. It is doubtful whether Healy ever told Biggar and Davitt of Parnell's resentment at what for the moment looked like their neglect, for his followers deluded themselves and each other in proclaiming the most sensitive and vulnerable of individuals to be a superman. According to Justin McCarthy, "he was not liked by his party as a whole, but, like or dislike, all bowed to him because all felt that he was the one man who knew what to do in moments of difficulty and that he was always right." He owed his ascendency to his strength of will and an iron self-control which banished every human sentiment and feeling from his public life. The rhetorical, emotional Irish politician who on the public platform wept over his country's wrongs, regarded him not as a man but as a phenomenon.

The entire population of Cork came out into the streets to welcome Parnell. He was given a royal reception, with public processions and banquets, and there was only one note of dissension, when a group of extreme Fenians presented him with an address, saying that, impelled by the conviction that it was useless to look for any practical national good through the means of parliamentary representation, they had determined as a political party to take no part in the coming elections, and consequently no part in the adoption, rejection or support of the parliamentary candidates.

The cooperation of Dr. Carroll on the other side of the Atlantic had strengthened the supreme council of the I.R.B. in their opposition to Parnell. In 1880 they withdrew the resolution that any Fenians of the rank and file might at their own risk take part in the parliamentary movement. From now onwards no Fenian adhering to the rules of the council was allowed to have dealings with the constitutional party. This was a direct hit at the New Departure, and Michael Davitt resigned from the council.

After being presented with this address on landing at Queenstown, Parnell had not very long to wait before the Fenians came out into the open against him. Instead of the rest cure which he badly needed, he was faced with an electioneering campaign in which there was a lack of both candidates and funds. The *Freeman* still extolled the Whig Home Rulers, and Mr. Shaw, the careful manager of the Munster Bank, controlled the exchequer of the Home Rule party. Forty thousand pounds had been collected in America, but the Land League was dominated by Fenians, and Brennan, the secretary, adhered to the rules of the organization and declared that not a penny was to go towards helping a parliamentary candidate. His uncle, Pat Egan, who was acting as treasurer, proved to be more amenable, but it must have been very irritating for Parnell to have to plead and persuade in order to be granted a thousand pounds of the money he had collected himself.

Now began the breathless turmoil of a hurried electioneering campaign in which there was not a moment to lose. At times like this Parnell showed himself to be truly great, for he was a superb fighter. No place was too remote, no journey too fatiguing, to prevent him from attending any meeting where his presence might help his candidate. Special trains bore him to every part of Ireland. He himself stood for Cork city, Meath and Mayo, where his nominal opponent was George Brown, though in reality he contested the seat in order to oust O'Connor Power, who in his jealousy was trying to make trouble in the party. His days were spent at public meetings, his nights in draughty trains, and for ten days he did not sleep in a proper bed. He was living on his nerves, and he was so determined to win that his thin, delicate frame seemed possessed of a superhuman strength. It was only owing to lack of funds that he was unable to make a clean sweep of the Whig landlords who had adhered to the principles of Isaac Butt, but nevertheless he struck them many a hard blow. In Roscommon, James O'Kelly, an adventurous Irish-American journalist who had participated in every war and revolution which had taken place in the last fifteen years, succeeded in ousting the O'Connor Don, the chief representative of the old Catholic aristocracy; and in Wexford Parnell nominated John Barry, the ex-Fenian manufacturer who had won him the support of the Home Rule Confederation of Great Britain, in opposition to the chevalier Keyes O'Clery, a well-known champion of Catholic interests. At this election the physical-force men came out against Parnell for the first time, for they were determined to have a thrust at John Barry, who in their eyes had proved himself a traitor to their cause. The hustings presented the incongruous spectacle of the extremists and the priests united in denouncing Parnell's candidate.

On Easter Sunday, April 13th, which in Parnell's eyes was always an unlucky day, he went down to Enniscorthy to speak in favor of his two candidates for County Wexford, but he had barely mounted the platform before he was attacked by a mob of screaming hooligans. Young John Redmond, who barely knew him in those days, describes the scene:

"I was at Enniscorthy with him. It was an awful scene. There were about four thousand to five thousand people there. They all seemed to be against him. I remember one man shouting, though what he meant I could not tell: 'We will show Parnell that the blood of Vinegar Hill is still green.' The priests were against Parnell. Parnell stood on the platform, calm and self-possessed. There was no use in trying to talk. He faced the crowd, looking sad and sorrowful but not at all angry; it was an awful picture of patience. A rotten egg was flung at him. It struck him on the beard and trickled down. He took no notice of it, never wiped it off and was not apparently conscious of it. He faced the crowd steadfastly and held his ground. One man rushed at him, seized him by the leg and tore his trousers right up from bottom to top. There was no chance of a hearing, and we got away from the platform and went to the hotel to lunch. Parnell ate a hearty lunch, while a waiter was busy stitching his trousers all the time. It was a comical sight. Afterwards we went for a walk. We were met by a hostile mob and I was knocked down and cut in the face. I got up as quickly as I could and made my way to the railway station. When

Parnell saw me, he said: 'Why, you are bleeding. What is the matter?' I told him what had happened and he said, smiling: 'Well, you have shed your blood for me at all events.'" These were his first friendly words to a young man who afterwards proved himself to be the most devoted of his followers, one of the few who defended his name when the majority of his party tried to drag it in the mud.

No wonder Redmond was impressed by that awful picture of patience. For someone so proud and fastidious, who disliked even a friendly crowd and flared up at the slightest insult, it must have been torture to have to control himself from hitting back at the first man who dared to lay hands on him. Parnell, like most of his countrymen, was quick with his fists, and if the incident had occurred during one of his early electioneering campaigns he would probably have given way to his natural instincts, but by now he had learned that a statesman's feelings must be blunted and his skin hardened to any form of abuse. To have pandered to a crowd who were spoiling for a fight would have been unwise tactics, and afterwards he never complained, beyond saying that his supporters as well as the police stood by like a flock of sheep and looked on.

It was in Parnell's interests to make light of any opposition he encountered. Cardinal McCabe and the leading bishops, with the exception of Dr. Croke, were all against him. In the great Catholic city of Cork only two young curates could be persuaded to speak on his platform, but his heroic behavior at Enniscorthy, when he had replied to his chairman's advice to retire by saying, "I will say a word for John Barry if I stand here all day," had so impressed the local clergy that in the end they deserted the Catholic nominee and rallied to him at the poll. All during the campaign Parnell took great pains to deny that the extremists and the priests were against him. He maintained "that it was only the case of a few individuals, and that, anyway, everyone was welcome to express his opinion on the Parnellite policy." For a little while he would have to exercise tact and patience, but the great mass of the people were at his back and the others would soon be brought to heel.

He resented bitterly the way in which the priests interfered in politics, but as a Protestant he dared not say a word about the undue influence which they exercised over their parishioners. Only once during a recent election, through a slip of the tongue, he had referred to the clergy as "those fellows," and all during his career he had to contend against the Vatican intrigues and the constant cabal engineered by the Tory bishops and the members of the leading Catholic families.

For Parnell the election of 1880 was a tremendous personal triumph; while Gladstone made his royal progress from Midlothian back to Downing Street, the young Irish leader was returned for all three constituencies he had contested. In spite of the empty exchequers, his candidates scored the most astounding victories. T. D. Sullivan, Edward Leamy, Justin McCarthy (M.P. since a by-election the previous year), Thomas Sexton, John Barry, Lysaght Finnegan, the O'Gorman Mahon (who had taken part in the historic election of 1829), James O'Kelly, T. P. O'Connor and John Dillon, were all returned to Westminster. Only Healy, who had supervised and organized the electioneering campaign, had refused to be nominated, though later in the year he was prevailed upon to stand for the borough of Wexford.

This election made Parnell the idol of his people. When he drove up to a country meeting in an outside car the jarvey had to protect him from the crowds who gathered round, kissing his hands, stuffing amulets into his pockets, bringing him homely, simple gifts—a cackling hen in a basket, a handful of eggs or a bunch of shamrock—overwhelming him with their effusive demonstrations of affection, which made him feel embarrassed, almost angry with the people who loved him so much, and whom he loved also in that queer, repressed manner which made it impossible for him to give more than a shy smile in response, that peculiar, gentle smile which only the country people in Ireland knew. For Parnell loved the Celtic peasant as he never loved any of his colleagues, with the exception perhaps of Joseph Biggar and, in later years, James O'Kelly.

On polling day Mr. Shaw was still the leader of the Home Rule party, but on May 17th the Irish parliamentarians met in Dublin to nominate their leader, and Parnell was elected by a majority of five votes. Eighteen members voted for Shaw and twenty-three for Parnell. From now onwards the Nationalist party was to sit in opposition to whatever Government was in power, for although the whole of Ireland had rejoiced at Lord Beaconsfield's defeat, Parnell was inclined to be skeptical over Liberal promises. Among the new members of Parliament who voted for Parnell was a certain Captain O'Shea, who, together with the O'Gorman Mahon, represented the County of Clare.

CHAPTER SIXTEEN

THE same circumstances which in 1874 gave Parnell the opportunity to contest County Dublin now enabled Captain O'Shea to be returned for County Clare, for the impoverished state of the parliamentary funds forced the Nationalists to accept any candidate who was willing to pledge himself to their principles as well as paying his own electioneering expenses. Captain O'Shea was eminently presentable, but he was Irish only in name, for all his interests were centered in England. His father, a hard-working Dublin solicitor who had amassed a considerable fortune at the expense of his thriftless landlord clients, realized the height of his ambition when he managed to send "Willie" to Oscott and to buy him a commission in the 18th Hussars. "First become a smart officer, secondly, do what the other men do and send the bill in to me" was his parting advice to a son who followed his instructions so faithfully that in the space of a few years he was presented with a vast pile of debts. Poor Mr. O'Shea, slaving in his dusty Dublin offices, had many difficulties to contend with. He had a tiresome, elegant wife who never let him forget that she was a papal countess in her own right, and an invalid daughter with religious mania. All his family despised Ireland for the simple reason that whereas in London, Paris and Madrid (where the O'Sheas had connections) they were accepted at their full value, in Dublin they were never able to penetrate the sacred precincts of Viceregal Lodge. Matters did not improve when Willie O'Shea fell in love with the thirteenth child of an impoverished English parson, even if the parson was the aristocratic Sir John Wood, living in a great dilapidated mansion in Essex. At first the Woods did not consider the young Irishman to be much of a match for their lovely daughter, but when old Sir John died, leaving his family practically penniless, Katherine accepted her persistent suitor, who for her sake had given up the army and accepted a partnership in his uncle's Spanish bank. Willie's business enterprises were doomed to failure, for, though he was popular with his sporting, racing friends, he was not a man to inspire confidence. His father died, and with him went the one reliable source of income. He quarreled with his uncle and decided to try his fortune at managing a stud farm. He was declared bankrupt, and by the irony of fate it was his wife's relations who had to come to his rescue. Her uncle, Lord Hatherley, was Lord Chancellor, and, though he declined to avail himself of Willie's valuable services, he was willing to give financial assistance to his niece. There was also a rich old aunt called Mrs. Benjamin Wood, to whom the young couple could always appeal when in distress.

During the first years of her married life Katherine found herself thrown from pillar to post, at one moment living in affluence and luxury, with a French lady's maid and a private carriage; the next moment nursing a sick husband in furnished rooms off the Harrow Road. By the time she had given birth to three children she was completely disillusioned, for Willie was a born bachelor, whose idea of a perfect married life was to plant his wife and children in the country while he lived in London, only paying them occasional visits. Katherine refused to be ignored, and, being a sensible, practical woman, she decided to make herself indispensable by cultivating the rich business men who might be useful to him. She despised her husband, but she still loved him in a purely physical way. She was a very physical person, full-blooded and robust, and you had only to look at her deep bosom, her beautiful, sensuous mouth and wide, curving nostrils, to know that here was a woman who would appeal to almost any man. But sometimes she marred her sexual attraction by an oppressive intellectuality. Her youth had been spent in cultured, artistic surroundings. Scholars and poets had frequented her home at Rivenhall, and she had very little in common with her flippant, gregarious husband, who liked to fill his house with loud-voiced racing-men and titled foreigners whom he had picked up in the different European capitals where he was so very much at home. At twenty-five William O'Shea must have been a delightful, irresponsible being, but age did not improve his qualities. His flippancy had hardened into cynicism, his childish vanity in insisting on his wife attending certain social functions had degenerated into a calculating snobbery, in which he used Katie and her relations as pawns in his various business enterprises. He was brilliant and superficial, insincere and unreliable, and, though his considerable social gifts made him welcome in many circles, most people fought rather shy of his intimacy, for there was something shifty about O'Shea in spite of his ready laughter and witty, caustic speech. For several years this ill-assorted couple led an improvident, precarious existence, tiding over periods of financial difficulty, thanks to devoted servants, whose wages were rarely paid, and miraculously patient creditors, on whom Katherine bestowed her most enchanting smiles.

Willie became involved in mysterious business concerns which took him for many pleasant trips abroad, and finally Mrs. Benjamin Wood, who lived in a rich and rigid seclusion at Eltham, offered a home to her neglected niece by buying her a house in the precincts of her park and settling a regular income on her and her children. The only condition the old lady imposed was that Katherine should be her constant companion. It was not a very attractive proposition for a high-spirited, young woman, but after years of constant struggle any secure anchorage was welcome. So the late 'seventies saw Mrs. O'Shea settled in a comfortable villa at Eltham, with a husband in bachelor lodgings in London who only visited her for the week-ends. To quote her own words: "The wearing friction caused by our totally dissimilar temperaments began to make us feel that close companionship was impossible." Yet still he had that curious physical hold over her, so that years later, when the whole world knew Parnell to be her lover, O'Shea complained to Labouchere that whenever Katie visited his flat in Victoria Street she insisted "on renewing our old relations." Therefore it was not only for her children's sake that Katherine kept on amicable terms with her husband.

She was also an ambitious woman, and she still thought that, given a proper chance, Willie could make a brilliant career. He was now interested in some Spanish mines which, with a certain amount of capital, could be made into a paying concern, and it was in her interest to help him to the best of her ability. Christopher Weguelin, an old friend of the family who had always shown himself disposed to take more than a friendly interest in her pecuniary difficulties, was easily persuaded to invest a considerable amount of money in Willie's sulphur mines, and he was influential enough to get a number of able business men to follow his lead. A company was promoted, and the only condition imposed by the chief director was that Willie should be sent to Spain as general manager. Needless to say, his wife remained behind, and Mr. Weguelin was amply rewarded for having secured Willie a very handsome salary. It was all done quite openly, for by now the O'Sheas were frankly cynical with one another. Willie was very happy in Spain; being the complete cosmopolitan, he enjoyed Continental life, and, whenever he ran short of funds or machinery for the mines, he would write to Katie to use her influence in stating his demands before the board. The dull routine of Katherine's life at Eltham was now constantly interrupted by little trips to London, with pleasant dinners at Mr. Weguelin's house, where she would delight her host and his friends by cooking them one of her gorgeous beefsteak pies for which she had been famous since girlhood. In spite of her intellectual leanings she was thoroughly domestic, skilled in all the housewifely arts, and it was her warm "mothering" quality which endeared her to the hard business men who constituted her husband's boards of directors. When she forgot to be "one of the brilliant Wood sisters" and was just her charming natural self, with her round, merry face crinkled in laughter and her large dark eyes sparkling with fun, then no high-spirited girl could be more enchanting than she.

Willie's business enterprises were only successful in the prospectuses, and even Christopher Weguelin's infatuation for Katie could not blind him to the fact that he would be made responsible for substantial losses. At the end of eighteen months Willie was recalled and the relationship between his wife and Mr. Weguelin grew noticeably cooler. Maybe he considered that his temporary bliss had been purchased at a rather expensive price.

Once more the young couple attempted to resume their family life at Eltham, but the result was constant friction. Willie's thoughts now turned towards a political career, for as M.P. he would be *persona grata* on many a director's board, where as plain Captain O'Shea he did not stand a chance of being admitted. His wife was delighted at the idea, and again acted as intermediary in wheedling the necessary money out of her rich aunt. O'Shea was the typical political adventurer who, though devoid of any Nationalist principles, chose to style himself as an Irish Home Ruler for the simple reason that it was both easier and cheaper to become nominated to an Irish constituency than to an English one. The O'Gorman Mahon, that picturesque old soldier of fortune whose swordsmanship was famous all over Europe, had been nominated for County Clare, mainly because he had been one of the champions of O'Connell in the stormy elections of '29. It was he who now obtained for O'Shea the honor of standing with him on condition of his guaranteeing all the electioneering expenses.

The Clare farmers looked somewhat askance at the overdressed young London dandy when the veteran duelist brought him on to the platform at Ennis, and Parnell's comment on first seeing O'Shea was, "That's just the kind of man we don't want in the party." But time ran short and money ran shorter, so O'Shea and the O'Gorman were left to canvass Clare, and after they had kissed every pretty girl from Blackhead down to Killaloe, and drunk lashings of Irish whiskey, which poor Willie loathed, they were returned with a thumping majority.

Meanwhile Katherine O'Shea spent long quiet days in her garden at Eltham, driving out with her old aunt, who still wore the early Victorian fashions of her youth, sitting in those hushed tapestry rooms, where the sunlight was never allowed to shine, and occasionally entertaining Mr. Meredith to tea, for the famous novelist was paid three hundred pounds a year to come down once a week to read aloud to Mrs. Wood. No wonder she looked forward to Willie's letters, and now that Christopher no longer played a leading rôle in her thoughts she rather enjoyed the prospect of entertaining as the wife of an Irish M.P. She knew nothing of Ireland or of Irish affairs, but when Willie returned from Clare, they invited the O'Gorman to dinner at Greenwich, and she was soon captured by the old man's infectious enthusiasm for his country. He had such merry blue eyes and such a musical voice that she forgot to be annoyed when he informed her with the grand air of a conqueror that he was practically penniless, and that her husband had guaranteed their joint expenses, which had totaled two thousand pounds. It was here that for the first time she heard Willie and the O'Gorman discussing Mr. Parnell, describing him as a reserved, aloof young man who had ruined his health through overwork and who treated with a freezing hostility anyone who dared to suggest that he should take care of himself. Whenever Parnell's name had cropped up in conversation with her brother Evelyn, or her uncle, Lord Hatherley, they had always talked as if he were a dangerous agitator determined to undermine British prestige; but now the O'Gorman turned to her with a twinkle in his eyes, saying, "If you meet Parnell, Mrs. O'Shea, be good to him. His begging expedition to America has about finished him and I don't believe he'll last the session out." And Willie looked across at her and said in his bland, smiling way, "We will give some political dinners and we will ask Parnell, though I am afraid he may not come." She did not answer, but she mentally decided that if she gave any dinners to the Irish party, she would make a point of getting their leader.

The new Parliament met, and the O'Sheas launched out on a series of small dinner-parties at Thomas's Hotel in Berkeley Square. But, though Mr. Parnell was invited to every one of these dinners and on one occasion had even accepted the invitation, he invariably failed to turn up at the last moment. It was galling for Katherine when her guests made laughing allusions to the "vacant chair," though they vied with one another in telling her stories of Parnell's inaccessibility and of his dislike for social intercourse, of how he refused the invitations of the most important political hostesses and went so far as to pass his own relations in the street, without making them the slightest sign of recognition. Katherine was both ambitious and determined, but not one of her guests realized the strength of her determination when she said one evening in her gay, childish way: "The uncrowned King of Ireland shall sit in that chair at the next dinner I give."

At this time Parnell was suffering from a nervous reaction following the strain of his American tour and of the General Election, and even a holiday at Avondale could not cure his insomnia. For a few days he tried to forget politics by immersing himself in the business of his estate, seeing to his sawmills and stone quarries and shutting himself up in his laboratory, where he would spend hours in trying to extricate a fraction of gold from the quartz of his own hillside. He went fishing with Arthur Dickinson and riding with Emily, but it was impossible for him to find any peace. Healy was always at hand with letters and petitions which had to be answered, and Michael Davitt was constantly worrying him about a new scheme of land purchase which proposed that when a landlord consented to sell a holding to a tenant, the executive of the Land League should advance the tenant whole or part of the purchase money, with the stipulation that an annuity of five pounds was to be charged for every hundred pounds advanced. Parnell agreed that land purchase aided by State credit should be made a new plank on the Land League platform, and he decided that twenty years' rent was the fair price to be paid for a holding. The unpractical revolutionaries who clamored for the annihilation of every landlord considered the price too high, and after a good deal of unnecessary wrangling Davitt refused to sign his name to the new program. At the same time Anna arrived in Ireland for the purpose of founding the Ladies' Land League, a scheme to which her brother was bitterly opposed. The idea had originated with Fanny, who had allowed herself to be influenced by the militant feminists, who abounded on the other side of the Atlantic, and, once his sisters had secured Davitt's support, Parnell was hardly in the position to veto their patriotic efforts. Exhausted and depressed, he had no one to turn to in his loneliness, for, though Emily attended to his creature comforts, she was far too self-centered to take much interest in his gloomy moods; she had enough worries of her own without listening to Charlie's political grievances.

He moved to Dublin, where he was pursued by a beautiful American who had followed him across the Atlantic, but, though she waylaid him every day in Morrison's Hotel, she never got a kind word out of him. The beginning of the session saw him back at Westminster, looking so gaunt and ill that well-meaning strangers would stop him in the lobbies in order to make enquiries after his health. His heart and chest had always been delicate, and the high tension at which he had been living during the past months had aggravated his condition. He was in such a state of nerves that he could not bear to be left alone at night. And sometimes he would sit up till dawn in the Westminster Palace Hotel before he could summon up the energy to return to his own rooms.

Mr. Gladstone was now Prime Minister, with Lord Cowper as Lord Lieutenant of Ireland and Mr. Forster as Chief Secretary. This last appointment was a popular one, for Mr. Forster was well known as the friend of Ireland, who had done such noble work during the famine days, and during the first months of his term of office he showed his good intentions by introducing the Compensation for Disturbance Bill, which proposed that an evicted tenant should be entitled to compensation if he could prove to the satisfaction of the court that he was unable to pay his rent, not from thriftlessness or idleness, but on account of the bad harvests, and that he was willing to continue his tenancy on just and reasonable terms, which had been unreasonably refused by the landlord. Every Irish Nationalist supported this measure, but twenty Liberals voted against it and twenty walked out.

Crippling amendments were suggested, and in the end the Bill was rejected by the Lords. This unconsidered action on the part of the Upper House revived outrages and riots all over Ireland.

It was on a fine July afternoon during the second reading of Mr. Forster's Bill that Parnell, worn and harassed over a hundred different matters, was handed a card saying that two ladies, who would like to see him, were waiting outside in Palace Yard. One of the ladies was Mrs. O'Shea, the woman who had so persistently bombarded him with invitations and whose husband was the overdressed dandy whom the O'Gorman had foisted on Clare for lack of a better member. It must have been with mingled feelings of boredom and irritation that Parnell stepped out into the sunlight to greet Mrs. O'Shea.

CHAPTER SEVENTEEN

SHE was so different from what he had expected. Here was no strident, self-possessed female determined to hunt her quarry down, but a shy, diffident young woman who blushed when she addressed him and then smiled a happy, trusting smile, radiating kindness and goodwill. There was something very warm and gentle about those great dark eyes which gave him such a direct, candid look; something very appealing about that small round head where the curls clustered so thickly under the fashionable bonnet, giving her a young, curiously girlish appearance.

To the tired, sick man, Katherine O'Shea looked so gloriously healthy, so vital and reassuring. Her sister, Mrs. Steele, was sitting beside her in the carriage, but he was unaware of her existence. From the first moment he was fascinated by that gay, alive little face, that deep, rich voice which, like the rest of her, was warm and soft and comforting. Over thirty years later, when Katherine O'Shea was a feeble old woman with her mind sagging under the weight of her misfortunes, she could still recapture the wonder of their first meeting, "of how he came out into Palace Yard, a tall, gaunt figure, thin and deadly pale, and how he looked straight at me, smiling, with his curiously burning eyes looking into mine with an intentness that threw into my brain the sudden thought, 'This man is wonderful and different.'"

It was a case of love at first sight. After nine years of varying periods of chastity and promiscuity, Parnell gave way to an infatuation for which there is no justification or explanation beyond the fact that he was a miserably lonely man snatching at his one chance of happiness. Nine years before he had adored a young girl with all the emotional enthusiasm of youth; now he needed a woman who was mistress, mother, nurse, and in Katherine O'Shea he found the three incarnate. She only failed when she set herself out to be his political Egeria.

That first meeting in Palace Yard had all the sweet savor and sentiment of the romantic 'eighties, those days of romantic epics, romantic paintings, romantic politics and romantic loves. But there was nothing romantic about the setting, with the policemen on duty in the Yard involuntarily overhearing every word of the conversation—policemen who all had a sneaking liking for Mr. Parnell, though they never knew when they might be called upon to expel him from the House. One can picture Parnell standing by the Gothic archway, shading his eyes against the glaring sunlight, then moving quickly forward with his nervous, springy walk, his straggling chestnut beard accentuating the hollow of his cheeks, his dark cut-away tweeds hanging loosely from his emaciated frame; the cold, rather elaborate courtesy of his first greeting to the two young women sitting in an open carriage, looking at him rather timidly from under the shadow of their pale pink parasols. Then Parnell smiles a disarmed, disarming smile.

It is hard to visualize how a man so shrewd and balanced in his political life could have walked out into Palace Yard and, within five minutes, lose his heart to a pretty, plump young woman who had no pretensions to great beauty, and who had come here to pursue him as so many English and American women had pursued him before. She referred lightly, half teasing, to the way in which he always kept away from her parties, and if she had any doubts as to the wisdom of her visit, she was fully reassured when he begged her to allow him to come and dine as soon as he returned from Paris, where he had to go for his sister's wedding. While saying good-by, she dropped the rose she was wearing in her bodice. He picked it up, lifted it to his lips and put it in his buttonhole. After his death it was found carefully done up in an envelope, treasured among his most private papers.

There must have been something extraordinarily magnetic about Katherine O'Shea to have fascinated Parnell even at their first meeting—some intensely human, sympathetic quality. Later he allowed himself to be subjected by her dominant personality, till she obtained both a mental and physical ascendency

over him, but his first attraction was probably based on something much simpler, much more rudimentary—one of those inexplicable contacts which warm the heart and give a new meaning to life.   From the very first he felt that with her he could
find the happiness and peace which had always been denied him.
He was obsessed by the longing to see her again, and even before he left for Paris, at the very height of the struggle over
the Compensation for Disturbance Bill, one finds him writing
to her from the House of Commons: "We have all been in such
a disturbed condition lately that I have been quite unable to
wander further from here than a radius of about one hundred
paces allows, and this notwithstanding the powerful attractions
which have been tending to seduce me from my duty towards
my country in the direction of Thomas's Hotel."

When he returned from Paris he wrote again, and within a
week Mrs. O'Shea had vindicated her pride—the "Uncrowned
King" was the guest of honor at a small dinner-party where
both her sister and Mr. Justin McCarthy were witnesses to her
triumph.   Willie was delighted at her success; it was to his
advantage to be on friendly terms with the chief, though he
was utterly out of sympathy with his Land League policy.   At
heart he was a Whig and an adherent of the safe, slow-going Mr.
Shaw, but he had voted for Parnell partly through the instigation
of the O'Gorman Mahon, and partly because he saw more chance
of making a career by identifying himself with a party daily
growing in strength.   At least Parnell was a gentleman, which
was more than could be said of most of his lieutenants, those
able young men whom the Parnellite party had gathered from
the ranks of small tradesmen, obscure journalists and Government clerks; men of whom O'Shea would say in his caustic
manner, "I may rejoice in, but I cannot sit with, unvarnished
genius."

Even if Parnell never had any real liking for O'Shea, even if
he always felt towards him as he did on the occasion of their
first meeting in Clare—that here was just the kind of man he
did not want in the party—still, there was no denying that

O'Shea was a very agreeable host, a witty raconteur with an astute knowledge of the world and a keen appreciation of the good things of life. As Katherine was determined that her husband and Parnell should be friends, both men agreed to adopt the outward semblances of an intimacy which never existed. The O'Sheas were curiously lacking in moral backbone, and Mrs. Steele, who, as Katherine's favorite sister, played a considerable part as liaison officer between her and Parnell, was ill-rewarded when, ten years later, in the case of O'Shea *versus* O'Shea and Parnell, the defendant accused her of having committed adultery with her husband. These accusations were never substantiated by either Katherine or her lawyer, though it is hardly credible that any woman would launch such a scurrilous attack on her own sister without having conclusive proofs of her guilt. And, even so, she would not have been justified in bringing the action when for years she must have been fully aware of the relationship. There were times when she even took advantage of this questionable intimacy, for Anne Steele was always the chief peacemaker in the O'Shea matrimonial differences.

From the day when Charles fell in love with Katherine, he became entangled in a life of constant lies and subterfuges, of humiliating pretenses which had to be kept up before the outside world. These pretenses meant nothing to Katherine, whose complicated married life had only been rendered possible through a series of sordid intrigues. She had preserved through it all that radiant youthful quality which rendered her capable of giving Charles moments of happiness which compensated him for all those niggardly, deceitful actions so galling to an honorable and fastidious man.

The first dinner-party at Thomas's Hotel sealed their intimacy, and later in the evening, as they sat together at the back of a box at the Gaiety Theatre, Katherine had a feeling of complete sympathy and companionship "with that strange, unusual man with the thin face and pinched nostrils, who sat beside me staring with that curious, intent gaze at the stage, and telling me in a low monotone of his American tour and of his broken health."

He was not the young, triumphant lover sweeping her off her feet; he was an ill, tired man coming to her for sympathy and affection, irresistibly drawn by her glorious health and super-abundant vitality. They were both intensely passionate people, and it must be laid to the credit of Katherine O'Shea that for many months she fought against giving way to the love which she felt for Parnell from the first moment she met him, but it was hard to resist a man who was starved for affection and who had suddenly realized that in her he had found a woman whom he could not only love but trust, with whom he felt so utterly at ease that even an occasional silence was dangerous in the "complete sympathy" it evoked between them.

She could not help taking advantage of every opportunity to see him, and from now onwards they met at her sister's house, at Thomas's or at the Westminster Palace Hotel, where he had taken a suite of rooms. They would have tea in his private sitting-room and he would talk to her of the things which interested him—politics, the condition of the Irish peasants, his experiments in mineralogy. He was not a witty or an amusing man, but with her there was no need to make conversational efforts. And at times, when he was so tired that his brain refused to function, he would just lie on the sofa and listen to her bright, effortless chatter and hearty, ringing laughter. She would arrange the cushions behind his head and bring him flowers to brighten his dreary rooms, and pour out the tea and minister the hundred little feminine attentions which he had never known. But they met chiefly in the House of Commons, for the Parliament of 1880 remained in session till the beginning of September, and all during August, Mrs. O'Shea was to be found every Wednesday afternoon sitting in the Ladies' Gallery. If the evening meetings were not important, she could be seen leaving the House with Mr. Parnell. A hansom cab would be hailed from the ranks, and they would drive down to Richmond or Mortlake in the cool of the summer's evening.

During the last few years Parnell had sacrificed every hour of his life to his political interests. Now he found all the excitement of a stolen holiday in those few hours in which he managed to escape both from his colleagues and the House. Whether they dined in a little restaurant overlooking the Thames or rested in the Mortlake meadows, Katherine managed to invest the scene with a romantic atmosphere, a certain lyrical quality which enchanted him.

It was not long before his colleagues noticed his sudden absences. And Tim Healy, who as his private secretary was always dogging his footsteps, commented to his brother: "There must be a lady in the case, else he would not be in such a hurry to leave the House as he has been two or three times this week."

The Westminster Palace Hotel was always crowded with Irish members, who did not enjoy the fact that Parnell never bothered to acknowledge their greetings when he passed through the hall with a lady friend. They were still more irritated when Captain O'Shea, whom they all disliked on account of his "Whiggishness," boasted that he was on intimate terms with the chief. But not one of them, not even Justin McCarthy, who as a warm friend of Mrs. Steele was frequently present at the small dinner-parties that took place at her house, ever contemplated the idea that there might be anything more than a mild flirtation between their chief and Mrs. O'Shea.

When Mr. Gladstone formed his Cabinet in the spring of 1880, his attention was focused on the unraveling of the Gordian knots of Lord Beaconsfield's Eastern policy. In his opinion the Irish question had been solved by the Land Bill of 1870 and the disestablishment of the Irish Church; but before he had been a month in power "a social revolution with the Land League for its organ in Ireland, and Mr. Parnell and his party for its organ in Parliament, rushed upon him and his Government like a flood." The Irish executive, under Mr. Forster's kindly domination, made a noble effort to govern the country without coercion, but all their good intentions came to nothing when the Compensation for Disturbance Bill was thrown out by the Lords. The landlords were once more victorious, and they took advantage of the situation by raining evictions on their unfortunate tenantry. But the Land League had been growing in strength, and Parnell declared to the ministers that, unless they gave him assurances that during the next session they would bring forward some measure of Land reform, they would get little help from him in quelling the outrages which had broken out all over the country. He declared that the Government had been half-hearted, and that if they had shown any grit the Lords would never have dared to have thrown out the Bill. But the Liberal leaders refused to make assurances. In the Upper House even the members of their own party had declared against them, and it was now decided that, with regard to Ireland, there were no more concessions to make. Not many months were to pass before they realized their mistake, for Parnell and his lieutenants roused the whole of Ireland. In Biggar's words, it "was to be war to the knife," and during the following session that sagacious observer, Sir Henry Lucy, recorded "that the House of Commons is perfectly helpless under Mr. Parnell."

Meanwhile Michael Davitt had crossed the Atlantic in order to defeat the schemes of Dr. Carroll, who, owing to his personal enmity to Parnell, was bent on undermining the policy of the New Departure. The supreme council of the I.R.B. did everything in their power to help him, but, in spite of their intrigues, Davitt triumphed in his mission, for he had a formidable ally in Patrick Ford, that sensation-mongering Irish patriot who had opened the coffers of his "skirmishing" fund for the benefit of the Land League. As a result, copies of his paper, the *Irish World,* circulated in every Connaught village, and every page contained some vitriolic outburst against the landlords and the British Government. Davitt was accepted by the extreme revolutionists who had been inclined to fight shy of Parnell, who was too much of an English gentleman for their liking, and it was in these so-called closed circles of the Clan-na-Gael that he first came across the sinister figure of Le Caron, *alias* Beach, who was regarded as one of the most trusted members of the Clan until the day when he stood up in a witness-box of the London Law Courts, revealing himself to be an agent of the British Government.

While Davitt toured the continent from the Atlantic to the Pacific, prognosticating the overthrow of Irish feudalism, Dillon concluded his successful lecturing tour and returned to his own country with some very substantial earnings to be added to the budget of the League.

The session ended, Parnell crossed over to Ireland, and the country reechoed with his slogans: "Hold the Harvests" and "Keep a Firm Grip on your Homesteads." The people were starving and desperate and they knew that there was no relief to be expected from the Liberal Government. Only the Land League could help them, and they pinned their faith on to the young Protestant landlord who on September 19th mounted the platform at Ennis to lay down the lines of his policy.

The little square of Ennis was dense with people, a wild inflammable mob of Celtic peasants, very different from those apathetic, downtrodden serfs whom Parnell had addressed at the first Land meetings; and he spoke to them in that clear, passionless voice which thrilled them, as one thrills at the touch of a cold steel blade.

"Depend upon it, the measure of the Land Bill next session will be the measure of your activity and energy this winter. It will be the measure of your determination not to pay unjust rents; it will be the measure of your determination to keep a firm grip on your homesteads; it will be the measure of your determination not to bid for farms from which others have been evicted and to use the strong force of public opinion to deter any unjust men amongst yourselves—and there are many such—from bidding for such farms. Now, what are you to do to a tenant who bids for a farm from which his neighbor has been evicted?"

He paused, with his dark, inscrutable eyes fixed on some distant point, as if he were quite unaware of the surging crowds below him, who now cried out: "Kill him! Shoot him!" And in his quiet, expressionless voice he went on: "Now, I think I heard someone say 'Shoot him,' but I wish to point out to you a very much better way, a more Christian and more charitable way, which will give the lost sinner an opportunity of repenting."

The people stared at him, wondering what was coming next, for this was so different from the fierce outpourings of his lieutenants. They saw his face harden, his eyes become like flints, while with every sentence his voice gained in volume—an icy, penetrating voice, every syllable incisive as the cut of a knife: "When a man takes a farm from which another has been evicted you must show him on the roadside when you meet him, you must show him in the streets of the town, you must show him in the fair and in the market-place and even in the house of worship by leaving him severely alone. By putting him into a moral Coventry, by isolating him from his kind as if he were a leper of old, you must show him your detestation of the crime he has committed, and you may depend on it that there will be no man so full of avarice, so lost to shame, as to dare the public opinion of all right-thinking men and to transgress your unwritten code of laws."

His speech was hailed with wild enthusiasm, for he had handed the farmers a new weapon with which to carry out a bloodless revolution.

The first victim of this moral Coventry was Lord Erne's agent, a certain Captain Boycott, whose name has given a new word to the English dictionary. He was a hard taskmaster who, after refusing to grant any reductions of rent, threatened his tenants with eviction. Through the power of the Land League, his servants and farm laborers were terrorized into leaving his service, the tradesmen were forbidden to sell him goods, and the very postmen were cautioned not to deliver his letters. His crops were left ungathered, and they were only saved by a band of Ulster Orangemen who took the opportunity of making a demonstration in Connaught. This invasion of fifty Orangemen on the shores of Lough Mask would have had unfortunate results if the Government had not sent a large detachment of both military and police to protect Captain Boycott and his crops. After a few unpleasant weeks the captain was sensible enough to leave the country.

In spite of his calm, measured words, Parnell's speech at Ennis was a deliberate incitement to treason. He fired the first gun of the social revolution which "rushed upon Mr. Gladstone and his Government like a flood." Then he returned to Dublin, from where he wrote to Mrs. O'Shea, "I cannot keep myself away from you any longer, so shall leave to-night for London."

CHAPTER EIGHTEEN

"IRELAND for the Irish and the land for the people," was the Land League's rallying-cry, but according to Mr. William O'Brien "this phrase bore three different meanings for the different schools of agitators. For the mass of the Irish tenantry, as well as for Mr. Parnell and his parliamentary followers, it meant the conversion of the four hundred and fifty thousand rent-paying tenants into proprietors of their own holdings by State purchase; for the small holders of the province of Connaught, among whom the agitation originated, it meant not merely the purchase of their existing holdings, which were too small and poor to support life, but the restoration to the people's use of the enormous tracts of rich grazing lands from which their fathers had been extirpated in the famine clearances; and the land for the people had still another meaning for Mr. Davitt, for whom it spelt nationalization of the land as contemplated in Mr. Henry George's enticing 'dreams.'" Davitt was still the high-minded idealist who, in spite of being born of peasant stock, never seemed to understand the mentality of his own people, who worshiped him as a man but neither understood nor cared about his theories. He advocated an alliance with the democracy of England. He dreamt of the day when the workers all over the world would be united against capitalism, but the farmers of Munster and Connaught could not be prevailed upon to show any interest in the sufferings of the British factory workers, and when in his high-flown, passionate speeches he inveighed against the feudal system, the people reacted, in their own primitive way, by killing and maiming the landlord's cattle and poisoning his dogs and horses. No righteous Englishman was more horrified by these crimes than Michael Davitt, for not only was he aware how much they prejudiced the Irish cause in America, but he was also so tender-hearted that he was unable to contemplate any form of suffering, and on his return to his own country he set out on a crusade to denounce

Agrarian outrages. Parnell, on the contrary, did nothing to mitigate these excesses. During the previous session he had given a warning to the Government, and, if Mr. Gladstone chose to ignore the warning, then let all the moonlighters of Kerry and Connemara do their worst. When a country was fighting for its life, any means of warfare was justifiable, and, though all his innate fastidiousness must have revolted at the crimes, he deliberately shut his eyes to the way in which the ardent Land Leaguers were terrorizing the countryside. Farmers who had incurred their enmity were dragged out of their beds at night and threatened at the point of a gun, and unpopular tradesmen had their shop-windows smashed and their stores rifled. In the great domains of the evicting landlords, the cattle were houghed and mutilated, pits were dug at night in the middle of the carriage roads, agents lived in continual fear of their lives, while their masters either existed as virtual prisoners in their own homes, guarded by detachments of the Royal Irish Constabulary, or else took a speedy departure for Dublin or London.

In George Moore's *Parnell and His Island* one reads of the reign of terror which heralded the downfall of feudalism in those great deserted houses—with the blinds drawn down, the mildew encroaching on the walls, and the dust-sheets shrouding the chairs—from which the owners had fled in haste; derelict properties where only the agent and his family still made a brave attempt to lead a life of refined gentility, while threatening letters arrived by every post and graves were dug in front of their doors.

Poor Mr. Forster's noble intentions were weakening. At the very outset of his career as Chief Secretary, when he had allowed his Compensation for Disturbance Bill to be mutilated by amendments, Parnell had turned on him in the House of Commons, crying, "Unstable as water, thou shalt not prevail." Speaking at Galway on October 29th, the Irish leader went still further in deprecating the methods of the kindly-hearted Quaker. "I expressed my belief at the beginning of last session that the present Chief Secretary, who was then all smiles and promises, would not have proceeded very far in the duties of his office before he would have found that he had undertaken an impossible task to govern Ireland, and that the only way to govern Ireland was to allow her to govern herself." It was in this speech that he declared that, though he wished to see the tenant farmers prosperous, he would not have taken off his coat and gone to his work if he had not known that they were laying the foundation in this movement for the regeneration of their legislative independence. Unfortunately both for himself and for Ireland, Mr. Forster was speedily coming to the conclusion that he had undertaken an impossible task in attempting to govern Ireland without suspending the Habeas Corpus Act. He had set his heart on ruling the country by the ordinary laws, but in the offices of Dublin Castle and in the smoking-rooms of the Kildare Street Club, both officials and landlords soon convinced him that the only chance of pacifying the country was to crush the growing power of the Land League. As late as October 1880 one finds Lord Cowper writing to the Cabinet: "I would preserve freedom of speech to the very utmost as long as it is confined to general subjects, such as abuse of England, abuse of the Government or advocacy of political measures, however unpracticable; when it has the immediate effect of endangering the lives or property of individuals it should be stopped." Lord Cowper was convinced that, even if Parnell did not instigate the outrages, he was guilty of conniving at them. In his opinion Parnell was the center of the disturbance, and in later years he admitted that "the Irish Executive had feared Parnell because he had united all the elements of discontent, because they never knew what he would be up to and they felt he would stop at nothing." In spite of all the talk about Home Rule, both the Lord Lieutenant and the Chief Secretary thought that the Land League's real aim was separation. They disregarded the fact that before the potato crop had been gathered in, before the newly sown potato called the "Scottish Champion" was ripe for consumption, the majority of the population of Connaught had been subsisting on the meager rations of Indian corn dealt out by the various

charitable organizations; that in the midst of all this poverty
and starvation, ten thousand four hundred and fifty-seven people
had been thrown out on the roadside, and that a hungry, desperate man needed very little incitement to revolt.

There were many just and broad-minded Englishmen who
realized that the Irish question could only be solved by some
drastic measures of reform. On December 3rd, *The Times* published a letter from General Gordon written while on a visit in
Ireland, in which he said: "I have lately been over the south-
west of Ireland in the hope of discovering how some settlement
could be made of the Irish question, which, like a fretting cancer,
eats away our vitals as a nation. . . . No half-measured Acts
which left the landlord with any say to the tenantry of these
portions of Ireland will be of any use. They would be rendered,
as the last Land Acts of Ireland have been, quite abortive, for
the landlords will insert clauses to do away with their force.
Any half-measures will only place the Government face to face
with the people of Ireland as the champions of the landlord
class."

General Gordon's solution was that, at a cost of eighty millions, the Government should convert the greater part of the
south-west of Ireland into Crown land, wherein landlords should
have no power of control, and he added: "For the rest of Ireland,
I would pass an Act allowing free sale of leases, fair rents and
a Government valuation. In conclusion, I must say that from
all accounts and my own observation the state of our fellow-
countrymen in the parts I have named is worse than that of any
people in the world, let alone Europe. I believe that these people
are made as we are; that they are beyond belief loyal, but at the
same time broken-spirited and desperate, living on the verge
of starvation in places where we would not keep cattle."

But, though this letter made a great impression in certain
quarters, there were very few Englishmen who would have
consented to be taxed in order to supply the Irish peasant with
his own freehold.

It was sad that Mr. Forster should have allowed himself to

fall under the influence of the landlords of the Kildare Street
Club to the extent of committing one of those unfortunate
blunders which occur so frequently in the history of British rule
in Ireland. All the rusty machinery of officialdom was set into
motion, red tape was flourished, the dust was shaken off the
archives and officials worked overtime when the Liberal Government decided to prosecute the leaders of the Land League. On
November 2nd, Charles Stewart Parnell, M.P., John Dillon,
M.P., Joseph Biggar, M.P., T. D. Sullivan, M.P., Thomas Sexton,
M.P., Patrick Egan and Thomas Brennan, as well as seven subordinate officials of the League, were named as traversers for
conspiring against the Crown in preventing the payment of rent
and the taking of farms from which the tenants had been evicted,
for resisting the process of ejectment and creating ill will among
Her Majesty's subjects. This information was filed in the
Crown Office of the Queen's Bench, Dublin, and no more unfortunate indictment had been filed since the repeal days of the
'forties, when Daniel O'Connell and the eleven traversers drove
in triumph to Richmond Prison. The Land Leaguers knew that
not a single jury in Ireland could be brought to convict them,
and the extremists were openly exulting in what they anticipated
as a crowning victory for the League, but sensible, hard-headed
business men like Joe Biggar were seriously angry with that
"damned fool Forster" and "those damned lawyers" who were
wasting the public money, and Parnell voiced these feelings at a
public meeting in Dublin when he said: "I regret that Mr.
Forster has chosen rather to waste his time, the money of the
Government and our money in these prosecutions." He was
entertaining an American journalist to lunch at the Imperial
Hotel in Dublin when he was served with a writ, which he
received with his usual courtesy, but the writ itself was barely
glanced at, and he went on with the ordering of his meal as if
that were the matter of vital importance.

The failure of the Sligo prosecutions might have warned
Forster of the folly of his act, but, as Mr. Gladstone said in
later years, "Mr. Forster was a very impracticable man placed

in a position of great responsibility." The Cabinet was divided over the Irish question. Before it was six months old the Duke of Argyll was pulling in one direction and Mr. Chamberlain was pulling in another, for Her Majesty and Mr. Gladstone had been forced to accept the ex-Mayor of Birmingham as the President of the Board of Trade. With the possible exception of John Bright, there was not a single member of the Cabinet who had any profound knowledge on the Irish question, and it is a curious fact that whereas Mr. Disraeli had never even crossed St. George's Channel, Mr. Gladstone spent only one week in the country whose affairs threatened to overwhelm the last decade of his life. In the Government of 1880, Joseph Chamberlain and Sir Charles Dilke represented the high-water mark of English Radicalism, and, because of their alliance with Parnell over the Mutiny and Prison Bills, they were known as the "Attorney-General and Solicitor-General of the Irish party." Combined with Mr. Bright they made a firm stand against coercion.

Curious political friendships were formed in the Parliament of 1880, and among the most curious was the occasional alliance between the Irish Nationalists and the members of the fourth party, which consisted of Lord Randolph Churchill, Mr. Arthur James Balfour, Sir Henry Drummond Wolff and Mr. Gorst. Though Parnell was now the leader of the Irish Nationalist party, his personal following only numbered about thirty, and he had not enough men to move the adjournment of the House, which was by far the most effective form of obstruction. The Parnellites and the fourth party supported one another, and a cynical onlooker could have found a certain amount of amusement in watching the son of a Tory Viceroy conspiring with the notorious agitator. It was rumored that the hard, taciturn Irishman, who so rarely unbent to any of his colleagues, had a personal liking for Lord Randolph, who was so much better informed on the Irish question than any member of the Cabinet. An occasion when they did not act together was over the Bradlaugh controversy, when Parnell supported Gladstone in stating that the atheist member for Northampton had a right to be admitted to the House, though he added that "personally his tenets were odious" to him. In his support of Bradlaugh he risked incurring the disapproval of many of his Catholic countrymen; and it was an act for which Cardinal Manning never forgave him.

Parnell had many difficulties to contend with during the session of 1880. The moderate Home Rulers were still determined to oppose him, and there was jealousy in his own ranks, for O'Donnell deserted him and sat with Shaw on the Liberal benches. According to Tim Healy, "Parnell had a number of enemies in the party, watching his every movement, for O'Connor Power and others wished his downfall as heartily as O'Donnell or Shaw." With O'Donnell it was merely a question of injured vanity. He had a brilliant but warped mentality, and he suffered from the delusion that he was born to be a great leader. This idea preyed on his mind, till in 1880 he wrote a letter to the *Freeman's Journal* saying that there "was patriotism in other halls than those of Avondale." But the secession of O'Connor Power was a far more serious matter. He was among the chief organizers of the Home Rule Confederation of Great Britain and one of the most powerful orators in the House of Commons, and, though he had always disliked Parnell, it was not a matter of personal feeling or of thwarted ambition which finally led him to the Liberal benches. He was genuinely convinced that the Land League agitation was detrimental to the campaign in favor of Home Rule, and he deplored the day when the Agrarian question was given pride of place before the national ideal.

But in the Parnellite party were some raw, untried young men who were destined to leap into fame during the next six months and others who had already established themselves as orators, speaking from Irish county platforms—men like Thomas Sexton and John Dillon, whose fierce, passionate utterances and sensitive faces had captured the imagination of the crowd. Then there were the representatives of the older school, men like Justin McCarthy and T. D. Sullivan, who brought the

serenity and dignity of age to the new movement, while behind
Parnell, watching his every step, criticizing but adoring, slaving
for him, writing his interviews, drafting his speeches, warding
off the inopportune reporter, the presumptuous constituent, was
the indispensable Mr. Healy, the newly elected member for
Wexford. Yet the day was to come when Mr. Parnell would
draw down the curtains, screening his private life from Mr.
Healy's inquisitive stare.

CHAPTER NINETEEN

More tragic than any of the circumstances which caused his downfall was the treatment which Parnell's love-letters received at the hands of the woman to whom he confided his most secret thoughts with such implicit trust. There is no fine phrasing or ornamentation in these letters, nothing which entitles them to a place among the great love-letters of history: they are the genuine, simple outpourings of a man who had no great gift of expression, no profound culture; a man groping for similes and epithets with which to convey the measure of his love, and falling back upon the old hackneyed expressions which belong to every class and to every age— "My queen, my love, my own wife." Private, intimate little notes scribbled on boats, in trains, in bleak hotel parlors at the end of a country meeting; written at times when mind and body were so utterly exhausted that he had only one longing—to be back in the peace and quiet of her sitting-room at Eltham. Over twenty-three years after his death, she chose to violate both his love and trust by publishing these letters, to be read by a generation for whom he was already an historical figure, the enigmatical central figure of a great tragedy. Only the words of poets can bear to be disinterred from the ashes of their love, and for critical or indifferent eyes Parnell's letters revealed the mind of a mediocre bourgeois lover who called his mistress "Queenie" and signed himself "Your King." It is pathetic that the proud and reticent man, who loathed any form of notoriety, should after his death have been the victim of the most vulgar form of publicity, all because of the tragic disintegration of the mind and fortunes of what had once been a charming and brilliant woman.

When Parnell fell in love with Katherine O'Shea in the summer of 1880, she was thirty-five years old, a virile full-blooded woman, tied to a husband whose visits to Eltham were of a very desultory character, ignored by all the more prominent members of her family, who had made it quite clear that they had no interest in either her or her job-hunting husband, and utterly dependent on the passing humors of an octogenarian aunt. She was attractive and ambitious, and in her drab and monotonous life she had no scope or outlet for her many talents. It was not very enlivening to have to spend one's evenings in reading aloud to a rather deaf old lady who could never be thwarted or contradicted, and who had always to be guarded from the other Wood relations, who hoped to benefit by her will.

Katherine was a very businesslike person, and she was determined that both her own and her children's futures should be assured. For several years Captain O'Shea had not contributed one penny to the maintenance of his family, and on several occasions "dear Aunt Ben" even went so far as to pay the rent of his lodgings in the Haymarket. There are not many charming young women who would have resigned themselves to the force of circumstances as gracefully as Katherine O'Shea. She was by nature kind and affectionate, and she was genuinely fond of her old aunt and devoted to her children. While other women might have become soured and embittered, she remained blithe and light-hearted, though her moral sense was rather warped after thirteen years of married life with Willie. According to her own testimony, Willie's position in her home was that of a stranger. Barring his Sunday visits to his children, he rarely came to Eltham except on her direct invitation. This statement must be taken with a grain of salt, when one considers that it was he, and not Katherine, who first invited Parnell to Wonersh Lodge, and that the only quarrels which marred the harmony of her relations with Parnell were always caused by his jealousy regarding her intimacy with her own husband.

The Parliament of 1880 must have been still sitting when the Irish leader came for the first time to stay at Wonersh Lodge, and, curiously enough, it was Katherine who tried to put obstacles in the way of his visit by urging that her house was small and shabby, and that her noisy children would be sure to get on his nerves; but O'Shea, both shrewd and observant, was fully aware that his chief was attracted by his wife, and he foresaw many pleasant possibilities. If Katie played her cards well and discreetly, there was no reason why he should not become Parnell's right-hand man, and once he was in that position he would be worth quite a good price to the Liberal party, for there was many an Irish Nationalist who had ended his career on the Treasury Bench at Westminster.

One hears of Parnell "in his gentle, insistent way" having urged his invitation to Eltham, but that is hardly likely, when the captain was only too proud and honored to have him staying in the house—a house where, incidentally, he did not contribute so much as a bottle of whiskey.

At first Katherine protested against this visit, for she realized the danger of being under the same roof with the man whom she had loved from the day of their first meeting, but her protestations were very half-hearted and her husband was deliberately encouraging her to give way to her feelings.

To-day, couples like the O'Sheas flourish in every London square. They have grown up in a simpler, franker age. But in the 'eighties the rigid morality of Her Majesty's Court, the impeccable morality of Mr. Gladstone, the influence of theologians like Pusey and Keble, inflicted a high standard of decorum on the upper classes of England, and, because of all the draperies, hypocrisy and surreptitious excitement, romance flowered behind the heavy plush curtains of the Victorian home, where conjugal ties were respected and where a divorced woman was excluded from the visiting-lists of both Putney and Mayfair.

In the O'Shea *ménage* there was only one important person to be considered, and, when Katherine tried to put obstacles in the way of Mr. Parnell's visit, it was not Willie she was thinking of, though she had always tried to be a good wife according to his rather peculiar standards. It was her dear Aunt Ben whom she was worrying about: that kindly, tyrannical old lady, who would be quite capable of disinheriting both her and her children if there was the slightest breath of scandal attached to her name. Aunt Ben had always objected to gentlemen staying in her own house, and she would be sure to disapprove of her niece entertaining male guests at Wonersh Lodge, when her husband was so irregular in his visits. The O'Sheas had always been careful to keep their quarrels and misunderstandings to themselves, for Mrs. Wood belonged to a generation where outward appearances were kept up even at the cost of heartache and inward humiliation. And, though she was quite shrewd enough to see how matters stood, she never referred to the young couple's matrimonial differences from the day when she first offered her niece a home, saying that "the arrangement would be more seemly now that the captain was obliged to be so much away."

From the very beginning Katherine was aware that her growing intimacy with Mr. Parnell might end by endangering the security of her existence, and she valued that security to the extent of forcing him to accept her love at her own terms, which entailed the countless devices, subterfuges and compromises necessary to propitiate both Willie and Aunt Ben. It is rather sordid and pathetic that her careful regard for both her own and her husband's reputations should have been dictated by financial considerations. All her life she had been haunted by the fear of poverty, and at times that fear had become an actuality. Circumstances had accentuated her failings, and, in spite of all her kindliness and warmth and craving for affection, she was at heart an ambitious, calculating materialist, whom not even the most passionate love-affair could transform, who was utterly incapable of any heroic sacrifice, and who, while accepting with complacency her lover's political position, never had any real interest in the country whose destiny he was shaping.

She was so careful to conform to the accepted standards of respectability, and he, who had so much to lose, never once envisaged the possibility that his love for an Englishwoman married to one of his colleagues might in any way jeopardize his career. In his eyes a man's private affairs had nothing to do with his public life. He had never encouraged the intimacy of his colleagues, and not one of them was in a position to question his movements. If he chose to disappear, be it for an hour or for a week, not even Tim Healy was allowed to know his whereabouts.

When he gave up his Bloomsbury lodgings and took a permanent suite at the Westminster Palace Hotel, he identified himself as the leader of the Irish party, who, since the days of Isaac Butt, had made the place their headquarters. To the outside world it looked as if he had very few interests further than the division lobby of the House, but now he was not so ready to join his colleagues in their little dinner-parties at Gatti's, and when Biggar with a kindly wink would sidle up to him, suggesting in his raucous voice "a bit of physical distraction with the fair sex," he would excuse himself, pleading a previous engagement—maybe a dinner with Captain O'Shea, that supercilious Whig who always made a point of dressing very elaborately even when he had to spend most of the night sitting below the gangway. None of the Irish members could understand why their chief should show so much courtesy towards a man who was nothing more than a nominal Home Ruler, who openly denounced the Land League and was rumored to be in alliance with the Liberal whips. Among their number were certain inquisitive-minded journalists, ferret-nosed reporters who took the trouble of turning the pages of the visitors' book in the Ladies' Gallery, where they were edified to notice the frequency with which Mr. Parnell entered the name of Mrs. O'Shea, whose husband evidently had other things to do than to procure her admission orders for the House.

All Parnell's biographers have laid great stress on the way in which he tried to keep his love-affair a secret from his colleagues. One of them goes so far as to state "that he never dared to appear in public with the lady who was his companion and friend, except in the grounds of her suburban residence, and that when he did go abroad with her, it was in the darkness of evening." This can scarcely have been true, when not only was she a frequent visitor to the House of Commons, but also his habitual guest at the Westminster Palace Hotel—the one place where he was bound to run into members of his party.

Katherine was also on friendly terms with several of his colleagues, especially Justin McCarthy, who very soon realized that his young leader had better things to do than to spend his Sundays in the family circle at Gower Street. Before long the rawest recruit to the Parnellite party must have been aware that the chief was attracted to Mrs. O'Shea.

But such was Parnell's domination over his followers that not one of them dared to criticize his behavior or to question his movements, and it was not for their benefit that he developed into the mystery man of the English Press, who assumed strange names and disguises which led to a hundred misinterpretations. It was rather in order to satisfy the standards of decorum as decreed at Eltham, in order to evade the irrepressible journalists and detectives who dogged his footsteps and shattered his nerves far more than all the murderous warnings of the extremists, who had been against him ever since his *débâcle* at Enniscorthy. The commissioner of the Dublin police had the ungrateful task of employing detectives to shadow the notorious agitator, and at the same time to protect him from the various conspiracies which threatened his life.

Neither Parnell nor Davitt ventured out unarmed, and, according to Detective Mallon, Davitt's revolver was actually loaned to him by the police, "who had unearthed the suspicion of a plot for his assassination at the hands of his erstwhile *confrères* of the Fenian movement."

There is a story told of a respectable Tory who, having the same initials as Parnell, came into the cloakroom of the House of Commons and took what he believed to be his overcoat. When he put his hand into the pocket he touched the cold steel of Parnell's six-chambered revolver. Gone were the days when the House of Commons was "the most exclusive club in Europe."

Parnell was fond of joking on the subject of his revolver, and he would delight in telling of how, when he was once traveling in a first-class carriage from London to Holyhead, his fellow-passengers began discussing the anti-rent agitation, and how one old diehard who sat next to him, happily oblivious of his identity, began to use the most abusive language, describing him as a renegade to his own class, who ought to be shot for stirring up the country against the landlords. Then Parnell would chuckle softly to himself and say, "Think, if he had known that he was sitting close up to a six-chambered loaded revolver in my right-side pocket!"

But in spite of his utter fearlessness and personal bravery, he was far too nervous and highly strung not to be affected by all the watching and spying to which he was constantly subjected, and there is no doubt that at a certain period of his life Parnell was afflicted with persecution mania.

He exercised a tremendous control over his nerves, and all during the autumn and winter of 1880 81, when, according to Mrs. O'Shea, he was so broken down in health that "he would fall asleep from sheer weakness" while sitting in a chair, not one of his colleagues seems to have been aware that he was a sick man; they saw him in Ireland swept along by the force of the great Agrarian agitation, fired by the enthusiasm of the crowds, speaking at Ennis, Longford, Galway, driving through the streets of Cork, where every window, roof and pavement was crowded with cheering people, until, according to an eye-witness, it looked as if "every brick in the walls of the city was a human face." He was so modest and diffident about it all, and yet so confident in the future, so impervious to the ugly threats of the extremists. Not one of the men who saw him that day in Cork would have thought of him as a tired, exhausted man; on the contrary, he looked absurdly young and boyish, greeting the enthusiasm of the crowds with his ingenuous smile.

T. P. O'Connor describes visiting Parnell at Avondale in the early autumn and finding him in splendid condition, with the air of a highly trained athlete. In fact he looked so well that T. P. complimented him both on his looks and figure, and he answered in his quiet, half-joking way, "Yes, I am in very good condition—quite equal, I think, to five years' penal servitude from old Forster."

And yet it was from Avondale that he wrote those lonely,

pathetic letters to Mrs. O'Shea, enclosing her some dried sprigs of heather he had picked on the moors of Aughavanagh, and assuring her "that you are the one dear object whose presence has ever been a great happiness to me." With her he could relax and be at peace, and so great was his obsession that he would cross over to London sometimes only for a day or a night in order to spend a few hours in her company. By the end of October they were lovers, her scruples had been overcome, and from now onwards she possessed and dominated him, dragging him down to her own level, forcing him to conform to her own standards.

CHAPTER TWENTY

Mr. Forster introduced his Coercion Bill on Monday, January 24th, and on the following day the fourteen traversers were acquitted in the Four Courts of Dublin. The mockery of the Sligo prosecutions had been reenacted on a larger and more expensive scale. In a moment of panic, the executive of Dublin Castle had irrevocably committed itself to a senseless exhibition of force. And, now that the State trials had failed, Lord Cowper and Mr. Forster had no other alternative but to revert to coercion, that old familiar remedy for reinstating Government prestige.

Mr. Parnell ruled supreme in Ireland, and so great was his power that even Mr. Gray of the *Freeman's Journal* had deemed it prudent to accept his leadership. When the people heard that their beloved chief was to be put on trial, popular feeling rose to such a pitch that the Government took elaborate precautions against any attempted demonstrations. Cordons of armed police were posted at every entrance to the Four Courts. Constables on horseback patrolled the quays in order to break up the crowds which kept forming in the hopes of catching a glimpse of the traversers. And it was only through the Nationalist Press having warned their leaders to give the Government no excuse to resort to force that the twenty days of the trial passed without a single riot.

Parnell was the only person who suffered through the enthusiasm of the crowds, and he could be seen in the evening, hurrying through the dirty slums that lay behind the quays, avoiding the cheering multitudes which lined O'Connell's Bridge.

At country meetings both Michael Davitt and John Dillon, and in later days William O'Brien, were all capable of rousing popular enthusiasm, but for the Dubliner there was only one leader, and when the newsboys hawked their wares they shouted "Trial of Parnell," as if the other traversers were of no account. The love and interest of the people were centered in the austere-looking man who sat in court wearing a small skull-cap. This

159

cap drew the attention of every local painter and caricaturist, and it was worn for the prosaic reason that the wearer had shaved his head in the hopes of stimulating the growth of his hair, which was beginning to become thin on the top. He would sit quite indifferent to the proceedings, quite oblivious to the women who paid vast sums to reserve a seat in his vicinity, so that they could press flowers and messages of affection into his hands. Occasionally he would make some joking aside to one of his colleagues. But on the whole it was such a waste of time, this absurd trial which kept him away from Parliament and Eltham, and even in the middle of the proceedings he would manage to snatch a few days in England; for Captain O'Shea was spending Christmas in Madrid, and his wife was not only lonely, but jealous of every paragraph in the *Freeman's Journal* which hinted that Mr. Parnell was besieged by female admirers. Curiously enough, her hysterical and unreasoned jealousy tightened her hold over her lover, for hers was one of those nervous natures on which any emotional excitement reacted physically, and when Parnell saw her, worn and hollow-eyed, compassion made him even more adoring than when she radiated health and vitality.

After a hearing of twenty-one days the trial ended with a verdict of ten to two for an acquittal. Coercion was now inevitable, and Davitt, who was still a "ticket of leave" man, was bound to be the first victim.

As they walked out of the Four Courts, acclaimed by the jubilant masses, Parnell turned to Davitt, saying: "We have beaten them again and now they will go for you." A week later the prophecy was realized.

Meanwhile it looked as if the League had triumphed once more, and the dollars came pouring in from America, where Patrick Ford, of the *Irish World,* was conducting a campaign in aid of the Agrarian agitation. During this period Parnell was in close alliance with the Irish-American extremists. The days were over when he would refuse to identify himself with the leading spirits of the Clan-na-Gael; now he played them off against the physical-force party which had declared against him in Ireland, and, whatever might be his private opinion regarding their methods, he never allowed himself to overlook the men whose dollars had laid the foundations of the Land League. He was always ready to despatch gracious cablegrams, thanking the *Irish World* for their "constant cooperation and substantial support" and to grant interviews to their reporters—interviews which were usually composed by the ubiquitous Mr. Healy.

With a full exchequer and the blessings of the Church, the Land League could become omnipotent, and Parnell's dream of a united Ireland seemed about to materialize when the powerful archbishop of Cashel and the bishops of Meath and Clonfert openly championed the Agrarian movement in face of the bitter opposition both of the archbishop of Dublin and the English cardinals.

In Ireland the Land Leaguers were victorious and Parnell was the hero of the hour, but at Westminster Mr. Forster was busy on his Coercion Bill; Mr. Chamberlain and Mr. Bright had laid aside their scruples, and the great champion of liberty who had evoked with magic words and sublime oratory the hapless state of the enthralled Balkans, who had been the first to acclaim the champions of "redeemed Italy," was the virtual head of the Government which proposed a Coercion Bill, by which a country was to be strangled into submission.

In the speech from the throne on January 6th, 1881, the suspension of the Habeas Corpus Act was declared necessary on account of an "extended system of terror which had been established in Ireland and which had paralyzed almost alike the exercise of private rights and the performance of civil duties."

In one of Mr. Gladstone's memoranda, written in later years, one finds the following note: "Forster allowed himself to be persuaded by the governmental agents in Ireland, that the root of the evil lay within small compass; that there were in the several parishes a certain number of unreasonable and mischievous men; that these men were known to the police and that if summary powers were confided to the Irish Government by the exercise of which these objectionable persons might be removed, the evil would die out of itself. I must say I never fell into this extraordinary illusion of Forster's about the village 'ruffian.'"

But, whatever might have been Mr. Gladstone's doubts, he allowed them to be overruled by Lord Cowper and Mr. Forster, and one cannot but pity the Chief Secretary who, after undertaking his present duties with such manifestly good intentions, was now forced to urge measures which must have been in direct opposition to his strong Radical tendencies. Greater men than he had failed to govern Ireland, that festering sore in the heart of the Empire, and it is not surprising that he should have lost some of his kindliness of heart and breadth of vision, encompassed by the corrupt officialdom of Dublin Castle. But even the most vehement of the Land Leaguers was ready to pay a tribute to the courage of "Buckshot" Forster, who in 1881 set out to make a tour through the most disturbed parts of the country without as much as summoning one extra policeman or taking the simplest precautions for his own safety.

The Protection for the Person and Property (Ireland) Bill was the first bill to be introduced in the new session, regardless of the fact that in principle both the Prime Minister and the Chief Secretary and half the members of the Cabinet were opposed to government by coercion. It was introduced at the very time when a commission, under the presidency of Lord Bessborough, was making a thorough enquiry into the Irish Land question—an enquiry which was to result in a momentous report declaring in favor of the "three f's." This decision, which first struck Mr. Gladstone as "incredible," determined the drastic reforms of his great Land Bill, a measure which many people declared might never have been passed if more members had understood its significance.

The speeches at the beginning of the session make dreary reading. The Irish members were pledged to oppose coercion to the bitter end. Obstruction was rampant, and, due to their numerous amendments, the debate on the Queen's speech was drawn out during a fortnight. But after the motion that leave to introduce the Bill should be given the whole tone changed. Even Mr. Forster's speech proving the necessity of coercion was delivered in a fiercely passionate manner. He was passionate and pathetic at the same time, for he admitted that it gave him the keenest sorrow to ask for extraordinary powers, that it had been for him a most painful duty, which he had never expected to discharge, and if he had thought that this duty would devolve on the Irish Secretary he would never have held office.

On the following day, January 25th, the day of Parnell's acquittal, when Mr. Gladstone moved that the Coercion Bill should have precedence of all other business, the Irish members offered such violent opposition that they kept the House sitting all through the night till two o'clock the following afternoon. In the early hours of the morning they were strengthened by the presence of their leader. He had crossed over from Ireland in a raging gale, and when the members on the Treasury Bench returned to their seats, after snatching a few hours' rest, they found the honorable member for Cork sitting in his place, so elegant, bland and self-assured that it seemed hard to believe that only twenty-four hours had passed since he had stood in the dock accused of treason against the Crown.

The battle over the Coercion Bill was a long, grim struggle, in which the Irish members were ordered to speak as often and for as long as they could. Their business was to obstruct, not to orate, and Mr. Gladstone commented that they "sometimes rose to the level of mediocrity and more often groveled amidst mere trash in unbounded profusion." But this was hardly a fair criticism. When one turns over the pages of Hansard, amidst a series of dreary speeches delivered by men suffering from want of sleep, faced by the uninspiring audience of several snoring Liberals, one suddenly finds some fresh oasis watered by the sparkling wit of "Tim" and "T. P."—the *enfants terribles* of the Irish party.

Sir Henry Lucy writes: "When Healy made his appearance in the House, it was said his introduction was due to a rare pleasantry on the part of Parnell, but then T. P. was judged the most insupportable of the Irish members. Both bring on to the floor of the House of Commons the manners and habits of thought of the Irish peasant." Yet both these men lived to be two of the most popular members of the House.

Mr. Labouchere, designated as "the Christian member for Northampton" in contrast to his colleague, Mr. Bradlaugh, was one of the few Radicals who remained true to his principles in resisting the Bill, and with merciless sarcasm he showed up the ridiculous exaggeration of Mr. Forster's statistics regarding the increase in criminal outrages, but, though history relates that during Mr. Labouchere's speech the face of the Prime Minister grew clouded and disturbed, public feeling in England was so bitter against the Irish that even the Radical members for manufacturing towns and old friends of Ireland like Mr. Bright made vigorous speeches in support of the Bill. One realizes the intensity of that feeling when one glances through the old newspapers and sees the way in which the most stern and unbiased leader-writers delighted in abusing the Parnellites.

On Monday, the 31st, the Government declared their determination to close the debate on the motion for leave to introduce the Bill, but that night Parnell announced quite calmly that he would not allow a division to be taken. It was to be a fight to the finish, and he cabled to the *Irish World:* "The present struggle against coercion will, please God, be such as never has been seen within the walls of Parliament."

During forty-one hours a handful of Irish members defied the united Liberal and Conservative forces. Even the weather seemed to participate in the bitter struggle, for wild tempests swept the Irish Sea, dislocating the shipping and preventing the sorely needed Nationalist members from rejoining their colleagues. Snow littered the London streets, and in the draughty lobbies disgruntled members waited for vengeance to be wreaked on the offending Irish minority.

It was only at one o'clock on Tuesday morning, when Mr. Gladstone showed his determination to resist the usual Irish method for adjournment, that the calm and tranquillity of the

House gave way. For the first time Gladstone and Parnell confronted one another as open enemies. The Grand Old Man saw his power menaced by a cool, defiant young agitator who, according to Sir Stafford Northcote, "looked upon himself as an equal power competing with the power of the throne." The most superb actor of the day saw himself forced to play a rôle unworthy of his talents. For over half a century he had posed as "Perseus delivering nations from their chains," and now Mr. Parnell, in the mildest of tones, was asking him to prove whether there was urgency "for this cruel, wicked, wretched and degrading measure."

The whole affair was degrading; the accepted traditions and cherished liberties of the House were being dragged in the mud; relays of Liberal and Conservative members were mobilized to remain in their seats, while a succession of verbose Irishmen exhausted their vocabulary in speeches which were little more than mere tests of endurance. Mr. Biggar beamed on the House as if he were full of the kindliest intentions, and after twenty-two hours Mr. Parnell addressed the Speaker with "a sweetness of manner which contrasted with the strength of his language." By then, most of his opponents had lost both their tempers and their manners, and it was in the midst of thunderous glances, and subjected to constant interruptions, that the Irish leader made his quiet, calm and collected speech. That master of satire, Sir Henry Lucy, declares that "his mincing manners might have allured to his touch the most timid mouse, and there was a delightful unconsciousness about him of all that had happened in Ireland and of all that might be happening at that very hour. The whole thing was, according to his way of putting it, an abstract question, to be argued quietly in the House of Commons. There was the Land League and there were the landlords. They differed as people of diverse interests do. Only one could be right, and Mr. Parnell undertook to show that it was not the landlord." He was so polite, so exasperatingly polite, that Sir Henry regretted that "the Strangers' Gallery could not have been crammed with Irish peasantry, who might have found it hard to recognize the leader whom they were accustomed to see with pale face and quivering lips, denouncing England and all that's English."

Parnell was a consummate tactician; there was nothing to be gained by losing his temper, and, while Mr. Gladstone might allow himself to launch Olympian thunderbolts, and Sir William Harcourt might descend to the grossest forms of abuse, he remained smiling but inexorable, courteous but adamant, the general of a small but highly disciplined army, where not a single man dared to disobey his orders and where every man had to speak even if he had nothing to say. He was to be seen prowling along the corridors keeping a watchful eye on anyone who showed the slightest sign of shirking his duties, and such was the strength of his will that many a Whig Home Ruler on his way to a comfortable bed was prevailed upon to return to his seat as one of his supporters. By the Tuesday evening the House was uproarious, and the Conservatives protested that the Speaker should put an end to this wilful obstruction. Then the Parnellites suddenly changed their tactics, and, after spending the best part of twenty-four hours in proposing motions for adjournment, they proceeded to debate the main question with unflagging energy. But the fate of obstruction was sealed. Already at noon, the Speaker, Mr. Brand, had come to the conclusion that "it was his duty to extricate the House from the difficulty, by closing the debate of his own authority and so asserting the undoubted will of the House against a rebellious minority." He sent for Mr. Gladstone and told him that he would be prepared to put the question, in spite of obstruction, on the following conditions: "Firstly: that the debate should be carried on until the following morning, his object in this delay being to mark distinctly to the outside world the extreme gravity of the situation and the necessity of the step which he was about to take; and, secondly: that the Prime Minister should reconsider the regulation of business, either by giving more authority to the House or by conferring authority on the Speaker." So it came about that the ancient liberties and privileges of Westminster were finally strangled by the "iron hand of *clôture.*"

At four in the afternoon Mr. Gladstone summoned a Cabinet council, and, when Parnell saw the harassed ministers hurrying along the corridor on their way to the Speaker's library, he knew that something violent was about to happen, but even he did not contemplate the possibility of the Speaker adopting summary powers. Mr. Brand took a well-earned rest, leaving Dr. Playfair to deputize for him, and it was only at nine o'clock on Wednesday morning, after Mr. Parnell had been forced to retire for a few hours' sleep and after Mr. Sexton had achieved a *tour de force* by addressing a nearly empty House for over three hours, that the Speaker made his momentous entry with a great roll of paper in his hand.

From one moment to another the ministerial benches became crowded, there was an atmosphere of tense excitement, and when Mr. Brand announced that he was about to close the discussion, his decision was greeted with wild cheers. The Irish members were dumbfounded, for, though they had had uneasy presentiments, they had never expected this *coup d'état.* Taken utterly by surprise, they were forced to participate in the farce of a division. But immediately afterwards Mr. McCarthy, the deputy chairman of the party, rallied his forces, and one and all they rose to their feet shouting, "Privilege! Privilege!" while the members of the victorious Government looked extremely embarrassed and disturbed. Peace was restored when the Parnellites marched out of the House in single file and the motion was adopted without a single dissenting vote.

Meanwhile, Healy had carried the news to Parnell, and when his followers retired to the conference-room they found him calm and self-confident, wearing his usual placid smile, very different from the Parnell who not so long ago had greeted O'Donnell, after the twenty-six hours' sitting, with a white, distorted face and furious, hissing voice. In the last years he had learnt to hold himself in perfect control; he was the leader whose duty it was to encourage and reassure his young lieutenants now suffering from the inevitable reaction following a hard battle. They had lost, but they had put up a fight "such as never had been seen within the walls of Parliament."

Parnell's cablegram to his American supporters had been no idle boast. As *The Times* once said, "He might prophesy with safety because he had the power of fulfilling his prophecies."

CHAPTER TWENTY-ONE

THE Irish members lost no time in challenging the Speaker's right to assume arbitrary powers, and the whole of the Wednesday was wasted in motions of adjournment, but Thursday morning found them in the depths of gloom and despair at the news of Michael Davitt's arrest. That day Parnell realized there was little to be gained by further resistance to the Coercion Bill. The temper of the House was such as to preclude any sense of fairness towards a troublesome minority. The all-night sittings, the constant obstruction and personal taunts of the Irish members, had ended by infuriating the most unbiased Englishmen. When Parnell stood up in the House to ask the Home Secretary in which way Michael Davitt had violated the conditions of his ticket of leave, Sir William Harcourt did not even answer his question, and the Liberal benches presented the extraordinary spectacle of members cheering because a crippled invalid had been sent back to the horrors of penal servitude.

If the Irish executive had taken the trouble to peruse Mr. Davitt's speeches, they would have found that he was the first to condemn any form of outrage, but after the humiliation of the State trials they were regardless of justice. Besides, they were afraid of Davitt, who was preaching the doctrines of the Land League in the heart of Ulster, where the new movement was making considerable headway. Sir William Harcourt justified his summary arrest by telling the House that "Mr. Davitt's conduct was not such as to permit his retention of his ticket of leave," but when Parnell confronted him with that hard, cold look in his eyes, and in his slow, dragging voice asked him to specify what conditions he had violated, then he could find no answer. The Speaker, who had definitely ranged himself on the side of the majority, came to his aid by calling on Mr. Gladstone to propose the new urgency resolutions; but the Prime Minister had barely concluded a sentence when the Irish benches showed the first signs of battle. Mr. Dillon interrupted to ask further questions regarding Mr. Davitt's arrest, and, though the Speaker ignored his demands, he refused to give way and claimed his privilege of speech. In spite of acting within the laws of Parliament, he was named amidst the deafening shouts of the opposing parties, and his refusal to leave the House until the Sergeant at Arms had summoned a retinue of doorkeepers and messengers to help in a forcible ejectment if necessary, was a signal for Parnell to commit a drastic action. Dillon asked him "not to involve the party on my account but to let it be my affair alone." But Parnell quite deliberately told him to "go on," for he knew that, following the strain of the past few weeks, most of his younger followers were spoiling for a fight, and that dramatic deeds at Westminster gained warm applause on the other side of St. George's Channel. As soon as Mr. Gladstone rose to proceed with his speech, Parnell stood up and proposed "that the right honorable gentlemen be no longer heard." He was named for causing wilful and deliberate obstruction, and, when the division upon his suspension was called, twenty-nine of his followers protested against the legality of the proceedings by refusing to leave their seats as was compulsory according to the procedure of the House when the opinion of the members had to be tested in the Lobbies. They were suspended *en bloc,* and for the next half-hour the rest of the House had nothing to do but to watch the various ways in which the Irish members reacted to the touch of the Sergeant at Arms. There was a slight cheer from Radicals such as Henry Labouchere when Parnell, still adhering to his usual formal courtesy, made an elaborate bow to the Speaker before walking out of the House, but some of his supporters insisted on a formidable display of force before they could be ousted from their seats.

Later in the day three more Irish members were named, and it is curious to note that, in spite of having quarreled with their leader, both O'Connor Power and O'Donnell were among the suspended members.

It was only when there was not a single Nationalist, barring Mr. Shaw and a few of his adherents, remaining in the House,

that Mr. Gladstone was able to move his resolution, which proposed that "if a motion declaring the business urgent was supported by forty members rising in their places, then the motion
was to be put forthwith without debate, and that if carried by a
majority of not less than three to one, the regulation of the business was to remain in the hands of the Speaker." It was amaz-
ing to see with what alacrity members voted for the destruction
of their own rights of free speech, and how the terror of obstruction made them willing to invest the Speaker with omnipotent
powers.

Captain O'Shea was preesnt at this memorable debate, but he
took no part in the proceedings beyond voting against Parnell's
suspension. Maybe his intimacy with the Liberal whips did not
permit him to identify himself with an unpopular minority;
maybe he was beginning to suspect that his friendship with
Parnell was not a very fruitful one. During the previous autumn he had done everything in his power to encourage the
growing intimacy between his wife and the Irish leader, and
there had been times when he had flattered himself that he and
Katie would be able to persuade Mr. Parnell to adopt a more
moderate policy, which would be favorable both to the Liberals
and to the nominal Home Rulers, for Captain O'Shea's interest
was always focused on the Treasury Benches. He was the born
political agent, with a talent for intrigue and negotiation, and it
was to the Liberal party that he looked for a handsome income,
but first he must have a safe seat in Parliament, and he was
aware that the electors of West Clare were not likely to return
him a second time. They had only been won by the persuasion
of the O'Gorman Mahon, and it was doubtful whether the gallant octogenarian would fight another election. It was Parnell's
business to secure him a seat, and already, in the early days of
their romantic friendship, Katherine O'Shea would beg the Irish
leader to do everything in his power to keep Willie in Parliament, even though he was but a lukewarm supporter of his
policy, even though he openly denounced the Land League.
"Willie can be useful, very useful," said his wife, and Parnell

was only too ready to believe her. It seemed natural to her at first that she should make use of her influence by obtaining material benefits for her husband. All during their married life Willie had exploited her charm to his own advantage, and she was not even disgusted when, in order to obtain Parnell's consent on some particular point, he would tell her with brutal candor: "Take him back with you to Eltham, make him all happy and comfortable for the night, and just get him to agree." But she had to contend with Parnell's uncompromising disposition and intense possessiveness. From the moment when he became her lover he regarded her as his lawful wife, and his jealousy of Willie was that of a strict, exacting husband.

Nine years later, in the divorce courts, Katie was accused of having deceived Captain O'Shea, but if any man was deceived during those years it was Parnell. From the first she had assured him that Willie was her husband only in name, but there are many substantial proofs to the contrary—proofs that cannot be denied—and when, in the spring of 1882, she gave birth to a child, Captain O'Shea was convinced that he was the father. Parnell, the brilliant tactician and unscrupulous parliamentarian, whom the outside world regarded as so cold and unemotional as to be almost repellent, was curiously spontaneous and direct in his feelings, curiously naïve, and, once he had given his heart to a woman, there was no question of reserve, caution or regret. Katherine dominated and enslaved him, and when, at the height of his infatuation, he begged her to divorce Willie, regardless of the fact that as the leader of a Catholic nation he could never marry a divorced woman, she resisted his pleadings. Though Willie was notoriously unfaithful, she still had a queer kind of loyalty towards him, a loyalty that never wavered up to the day when he declared himself an enemy. Then there was Aunt Ben to be considered, and it was quite impossible to contemplate the scandal of a divorce while the old lady was alive. Katherine begged her lover to have just a little patience, for her aunt was old, so old that she could not be expected to live much longer.

If they only waited, everything could be arranged so simply, without endangering the children's future, without giving unnecessary pain.

But Mrs. Benjamin Wood came of a strong, healthy stock, a stock of hardy sea-captains and merchants, and she upset her niece's careful calculations by living for eight more years—eight momentous years, during which Parnell rose to such perilous heights of fame as to make his ultimate fall more dangerous and precipitous. He once told a turbulent mob in Galway, "I hold Home Rule in the hollow of my hand; destroy me, and you destroy Home Rule." And because an old lady in Eltham lived eight years too long, because the will in which she left her fortune to her dearly beloved niece was contested by numerous Wood relations, Katherine's hands were tied up to the time when her husband, after years of intimidation and blackmail, chose to bring an action for divorce, citing Mr. Parnell as co-respondent. An octogenarian lady living in a London suburb helped to seal the fate of Irish Home Rule. So long as her children's futures were insecure, Katherine refused to divorce her husband. So long as there was money to be extorted from Aunt Ben, the Captain was careful not to create a scandal. Well might it be said that Parnell was no match for the astute and worldly O'Sheas. He took the course of least resistance. He placed himself in Katherine's hands and abided by her decisions, but he refused to take any part in the dubious negotiations between husband and wife. According to Mrs. O'Shea's testimony, "he made no denials and he gave no assurances to Willie; he was prepared for my sake, and reluctantly enough, to keep up appearances with the outside world to avoid scandal, but he would have no ambiguities with my husband."

The affair developed in romantic, almost melodramatic, circumstances. From the day when he was arrested on the charge of treason, and all during the State trials, Parnell was constantly shadowed by detectives, and his correspondence was subjected to rigorous censorship. His letters to Katie had to be sent under cover to various addresses; they had secret assignations and a special code for their telegrams; their tenderest meetings took place in drab, almost sordid surroundings: the waiting-room of Waterloo Station was one of their favorite haunts, and sometimes Katherine would sit there until the early hours of the morning, when her lover would come and tell her how things were progressing in the House.

She may have failed to sacrifice herself to the tremendous issues at stake, she may have failed to ensure his political safety, but she never failed him in her love. She would spend all night in a draughty railway station, huddled over a burnt-out fire, just to have him near her for half an hour, to see that grateful, welcoming smile, those queer red lights brightening his eyes. When he left for Ireland by the morning mail, she would come up to the St. Pancras Hotel, and when he got away from the House in time to snatch a few hours' sleep before catching the train, he would find a delicious little supper prepared for him in his private sitting-room, his smoking-jacket and slippers warming by the fire, and she waiting, quiet and unobtrusive, never worrying him with unnecessary questions, never forcing him to talk while he ate his supper, but always sympathetic and understanding, interested in the smallest details which concerned him.

One of the secrets of Katherine's hold over Charles was that she never let him see her bored or indifferent. His health and comfort were her chief concerns, and nothing which might give him one moment's happiness was ever too much trouble. Her passionate scenes of jealousy and wild fits of temper only strengthened the bond between them, for both were exacting and unreasonable, and on the whole Charles suffered far more than she, for every separation was an agony when circumstances forced him to be in Ireland and he knew Willie to be at Eltham. Katherine was more adaptable, for in spite of being engulfed "by a fierce, bewildering force that was rising within me in answer to the call of his passion-haunted eyes," she remained with her feet very firmly planted on the ground.

Shortly after Davitt's arrest, Parnell was warned that it would be just as well for him to go abroad for a while, as the Government was being urged to imprison him on the grounds of sedition. Lord Cowper had come to the conclusion "that it would be desirable to break up the Land League," and Parnell's first reply to this threat was to transfer the funds from London to Paris, where Pat Egan was put in charge of all the financial transactions. The Lord Lieutenant realized that it was too late to stop the Land League meetings, that it would involve too great a change of front, and that it would be a difficult undertaking, as the people were well organized and able to alter the time and place of meeting very rapidly. In his letter of advice to the Cabinet he said, "To strike at the leaders is undoubtedly the right thing, and this is just what we have been accused of not doing. But openly teaching the doctrine of breach of contract, which is their real crime, does not, unfortunately, enable us to take them up. We are hampered in our action by an express agreement that we will not arrest any man unless we can say on our honor that we believe him to have actually committed or incited to outrage. This at first prevented us from attacking the leaders as vigorously as we might have done, but latterly some of them have been less cautious, and we have also prevailed upon ourselves to give a wider interpretation to our powers. For my part I should be inclined to interpret them very widely. . . . And there is hardly anyone whose detention policy would demand that I would not personally arrest."

When Parnell was advised to absent himself from public platforms until Gladstone was ready with his Land Act, he chose to take his enforced holiday at Eltham, the one place where his presence would be most likely to arouse suspicion. He was already in the habit of considering Wonersh Lodge as his home, and would think nothing of driving down after a late sitting at the House. These cold night drives, with supper in the early hours of the morning and no sleep till dawn, must have been very injurious to his health, but he was so dependent on Katherine that he could not bear to be separated from her for twenty-four hours. There was something very touching about this implicit trust, this boyish adoration, but Mrs. O'Shea must have felt rather helpless, not to say horror-stricken, when her lover arrived one night and asked her to hide him for a few weeks, as if it were the simplest thing in the world to hide a full-grown man in a small house full of servants and children. Luckily, Willie happened to be in Paris visiting his mother, the maids were both devoted and discreet, and if they had their suspicions they kept them to themselves, so for a fortnight Parnell evaded the Government detectives by enjoying a well-earned rest in Mrs. O'Shea's boudoir. She looked after him entirely herself, and both labored under the delusion that none of the servants knew him to be there. She nursed and mothered him, forcing him to take regular nourishment, cooking him dainty little dishes on the open fire, while he lay on the couch, white, inert and utterly worn out, watching her with that happy little smile which always greeted her slightest movements. The long-drawn-out trials, the struggle over the Coercion Bill, the sudden shock of Davitt's arrest, had frayed his nerves, and, like most highly strung people, he lived on his nerves; they supplied the driving-force which carried him through his arduous political campaigns, which spurred him on to those feats of endurance which were the envy of many a stronger man. Though he never spared himself in his public life, he was constitutionally lazy. He suffered from inertia caused by delicate health, and when his nervous strength gave way he lapsed into a state of apathy. He was really happy during this period of enforced idleness. Before him loomed the prospect of a Land League meeting in Paris where his five chief lieutenants were already awaiting his arrival. Those devoted followers of his who never gave him a moment's peace, who even tried to deny him the right to any life of his own—what matter if they were left in suspense for a little while? It was so hard to throw off his inertia, to leave the blessed peace of "Queenie's" boudoir for the uncongenial company of those well-meaning Irish patriots, and, while putting off the date of his departure from day to day, it never occurred to him to give them a sign of life.

In the Hotel Brighton, in the Rue de Rivoli, the Land Leaguers speculated on the strange disappearance of their chief. His letters accumulated in the post office of the House of Commons or in the pockets of Mr. Healy, whom a few days of the French capital had transformed into the complete *boulevardier*. The *Freeman's Journal* wrote up fantastic accounts of Mr. Parnell's movements. Reporters besieged the grounds of Avondale in the hopes that Mrs. Dickinson might enlighten them on her brother's whereabouts: and all the time he was quietly spending his time reading *Alice in Wonderland,* which he never thought in the least bit amusing but regarded as a serious and curious book.

The weather was bitterly cold and the fields were deep in snow when Parnell finally decided to leave for Paris, carefully choosing the Harwich route as the one where he was most likely to escape recognition; but he had reached no further than Lowestoft when he suddenly decided to return to London and to go to Paris via Dover the following day. It was characteristic of him to take the most elaborate precautions to ensure the secrecy of his movements and then suddenly to throw all discretion to the winds. But the detective who shadowed him on to the Calais boat had no warrant in his pocket. As long as the Irish leader was willing to behave himself, the Prime Minister had no intention of carrying out Lord Cowper's advice, for such a sensational arrest would only endanger the popularity of his coming Land Act, and Mr. Gladstone relied on his Agrarian policy to settle once and for all the grievances of the Irish people.

From Paris Parnell wrote to Mrs. O'Shea one of those formal, carefully worded letters which were intended to ward off the suspicions of Government spies and inquisitive husbands; a letter starting with "My dear Mrs. O'Shea," written as if he had left her house a fortnight ago on the occasion of his last appearance at Westminster, saying: "I did not know, when leaving you, that I was going—my departure was influenced by information of reliable kind that my arrest was intended, and that bail would be refused and I should be left in jail until Habeas Corpus was suspended, when I could have been again arrested. I think, however, they have now abandoned this intention, but will make sure before I return."

CHAPTER TWENTY-TWO

"MR. PARNELL has retired from the militant attitude he once assumed. His great power of sustained work and his unwearied attendance on the sittings of the House formed no small part of the secret of his success. He used to be the first to come and the last to go. He was always in his place ready to take objection to fresh points as they arose. He seemed as unassailable by fatigue as he was implacable in opposition. With such a leader, his followers would be ashamed to show hesitancy or plead fatigue. But Mr. Parnell has been an altered man from the day Davitt was arrested."

So wrote Sir Henry Lucy, commenting on the Irish leader's empty seat at Westminster, where a small band of Nationalists, led by T. P. O'Connor and Thomas Sexton, were still making brave attempts to resist the third reading of the first Coercion Bill. They were so obviously baffled and disappointed by their chief's desertion that on one occasion Sir William Harcourt gave free rein to his witty, caustic tongue, by quoting:

> *Bon Jean was a gallant gentleman,*
> *In battles much delighting.*
> *He fled full soon,*
> *On the First of June,*
> *But bade the rest keep fighting.*

The Home Secretary's sneers soon turned to alarm and bewilderment when both detectives and Press reporters cabled from Paris that Parnell was not to be traced and that the members of the Land League executive were in complete ignorance of his movements.

While Sir William Harcourt and the heads of Scotland Yard were mystified by Parnell's disappearance, the emotional Irishmen who had been sitting in Paris without any news of their chief were worn out with anxiety and fear. Over a week had passed without bringing them any nearer to solving the mystery.

In Healy's pockets reposed a bundle of letters addressed to Parnell, which some instinct had warned him not to open in spite of the fact that he had full authority to deal with all the chief's correspondence. They were letters addressed in a woman's hand, stamped from a post office in Holloway, and when his colleagues asked him whether he could produce any document which might clear up the matter, he was forced to admit that he held letters which he regarded as private. After a long debate he was prevailed upon in the national interest to hand over one of these communications in the hopes that it might afford some clue as to Parnell's whereabouts. But he declined to take any responsibility in the matter. He was not a member of the Land League executive, and had come to Paris purely in the capacity of Parnell's private secretary; therefore it devolved on Dillon and Egan to open the letter, and it was agreed that they were to maintain the strictest secrecy regarding the contents, merely giving the other members the necessary clue.

These communications had nothing to do with Mrs. O'Shea; they were a legacy from the days when, in sheer loneliness and depression, Parnell would seek momentary relaxation and female companionship in any provincial bar and music-hall. Being a man of normal passions but of intense reserve, he deliberately indulged in these casual, promiscuous affairs, where the affections played no part. But the most passing episode is apt to have undesirable consequences, and the letter that Dillon and Egan were forced to read was the last of a series of begging notes from a barmaid who had given birth to what she claimed to be Parnell's child. As the chief rarely bothered to look through his correspondence, and always maintained that it was quite unnecessary to reply to the majority of his letters, it is more than likely that he was in complete ignorance of this unfortunate misadventure. It is purely by chance that "Lizzie of Blankshire's" pathetic communications lay in Mr. Healy's pocket; they might just as well have been collected by Parnell at the House of Commons, taken down to Eltham and flung on to Mrs. O'Shea's writing-desk, with the words, "Queenie, do see to these, and answer those which don't answer themselves." She would scarcely have been edified by her lover's lack of discrimination.

There is evidence that Parnell made ample financial amends for his temporary neglect, and this letter, evoking a rather sordid episode, would be totally unimportant in his life were it not for the way in which it influenced his relations with two of his principal lieutenants.

Dillon, who was by nature chaste and very religious, must have been profoundly shocked by this revelation of the private life of a leader whom he regarded with unbounded admiration and of whom he wrote, "In my judgment Parnell was, next to Bismarck, the greatest political genius of the nineteenth century. The difficulties by which our movement was beset in its earlier stages were beyond belief, and it would have been wrecked not once, but a hundred times, were it not for Parnell's wonderful acumen and clear-sightedness. There was none of us who could at all compare with him in that respect."

Parnell never forgave Dillon for having opened one of his letters, and when, later in the year, they differed over the Land Act, the knowledge that Dillon was in a position to criticize his behavior inspired him to an active dislike of a man whose popularity in Ireland was only second to his own. He ignored the extenuating circumstances which had forced him to intrude into his private affairs, he ignored the fact that Pat Egan shared the responsibility, for in his eyes Egan was merely a useful link in holding together the complicated machinery of the Land League—one who could be relied upon to do the dirty work with which he did not care to soil his hands. It was Egan who, as an ex-Fenian, possessed inside information on those dubious patriotic societies and associations which flourished in the Dublin underworld; Egan who tracked down, bribed or intimidated the secret agents whom the supreme council of the I.R.B. paid to make propaganda against the constitutionalists; Egan who supplied Richard Pigott with several hundred pounds in the days when, as editor of the *Bankrupt Irishman,* the wretched black-mailer extorted money from Dublin Castle, the Fenians and the Parnellites. It was Egan, scrupulously honest, ardently patriotic, who kept careful account of every penny supplied by the Clanna-Gael, but the little Dublin baker, who ended his extraordinary career as the United States Minister to Chile and the trusted confidant of the dictator, Balmeceda, was never considered as an equal by Parnell; he was just a tool to be used as long as he served his purpose.

Dillon was different; like Davitt, he was both a fanatic and an idealist, and idealism was apt to be dangerous when it led men to deliver wild, injudicious statements on public platforms, when it made them averse to any form of compromise or bargain. Parnell, who had acquired a consummate mastery of parliamentary tactics, was a keen bargainer. At times he was hard, perhaps a little unscrupulous, but his dislike of the English never made him miss an opportunity for advantageous negotiations. The main issues at stake remained the same, the battle would continue until Home Rule was won; but the weapons were laid aside while he wrested yet another concession for his country from an unwilling Government.

This incident in Paris had another important result, in so far as it led Tim Healy to offer his resignation as his private secretary. In the opinion of one of their colleagues, "Tim was the most necessary secretary to the most necessitous principal that ever existed," for in those days he was loyalty personified, the first to volunteer for any dangerous enterprise, the last to covet any personal reward; but he soon discovered that it was a very thankless job to be Parnell's secretary.

When Dillon and Egan returned from their consultation with a look of settled gloom on their naturally melancholy faces, they proposed that Healy and Biggar should start at once for London and search for Parnell at an address in Holloway taken from the letter. This proposal was agreed to, but the two delegates had hardly started for the Gare du Nord when their cab crossed another one in which sat Parnell.

As soon as he arrived he retired to his room, offering no word of explanation or excuse to his colleagues. It had not taken many years for a modest, self-depreciating young man to develop the tactics of a dictator, and when Katherine had urged him to send a message explaining his delay, he had replied, half laughing: "You do not learn the ethics of kingship, Queenie. Never explain, never apologize. I could never keep my rabble together if I were not above the human weakness of an apology."

Few of his colleagues realized that he had been under danger of arrest, a circumstance which could have justified both his absence from the House of Commons and his mysterious disappearance. But Parnell was not given to confidences. The numberless attempts made on his life by half-crazy revolutionaries were kept as strictly secret as the fact that he had been shadowed up to the door of his hotel by what he believed to be a spy of the British Embassy. The Irish members only learnt of this when, several months later in the House of Commons, he publicly charged Sir William Harcourt with having "had him shadowed in Paris by persons from the Embassy." Harcourt admitted that he had been watched, though the agents had been selected by the Home Office without consulting the Foreign Office or the Paris Embassy, an oversight which led to friction between the Home Secretary and Sir Charles Dilke, Under Secretary for Foreign Affairs.

When Parnell reached his room, he found an unpleasant surprise awaiting him. Beside his pile of unopened letters lay one with the seal broken, accompanied by an explanatory note from John Dillon. Parnell was the last man to make any allowance for what he looked upon as deliberate spying, but only for a moment did he allow himself to be governed by his rage, and it cost him the services of an invaluable secretary. When Healy knocked at the door, he half opened it with a look of cold anger on his face, snapping out, "Who do you want?" And when the emotional Tim, who had gone through hours of agony, replied, "I am glad to see you. We were worried about you," he merely closed the door in his face without troubling to answer. Three days later, when they were back in England, Healy told him that he could no longer act as his secretary.

The Paris conference passed off in perfect harmony, and everyone did his best to forget an unpleasant incident. Both Dillon and Egan preserved the utmost reticence over the contents of the letter, and Parnell, who never let his private feelings interfere in his political calculations, was the first to propose John Dillon as Davitt's successor in the organizing of the Land League. There was nothing small or petty about him and he was always generous in rewarding the ability of his lieutenants, always ready to give every young member a chance to distinguish himself. That evening, as he presided over a gathering of men whose nerves he had unstrung and whose time he had wasted, he was at his most charming, his most considerate. He listened to their suggestions, seeking their advice, appreciative, almost flattering in his deference to their opinions, chaffing Biggar with his quiet, subtle humor, smiling his slow, gentle smile, which had such indefinable fascination. Dillon notes in his diary that he never had "the slightest side." It was not necessary. The magnetism of his personality commanded respect, implicit obedience and a blind, uncomplaining devotion.

At times he allowed himself to be influenced by his colleagues. He was hardly back in the House of Commons before James O'Kelly, the fat, jovial Irish-American whose gift as a journalist did not include political insight, persuaded him to make another trip to Paris in order to meet the prominent French journalists and writers who might be persuaded to rouse public feeling in their country with regard to Ireland. One marvels that Parnell could have taken this suggestion seriously, but during this period there was nothing to be gained by obstruction in the House. Sir William Harcourt had introduced the second Coercion Act, the Arms Bill, which gave power for the search for and the prohibition of arms, and though Sir Charles Dilke records in his diary that Gladstone, Bright and Chamberlain fought hard in the Cabinet against this Bill, "the autocratic Home Secretary carried the day, with one of his memorable epigrams, saying, 'Coercion is like caviare; unpleasant at first, it becomes agreeable with use.'"

This view was evidently popular, for the Bill was passed by a thumping majority and Mr. Gladstone appeased his conscience by the preparation of his Land Act.

There was nothing to be gained at Westminster, and propaganda was always a useful weapon for poor and struggling nations; so argued James O'Kelly. Parnell returned to Paris to meet Monsieur Victor Hugo and the Marshal MacMahon, who, while professing to have "the deepest sympathy with struggling nationalities," never got further than voicing beautiful sentiments at social gatherings where the Irish leader felt very ill at ease. O'Kelly gave racy interviews in his name and trailed him round the left wing *salons* and newspaper offices. Henri Rochefort of the *Intransigeant* declared that he was as greatly moved by shaking hands with Mr. Parnell as he was when he embraced Garibaldi. But even this pretty tribute did not benefit either Ireland or the Land League, and his trip is only memorable in so far as it brought about a meeting between Parnell and Clemenceau—a meeting which ripened into friendship when the latter visited England.

It was hardly likely that the princes of the Catholic Church would approve of the Irish leader fraternizing with men like Rochefort and Clemenceau, and one finds Cardinal Manning writing to Archbishop Vaughan:

"The Irish affairs are, I think, playing out. Parnell's Paris expedition is a showing of cards, which has damaged him and his works. But the agencies in America are serious. Gladstone has met his nemesis."

The last words were prophetic. When Gladstone introduced his Land Bill on April 4th, he spoke to unsympathetic Irish benches. Conciliation had come too late, and, though the terms were such that some of the older members who had supported Butt in his modest demands for Land reform could hardly believe them to be true, the extreme Nationalists turned their backs on both Mr. Gladstone and his Land Act.

CHAPTER TWENTY-THREE

LORD MORLEY describes the Land Act of 1881 "as the carriage of a single measure by a single man. Few British members understood it, none mastered it, the Whigs were disaffected about it, the Radicals doubted it, the Tories thought that property as a principle was ruined by it, the Irishmen when the humor seized them bade them send the Bill to line trunks." And yet this Bill, which received so little appreciation, gave the Irish tenant farmer all that he had clamored for during half a century: fair rents to be fixed by the land courts at intervals of fifteen years; free sale, giving all yearly agricultural tenants the right to sell their holdings for the best price they could get; fixity of tenure, so that no tenant could be evicted as long as his rent was paid and the conditions of his tenancy observed.

It was a drastic revolutionary measure, which twelve years later Mr. Gladstone himself admitted "would never have been on the statute book but for the existence of the Land League." It sounded the death-knell to feudalism, "making landlordism intolerable for the landlord," bringing the Prime Minister into collision with the Upper House and into disfavor with the Queen, while, instead of being rewarded by the humble gratitude and thanks of the Nationalist party, this Bill was greeted with frigidity by Mr. Parnell, with mocking taunts by Mr. Biggar, with criticism by Mr. Healy and open opposition by Mr. Dillon—not that Mr. Dillon had much opportunity of voicing his disapproval in public, for by the beginning of May he was clapped into Kilmainham Jail, the first prominent victim of Mr. Forster's Coercion Act. Mr. Gladstone's Bill could not work miracles, and, though seasoned Nationalists like A. M. Sullivan and O'Connor Power, who for years had used the "three f's" as the chief plank in their parliamentary platform, gave open support to the measure, the majority of Irishmen were too embittered by the numberless evictions which had occurred during the winter, and the brutality with which the armed police were terrorizing the country, to abandon their hostility to a coercionist ministry.

Parnell was well aware that the Bill deserved a more friendly reception. When in 1880 he told the Clare farmers that "the coming measure of Land reform" would be the measure of their energy that winter, he never in his wildest dreams had expected such a complete surrender on the part of the Government. But there was division in his ranks, and the very possibility of his coming to terms with the British was sufficient to arouse John Dillon's righteous but most embarrassing wrath. Old Fenians such as Brennan and Biggar regarded the Bill with suspicion, thinking that if the grievances of the people were redressed there would be an end to Home Rule. On the night of April 7th, Mr. Gladstone had barely started to unfold his scheme before the member for Cavan turned to Parnell with one of his most impish smiles, commenting in a very audible voice on what he considered to be a thoroughly bad Bill, and an answering smile, sly and humorous, testified that, though Mr. Parnell considered it "a good Bill," he was not going to accept it wholeheartedly lest the Government should feel they had conceded too much. Any elaborate show of enthusiasm on his part would wreck the Land Act in the Upper House. So, with Dillon pulling in one direction and Healy pulling in another, he remained a passive spectator, while a sparsely filled House listened with indifference to the veteran Prime Minister grappling with the intricacies of Irish Agrarian law. Whenever the Bill was in danger the Parnellites came to the rescue; at other times they made it the target for the most unsparing criticism; their approval was cool, their support was vacillating, and, though there were times when, according to Sir William Harcourt, "Parnell seemed disposed to become a Christian," he never had any intention of risking dissension in his party by championing a measure which might prove to be totally inadequate when tested in the Land courts. A certain clique of extreme Nationalists was trying to undermine his authority by spreading the rumor that he would take the moderate course in accepting the Bill; these men, who had been raised to power by the Land League, were afraid lest a measure so favorable to the tenants might crush their movement. In picturesque language, they feared that "if the yoke of landlord ascendency were made lighter, the people of Ireland would once more bow their heads beneath it and consent once again to accept the position of living as slaves." This was the genuine opinion of a few high-minded idealists such as Mr. Dillon, but the majority were chiefly influenced by the salaries they drew from the exchequers of the League. Though the dollars were still pouring in, Patrick Ford hinted very plainly in the columns of his paper that Irish America expected something more dramatic from Mr. Parnell than a tame acceptance of Mr. Gladstone's proposals, and the fire-eating patriots on the other side of the Atlantic were loud in favor of a "No Rent" campaign.

The situation was critical, and at first it seemed as if the Prime Minister's magnanimous Land Act would end by destroying the unity of the Irish party. During the Easter recess Mr. Parnell did nothing beyond summoning a convention in Dublin, where he declared that every member of Parliament was to be left free to take any course he pleased. So, while A. M. Sullivan supported the measure and Healy proposed amendments, proud of parading his unique knowledge of Agrarian law, while Dillon denounced it and Archbishop Croke, speaking for the majority of the tenant farmers, demanded a fair trial for the Bill, the leader kept his own counsel and awaited developments.

Then followed the imprisonment of Dillon and of Father Sheehy, one of the most popular priests in Ireland, and public feeling was roused to such a pitch that Parnell, without consulting any of his followers, decided on an action which at first seemed to be ill-considered and imprudent, but which later proved to be the superb tactics of a parliamentary opportunist. For Parnell was first and foremost a parliamentarian. He hated Westminster, he spent as little time there as possible, and yet it was his natural fighting-ground. Popular platforms and idolizing crowds held no appeal for him, and it was in adverse circumstances, pitted against the greatest parliamentarian of his day, that he fought and won his most daring victories. His sudden declaration that he had decided to take no responsibility for the Bill came as a bombshell to many of his adherents. Shortly before the second reading of the Bill, he strolled in, late as usual, to the Committee Room 15, where the Irish party held their conferences, and declared without any preliminaries: "Gentlemen, I don't know what your view on this question is. I am against voting for the second reading of the Bill. We have not considered it carefully. We must not make ourselves responsible for it. Of course I do not want to force my views upon anybody, but I feel so strongly on the subject that if a majority of the party differ from me, I shall resign at once."

The result of this terse declaration was that thirty-five Home Rulers followed Parnell's lead in abstaining from voting, while twenty-four joined the majority. The small clique of malcontents who had been grumbling against their chief were checkmated, the prisoners of Kilmainham were momentarily mollified, Mr. Healy was allowed to continue proposing his amendments and the moderate section of the party were told that the Bill was safe, that abstaining from voting was merely a question of tactics and that they could do as they wished. A. M. Sullivan, who had been one of the first to protest against what he called a "highhanded act on the part of our leader," afterwards admitted, "Many of us are inclined to be carried away by what we think a kindly and generous act. Parnell is never carried away by anything. He never dreams of giving the English credit for good intentions. He is always on the look-out for the cloven foot. He distrusts the whole lot of them and is always on the watch. They have got their match in him, and serve them right. It's not poor Isaac Butt they have to deal with, or even O'Connell. Parnell is their master as well as ours."

But was Parnell really interested in the Land Bill? According to Tim Healy, there were times when he gave it but scant attention, absenting himself for days in the middle of the session. Private domestic worries took his thoughts away from the fate of a million tenant farmers. At Eltham, Captain O'Shea was beginning to show himself in his true colors, and his visits to his neglected wife became more frequent when it dawned on him that Mr. Parnell had found a very comfortable home at Wonersh Lodge. A portmanteau left in his room, the gossip of servants, sly observations on the part of one or two of his colleagues, were sufficient to make the injured husband aware that Katie was not conducting this affair with either discretion or good sense. It was galling to his self-esteem to find that she had lost her heart to this dry, silent Irishman who, according to his standards, was totally deficient of either charm or grace of manner. He was peculiarly sensitive about his reputation, he prized it highly, and as yet he had derived no material advantages to compensate him for being made ridiculous in the eyes of the world. So, in the late spring, Captain O'Shea came down to Eltham, provoked a scene with his wife, and, for the first time in their married life, played the part of the heavy, jealous husband. Katherine very naturally resented his daring to lecture her on morals and conventions, and in a moment of fury she confessed the whole story of her love for Parnell. This open defiance cost her a heavy price; she had played into Willie's hands, giving him every opportunity to exercise his pretty talent for blackmail, and his first move was to challenge Parnell to a duel—a suggestion which must have originated with the O'Gorman Mahon, who was always regretting the good old days when a gentleman avenged his honor with the sword. It was disappointing for O'Shea to find that Parnell was quite willing to fight, even going to the lengths of suggesting suitable meeting-places near Boulogne or Calais, and the gallant Captain, who had no wish to risk his life for the sake of a wife in whom he had never felt any proprietary interest, had to resort to working on Katie's fears for her lover's safety in order to prevent a duel which might have disastrous financial consequences for both them and their children. Anne Steele, the favorite sister and cherished sister-in-law, ran between husband and wife, suggesting, intriguing and bargaining. But Parnell kept aloof from the whole proceedings. If O'Shea wanted to fight, he was ready to meet him, even if all the Catholic hierarchy of Ireland were to rise against him in disapproval; but if, as Katie and Anna seemed to think, the noble Captain's complaisance was to be bought for a consideration—well, then he was willing to pay, though he refused to have a hand in the dealings. There must have been moments when he was revolted by the pettiness and sordidness of the whole affair, the miserable nagging which took place between the woman whom he adored and the man with whom he was forced to maintain an outward semblance of friendship. But in his infatuation he was ready to pay or promise anything that might ensure his happiness with Katie. As naïve and helpless as a boy in the throes of his first love-affair, he deliberately shut his eyes to a degrading compact. In a way it was a relief to have the whole situation defined on a clear basis, so that he might be spared some of those tiresome subterfuges and explanations which Katie called "preserving the appearances."

Years later, William O'Brien told Michael Macdonagh of the *Freeman's Journal* that Parnell could have cleared himself of half the charges of which he was accused in the divorce courts by producing the counterfoils of his cheque-book, showing the various sums of money paid into the account of Captain O'Shea. But Parnell was never eloquent in his own defense. All during his career, whether he was indicted of crime by Mr. Forster in the House of Commons or by Mr. Houston in the columns of *The Times;* whether he was accused by the extremists of selling himself to Gladstone or by the Liberals of intriguing with the Conservatives, he never gave any justification either of his methods or his actions.

After this bitter quarrel, Katherine O'Shea states that she and her lover "were one without further scruples, without fears and without remorse." The words are romantic, but the circumstances were the reverse. A bargain was concluded, and, though the details were never made public, it is believed that Captain O'Shea received six hundred per annum, not to mention the occasional *douceurs* his wife contributed from her aunt's exchequer. But it was not only a question of money; the Captain was ambitious, and from now onwards Parnell was forced to further the parliamentary career of a man whom he despised as a political mountebank.

So, while Mr. Healy persuaded an admiring Prime Minister to adopt the famous Healy Clause (to protect the tenants' improvements from rent), and while Mr. Dillon issued bitter manifestos from Kilmainham Jail, Parnell embarked on a life that subjected him to a continual mental and physical strain.

Ten years later, Wilfrid Scawen Blunt, an Englishman who was no friend of the O'Sheas, wrote: "Parnell's devotion to Mrs. O'Shea and the worry of his public life were too much for him, and she really hastened his end by her exigencies." There are still men living who knew her in her prime, who remember her as a gay, witty creature, a great talker with an insatiable craving for admiration, and, though her most friendly critics admit that she could never have been considered a beautiful or stately woman, yet she had a certain quality which made one notice her in a crowded room. There is an old solicitor who, over fifty years ago, used to be her traveling companion on the Eltham railway, and who still remembers the warm, friendly smile and "winning" manner with which she greeted the merest stranger. He described her as "unusual," and in that word lay the secret of her charm—that indefinable charm and magnetism that enslaved Parnell.

Every night when he left the House of Commons he would either drive down to Eltham or join her at one of their strange meeting-places. He discussed everything with her, and those sudden, drastic decisions, with which he would stun both the extremists and the moderates of his party, were all carefully weighed and considered during those *tête-à-tête* suppers, with the early morning light already filtering through the window-curtains. When the meal was over, he would relax in his favorite armchair, light a cigar, and gaze at her for a moment or two without speaking. And it was such a tender, trusting gaze that there must have been times when she wondered if she quite deserved that trust. The very domesticity of her surroundings appealed to him, for he had never known those everyday comforts which are the privilege of a family man, and, though Katie was preeminently social and her real ambition would have been to shine as a political hostess, the qualities which chiefly attracted her lover were her homeliness and her simplicity. With her he could talk in an easy, effortless way on any topic that passed through his mind—Gladstone's speech that evening, Healy's latest amendment, his agent's letters regarding the development of his saw-mills and slate quarries. Then he would begin to reminisce about his youth at Avondale, saying, "One day, Queenie, I must show you my home," and for a few moments they would forget Willie's existence, and the children sleeping upstairs, and Aunt Ben, who was probably already awake in the big house on the other side of the park.

They forgot all those ties for one happy week in the early summer, when they escaped to Brighton under the pretext that Katie had to find summer lodgings for her children. It was the first of their surreptitious honeymoons, and Parnell—or "Mr. Stewart," as he was registered in the hotel—went to the lengths of cutting off his beard with a pair of nail scissors in order to avoid being recognized. Parliament was still in session and the news from Ireland was disquieting, but for those few days he was just the ardent, possessive lover absorbed in his own happiness. The only cloud to mar that happiness was when he found that Katie was not only unable to swim owing to a weak heart, but was also sick as soon as she got into a boat, and there is a story told of how he once persuaded her to go fully dressed into the sea in the fond belief that it would do her no harm if she had her clothes on. Maybe she was compensated for her discomfort and her fears when he lifted her into his arms and carried her, with all the weight of her soaked clothing, back to the shore, kissing her wet hair and whispering words of endearment into her ear.

The week at Brighton passed all too quickly and there were

meetings at Cork and Dublin that could no longer be delayed. When Parnell crossed over to Ireland, the enormous crowds awaiting him at Kingstown pier failed to recognize their chief as a beardless young man descended the gangway. All over the country the people were clamoring for the release of the Kilmainham suspects, and the *Irish World* was circulating in every cottage, advocating the expediency of a "No Rent" manifesto. Parnell was beginning to realize the danger of Mr. Ford's inflammatory literature; it was high time that his party had a newspaper whose opinions he could dictate, for the *Nation* was a family affair run by the Sullivans, and the *Freeman,* which had pledged itself to uphold his policy, was very vacillating in its support. There was a group of so-called Nationalist papers owned by Richard Pigott which, under the cover "of Fenian idealism," conducted a subtle propaganda against his party, and it was to buy off the ill will of this fraudulent journalist, as well as to obtain an organ in the Irish Press entirely under his own control, that Parnell paid the considerable sum of three thousand pounds for a group of bankrupt newspapers. This money was advanced by the Land League funds, while the running expenses were to be covered by a bank overdraft on his private credit. It is somewhat ironical that the dollars contributed by Mr. Ford's skirmishing fund should have financed a journalistic enterprise that doomed the circulation of the *Irish World*.

This newspaper project, sponsored by Parnell and Egan, was opposed by John Dillon, who, having differed from his leader on the Land Bill, quite naturally refused to identify himself with a paper which was bound to support Parnell's policy. At first his antagonism seemed serious, and William O'Brien, who had been approached with the offer of the editorship of *United Ireland* (as the paper was to be called), refused to consider the post until Dillon personally assured him that he would offer no active opposition. The Parnellite party, which abounded in heroic, self-sacrificing patriots, offered no finer type of pureminded idealist than William O'Brien. From the day of August 13th, when the first number of *United Ireland* appeared in print, to the day when Mr. Gladstone first declared himself in favor of Home Rule, O'Brien fought an almost single-handed battle against the executive of Dublin Castle. There were times when his paper was deluged by prosecutions and actions for libel, when it was edited behind prison walls or from a foreign capital, but month after month its circulation grew, till it was read by every Irish Nationalist throughout the world. Before he embarked on the enterprise he warned Parnell that if the object of the paper was to preach moderation he was the last man to be placed at the helm. They were discussing the future of the journal while dining at Romano's, which was one of Parnell's favorite restaurants, and, according to O'Brien, he would sit there for hours, "never ordering anything more *recherché* than a Bordeaux pigeon or a glass of Rhine wine. While it was characteristic of the man that, although he would give no fresh order and would occupy a table until after the last supper-party had quitted the place, there was not a waiter who would not hang obsequiously upon his lightest word or order." It was a strange place in which to discuss seditious politics, and Parnell answered O'Brien with a smile, "You are to go as far as ever you please, short of getting yourself hanged—or us, you know," alluding to the responsibility of himself, Biggar and Egan as co-directors.

Through all his difficulties Parnell remained optimistic, for he believed that the attitude of the Kilmainham party as regards the *Irishman* project was based upon insufficient information or misapprehension, and that in the end it would have the entire support of the Land League. He proved right, for O'Brien's fiery pen convinced the most uncompromising Nationalist that the newspaper was from "crest to spur a fighting organ."

The summer session was nearing an end, and, after walking out at the third reading of the Land Bill, Parnell wound up his parliamentary activities by being suspended for disregarding the authority of the House. In one of those tensely dramatic scenes which he deliberately staged for the benefit of his Celtic public, he demanded a day for discussing the behavior of the Irish executive since the enforcement of the Coercion Act. When his demand was refused, he said, "The ministry of the day, of course, always gains the sympathies of the powers that be in this House, and if we may not bring the cause of our imprisoned countrymen before the House, I may say that all liberty and regard of private right is lost in the assembly, and that the minister of the day has transformed himself from a constitutional minister into a tyrant."

The Speaker named him at once; Mr. Gladstone rose to move the motion for his suspension, but he shouted in defiance above the angry cries of the outraged Liberals, "I shall not await the farce of a division. I shall leave you and your House and I shall call the public to witness that you have refused freedom of discussion."

That same night he crossed St. George's Channel, and there was not a single malcontent in the party who dared to accuse him of conciliatory methods. He had been suspended for advocating the cause of the very men who, while in prison, had been trying to undermine his authority. His strategy had been brilliant, and, now that the Land Bill was ready to go through the usual process of mutilation by the Lords, the people of Ireland were to be taught to accept it with judicious discrimination, neither by rushing into the courts nor by flouting its advantages, but by testing it in selecting certain cases to be put on trial. Here again the strategy was brilliant, but it was hardly likely to find favor with Mr. Gladstone, and when Parnell left for Ireland he was doomed to a long separation from the one being whom he loved and cherished—a woman who now held him with the strongest tie of all, having but lately told him that she was to be the mother of his child.

CHAPTER TWENTY-FOUR

"Mr. Parnell desires to arrest the operation of the Land Act, to stand as Moses stood between the living and the dead; to stand between them not as Moses stood, to arrest, but to spread, the plague. If it shall appear that there is still to be fought a final conflict in Ireland between law on the one side and sheer lawlessness upon the other; if the law, purged from defect and from any taint of injustice, is still to be repelled and refused and the first conditions of political society to remain unfulfilled, then I say, gentlemen, without hesitation, that the resources of civilization against its enemies are not yet exhausted."

So spoke Mr. Gladstone on October 7th, at a great mass meeting in Leeds, and his words of warning sped across the Irish Sea. During the past months he had been watching Parnell's movements with increasing suspicion, for it looked as if the Irish leader meant to present test cases which the Land Commission must refuse and then to treat their refusal as showing that they could not be trusted and that the Bill had failed. At the Land League conventions held in Dublin and Maryborough during the month of September, Mr. Parnell had stressed the fact that the test cases selected for the Land Commission should not be the most rack-rented tenants, but rather tenants whose rents hitherto had not been considered cruel or exorbitant. The average scale of rent was still too high and required almost universal reduction; therefore a rack-rented property did not supply the court with a fair case. In Mr. Gladstone's opinion, Parnell was deliberately trying to thwart the Government in their conciliatory measures, and he was now willing to lend a listening ear to the Irish Secretary, who was firmly convinced that the only way of pacifying the country was by proclaiming the League and arresting its president. The Prime Minister ignored the fact that, by giving a fair test to the Land Bill, Parnell was acting in direct opposition to the advice of his American allies; that, during the first day's discussion at the Dublin convention, his voice was the only one heard "that was not for the scornful and uncompromising rejection of the Act," and that it was only when the fiery upholders of the Kilmainham party had exhausted their rhetoric that he was able to convince his listeners to vote in favor of his own resolution. As calm and unmoved as if there was not one breath of opposition amongst those fifteen hundred delegates assembled in the Rotunda, he said in his quiet matter-of-fact way: "I myself don't believe the Act will stand the test, but we should be assuming an unreasonable and indefensible position in the eyes of the world, and I venture to think in our own eyes also, if we refused to test this measure." And at the end of a three days' session, the convention, which had listened to his opening address in frigid silence, carried his resolution by an overwhelming majority. John Dillon, who had been released from Kilmainham in broken health, now added to the tenseness of the situation by announcing at a public banquet that, owing to his hostility towards the Land Bill, "the only honorable course for me is to retire from public life for a couple of months and leave those who believe in the policy, unembarrassed, to carry it out." He was still chivalrous and loyal towards a leader "whose generalship and political skill" he had never more admired than at the present moment. But unfortunately Parnell had disliked him ever since the Paris conference, and his dislike had deepened into distrust, though he never voiced these feelings to anyone except Mrs. O'Shea. On the contrary, when he discussed the situation with his colleagues, he was very gentle and indulgent in his attitude towards Dillon, excusing him on the grounds of ill health. And when they became politically reconciled, he always looked upon him as his second in command. Mr. Gladstone was the unwitting peacemaker, for when he denounced Parnell amidst the torchlight processions and rejoicing multitudes of Leeds, he took advantage of the recent differences between the Land League leaders by upholding Mr. Dillon "as one who will not give up his extreme national views, but neither will he take upon himself the fearful responsibility of attempting to plunge his country into permanent disorder and chaos by intercepting the operation of the Land Act. I claim him as an opponent, but as an opponent whom I am glad to honor."

This speech forced Mr. Dillon to come out of his retirement in order to free himself "from the contamination of Mr. Gladstone's praise," and two days later his tall, picturesque figure was to be seen once more on the popular platform.

How Parnell hated those popular platforms and the frenzied crowds, whose enthusiasm forced him to make the kind of speeches which he knew would ultimately land him in jail! With quiet sarcasm he remarked, "Having been during several years of my political life considerably in advance of the rest of the country, I am exceedingly pleased to find, as a result of my excursions during the last few weeks, that the rest of the country is considerably in advance of me." With the same ironical humor he once curbed the overheated ardor of his lieutenants by saying quite simply, "Of course, I have never been a Parnellite." And had he been able to follow his own inclinations instead of pandering to the passions aroused in the country, he would have made no more speeches till the test cases had come into the Land courts. In the month of September, when Avondale was looking its loveliest, with the beech-woods turning gold and the grouse in flight over the heather moors of Aughavanagh, he closeted himself in the Land League offices in Dublin, looking through old blue-books and memoranda, searching for suitable test cases to be put up for trial. His two objects, of utilizing the Act, but of utilizing it under the supreme influence of the League, were being carried out in the South, but in Ulster his power was not yet omnipotent. Thirty thousand tenants rushed into the Land courts, disregarding his advice to hold back, and when at the beginning of the month he deliberately challenged the Government by putting up a candidate in opposition to the Liberal nominee at a by-election in County Tyrone, not even his presence nor the eloquence of "Tim" and "T. P." could persuade the Ulstermen to forsake their faith in their Whig allies. Mr. Gladstone rejoiced in what he considered to be a great victory demonstrating that Parnell's influence was on the wane; but Mr.

Forster, worn out with work and embittered through failure, reminded him that "Tyrone is in Ulster and that Ulster is not Munster or Connaught." The Chief Secretary cherished no illusions about Mr. Parnell's waning power, for he happened to have been in Dublin when the chief was welcomed back from the North with bands, banners and torches, when the populace, wild with enthusiasm, dragged his carriage from College Green to the Rotunda. Disquieting reports from all over the country proved that never since the days of O'Connell had a leader been so firmly enthroned in the hearts of the people. When Parnell visited the town of Cork, his constituents almost tore one another limb from limb as they surged around the platform, and, carried away by their wild cheering, he allowed himself to make one of those unguarded speeches, using words which were perilously near to treason, saying, "Those who want to preserve the golden link of the Crown must see to it that it shall be the only link connecting England and Ireland."

And all the time while he was working out the test cases with Tim Healy, and appearing on the Land League platforms, he knew that the movement could not be sustained at the present pitch, and that the Irish-Americans who supplied the funds would only be placated by his offering himself up for temporary martyrdom. As a victim of the Coercion Act, lodged in Kilmainham Jail, he would earn the allegiance of every Fenian extremist. But was it worth the price? He had not changed since the days when he confessed to Michael Davitt his horror of solitary confinement, and now, coupled with his fear of imprisonment, was the misery of being separated from Katie at the time when she most needed him. His heart must have been very heavy during these days when he had to fight to consolidate his leadership; days when he was so overworked that he had barely time to write her a few hurried lines. "My dearest Katie must have been very lonely. Her husband has been so busy he has not even had time to sleep, but he has never been too busy to think of her." Or, "My dearest little Wifie,— Your husband has been very good since he left you and so long-

ing to see you again. He has kept his eyes, thoughts and love
all for you, and my sweetest love may be assured that he always
will." It cannot be said that Mrs. O'Shea contributed towards
alleviating his worries, for her pregnancy upset her whole nervous system, and she gave way to morbid fears and fits of hysteria,
which were all too often communicated to her letters.

In his life of Joseph Chamberlain, Mr. Garvin states that during the autumn "Parnell was deliberately provocative to an extent
that no motive solely political could explain. He desired not to
avoid arrest but to court it, to make it inescapable. The reason
was that on account of his child not yet born he was in an unbearable extremity. Humanly he could not remain free without
making his tenderness the sure cause of his detection. If he
meant to remain a political leader and yet communicate with
the woman he worshiped through the time when she was herself in fear, his only resorts were prison and invisible ink."

On the other hand, Mr. William O'Brien, one of the few men
whom Parnell both liked and trusted, is emphatic in declaring
that he actively resented the forces that were driving him to
adopt an attitude that would ultimately lead him into jail. It
will never be known to what extent Parnell was involved with
the American extremists. However ruthless and dictatorial he
might be in his dealings with his own party, he was always
tactful and conciliatory with the executive of the Clan-na-Gael.
He neither countenanced outrages nor did he condemn them,
and Mrs. O'Shea writes that "all during 1881 he was privately
ascertaining for himself how far the 'reactionaries' could be
trusted to do the work he wished without becoming too greatly
involved in the tactics of the 'invincibles' proper." She hints at
mysterious papers, so incriminating that he did not dare to carry
them on his person, and secret documents that she kept locked
inside a hollow gold bracelet that never left her arm. But not
one of the Government spies was able to trace any connection
between the Nationalist leader and the physical-force men. As
O'Brien said, "He was one of the slowest of mankind to go into
a position of danger, but, once in it, Leonidas was not more

unshakable at his post." The Leeds denunciation forced his hand, for he was bound to make a warlike reply, even though he remembered that O'Connell had met his Waterloo on the day of his Mallow defiance.

On the Saturday following Mr. Gladstone's speech, Parnell was at Aughavanagh shooting grouse with James O'Kelly and he never saw a newspaper till the Sunday, when he met Barry, Redmond and Healy at Rathdrum station. There was to be a big meeting at Wexford, where he was to be presented with the freedom of the city, and during the short railway journey Healy read him the menacing passages from the Prime Minister's speech, while he made hasty notes framing a suitable reply. This impromptu speech has come down to history as one of his most famous utterances.

Wexford has always been fiercely Nationalist; memories of Vinegar Hill and Father Murphy are still treasured by the townspeople, and Healy records that when Parnell drove through the narrow streets, "his carriage was bombarded with flowers, the women threw their handkerchiefs from the windows and the people cheered madly." The scene was set and there was no possibility of drawing back. When he mounted the platform to address the gigantic crowds in the quiet cultured accents of a man who was about to take part in a university debate, he deliberately used words that could be construed as an incitement to treason, beginning: "You have gained something by your exertions during the last twelve months, but I am here to-day to tell you that you have gained but a fraction of that to which you are entitled, and the Irishman who thinks that he can now throw away his arms just as Grattan disbanded the volunteers in 1783, will find to his sorrow and destruction when too late, that he has placed himself in the power of the perfidious and cruel and relentless English enemy." Then he went on to defy the warnings of "that masquerading knight errant, that pretending champion of the rights of every other nation except the Irish, who used brave words which had a ring about them like the whistle of a frightened schoolboy on his way through a churchyard at night."

His voice became louder, clearer and harder as he declared: "It is not in Gladstone's power to trample on the aspirations and rights of the Irish nation . . . and I trust, as the result of this great movement, we shall see that, just as Mr. Gladstone by the Act of 1881 has eaten all his own words, has departed from all his formerly declared principles, now we shall see that these brave words of the English Prime Minister will be scattered like chaff before the united and advancing determination of the Irish people to regain for themselves their lost land and their legislative independence."

At Leeds, Gladstone had eulogized the statesmanship of O'Connell and Butt, dismissing Parnell as nothing more than a dangerous agitator. The Irish leader took up the challenge by saying, "In the opinion of an English statesman, no man is good in Ireland until he is dead and buried and unable to strike a blow for Ireland. Perhaps the day may come when I may get a good word from English statesmen as being a moderate man after I am dead and buried."

But after his last words were drowned amidst the enthusiastic cries of his audience, he turned to Healy and said in a tense whisper, "Tim, we have pushed this movement as far as it can constitutionally go." There was no longer any hope of avoiding jail, for Gladstone was in a temper and would let "Buckshot" do as he liked. That night, at the Imperial Hotel at Wexford, the frugal and abstemious leader, who usually contented himself with a half-bottle of Moselle, entertained his colleagues to a champagne supper. He was not a cheerful host; for a man of his temperament, confinement in Kilmainham was a gloomy and terrifying prospect, and he sat in utter silence till one of his guests asked him somewhat tentatively, "Do you think, Mr. Parnell, that you are likely to be arrested after your speech to-day?" He glanced up from his plate, and for a second those queer red lights flickered in his eyes, then he said very quietly, "I think I am likely to be arrested at any time—so are we all.

A speech is not necessary. Old Buckshot thinks that by making Ireland a jail he will settle the Irish question." "But suppose they arrest you, Mr. Parnell, have you any instructions to give us? Who will take your place?"

There was a slight pause, and the leader lifted his glass of champagne to his lips before he answered, in the same slow, quiet voice, "Ah, if I am arrested, Captain Moonlight will take my place." And, as he spoke, he could hear the hoarse and excited cries of the populace who were waiting for him to appear at his window.

The following day Mr. Forster crossed to England for a Cabinet council, having previously arranged with the Irish commander-in-chief that if Parnell's arrest was consented to he would telegraph the one word "Proceed."

Worn out with anxiety and sick at heart, Mrs. O'Shea waited at Thomas's Hotel for a message from her lover. He had warned her that it might be impossible for him to escape arrest, and in his last letter he had hinted that " 'something' may turn up at the last moment which will prevent me from rejoining you next week-end."

On Wednesday Parnell was still at liberty, addressing a convention at Kildare, promising to speak at Naas the following day, and returning to Dublin in the evening to discuss the situation with his colleagues. William O'Brien gives us a vivid picture of that last evening, of Parnell eating his chop in his cheerless hotel sitting-room, surrounded by an excited group of members of Parliament, organizers and priests, to all of whom he listened with "patient, long-suffering attention." Only by one remark did he show how much he resented the idea of going to prison. Turning to a member who spoke contemptuously of coercion, he said in an icy tone, "I dare say you were born to be crucified; I was not. I am for winning something for my country all the time."

At eight o'clock on the following morning, Thursday, October 13th, Chief Detective Mallon, superintendent of the Dublin police force, knocked at the door of Morrison's Hotel. He bore a warrant for the arrest of Mr. Parnell, but consented to wait in the hall until his prisoner had been awakened. The story of how Pat, the boots, begged the chief to escape by the back of the house, even at the risk of his being made responsible for his flight, has been immortalized into one of the most popular ballads of the Dublin streets; but Parnell refused to take advantage of Pat's loyalty. There was no point in evading arrest, and he was quite calm and prepared to receive the visit of the police. Only the unpleasant effort of rising early on a raw October morning made him somewhat reserved in his greeting. He dressed slowly and deliberately, and refused to step inside the waiting cab before he had queried every detail of his account, even to the extent of obtaining a ten per cent reduction on the bill.

Chief Detective Mallon, who, according to William O'Brien, "was not wholly corrupted, but had a good deal of the original Nationalist at heart," did not relish the task of having to arrest "the uncrowned King of Ireland," and he treated him with a respectful courtesy. His one idea was to get him to Kilmainham as quickly and as quietly as possible before the news of his arrest had penetrated to the public. But, under Mr. Forster's régime, the presence of armed force was such an everyday occurrence that when the closed cab, followed by two outside cars filled with policemen, passed through the streets of Dublin, it attracted little or no attention.

It was only when the prison officers of Kilmainham proposed to go through the usual form of searching him that Parnell really lost his temper. "How dare you!" he cried, with his face convulsed with rage, and there was a look in his eyes that made the head warder desist in his search. Afterwards, one of his colleagues asked him, "What would you have done if the warder had persisted?" "I should have killed him," he replied in a furious whisper; then he collected himself, and added with one of his most charming smiles, "Poor old fellow, how he would have been surprised!"

But none of this indignation transpired in the note addressed to Mrs. O'Shea which Mallon posted for him shortly after his arrest. It was just a few hurried lines to tell her to be brave and not to fret, that the only thing which made him worried and unhappy was that his arrest might hurt her and their unborn child, ending up, "You know, darling, that on this account it will be wicked of you to grieve, as I can never have any other wife but you, and if anything happens to you I must die childless. Be good and brave, dear little wifie, then.—Your own husband."

CHAPTER TWENTY-FIVE

"TELL the Irish people I will consider they have not done their duty if I am soon released," was Parnell's first cryptic message from Kilmainham. It was addressed to a reporter of the *Freeman's Journal* and was a subtle warning to the Irish executive that from now onwards the country was to be left to the tender mercies of "Captain Moonlight." The news of his arrest, which plunged the whole of Ireland into mourning, was welcomed in England as "by far the most popular step which the Government has taken." The Prime Minister was hailed with enthusiasm when he appeared at the Guildhall to receive the freedom of the City of London only a few hours following this sensational arrest. He broke the news to his audience by a statement which was more effective than accurate, saying, "Within these few moments I have been informed that towards the vindication of the law, of order, of the rights of property, of the freedom of the land, of the first elements of political life and civilization, the first step has been taken in the arrest of the man who has made himself beyond all others prominent in the attempt to destroy the authority of the law, which would end in bringing nothing more nor less than anarchical oppression exercised upon the people of Ireland."

The pre-arranged appearance of a Treasury messenger bearing a despatch confirming the arrest to which Mr. Gladstone had given his official sanction eighteen hours previously proved to be highly popular with the Mayor and Corporation, for it gave them the delightful sensation that they were sharing in the secrets of the Cabinet, though at that very moment the newsboys were shouting "Arrest of Parnell" all over the London streets—an arrest which was later to be recognized as the main blunder in England's relations with Ireland during the nineteenth century.

Though many of his colleagues assert that Parnell deliberately courted imprisonment, his feelings during the first days of cap-

tivity were those of outraged pride and indignation against his
jailers. His remarks to Brennan and Kettle (the only members
of the original Kilmainham "party" whom the Government had
not thought fit to release) were those of an angry and humiliated
man, and there was nothing jocular about him when he said,
referring to Mr. Gladstone, "I'll live yet to trample on that old
man's grave." He was one of those people who forgive anything
in anybody except a slight against themselves, and he never forgave the Prime Minister for treating him as if he were one of
Mr. Forster's "village ruffians." Years later, in the days of the
"Union of Hearts," when his portrait, together with that of Mr.
Gladstone, was to be found wreathed in shamrock on the walls
of every Irish cottage, he still harbored his old resentment, and
on his memorable visit to Hawarden, while touring the castle
domain with Mary Gladstone, he enquired, with one of his
blandest smiles, where her father kept his dungeons.

But it is doubtful whether William O'Brien is justified in stating that Parnell's personal resentment at his arrest influenced
him in the launching of a "No Rent" manifesto a few days
following his arrival at Kilmainham. That he had no intention
of doing anything of the kind when he first entered prison is
testified by a private letter to John Dillon, dated October 13th:

"Some of our friends are anxious for a change of policy on
account of my arrest. I am, however, very strongly of opinion
that no change should be made, at all events until we can see
whether we can keep the tenants out of the court. I would
recommend that the test cases should be proceeded with and
that no means should be left untried to protect by mortgage the
sale of the interest of the more substantial class of tenants. If
we can do this, and if the Government do not suppress the
organization, we can, I am sure, maintain and strengthen the
movement."

But circumstances forced him to commit one of the biggest
mistakes of his career. In the following days the leading spirits
of the Land League were clapped into jail, and Sexton, O'Kelly,
O'Brien and Dillon were among the hundred suspects who

joined him in Kilmainham. Warrants were also issued against Biggar and Healy, but both managed to evade arrest, the former by escaping to Paris and the latter to America.

The leaders of the movement were crowned with the halo of martyrdom, the League itself was suppressed, and for two days Dublin was given over to the police, who perpetrated such brutal atrocities that even the Conservative Press denounced them in horror. Having feared the danger of a riot in O'Connell Street, a detachment of constabulary charged headlong into the people, striking right and left regardless as to whether they were respectable citizens or would-be rioters, strewing the ground with the bodies of women and children; and when members of the Corporation complained to the Chief Secretary, his only answer was that "clearing the streets was not a milk-and-water business."

Kilmainham was a haven of peace compared with the Imperial Hotel, where the cries of the wounded reechoed from the street, and, whatever Mr. Forster's mistakes might have been in bludgeoning the crowd, there was no denying that his prison regulations were very humane. After one night spent in a cell, Parnell was removed to the infirmary ward, where he had two light and airy rooms placed at his disposal. His colleagues were allowed to mess in his sitting-room, where they partook of excellent meals procured at their own expense from a neighboring restaurant. Gifts of every kind poured into the prison, from the hares and pheasants poached by Land League farmers to the superbly worked eiderdowns, embroidered caps and woolen vests presented by patriotic ladies. Unfortunately, most of these ladies showed a predominant fondness for the "wearing of the green"—a color that Parnell not only regarded as unlucky, but which he also objected to from a fear of arsenic poisoning. He would often say, "How can you expect a country to have luck that has green for its color?" and nothing would persuade him to wear or to touch anything of that shade. Discipline seems to have been very lax at Kilmainham, judging by the amount of documents that were smuggled in and out of the prison, where

William O'Brien never failed to produce his editorial column and leading articles for *United Ireland*.

Mr. Forster had rather a strange way of preserving the freedom of the Press, for, though the paper was never openly suppressed, the members of its staff ran the risk of being imprisoned at a moment's notice, and during the next few months *United Ireland* had to endure many vicissitudes, being printed one week in Dublin or Glasgow and the next in Manchester or Liverpool, until it was finally forced to seek the safety of the French capital, from where it was smuggled over to Ireland, carefully stowed away amidst the cargo of the Boulogne fishing-fleet.

It was Messrs. Ford and Egan who were chiefly responsible for the launching of the "No Rent" manifesto—a measure to which Parnell would never have resorted if his leading lieutenants had been at liberty; but Mr. Forster left him no choice but to seek an alliance with the extremists. O'Kelly, who was one of his most devoted colleagues, was opposed to the whole project, and, curiously enough, John Dillon, who had inveighed with so much bitterness against the testing of the Land Act, was now foremost in condemning "a strike against rent, which could never be carried out without the help of the priests, who could not support such a barefaced repudiation of debt." But the majority of the Kilmainham party were in favor of the manifesto, and, against his own better judgment, Parnell signed the document drawn up by William O'Brien, in which the leaders of the suppressed Land League called upon the tenants "to pay no agrarian rents under any circumstances, until the Government has restored the constitutional rights of the people." As T. P. O'Connor writes, "At last the extremists whom Mr. Parnell had successfully opposed were victorious. When Mr. Gladstone and Mr. Forster became their allies they were for the first time irresistible."

But it was an unfortunate day for the Irish leader when he played into their hands, for the manifesto was denounced by the priests and ignored by the people, and even the Nationalist archbishop of Cashel condemned it as an incitement to unlawful behavior. Later on Parnell commented with grim humor that the only place where the tenants were strictly living up to it was on his own estate at Avondale.

Even after the launching of the "No Rent" manifesto Parnell had very little to complain of in his treatment. The only thing he did not like was that the Government insisted upon sending a lot of police into the jail every night, two of whom slept under his door and two more under his window. He was now kept under a stricter surveillance, and was not permitted to receive visitors except in the presence of two warders, though Emily Dickinson states that, when she visited Charlie, the friendly jailers usually left them alone.

Parnell spent his time playing chess with the other suspects, and it was characteristic of him that his favorite opponent was a little Mayo farmer who invariably beat him with his slow peasant cunning. Strenuous games of ball took place in the prison yard and in the large central hall, and the only form of recreation to which the authorities objected was when he expressed the wish to try his hand at carpentering. Maybe the prison board did not like to take the responsibility of arming him with handsaws and chisels.

But in spite of the comparative comfort of his surroundings he chafed at the monotony of the routine, the long hours of solitude and the lack of fresh air, which was particularly injurious to a man of his constitution. Unlike Dillon and O'Brien, he was not a great reader, and, barring an occasional volume of history or Roman law, he was rarely to be found with a book in his hand. As he himself said, "Literature has no chance with me against the *Freeman*"; but when one is locked up in one's room at eight o'clock in the evening the bulkiest newspapers are quickly disposed of, and it was the long hours of the night which were particularly trying to a man who could never sleep till the early morning. It was then that he gave way to those dreadful fits of depression, when the movement and everything he had fought for seemed hollow and worthless; when, tortured with anxiety over Katie and their child, he would write those adoring, pathetic letters which have been judged so severely in the chronicles of history.

Katherine O'Shea must have suffered agony during those months of separation. Even if she had been in a normal state of health she would have found it hard to remain on friendly terms with a husband who openly rejoiced over her lover's imprisonment; but the situation was rendered intolerable when, for reasons best known to himself, O'Shea showed himself firmly convinced that he was responsible for her present condition. She herself writes, "Willie became solicitous for my health and wished to come to Eltham more frequently than I would allow. He thought February would seal our reconciliation, whereas I knew it would cement the cold hatred I felt towards him and consummate the love I bore my child's father." These words are an open avowal that, immediately after having given herself heart and soul to her lover during their Brighton honeymoon, she returned to Eltham and resumed relations with the husband whom she affected to despise. And however much she may have been prompted in the writing of her book, no one, however senile and blunted in feeling, would have written so simply about Willie claiming to be the father of her unborn child if he had not had some justification for his claim. A few months later, when this ill-fated child of love was dying in her arms, she writes again, "Willie was very good. I told him my baby was dying and I must be left alone. He had no suspicion of the truth, and only stipulated that the child should be baptized at once. . . . I had no objection to this." For not the least surprising thing about this cynical opportunist was that he was a devout and practising Catholic, and his Sunday visits to his children were always timed so that he could accompany them to Mass.

O'Shea still had a physical hold over his wife, and in her hysterical and abnormal condition she loathed him for all the times he had led her to betray her lover. Her letters to Kilmainham reflected that hysteria, that terror of being left alone with a man whom till lately she had looked upon with rather more than a friendly indulgence. His very presence now was a "daily torture," and in her distracted state of mind she blamed Parnell for having brought upon them this cruel separation, telling him that he was surely killing both her and their child— a fear that had been near his heart since the day of his arrest, for he admitted: "When I heard that the detectives were asking for me, a terror, one which has often been present with me in anticipation, fell upon me, for I remembered that my darling had told me that she feared it would kill her." And now he answered her anguished complaint by writing: "Rather than that my beautiful wifie should run any risk I will resign my seat, leave politics, and go away somewhere with my own Queenie as soon as she wishes. Will she come? Let me know, darling, in your next, about this. Whether it is safe for you that I should be kept here any longer." The following day he adds that "nothing in the world is worth the risk of any harm or injury to you. How could I ever live without my own Katie, and if you are in danger, my darling, I will go to you at once!"

These letters, which have been so bitterly condemned, can hardly be taken seriously, when one considers that at the moment of writing his one thought was to say something to soothe and comfort the woman whom he not only adored, but for whose unhappiness and ill health he was mainly responsible. They were the tender solicitations of a lover, which not even Katherine O'Shea had any intention of taking seriously. Still, it would have been fairer to his memory had she left these letters unpublished, or, failing this, had at least included her own share of the correspondence, which would have helped one to understand those protestations of affection written in invisible ink between the lines of a formal letter fit to be submitted to the most rigorous censorship, or transposed in a secret code sent under cover to a false address and smuggled out of Kilmainham in the pocket of a friendly warder. Even in prison Parnell was not free from the intrigues and subterfuges of his miserable infatuation. It was all very well for William O'Brien to talk of the pleasant little company that gathered round the chief's table, but the man who sat at the head of the table was most of the time oblivious to his surroundings. His thoughts were far away at Eltham, and as the time drew near for Katie's confinement he began to envisage the possibility of coming to some kind of agreement with the Government which would procure his release. The friends who visited him in prison described him as "looking pallid and worn with the monotony and confinement." He complained that though Kilmainham was infernally monotonous it was not a bit restful, that he was pestered about every fiddle-faddle, and that every soul who visited the place insisted on seeing him.

At the same time, he saw the movement which he had so carefully organized being handed over to a mob of hooligans and desperadoes. That old Fenian, Pat Egan, was at last coming into his own, handing out vast sums for the perpetration of crime and outrage, and foremost on the pay-list came the Ladies' Land League, under the presidency of Anna Parnell. Her brother had always suspected that this patriotic effort on the part of young Nationalist ladies would be more trouble than it was worth, and, now that the Land League was suppressed, these would-be revolutionary heroines had stepped into the breach and were squandering the party funds with a reckless abandon.

Ireland was in a state of anarchy; Agrarian outrages, which had diminished during the last year, were more frequent than ever. Crime was rampant, and Mr. Gladstone was slowly realizing that the man whom Mr. Forster had thrown into jail for inciting revolution was the only restraining influence in the country, while, on the other hand, Parnell was beginning to see that by summoning the forces of "Captain Moonlight" he had given power to a certain section of his followers whom from now onwards it would be difficult to control. The Irish executive still clamored for "more coercion," but in the Cabinet Mr. Chamberlain voiced his disapproval of their methods, while even the Opposition, momentarily forgetful of their own history with regard to Ireland, denounced Mr. Forster's régime.

The New Year saw the Land Leaguers still imprisoned in Kilmainham. February came, and Mrs. O'Shea underwent a long and painful confinement before giving birth to a daughter. The nervous strain to which she had been subjected during the months of her pregnancy had affected the child's lungs, for though at the beginning it seemed to be strong and healthy, it gradually grew weaker and weaker, till the doctor told her it had very little chance to live. Distracted letters flew between Eltham and Kilmainham, and now Katherine had only one wish at heart—that her lover could see his child before it died. It speaks for her strength of character that, instead of giving way to her grief, she used all her energy and resources to get him out of prison. She was once more her practical, normal self, and her "cold hatred" for Willie vanished as it dawned on her that his connection with the Liberal whips might facilitate negotiations with the Government. There was also her uncle, Lord Hatherley, who as an old colleague of Gladstone's might be in a position to furnish her with useful recommendations. It was not long before Mrs. O'Shea showed considerable talent as a political wire-puller, and the ultimate result of her exertions was the famous "Kilmainham Treaty."

At first Parnell disliked the idea of placing himself under an obligation to the Government. Any open negotiation would damage his reputation both with the Land League and with Irish-America. Lately Mr. Gladstone had been sending out tentative feelers to see whether the Land Leaguers were amenable to a compromise. The O'Gorman Mahon had been his accredited envoy, but the majority of the prisoners had agreed with John Dillon in declining to be released upon any understanding or condition whatsoever, and now, when Mrs. O'Shea "threw the whole strength of her influence on the side of conciliation,"

Parnell feared that by giving way to her pleadings he would place himself in a false position with his followers. Rumors had reached him of dissension in the Cabinet. If Chamberlain had his way, they would soon be released unconditionally, the Irish party would still preserve its old integrity, and there would be no disaffection among the extremists. At the back of his mind there was always the fear of the extremists; not that he was frightened for his personal safety, for this man of a hundred contradictions, who was absurdly nervous of any contagious disease, merely smiled before the threat of an assassin's knife. But he was frightened that the reins of Government were slipping out of his hands and that a band of reckless men and women were trying to rush the country headlong to disaster.

Katherine was actuated by only one motive. She wanted to see her lover free, to have him beside her watching by the cot of their dying child, to feel his arms once more around her. As she herself said, she had never before ventured to influence him in any way politically. But now she "urged upon him the greater good for Ireland likely to accrue in the making of immediate peace." Parnell was wax in her hands, but if there was any bargaining to be done with Gladstone, he insisted on getting the better of the bargain. The Land Act was still defective on two points—leaseholders were excluded and tenants were liable to be evicted for not paying the arrears that had accumulated in the bad times before 1881. If the Government released both him and his fellow-prisoners and passed an Act canceling arrears, he on his side was perfectly willing to withdraw the "No Rent" manifesto, to advise the tenants to settle with their landlords, and to help in "slowing down" the agitation. This was the basis of the treaty inspired by Mrs. O'Shea and negotiated by her husband, for one of the cleverest moves of this astute and subtle woman was to let Willie take the full credit for engineering a *modus vivendi* between Gladstone and Parnell. She did it all in good faith, but the Kilmainham Treaty gave the death-blow to the independence of the Nationalist party. Slowly but surely the Liberal wire-pullers sapped the integrity of Parnell's lieutenants; they succumbed to the wiles of Labouchere, to the ruthlessness of Chamberlain, and, most dangerous of all, to the awe-inspiring fascination of the Grand Old Man.

CHAPTER TWENTY-SIX

ONE day early in April, Parnell said to William O'Brien, "Don't pitch into me too hard, O'Brien, if, like Micky Calligy, I sign conditions and go out." [1] These words, which were spoken half in jest, were the only indication any of his lieutenants received regarding the impending negotiations.

On April 10th, Parnell was released on parole in order to attend his nephew's funeral in Paris, and it was during these ten days of liberty that Mrs. O'Shea finally triumphed over his scruples. That he was already half won over was evident not only by his words to O'Brien, but on his arrival in London he had a long political talk with Justin McCarthy, who, as vice-chairman of the party, had been deputizing in his absence. The question of arrears came up for discussion, and Parnell prepared McCarthy for the Kilmainham Treaty by telling him that he had every reason to believe that the increase in crime was entirely due to the inability of the poorer tenants to pay their rents, owing to the accumulation of arrears—that once an Act was passed canceling these old debts, then tranquillity and peace would be restored to the country and the Government would find that the renewal of coercion was not necessary.

McCarthy, accompanied by a delegation of the Home Rule Association, had met him at Willesden Junction, and five years later, during the proceedings of *The Times* Commission, this act of friendly welcome was construed as a meeting of dangerous conspirators plotting a nefarious murder. But even the most biased Tory had difficulty in picturing the bland and middle-aged historian in the rôle of Guy Fawkes. Unfortunately, amongst the group of trusted officials was a certain Frank Byrne, who acted as secretary of the association. This quiet, well-mannered clerk was in reality a leading spirit of the "Invincibles." It was he who procured the surgical knives from the out-of-work

[1] Micky Calligy was a little Mayo peasant who was said to have purchased his freedom by signing a promise of better behavior.

219

Colonial doctor and then sent them over to Dublin hidden in the folds of his wife's petticoat. It was he and two others who paid and directed the besotted criminals and misguided boys who carried out the callous butchery in Phœnix Park—the butchery that was doomed to wreck the judicious treaty that Parnell had not yet been brought to sign.

But after visiting Eltham, where Katie put his dying child into his arms and he saw how tired and worn she looked after her months of suffering, then he knew that he would never again have the strength to leave her. He was so loyal and warm-hearted where his affections were concerned that even his journey to Paris was no mere excuse to get him out of prison. Delia had lost her only son, and, as the head of the family, he felt it was his duty to assist at the funeral. It was more than a duty, it was an ordeal, for he hated the very proximity of death and disease. He was not a religious man, though when young he had professed to be a strong Episcopalian. On the whole he was too practical, too scientific and too self-analyzing to have any real faith, and on one occasion when he was participating in a religious discussion with one of his Catholic colleagues he said rather pathetically: "The only immortality a man can have is through his children." He was essentially a family man, one who would have been perfectly content to be immersed in the simple everyday interests of his home. When he first heard of the birth of his daughter, he wrote to Katie: "I shall love her very much better than if it had been a son. Indeed, my darling, I do love her very much already and feel very much like a father. . . . Will you not give her papa's best love and innumerable kisses?"

But his child died on the very day of his return from Paris, and while he sat in the dining-room at Eltham, working out the Kilmainham Treaty with O'Shea, Katie was sobbing her heart out in the nursery. Whatever may have been her moral shortcomings, she never lacked courage, and it was with a sad but smiling face that she kissed her lover good-by when he went back to prison.

Meanwhile O'Shea had been in communication with the Liberal ministers. Already, on April 15th, one finds him writing to Mr. Gladstone, but the Prime Minister had no intention of playing into the hands of a comparatively obscure Irish member who claimed to have influence not only with Parnell but with the priests. All he did was to forward his communications to Mr. Forster, who, while showing himself to be sympathetic on the question of arrears, refused to have any underhand dealings with the Irish leader. In his opinion the increase of outrages in no way justified a release which would look very much like a surrender on the part of the Government. The taunts of the Opposition had wounded the rugged Quaker's pride, and he suspected a powerful influence conspiring against him in the Cabinet, where Mr. Chamberlain was supposed to be keeping a watchful eye on the chance of a vacancy in the post of Irish Secretary. So it was to Mr. Chamberlain that O'Shea now went with his offers of mediation, and when the President of the Board of Trade "saw nothing in his proposal which did not deserve consideration," O'Shea became so sanguine of success that he already saw himself as Under-Secretary for Ireland. For the sake of his personal ambition he was willing to dissimulate his underlying hatred for Parnell—a hatred that had been very evident in his joy at his imprisonment. That Parnell never really trusted O'Shea is apparent in so far as it was to Justin McCarthy that he sent the confidential letter containing the stipulations for his release, asking him to take the earliest opportunity of showing it to Mr. Chamberlain but not to let it out of his hands on any account.

Meanwhile Chamberlain had come to the conclusion that O'Shea could be a very useful intermediary, for his personal sympathies seemed to be wholly on the Liberal side, and he showed himself only too willing to accept any crumbs that might fall from the Treasury Bench. So Willie was sent to Kilmainham to interview Parnell on his return to prison, and, because his chief was so "shifty" in his dealings, he insisted on his writing a letter addressed to him, which not only repeated the clauses mentioned in the letter to McCarthy, but also stressed the conciliatory attitude which Chamberlain declared to be necessary in promoting goodwill between the two countries. It read as follows:

"I was very sorry that you had left Albert Mansions [1] before I reached London from Eltham, as I had wished to tell you that after our conversation I had made up my mind that it would be proper for me to put Mr. McCarthy in possession of the views which I had previously communicated to you. I desire to impress upon you the absolute necessity of a settlement of the arrears question which will leave no recurring sore connected with it behind, and which will enable us to show the smaller tenantry that they have been treated with justice and some generosity.

"The proposal you have described to me as suggested in some quarters of making a loan, over however many years the payment might be spread, should be absolutely rejected for reasons which I have already explained to you. If the arrears question be settled upon the lines indicated by us, I have every confidence —a confidence shared by my colleagues—that the exertions which we should be able to make strenuously and unremittingly would be effective in stopping outrages and intimidation of all kinds.

"As regards permanent legislation of an ameliorative character, I may say that the views which you always shared with me as to the admission of leaseholders to the fair rent clauses of the Act are more confirmed than ever. So long as the flower of the Irish peasantry are kept outside the Act, there cannot be any permanent settlement of the Land Act, which we all so much desire.

"I should also strongly hope that some compromise might be arrived at this session with regard to the amendment of the tenure classes. It is unnecessary for me to dwell upon the enormous advantages to be derived from the full extension of the purchase clauses, which now seem practically to have been adopted by all parties.

[1] Captain O'Shea's London lodgings.

"The accomplishment of the program I have sketched would, in my judgment, be regarded by the country as a practical settlement of the Land question, and would, I feel sure, enable us to cooperate cordially for the future with the Liberal party in forwarding Liberal principles; so that the Government at the end of the session would, from the state of the country, feel themselves thoroughly justified in dispensing with further coercive measures."

This letter, in which there was no attempt to hide the fact that Parnell was resident at Eltham in Captain O'Shea's absence, must have made the Government aware of the close friendship between the Irish leader and Mrs. O'Shea, even if Scotland Yard had not already brought it to their notice. In the month following Parnell's release one finds Sir William Harcourt telling members of the Cabinet that "the Kilmainham Treaty would not be popular when it was discovered that it was negotiated by Mr. O'Shea, the husband of Parnell's mistress."

But the damaging part of the letter was the last paragraph, in which the Irish leader promised to cooperate with the Liberals, and there is no doubt that this promise would have involved him in serious difficulties with the extreme members of his party had not the Phœnix Park murders shattered the very basis of the treaty.

O'Shea took it upon himself to present this document in person to Mr. Forster, who was inclined to be skeptical both of his trustworthiness and of Parnell's good intentions. After reading the letter carefully, the Chief Secretary refused to give him any opinion on the contents, merely asking him "if that is all Parnell has to say." O'Shea, who was only concerned with his own welfare, offered to supplement or change any words or expression that might not please the Cabinet, but he added that, even if the words were at fault, the substance was "that the conspiracy which had been used to get up boycotting and outrages would now be used to put them down, and that there would be a union with the Liberal party." He omitted to mention the fact that Parnell considered the settling of the arrears question to be far more important than the release either of him or his fellow-suspects. And he committed his chief still further by saying that he was going to make use of Sheridan (a notorious outrage-monger and one of Egan's paid agents) in helping him to put down the agitation.

In the eyes of the Chief Secretary, the very mention of Sheridan proved that Parnell was responsible for the campaign of outrage and intimidation, and he gave no assurance to O'Shea beyond telling him that he would show the letter to the Cabinet. When he forwarded an account of this interview to Mr. Gladstone, he commented that he "had expected little from these negotiations," therefore it must have been somewhat of a shock to find the Prime Minister not only highly gratified, but alluding in extravagant terms of delight to a transaction in which Parnell had definitely made the better bargain. He wrote: "This is a *hors d'œuvre* which we had no right to expect, and, I rather think, have no right at present to accept. . . . On the whole Parnell's letter is, I think, the most extraordinary I ever read. I cannot help feeling indebted to O'Shea." Through the ability of his wife, Captain O'Shea was at last on a confidential footing with the leaders of the Government, and an amicable atmosphere pervaded Wonersh Lodge, where Mr. Parnell's room was already being prepared for his arrival.

But the Irish executive refused to see eye to eye with Mr. Gladstone and Mr. Chamberlain, who between them had persuaded the Cabinet to renounce coercion and release those of the suspects who were still in prison. On May 2nd, Lord Cowper and Mr. Forster handed in their resignations. Dillon, O'Kelly and Parnell bade farewell to the governor of Kilmainham, and Sir William Harcourt, much against his will, signed an order for the release of Michael Davitt, a decision which aroused the indignation of the Queen.

For a moment it looked as if the clouds were lifting over Ireland and as if Mr. Gladstone could turn a weary glance to other quarters of the Empire—to Africa, where British interests were being threatened by Egyptian Nationalists and over-patriotic Boers.

It was a lovely spring day when O'Kelly and Parnell drove through the woods of Avondale, with the ground all carpeted with bluebells and the first azaleas already blossoming amidst the larches. The tenants came rushing out of their cottages crying with joy to see their master home again, and one old woman seized him by the hand, kissing it over and over again and crying, "Oh, Master Charlie, are you back to us again?" The emotional O'Kelly, who was very near tears himself, thought Parnell the most callous fellow he had ever met, just because he remained so calm and unmoved by all these demonstrations of affection. His remarks were as matter-of-fact as if he had only been out for a morning's walk, and, according to O'Kelly, the meeting between him and his sister Emily was so casual as to be almost icy. She greeted him quite calmly: "Ah, Charlie, is that you? I thought they would never let you back again," and he answered with a smile: "Well, what did you think they would do to me?" And she said in the same quiet, unemotional voice: "I thought they would hang you." But, though the aloofness of the Parnells might seem inexplicable to the demonstrative Irish-American journalist, their own people knew and loved them for their kindness and generosity and their extraordinary consideration to the humblest of their tenants.

This outward indifference and rigid self-control was never more evident than when Parnell took his customary place in the House of Commons on the evening of May 4th. He arrived as the Chief Secretary was in the midst of giving the reasons for his resignation, and for some seconds the deafening cheers of the Irish members interrupted Mr. Forster's speech. Parnell bowed to the Speaker, and, without looking to right or left, he moved slowly across the floor of the House to his usual seat below the gangway. Gladstone's devoted daughter, who was watching the scene from the Ladies' Gallery, comments in her diary:

"Went to the House to hear Forster's farewell speech. It was not a happy one. He was nervous and not wise and the suspects came in at various times, Dillon looking deathly, O'Kelly fat and jolly and Parnell indifferent. It all looked very nasty. The Tories had all their stings out. Parnell, however, substantially acknowledged the change in his tactics."

But, whatever might be Parnell's change of tactics, Mr. Forster frankly acknowledged him as the victor of the hour when he said:

"A surrender is bad, but a compromise or arrangement is worse. I think we may remember what a Tudor king said to a great Irishman in former times, 'If all Ireland cannot govern the Earl of Kildare, then let the Earl of Kildare govern Ireland.' If all England cannot govern the member for Cork, then let us acknowledge that he is the greatest power in Ireland to-day."

Very little was said that evening about the Kilmainham Treaty, and Parnell's fellow-suspects were still in ignorance as to the conditions of their release. But the chief was well aware that if those conditions were ever made public he would be ruined in the eyes of the extremists. Up till now he had been able to dominate them; he had held them with his back to the wall. But, as he said to Katherine O'Shea, "If I turn to the Government, I turn my back upon them, and then . . . ?" It was not a pleasant prospect even for the most fearless of men, and the Park murders following so closely on the negotiations left him no choice but to identify himself with the side of law and order.

Now that Mr. Forster had resigned, it was unofficially stated that Mr. Chamberlain would take his place. He more than anyone else was responsible for the new policy of conciliation. Together with Sir Charles Dilke he had made a firm front against coercion, but the Prime Minister had never forgiven him for an article written in the *Fortnightly Review,* in which he had acclaimed Mr. Gladstone's election manifesto of 1874 to be the meanest public document that ever in like circumstances had proceeded from the pen of a statesman of the first rank. The exigencies of politics had forced the Prime Minister to have

the Birmingham magnate in his Cabinet, but he had no intention of letting him reap the glory of a successful Irish policy,
and when Lord Spencer accepted to be Lord Lieutenant for a
second time, it was decreed that Lord Frederick Cavendish, Lord
Hartington's younger brother and Gladstone's nephew by marriage, should succeed Mr. Forster as Chief Secretary. This was
a popular appointment, for Lord Frederick was known to be
"one of the most modest and best men in the House and a thorough supporter of the new policy." But many pages of English
history might never have been written if Joseph Chamberlain
had gone in his place and met the assassins of Phœnix Park.

Meanwhile the political horizon looked serene, and the woman
who had been responsible for engineering the negotiations sunned
herself once more in her lover's presence. On Saturday, May 6th,
Parnell, Dillon and O'Kelly went down to Portland to meet
Davitt on his release from prison. They were all in a happy,
optimistic mood as they traveled back to town. The infectious
jollity of O'Kelly communicated itself even to Dillon and Davitt,
and Parnell gaily joked about the future, declaring that in the
first Home Rule Cabinet in Dublin he would make Sexton
Chancellor of the Exchequer, Dillon Home Secretary, O'Kelly
head of the National Constabulary Force, and Davitt Director
of Prisons. But, apart from the joking, both Dillon and Davitt
felt slightly suspicious of the way in which he deplored the recent
outrages in Ireland. He was especially bitter against the Ladies'
Land League, and, when Davitt praised his sister for keeping
"the ball rolling," he snapped out, "I don't want her to keep
the ball rolling any more. The League must be suppressed or
I will leave public life." According to Davitt, he spoke about
anarchy as if he were a British minister bringing in a Coercion
Bill.

Parnell had good reason for fearing the activities of the secret
societies that had sprung up under the régime of coercion. At
the very hour when he and his colleagues were traveling back to
London, the assassins were already waiting beneath the chestnut-
trees of Phœnix Park. All during the winter the Invincibles

(the members of a murder club founded in the previous year) had laid plots for the assassination of Mr. Forster, and he is supposed to have had no less than nineteen miraculous escapes. Now their vengeance was to be wreaked on the Under-Secretary, Mr. Burke, who as a permanent official of Dublin Castle had made himself unpopular in carrying out Mr. Forster's instructions, and it was an unfortunate accident that the unknown gentleman who accompanied him on the evening of May 6th happened to be Lord Frederick Cavendish.

The story of the murder is only too well known—of how Lord Frederick and Mr. Burke, after participating in the pageant of the Viceroy's state entry into Dublin and attending to their duties at the Castle, were quietly strolling home through the Park when they were stabbed by a gang of assassins in full sight of the windows of Viceregal Lodge. All that Parnell had worked for during the past years—his hard-won victory over the Irish executives, his alliance with the Prime Minister—was overthrown by this one dastardly act on the part of a gang of criminals.

CHAPTER TWENTY-SEVEN

THE London season was at its full height when the news of the Dublin murders crashed like a bombshell into the midst of diplomatic dinners and political receptions. The first reaction was one of stark horror and consternation, followed by a wave of loathing against the dastardly Irish who had been responsible for this butchery. It was not a time for tolerance or reasoning, and to the majority of the English people the whole of Ireland was incriminated in this outrage. The blind, bitter hatred that had swept the country at the time of the Manchester murders was once more prevalent, and public opinion was loud in its demand for repressive measures. The news which first circulated in the drawing-room of the Austrian Embassy, where a messenger from the Home Office found Sir William Harcourt, and which gradually spread among the thousand guests at an Admiralty reception, did not reach the suburban retreat of Eltham till the following morning, when Mr. Parnell opened the *Sunday Observer,* to find that the concessions he had wrested from the Government, and all his sanguine hopes of Home Rule in the near future, had crumbled beneath the knives of a gang of irresponsible assassins.

He was on his way to London to spend the day with Michael Davitt when he bought an *Observer* at the station, and Mrs. O'Shea, who had accompanied him to the train, describes how she saw him open the paper, glance at the headlines, and then suddenly turn quite stiff and rigid. She was so frightened that she called out to him and he turned to her with a chalk-white face and glazed, unseeing eyes. "Look!" he said, and pointed to the news. He seemed like a man in a trance, so strange and still, never answering her questions, beyond saying half to himself, "I shall resign. I can't go on." The train came into the station, and he still stood as if rooted in the same spot, clutching her hand so tightly that the rings dug deep into the flesh. "You are not a coward," she whispered, "you must go on." Then he seemed to regain control of himself and jumped quickly into the train.

At the Westminster Palace Hotel he found his colleagues all plunged in the deepest gloom. The unhappiest of them all was Davitt, who cried aloud that he wished he had never left Portland; even the indomitable Healy was so unstrung that he deliberately proposed that they should all resign their seats and go back into obscurity, as he believed the cause to be hopeless for a generation. Parnell was in no fit state to give guidance or advice; the six months of prison life had affected his health, and now this sudden shock had momentarily thrown him off his mental balance. His colleagues, who had always regarded him as a pillar of strength in any political crisis, now saw him giving way to a wild, raging despair. "How can I go on," he said, "if I am stabbed in the back in this way?" And it was only the quiet, measured counsels of Justin McCarthy which gradually brought him round to his senses. Biggar was the only member of the party who preserved a calm, almost brutal detachment, for in the eyes of the ex-Fenian the killing of two Government officials could not be considered in the light of a tragedy, and he did not approve of the manifesto sketched out by Davitt and revised by Parnell, in which the leaders of the suppressed Land League denounced the crime, and expressed the hope that the assassins would be brought to justice, ending with the words: "We feel that no act has ever been perpetrated in our country during the exciting struggles for social and political rights of the past fifty years that has so stained the name of hospitable Ireland as the cowardly and unprovoked assassination of a friendly stranger, and that until the murderers of Lord Frederick Cavendish and Mr. Burke are brought to justice that stain will sully our country's name."

It can be laid to Parnell's credit that, notwithstanding his gloom and despair, he carefully revised the document, eliminating all Davitt's purple patches and meticulously punctuating every line.

In his distracted state he seized upon every opportunity of

occupying his mind with small mechanical details—anything that
kept him from brooding over the disastrous consequences which
these murders might bring to bear on the future of his country.
There is no surer proof to show that he was not in full possession of his faculties than the fact that he despatched O'Shea with
a letter to Gladstone, in which he offered to retire from public
life if the Prime Minister thought that popular feeling in England would be propitiated by his resignation. But Mr. Gladstone, while suffering from the loss of one who was not only
a beloved colleague but also a member of his own family, still
remained one of the most moderate and far-sighted members of
his Cabinet, and his opinion was that if Parnell went, "no
restraining influence would remain."

Both Chamberlain and Dilke testify that the Irish leader was
in an overwrought condition when he visited them on that
memorable Sunday. It was McCarthy's suggestion that they
should consult some of their English friends in order to see
what could be saved from the ruins, and the first visit was paid
to the Under-Secretary for Foreign Affairs, whom they found
"perfectly calm and composed, and determined to be a Home
Ruler *quand même.*" It was rumored that either he or Chamberlain would now be offered the thankless post of Irish Secretary,
and, though Dilke expressed his willingness to accept the appointment if it was offered to him, he maintained that Chamberlain would be the wiser choice, for his unique experience of
municipal organization would enable him to destroy the corrupt
officialdom of Dublin Castle.

Just as they were leaving, Dilke drew McCarthy aside and
spoke of the "extreme unwisdom of allowing Parnell to walk
about the streets that day in London." He said "no one could
tell when someone might recognize him, and, thinking he was
responsible for the murders, make an attack on him."

Ten years later Chamberlain noted that when Parnell visited
him on that Sunday, the 7th of May, "he was white as a sheet
and apparently demoralized. At the time I thought he was
abjectly afraid for his own life, which he said was in danger.

'They will strike at me next,' were his words. He asked me, 'What shall I do? What shall I do?' I said, 'Your first duty is to denounce the assassins and to endeavor to ensure their apprehension.' He said he had offered to Mr. Gladstone to retire altogether from public life. I dissuaded him from such a course, which would almost justify suspicion of his complicity in a crime which I felt sure he detested."

But, whatever may have been Parnell's nervous fears, he was not concerned about his personal safety, and he refused to take any precautions even when Chamberlain repeated the warnings of his colleague. On leaving Princes Gardens, McCarthy suggested that it would be wiser to take a cab, but he answered sharply that he would do nothing of the kind, adding that he had done no wrong to anyone and that he intended to walk in the open streets like anyone else. On their way back to the hotel, some man from the top of a bus called out, "There's Parnell," but otherwise they passed unnoticed.

Two days later one finds the following entry in Lewis Harcourt's journal: "Parnell has applied for police protection, and in granting it W. V. H.[1] said he was glad that Parnell was now suffering himself some of the tortures he had inflicted on others during the past two years."

This application, which was made by O'Shea without the knowledge of his chief, must have been instigated either by Chamberlain or by Mrs. O'Shea, for it is hardly likely that if the Captain had been allowed to follow his own feelings he would have shown so much interest in Parnell's welfare. Chamberlain was genuinely convinced that Parnell was seriously anxious for the pacification of the country, and he realized what dangerous elements would be unloosed if the Irish leader met the fate of Lord Frederick Cavendish; therefore he took good care to impress on O'Shea the necessity of guarding him from all possible danger.

On the other hand, there was Katherine fearful for her lover's

[1] His father, Sir William Vernon Harcourt.

safety and astute enough to persuade her husband that not only was it essential for his career to be on friendly terms with his chief, but that it was also to his advantage to do everything in his power to protect him from his enemies. She was the only one who really knew of the dangers by which Parnell was encompassed now that he had signed the manifesto denouncing the Invincibles, for since he had made his home at Eltham she read all his letters before they were handed to his secretary, and every day she was harassed by some new threat of murder or warning letter. Most of these she kept to herself, only showing Parnell "enough to make him take some care of himself for my sake," and she admits that many a time "I was tempted to throw his honor to the winds and implore from the Government the protection he would have died rather than ask for himself." So there can be little doubt that when O'Shea made his application to the Home Office it was done with her full knowledge and agreement. The Captain quite plainly stated that his house at Eltham was Mr. Parnell's habitual residence, and he took good care to see that the police extended their protection to his own lodgings in Victoria Street. When he gave his evidence before *The Times* Commission, Parnell denied that he had ever given O'Shea any authorization to apply for police protection on his behalf, and said that it had been done entirely without his consent.

His refusal to take any precautions beyond the carrying of a revolver was little short of heroic, when one considers that during these days there was hardly an Englishman living who would not have rejoiced at his death. This wave of bitterness was at its height when the House of Commons met on Monday, May 8th, and John Redmond, one of the youngest members of his party, has left us a description of the scene:

"Inside the House, there was the stillness of the tomb. By a strange and mysterious instinct every member had come down dressed in black as to a funeral. Every available niche of room on the floor and in the galleries was occupied, and when Mr. Gladstone, looking strangely old and haggard, rose to move the adjournment of the House in consequence of the crime, a sort of shiver seemed to run through the entire assembly. Mr. Gladstone himself broke down. He had loved Lord Frederick Cavendish and he could barely articulate his words in expressing horror at the deed. When he resumed his seat, Mr. Parnell rose, pale and worn after his six months' imprisonment, but calm, erect and defiant. A strange, fierce murmur ran round the House, the like of which I had never heard. It could not be described as a growl, though it had in it a note of savage hatred. We looked up startled and knew not what was about to happen, but it suddenly died away into a silence so intense that we could almost feel it. What had this man to say?—this man, the indirect if not the actual cause of the murder? What right had he to speak? What right had he to be here at all? His very presence was an outrage! Never so long as I live shall I forget the looks of fierce detestation turned upon Mr. Parnell at that moment. We, his friends, tried to counteract all this by a cheer, but so chilled were we by the scene that it died away unuttered on our lips. Mr. Parnell, however, did not falter. In a few simple words, without any outward sign of the influence of the scene upon him, he expressed his horror at the crime, and sat down the most hated, distrusted and feared man in England."

It is not surprising that, following this ordeal, Parnell should have despaired of making any headway in the movement. After hearing Gladstone declare that so far as the Government was concerned, all previous arrangements and intentions had to be considered and to some extent recast, he turned to William O'Brien and said in a weary voice, "We have got to begin all over again," and with one last spark of hope he added, "Perhaps we may save the Arrears Bill." A new Coercion Act was inevitable, but it was introduced by Sir William Harcourt with a relish which was almost distasteful, and it reinstated all the worst provisions of Mr. Forster's Bill. Trial by jury was abolished in favor of trial by three judges specially chosen by the Lord Lieutenant. Curfew was enforced in the whole of the south of Ireland, and the police were free to search any house at any hour of the day or night. But the clause which was most open to abuse was the one which entitled a resident magistrate to act as a summary judge and to sentence any citizen to as much as six months' hard labor merely on the charge of intimidation. The Parnellites made a brave attempt to resist this iniquitous Act, but their leader knew that, with popular feeling against them, they could do little more than try to mitigate its severity. Labouchere, who had once more rallied to the Irish minority, denounced a bill which was not aimed solely at outrage but was directed at honorable members sitting opposite, and he constituted himself as a negotiator between the Parnellites and the Government by encouraging the confidences of Mr. Healy and bringing him into personal contact with Mr. Chamberlain. During the early summer there were many private meetings at "Labby's" house in Queen Anne's Gate, and sometimes Mr. Parnell would be persuaded to assist at one of these conferences. But, though Chamberlain was full of good intentions and genuinely opposed to repressive measures, Parnell had already discerned, with his flawless instinct, that whereas in the long run Mr. Gladstone might be brought to concede some sort of measure of Home Rule, Mr. Chamberlain would remain irrevocably wedded to his plan of local government.

Meanwhile his *protégé,* O'Shea, had shown himself to be a somewhat untrustworthy intermediary, for, when the Tories insisted on asking uncomfortable questions regarding the Kilmainham Treaty, an incident occurred which placed both the Liberals and the Irish leader in an awkward situation. During an acrimonious debate Parnell was handed a copy of the famous letter he had addressed to O'Shea from Kilmainham Jail, and when he read it aloud to the assembled House it was discovered that he had omitted the all-important paragraph in which he promised to cooperate with the Liberals.

Mr. Forster, embittered by the scurvy way in which he had been treated by his colleagues, who not a week after they had thrown him over had been forced to revert to his policy, now seized on his opportunity for revenge. Tim Healy describes how "he rose to his feet and shrieked, 'That's not the letter,'" and how "Parnell paled, and Gladstone's face mantled with pious resignation, while Chamberlain sat erect like a soldier who knew that the password had not been rightly rendered and that the guardroom yawned for a culprit."

The culprit was O'Shea, who had been so free with his words during his interview with Mr. Forster and who had shown himself only too ready to eliminate any passage which might be unfavorable to the Cabinet. Mr. Chamberlain may have objected to the insertion of a paragraph that showed so plainly that the Government was willing to pay for Mr. Parnell's support, and maybe it was on his advice that the words were deleted from the document, which unfortunately Mr. Forster had already seen in its original form.

O'Shea was now forced to read aloud the incriminating letter, and the hardened cynic, who had already visualized the possibilities of a Government post, made a pitiful exhibition of himself, as, stuttering and faltering, he tried to give the House some account of the Kilmainham Treaty.

Parnell muttered in disgust to Tim Healy, "This damned fellow will make a mess of it as usual." No wonder he was disgusted, for nothing could be more damaging than the publicity given to these negotiations. On his release from prison he had given an interview to the *Irish World* in which he had denied the reports of a pact with the Government, saying that he had never had any conversation with a member or agent of the Cabinet while he was out on parole, and adding that there was no truth in the rumor about the withdrawal of the "No Rent" manifesto. These disclosures would not only arouse the enmity of Patrick Ford, but they would also put him in a very delicate situation with some of his colleagues, who would not find it easy to forgive him for having purchased their freedom by coming to terms with the Liberals.

The tragedy of Phœnix Park sowed dissension among the Nationalists, for, now that all hopes of reconciliation had gone, every section reverted to its own policy. Dillon was more militant than ever, and his fiery speeches caused embarrassment to his leader, who at the moment considered it wiser to mollify English opinion. In the solitude of Portland, Davitt had been brooding over his pet scheme of the nationalization of land, and with a complete disregard of the critical state of affairs he now began to propound these theories to large audiences at Liverpool and Manchester. In Paris, Egan and Brennan and their section were furious at the idea of the League being converted into a "moderate Tenant Right association," with its headquarters in Dublin, and they demanded absolute control of the funds. Parnell told Labouchere, "The Fenians want one thing, the Ladies' League another, and I another. Therefore I shall limit my action to Parliament and leave the Government and the Fenians to fight it out in Ireland." The Crimes Act was to remain in force over a period of three years, and during this time it would be impossible to conduct an open movement in a country where one was liable to be clapped into jail if one uttered a single word derogatory to the Government. There was nothing to do but to "wait and then resume," for Parnell had no intention of returning to Kilmainham, though he told some of his more belligerent colleagues that "he had not the least objection to anyone else's going." For the moment he had no wish to make any speeches in Ireland, and it was against his express desire that the Dublin Corporation insisted on having a public demonstration when he and Dillon were presented with the freedom of the city. In a short, direct statement he warned his audience that public life in Ireland was rendered impossible for the three years during which the new Coercion Act was to last, telling them to concentrate their energies on that great object of reform which had always possessed the hearts of the Irish people at home and abroad—the restoration of the legislative independence of Ireland.

The situation was not so desperate, for Gladstone had been forced to resume coercion against his will and the Prime Minister's determination in carrying through the Arrears Bill proved that he was trying to keep his part of the pact. Dilke and Chamberlain had held out hopes of Home Rule, but it was only Gladstone's dominant personality which could carry it through.

So towards the end of May, after O'Shea had proved himself to be the tool of Chamberlain, one finds his wife assuming the rôle of intermediary between the Irish leader and the Government. Mr. Gladstone had already been informed of her relations with Mr. Parnell, not only by the extremely blunt-spoken Home Secretary, but also by one of his own private secretaries, George Leveson-Gower, who relates how he expostulated with his chief for negotiating through the O'Sheas, considering Parnell's connection with the lady, and how Gladstone fired in answer, "You do not mean to ask me to believe that a man should be so lost to all sense of what is due to his public position at a moment like the present, in the very crisis of his country's fortunes, as to indulge in an illicit connection with the wife of one of his own political supporters and to make use of that connection in the way you suggest!" But Mr. Gladstone possessed to the full one of the greatest qualities of the Victorian age—the capacity of deliberately closing his eyes to any unpalatable truths. His suspicions may still have been dormant when Mrs. O'Shea wrote to ask him whether he would be willing to have a private interview with Mr. Parnell, but they must have been definitely aroused when, on his refusing to incriminate himself by establishing personal relations with the Irish leader, she suggested herself as a trustworthy go-between. It is surprising that he should even have committed himself to the extent of meeting her at Thomas's Hotel in order to hear the proposals of Mr. Parnell. These proposals dealt with the amendments to the Land Act and the Arrears Bill, and suggested modifications to the Crimes Act. And though at the moment it was impossible for Mr. Gladstone to run counter to the wishes of the majority of his Cabinet, Mr. Parnell admitted that he had acted to the best of his ability. The negotiations of 1882 had no important results, but from now onwards Mrs. O'Shea was the accredited envoy between Gladstone and Parnell, and the Prime Minister was willing to believe that the relations between the Irish Nationalist and the charming woman who visited him at Downing Street were purely platonic.

Katherine O'Shea had obtained a complete ascendency over her lover. His health, which was already seriously affected by his imprisonment, now broke down entirely. At night he was once more subject to the nervous terrors of his childhood, and he would spring half conscious out of bed, waking up panic-stricken and bathed in sweat after some strange nightmare. These exhausting attacks were caused by acute indigestion, and Katherine nursed him back to health by superintending his diet and watching over him with a loving and untiring care. It was a sad, depressing spring, and, just as he was beginning to recover his normal equilibrium, the news of Fanny's death plunged him once more into the depths of despair. For years she had suffered from insomnia, and it was an overdose of a sleeping-draught which caused her death. With her delicate health and overstrung nerves she was totally unsuited to the political life she had embraced with such enthusiasm, and her warm, passionate nature had found its only outlet in a bitter, unreasoning hatred against England.

Perhaps it was as a tribute to the memory of his sister that, shortly after receiving the news of her death, Parnell reverted to his old methods of obstruction. After a stormy all-night sitting, he and sixteen members of his party were suspended for wilfully blocking the Crimes Bill, and they withdrew from the contest, "casting upon the Government the sole responsibility for a Bill which had been urged through the House by a course of violence and subterfuge, and which when passed into law would be devoid of moral force and would be no constitutional Act of Parliament."

But he was so tired of dramatic gestures which he knew were of no avail, so tired of watching and controlling every movement of his colleagues, many of whom he was beginning to regard with a suspicious distrust, that there were moments when he wondered whether it was worth while remaining at the head of a movement where some of his own followers would be capable of striking him in the back; whether it was worth while to lead an existence of continual subterfuge and deceit.

No one except Katherine knew of this terrible depression, which so often tempted him to the verge of insanity. She was the only witness to scenes which made her fear not only for his safety but for her own. There was one dark, stormy day at Brighton, in the middle of the summer, when they stood out on the pier watching the great waves sweeping over its head, and he suddenly turned towards her with a strange, wild light in his eyes, taking her up into his arms and holding her clear over the raging sea, murmuring, "Oh, my wife, my wife, I believe I'll jump in with you and we shall be free for ever." Instead of showing him that she was afraid, she just answered, "As you will, my only love—but the children?" and she saw the mad light die in his eyes before the tender, pathetic look she knew so well.

These fits of morbid depression were never so frequent as during the summer of 1882, and there were times when Parnell seriously contemplated retiring from public life, but then his pride would reassert itself—that cold, arrogant pride which dominated so many of his actions, which spurred him on to his greatest triumphs and which finally brought about his downfall.

CHAPTER TWENTY-EIGHT

WITH the return of coercion came the return of evictions, with the return of evictions came the increase in crime, and, in spite of Parnell's efforts to slow down the agitation, the year 1882 ended in a blaze of Agrarian outrages and murders.

The Irish leader had undertaken a thankless task in running counter to the wishes of the majority of his lieutenants, who were in favor of adopting a more militant attitude. But, at the risk of being accused of acting as policeman to Lord Spencer and the British Government, he was determined to adhere to a moderate policy. The failure of the "No Rent" manifesto had taught him that Maynooth [1] was more powerful than Fenianism, and he made a bid for clerical support by making all clergymen *ex-officio* delegates to all conventions which should meet for the selection of parliamentary candidates. He needed a strong Conservative element in the Nationalist party to counteract the Radicalism of Davitt and his associates. Up till now he had been a revolutionary from necessity, but never from choice. When he had won his Parliament in College Green, "he intended to treat the landlords fairly and honestly, to encourage them to live quietly among their own people, to give them a fair share of parliamentary honors, and make them happy in their own country." And once, when Davitt asked him, "Suppose you had your Irish Parliament, how would you begin?" he answered, with a very gentle smile, "Well, Davitt, I think I should begin by locking you up." He always displayed great tolerance and patience in his relations with Davitt, but when his refractory colleague, no longer content with propounding his theories on the English platform, had to travel to America in order to stir up trouble in the already troubled waters of the Clan-na-Gael, then his patience gave way, and in an interview with the *New York Herald* he definitely condemned the new theory of land national-

[1] Catholic College for the priesthood.

241

ization "as one which would never come within the range of practical politics." In private he commented with warrantable bitterness, "If I were Davitt, I should never define; the moment he becomes intelligible he is lost."

Davitt had no wish to split the party and to set himself up as a rival to his chief. He was just an unpractical idealist riding his pet hobby-horse, utterly unaware of the damage he was causing, and when Patrick Ford offered to finance a campaign in favor of land nationalization, he only accepted his support on condition that the *Irish World* would cease its virulent attacks on his leader.

When land nationalization failed as a popular stunt, Mr. Ford resorted to active dynamite propaganda, while the moderate section of the Clan-na-Gael, led by John Devoy, adhered to the policy laid down by the "New Departure."

Parnell was now determined to have absolute control over the party funds. He quarreled with Egan, who resigned in disgust at his moderate policy, and his next step was to suppress the Ladies' Land League by cutting off their bank account. This act, which earned him the undying enmity of his sister Anna, was bitterly resented by both Dillon and Davitt, and at the end of August he wrote to Mrs. O'Shea:

"The two D's have quarreled with me because I wouldn't allow any further expenditure by the ladies and because I have made arrangements to make the payments myself for the future. They were in the hopes of creating a party against me in the country by distributing the funds amongst their own creatures, and they are proportionally disappointed."

His ill health was beginning to warp his outlook, and the slightest suspicion of his colleagues was fanned by Katherine O'Shea, who in her jealous love resented any sign of defection from his leadership. Unconsciously she was responsible for estranging him from some of his most trusted followers. The pleasant little dinners at Justin McCarthy's and the jokes of old Joe Biggar no longer held the same attraction for him. Even his Irish shooting-parties with Redmond and O'Kelly were curtailed when a plaintive letter arrived from Eltham complaining of his temporary neglect. From now onwards his private life was that of a middle-aged valetudinarian pottering round a suburban garden, spending his holidays on the south coast; and even the riding which he still kept up for the sake of his health was merely an occasional canter across Keston Common, a sad come-down for one who had spent his youth hunting with the Meath and with the Ward Union. Slowly he was being dragged down to a bourgeois existence, learning to depend on the small, everyday comforts to which he had formerly been so indifferent, gradually allowing himself to be influenced, not only by his English environment, but by the woman whose natural wish was to see him at peace with her Government. She openly disapproved of the more violent passages in his speeches. She openly despised and disliked the majority of his colleagues, and her veiled aspersions on their loyalty preyed on him when he was in one of his morbid moods. There were so few he could trust. Healy, in spite of his effusive devotion, was too ready to intrigue with Labouchere and Chamberlain. T. P. was too ardent a denizen of Fleet Street to be entrusted with a party secret, Sexton was already an obvious Gladstonian, while O'Shea, whom Katie had forced him to accept as an intimate, was nothing more than a tool of Chamberlain. He must have had many a bitter smile to himself at Willie's blatant method of pumping him for the benefit of the Cabinet, and the Captain complained to Chamberlain that "Parnell is frequently in a moony, drifting state of mind nowadays, with which it is difficult to keep one's temper."

For Parnell it was a year of disillusion and illness, but he kept rigidly to his line of policy, uncompromising and inexorable, and seemingly undisturbed by the signs of mutiny among his followers. In the autumn he yielded to Dillon and Davitt in so far as to form a public organization to take the place of the suppressed Land League, but he insisted on personally revising every detail of the new constitution, in which Home Rule, and not the Agrarian question, was to be the chief issue at stake.

At the Dublin convention, which saw the birth of the National League, he treated Davitt's new scheme with an icy sarcasm, and, after several stormy meetings at Avondale, Brennan threw up his post as secretary and left the country; while Dillon, following the advice of his medical attendant, departed for Colorado.

Though Dillon's retirement was a serious loss to the Nationalist party, Parnell must have been secretly relieved to have seen the last of his most intractable lieutenant, and there must have been moments when he could have wished Davitt to have followed his example.

There was trouble on every side: intrigues in America among the dissentient members of the Clan-na-Gael; intrigues in London among the divergent elements in the Cabinet; intrigues in Rome, where a Catholic Whig named Errington was poisoning the minds of the cardinals and papal Secretaries of State against the patriotic priests of Ireland. The case of Errington was a curious one. As early as December 1881, Mr. Gladstone, alarmed by the Nationalist tendencies of some of the Irish bishops, sought the help and advice of Cardinal Newman, begging him to use his influence with the Supreme Pontiff in order to secure his intervention in discouraging agitation in Ireland. Mr. Gladstone was not at a loss to find an historic precedent for his demand. In 1844, at the time of the O'Connell manifestations, the Government of Sir Robert Peel had solicited the aid of Pope Gregory XVI, and, though the Prime Minister assured His Eminence that "Mr. Errington, who has brought the facts as far as he was able to the knowledge of His Holiness, is not our official servant, but an independent Roman Catholic gentleman and volunteer," it was known that the gentleman in question had come to Rome with a letter of recommendation from Lord Granville, the Foreign Secretary, while a year later it transpired that he was a secret English envoy to the Vatican. The Pope, who had always regarded the Land League with disfavor, was very willing to establish diplomatic relations with England, and Mr.

Errington had no difficulty in persuading him to assert his spiritual authority against the rebellious priests.

But events were to prove that Cardinal Newman had been right in warning the Prime Minister that he over-rated the Pope's power in political and social matters, and years later Mr. Gladstone confessed to Mr. Barry O'Brien, "The Errington mission was a very foolish affair. Spencer thought it might do some good and so I tried it. It did no good. It is absurd to suppose that the Pope exercises an influence in Irish politics." But in 1882 he was ready to descend to every kind of secret dealing and underhand negotiation in the hopes of solving the Irish question. By the end of the year, the good intentions of the Kilmainham Treaty were wearing thin. A by-election at Mallow, at which William O'Brien was returned by an overwhelming majority, showed the Government that the Irish leader was still determined to man his ranks with fiercely Nationalist candidates who would give no quarter to their Liberal opponents, and Sir William Harcourt wrote to Lord Spencer: "Gladstone still cherishes the illusion that the feeling of the people is changed and that Parnell is really converted. But the leopard has not changed his spots, and the Mallow election shows what is the real feeling of the people."

Mr. Gladstone was on holiday in Cannes, recuperating from the exhausting task of controlling the quarrelsome and dictatorial members of his Cabinet, when a Dublin police raid, on January 13th, 1883, resulted in the arrest of seventeen Invincibles. Then followed the sensational revelations of the Phœnix Park murders. The informer, that familiar figure in the Dublin underworld, once more stepped into the witness-box of the criminal courts of Green Street. In the hopes of saving his own skin, James Carey denounced his comrades, and the public learned with horror that Mr. Forster had escaped assassination no less than nineteen times, while the murder of Lord Frederick had just been a brutal and unnecessary accident. Though the Land League was not directly implicated, certain of its members were very much involved. Carey's job in the Dublin Corporation had been procured through the protection of Pat Egan. Byrne was the private secretary of the London branch of the League, and in constant contact with both McCarthy and Parnell, and certain dubious characters like Sheridan were shown to have a footing in both camps. Once more a wave of Irish phobia swept the country, and Mr. Gladstone, who had seriously been contemplating some form of local government for Ireland, realized that with the present state of public feeling it would be impossible to carry any measure of conciliation. The majority were on the side of the Home Secretary, who declared, "To create local bodies of a representative character in Ireland just now seems to me little short of madness. It is like handing revolvers to the Dublin assassins, thinking that, by placing confidence in them, you will induce them to behave well." And though Lord Spencer tried to administer the Crimes Act with justice and moderation, and though Mr. Trevelyan, the new Chief Secretary, was brave enough to expose the major iniquities of the landlord system, corruptness still prevailed in Dublin Castle, where the old machinery revolved on its well-oiled hinges. Chamberlain would have been the only man strong enough to crush the place-hunters and parasites who gathered round the Viceregal Court, but Gladstone had once more ignored his just claims to the post of Chief Secretary.

Meanwhile the Conservatives tried to profit by the anti-Irish wave that was threatening to engulf the Government. The thorny subject of the Kilmainham negotiations was once more brought up for discussion, and it was alleged that these negotiations had been carried on behind Mr. Forster's back. It was only natural that the former Chief Secretary should take advantage of the situation by seeking to expose, not only the man who had been the direct cause of his downfall, but also his old colleagues, who had not hesitated to make him a scapegoat for their own blunders. Popular sympathy was on his side, for the assassins had confessed that only a charmed life had protected him from their knives. But to rise in the House of Commons in order to deliver a savage and eloquent indictment of the leader of a small minority was a sad end to the career of a heroic and selfless philanthropist. Thirty-seven years had passed since Mr. Forster had risked his life in the famine-stricken bogs of Connaught, at a time when the man whom he now accused of "having connived at outrages and murders" was still an infant in arms, and the speech which sounded the death-knell to his political aspirations was neither wise nor dignified. The very cheers of the Opposition must have sounded incongruous to the ears of the old Radical, and they cheered, not because he was out to damage Parnell, but because every word he spoke reflected discredit on the Government. When he produced a pamphlet entitled *The Truth about the Land League,* a compilation of the more inflammatory and seditious speeches and articles of the Leaguers, showing that the man with whom Mr. Gladstone had bargained and with whom Mr. Chamberlain had intrigued was the "head of a rebellious and lawless agitation aimed at the very heart of the Empire," then old and young Tories shouted with enthusiasm. Mr. Bright, who had resigned from the Cabinet over the Egyptian question, commented in an audible aside to one of his colleagues, "The Tories dislike assassins much but the Government more."

Parnell sat in his usual seat below the gangway, his long pale hands resting listlessly on his knees and the ravages of illness drawing dark shadows on his face. He sat quite immobile and detached while Mr. Forster hurled his indictment with uncouth gestures and rough, unpolished voice, saying, "My charge is against the honorable member for the City of Cork. . . . Probably a more serious charge was never made by any member of the House against another member. It is not that he himself directly planned or perpetrated outrages or murders, but that he either connived at them or, when warned, did not use his influence to prevent them." At the word "warned" Parnell's voice cut in, hard, sharp and audible to the whole assembly. "It's a lie," he cried, giving one look of withering hatred to his opponent before relapsing once more into silence. At the end of Mr. Forster's speech the whole House expected Parnell to spring to his feet and deny the accusations. The Liberals called upon him to speak. Members of his own party begged him to make some kind of defense. Everyone waited, expectant, but only towards the end of the evening could he be prevailed upon to move the adjournment of the debate. Justin McCarthy states that he "did not want to answer Forster at all. We had to force him." And when he rose to speak the following day in the midst of a crowded House, with the Prince of Wales and Cardinal Manning as interested spectators in the gallery, he deliberately repudiated the right of the English people to judge or to condemn his actions. With a slow, trailing voice and frigid manner, he began: "I can assure the House that it is not my belief that anything I can say at this time will have the slightest effect on the public opinion of this House or upon the public opinion of the country. I have been accustomed during my political life to rely upon the public opinion of those whom I have desired to help and with whose aid I have worked for the cause of prosperity and freedom in Ireland, and the utmost I desire to do in the next few words I address to the House is to make my position clear to the Irish people at home and abroad."

Even Sir William Harcourt admitted that "Parnell's words, though detestable, were well conceived from his point of view. Posing as a man who would admit to nothing, apologize for nothing and give nothing—which is just what the Irish admire."

The speech which followed these opening sentences was delivered in the same uncompromising vein. What was England to him or to the Irish people, and what right had Mr. Forster to interrogate him—Mr. Forster, who was nothing more than a discredited politician who had been repudiated by his own party and whose administration of Ireland had been an ignominious failure; Mr. Forster, who above all others was fitted to administer the Crimes Act, to help Lord Spencer in the congenial work of the gallows in Ireland, to look after the secret inquisitions in Dublin Castle, to distribute the taxes which an unfortunate and starving peasantry had to pay for crimes not committed by themselves? Upon what did the accusation against him rest? Upon speeches and newspaper articles which he had not even read. But it was idle for him to try to strike a responsive chord in the House, just as it was impossible for him to stem the torrent of prejudice that had arisen out of the events of the past few days. And he ended his speech with, "The time will come when this House and the people of this country will admit once again that they have been deceived and that they have been cheered by those who ought to be ashamed of themselves; that they have been led astray as to the right mode of governing a noble, a brave, a generous and an impulsive people; that they will reject their present leaders who are conducting them into the terrible courses into which the Government appear determined to lead Ireland. Sir, I believe they will reject these guides and leaders with as much determination and just as much relief as they rejected the services of the right honorable gentleman, the member for Bradford."

This speech, which delighted Ireland as much as it exasperated England, turned the scale in the major events of the year, the Monaghan election and the Parnell Tribute, but Sir Charles Dilke was the only English statesman who was broad-minded enough to admit that as a tactician Parnell was equaled by no one except Gladstone. There were many who did not realize his extraordinary power when they listened to his short, terse speeches, so devoid of imagination and of all ornamentation. Men who had been used to the oratory of Gladstone found it hard to understand how one so lacking in eloquence could command the attention of the House. Parnell hated speechmaking, and, though he did not mind jumping up and asking some question on the spur of the moment, he would always avoid putting questions on the notice-paper if it meant waiting his turn. By taste and temperament he was totally unsuited to be a popular leader. He was so nervous that he could only be persuaded to speak under the greatest provocation. Usually he would leave the field to his young lieutenants, generous and ready in his praise and never grudging them their parliamentary laurels. When Davitt complained that he allowed too much self-advertisement among his followers, he answered good-humoredly, "Oh, you must let them show themselves off now and then a little, otherwise they might inflict the same speeches on you in Ireland."

He never conquered his dislike of public meetings, where the people would crowd round on every side, hemming him in, staring at him with that watchful, inquisitive look from which there was no escape. Even at the local banquets in the little Irish towns he would be pursued by those hundreds of staring eyes, when the whole populace would gather round the curtain-less windows gaping at him while he ate his dinner. Whether it was at a country railway station, on the Kingstown pier or in the Dublin streets, he was always the victim of the curiosity and importunate love of the people. As his visits to Ireland grew rarer, his hold on the public imagination strengthened, and Tim Healy relates how his meteoric descent on Monaghan, in June 1883, won him a seat in the heart of the Orange North.

Davitt and Healy had been the first victims of the new Crimes Act. On the charge of sedition they had been sentenced to four months' imprisonment, and Tim had barely been released a week before Parnell proposed to set him up as candidate at a by-election in Monaghan. In *Letters and Leaders of My Day* one finds an amusing account of the election, showing up one of the childish weaknesses of the chief.

"Before the Monaghan contest ended Parnell arrived, and threw himself wholeheartedly into it. His speeches were electrical. On the day before the poll we reached Castle Blaney. It was a 'fair' day at the end of June and very hot. The hotel was crowded, but the landlord gave Parnell and myself the best rooms—12 and 13. Twelve was small, so I had Parnell's luggage put into 13. When he came upstairs and saw the number, he banged at my door, crying, bag in hand, 'Look at that. What a number to give me!' I laughed and said, 'We can exchange, but you'll have the worst room.' He burst out, 'If you occupy 13 you'll lose the election.' The room was better than

12, and I told him so, but he maintained that the Tory hotel-keeper had allotted it to him purposely. . . . While making the exchange he repeated fiercely, 'Healy, you'll lose the election!'

"When I won next day, Parnell was overjoyed. . . . We toured the country that evening, and from our brake he shouted to every group at a cross-roads, 'Healy! Healy! Healy!' . . . Without side or snobbery, Parnell was a *grand seigneur*."

Healy was right in describing Parnell as having neither side nor snobbery. During these electioneering campaigns he would recapture his lost youth, and he was content to tour the country with no other luggage than a spare shirt, comb and toothbrush, wrapped up in a bit of newspaper. There is many an old farmer who can still bear witness to the charming simplicity and courtesy which he would display at the humblest village feast. Even when he was suffering from kidney trouble and in a wretched state of health, he was never known to refuse the rough food prepared with loving labor, and he was never too tired to listen to the endless stories told around the turf fire.

CHAPTER TWENTY-NINE

FINANCIAL difficulties were not the least of Parnell's troubles. What had been a handsome income for a private gentleman was hardly adequate for the leader of a party in which the majority of the members had no private means, and had not only to be financed in their electioneering campaigns but in many cases had actually to be kept. As the champion of Agrarian reform he was not in a position to exact rents from his tenants, and the impoverished condition of the people following the famine years of '79 and '80 made a continual drain on his purse. His personal liabilities were as heavy as ever, for old age had not taught his mother to practise economy and her debts still assumed formidable figures, while Emily was now a penniless widow who treated Avondale as her only home. His numerous schemes for improving his estate had proved to be nothing more than expensive hobbies; the Arklow quarries cost him thousands of pounds before they even started to pay, and his attempt to develop the gold resources of the Wicklow hills was a costly and unsuccessful experiment. His tenants lived in model houses, his saw-mills and gravel-pits were worked by the most up-to-date machinery, but his more unenterprising neighbors reaped profits which he never saw, and even a fourteen-thousand-pound mortgage on Avondale did little to alleviate his material difficulties. The situation looked very gloomy towards the end of 1882, when the mortgagee threatened foreclosure and Parnell was left with no other alternative but to file a petition for the sale of his old home. The news soon got abroad, and the archbishop of Cashel, who in spite of his denunciation of the "No Rent" manifesto had remained a firm adherent of the Parnellite party, was the first to propose a National Tribute to the leader as thanks "for the splendid public services by which he has earned the bitter hatred of every enemy of his country." Parnell's own reaction to the proposed Tribute was one of nervous pride lest it should result in a humiliating failure. The national fund which had been

started in an effort to pay the debts of Isaac Butt had met with
a feeble and hesitating response, and he always remembered
that O'Connell was said never to have passed a happy day after
he became a dependant on public subscriptions. In the present
despondent state of the country it was only too probable that
the appeal would meet with little success, but Parnell reckoned
without Mr. Errington, who unwittingly helped him to his
triumph.

While busily exploiting the channels of Vatican intrigue, this
renegade Home Rule member managed to convince the Sacred
Congregation *de propaganda fide* that the Irish people were losing their faith, preferring to follow the dicta of a Protestant
leader rather than the edicts of their cardinals. The Parnell
Tribute, which had been inaugurated by one of the leading
members of the Catholic hierarchy, led the Pope to believe that
this Irish Garibaldi "was imperiling the very salvation of the
people," and he despatched a letter to the Irish bishops condemning the Tribute and forbidding them "to subscribe or to
aid in raising subscriptions intended to inflame popular passions
and to excite the Irish people to rebellion against the laws."

Though the bishops had to comply with the wishes of Rome,
the bulk of the people refused to be dictated to in their politics,
and when the Nationalist newspapers published the fact that
the attitude of the Vatican had been inspired by an English
Liberal ministry, it became a point of honor for every patriotic
Irishman to subscribe to the Tribute. The subscription list
swelled to three times the amount required, till it was finally
closed at the sum of forty thousand pounds, and the presentation
of the testimonial at a banquet held at the Rotunda was the occasion for a great popular demonstration. Parnell's reply to Mr.
Forster, followed by the Vatican denunciation, had enhanced his
already fabulous prestige. His enemies had been discredited and
Davitt's scheme for a new settlement of the land question had
met with a cold reception from the tenant-farmers. In the National League, Parnell realized what had always been his ultimate ambition—a united Irish party incorporating men of widely

divergent views, where both bishops and Fenians accepted him as absolute dictator. Now that he found himself in supreme control his grip tightened, and the slightest opposition to his policy was ruthlessly suppressed. He declared that "in public life I prefer to deal with principles and not with men," and his own personal admiration for Davitt did not prevent him from denouncing his theories so forcibly that the "father of the Land League" decided to leave his country for a year rather than risk dissension in the party. Moderation was the keynote of Parnell's policy, and through the O'Sheas he had constant means of communication with the Cabinet, but Henry Campbell, who had succeeded Tim Healy as his private secretary, was probably the only one who knew how closely he was still in touch with certain Fenian elements both in Ireland and in America. He openly declined an invitation to preside at the Irish Convention at Philadelphia. Patrick Ford was against him, and the Clanna-Gael was divided in its allegiance, but few months passed without his sending some of his ablest followers to make propaganda in the States, and, when the Dynamitards financed by Ford and Finerty began their work of devilry, when attempts to blow up London public buildings caused a panic at Scotland Yard, Parnell never uttered a word against these outrages. In his eyes Ford was a "damned fool" and his plots so preposterous as to be almost laughable. With his peculiar sense of humor he would smile at the idea that had the attempt to destroy Charing Cross Station been successful several Irish members who were stopping at the hotel would have been blown to pieces; and when Randolph Churchill, one of the few Englishmen who appreciated his dry humor, remarked: "Well, Parnell, I suppose you would object to have a bomb thrown in the House of Commons? You would not like to be blown up, even by an Irishman?" he answered quite imperturbably, "I am not sure of that, if there was a call of the House." Though he never made the slightest effort to condemn the Dynamitards, he did not attempt to oppose the Explosives Bill, which the Government hurried through at a single sitting, and, while he allowed Healy and O'Brien to continue their vitriolic outbursts against the Irish Executive in the columns of his own newspaper, he carefully measured every word that he uttered on a public platform.

It is said that towards the end of 1880 he entered into a secret pact with the extremists of Cork City, which may account for the fact that his more violent speeches were usually addressed to his constituents. It is also noticeable that as soon as the Crimes Act made it imperative for him to moderate his language, he showed a marked disinclination to make any speeches in the Munster capital, where his Fenian supporters would resent a conciliatory policy. T. P. O'Connor recounts that he was even unwilling to take a part in the opening of the Cork Exhibition in the summer of 1883, and, unfortunately, the journalist ascribed his reluctance to the fact that he could not bear to be separated for another day from Mrs. O'Shea. When his friends finally persuaded him to attend this important ceremony, he traveled down to Cork just in time to visit the exhibition and attend the banquet before rushing back to Dublin by the next train. But, however averse he might be to popular demonstrations, the occasion of the presentation of the Parnell Tribute made it imperative for him to preside at a public gathering.

Barry O'Brien tells the story of the strange way in which Parnell received the Lord Mayor of Dublin and a deputation of leading citizens who called on him at Morrison's Hotel to invite him to the banquet and to hand him the check of £40,000. "At the appointed hour, the deputation arrived and were ushered into a private sitting-room, where stood the chief. The Lord Mayor, having been announced, bowed and began, 'Mr. Parnell—' 'I believe,' said Parnell, 'you have got a check for me.' The Lord Mayor, somewhat surprised at the interruption, said 'Yes,' and was about to recommence his speech, when Parnell broke in, 'Is it made payable to order and crossed?' The Lord Mayor again answered in the affirmative, and was resuming the thread of his discourse when Parnell took the check, folded it neatly, and put it into his waistcoat pocket. This ended the interview. The whole business was disposed of in five minutes, and there was no speech-making."

Even at the Rotunda banquet, Parnell never gave any direct thanks for the Tribute beyond saying, "I don't know how adequately to express my feelings with regard not only to your lordship's address, not only to the address to the Parnell National Tribute, but also with regard to the magnificent demonstration. I prefer to leave with the historian the description of to-night, and the expression of an opinion as regards the result which to-night must produce." There were many among the audience who considered this a short and ungracious way of thanking a warm-hearted and impulsive people. Sexton commented that a laborer would have acknowledged the loan of a penknife more gratefully, but Parnell believed in deeds, not in words. He neither criticized the attitude of Rome nor did he tender effusive thanks to the Irish priests who had been among the first to launch the Tribute. He merely stated the main lines of his policy, what he had achieved, and what he would be able to achieve for his people. The coming Franchise Act, by which household suffrage was to be extended to the country, would not only enable him to sweep Ireland at the next election, but it would practically put him in the position of arbiter between the two political parties in England. Definite and confident in his expectations, he asserted, "Beyond a shadow of doubt it will be for the Irish people in England—separated, isolated as they are—and for your independent Irish members to determine at a next General Election whether a Tory or Liberal English ministry shall rule England. This is a great force and a great power. If we cannot rule ourselves, we can at least cause them to be ruled as we choose. This force has already gained for Ireland inclusion in the coming Franchise Bill. We have reason to be proud, hopeful and energetic." These were the words with which he justified the gift which enabled him to retain the leadership of the party.

Meanwhile, the domestic situation at Eltham was undergoing a crisis. Captain O'Shea was becoming embarrassingly persistent in his demands for political promotion, and his wife impressed on her lover that at all costs Willie must be kept in Parliament. It was the necessary price to be paid for his silence, for it would hardly have pleased Mrs. Benjamin Wood to know that the two daughters born to her beloved niece in the spring of '83 and the autumn of '84 were the offspring of that "charming Mr. Parnell" who had been introduced to her as an intimate friend of the Captain's. This time there was no doubt as to who was the father, but Willie showed himself to be extremely obliging in acknowledging these somewhat belated arrivals in his family. And the pleasant way in which he tided over the difficulties showed that he recognized these new appendages to be valuable hostages in future blackmailing enterprises. In spite of these curious circumstances, the correspondence between husband and wife continued to be amicable and even affectionate during the years '82 to '84, and preserved amongst the Gladstone papers are some very revealing documents which show Mrs. O'Shea to have been quite as much concerned with her husband's political career as with the future of Irish Home Rule.

Among the foul accusations that have been hurled at Katherine O'Shea, none is so foul as the rumor that she was an agent hired by the British Government to seduce the Irish leader from his country's interests. But, though the accusation is base and groundless, it was she who was directly responsible for the alliance with the Liberals which sapped the independence of the Parnellite party. From the very first she was opposed to the men who were trying to push Parnell to extreme measures. Dillon and Davitt were probably never aware what a formidable enemy they had in Mrs. O'Shea, and in one of her letters to Gladstone, dated October 1882, she writes of Parnell: "It has taken me nearly two years to penetrate through his habitual reserve and suspicion of the Saxon sufficiently to induce him to make his views known at all, and thus shake himself free from the set by which he was surrounded, who certainly, whatever their wishes may be, have not a beneficial effect on their country when supported by anyone of influence."

From the year 1882, Mrs. O'Shea becomes an increasingly important figure. She proves herself to be a woman of considerable political sagacity, tenacious and determined beneath a soft feminine exterior, determined to further the ambitions both of her lover and her husband, as determined to penetrate the threshold of Downing Street as she had been to win the friendship of Mr. Parnell. There is evidence to prove that Mr. Gladstone made several unavailing efforts to substitute Lord Richard Grosvenor as the recipient of her confidences. It placed him in a somewhat ambiguous position to be in private communication with a woman who, besides being Mr. Parnell's accredited envoy, was the niece of an old colleague and the sister of a general in command of the Egyptian forces. She did not allow him to forget her connections when she wrote: "Our admiration of you has always been almost akin to religion in my family."

But as she was the only person who could claim to have any real influence with one of the most powerful forces in the political world, he was obliged to gratify her demands. She alone was in a position to produce telegrams from Parnell in which he promised to comply with her wishes and advice and not to permit himself to be drawn or pushed "beyond the limit of prudence and legality"; in 1885 she was in a position to promise Gladstone Mr. Parnell's support in four Ulster constituencies on the condition that the Liberal party adopted her husband as candidate for Mid-Armagh. And she did not hesitate to write: "Mr. O'Shea's being elected to a seat in the next Parliament is a matter of great importance for me."

From the very beginning of their friendship it was obvious that all Parnell's influence would not get Willie returned for Clare at the next election. No one was more cordially hated by his colleagues, and the fact that he resolutely refused to take the party pledge considerably aggravated the situation. He was, nevertheless, firmly convinced that he was invaluable both to the Liberals and to Parnell, and there were times when his inordinate vanity developed into megalomania, as when he wrote to Gladstone during the Kilmainham negotiations: "The person to whom Mr. Parnell addresses himself in many cases, much as I differ from him in serious matters of politics and policy, is myself. He considers, I believe, that I am not without insight about Irish affairs, necessities and possibilities, and he knows that no member of Parliament has nearly so much influence with the clergy of the county which that member represents as I have obtained. Eighteen months ago Mr. Parnell used every effort to induce me to take over the leadership of the party." It is hard to believe that a supposedly intelligent man should have been capable of inventing such a preposterous falsehood in the hopes of impressing Mr. Gladstone, and there is a further proof of his megalomania when, in September of the same year, he seriously thought that he would be eminently suited for the post of Irish Under-Secretary, "being more likely than most people to conciliate influential members of all parties."

One wonders how he ever came to contemplate the possibility of an Under-Secretaryship unless it had been suggested to him, either by his wife or by Mr. Chamberlain, and it is hardly likely that the member for Birmingham would have committed himself to such lengths, even though he was rather apt to overestimate both O'Shea's political capacity and his power to negotiate on Parnell's behalf. So much unnecessary bitterness and misunderstanding might have been spared if Chamberlain and Parnell had employed a more trustworthy intermediary, or, better still, have exchanged their views frankly and directly, but Parnell's elusiveness, his dislike of tying himself down to any definite commitments, his refusal to put on paper any proposal which might incriminate him with his party, led him to prefer an emissary who, though a man of straw, could be relied upon in his colossal vanity to make every suggestion as emanating from his own brain; whose statements on his behalf need not be considered binding, and who possessed a certain suppleness of mind which might enable him to discover just how far the Radical leader meant to go in his concessions. It was Katherine who first persuaded Parnell to send her husband to Chamberlain in the spring of 1884, and the member for Birmingham told Barry O'Brien how O'Shea came to him saying, "The Kilmainham Treaty has broken down. Do not you think that you and Parnell ought to try and come together again and to see if it is possible to do anything on the subject of Ireland? I think Parnell is anxious to have some sort of settlement."

Chamberlain was direct and straightforward in his proposals. He was willing to favor a large measure of local government, but he was definitely opposed to separate Parliaments, which in his opinion would endanger the unity of the Empire, and, though Parnell never considered his National Council scheme as a final settlement, it was a handsome concession to be offered at the end of two years of coercion.

The Franchise Act was barely on the Statute Book before the question of local government once more came on the tapis. There were signs and portents that the Conservative party was beginning to take into consideration the importance of the Irish vote. Lord Randolph Churchill had supported Mr. Gladstone in favor of the extension of the new franchise to Ireland, though the patrician element of the Liberal Cabinet had been loud in denouncing the "mud-cabin vote." Lord Hartington, Sir William Harcourt and Lord Spencer were still arch-Coercionists, though two years of administering the Crimes Act was beginning to teach the Viceroy that the suspension of the Habeas Corpus Act was no permanent settlement of the Irish question. He and his wife were practically prisoners in Viceregal Lodge, unable to venture forth without a military escort, and crime was as prevalent as ever. While Irish-American Dynamitards laid bombs beneath the Speaker's chair at Westminster, grim murders were enacted on the lonely lakes of Connemara.

Two years had passed since Parnell had told William O'Brien: "We must wait and then resume." Now that the new Reform Bill ensured him a following of eighty to ninety members in the next election he was ready to emphasize his demands and to sell the Irish vote to the bidder who offered the fullest measure of Home Rule.

During the intervening period there had been grumblings and murmuring at his enforced inactivity. Some of his lieutenants had grown too large for their shoes. Certain members whom he had dismissed from his party had revenged themselves by prying into his private life till it became impossible for him to spend a quiet week at Eastbourne or Brighton without having his footsteps dogged by spies. Refusing to admit to himself that his liaison was public property, he grew still more taciturn and reserved, rebuffing the slightest attempt at intimacy, avoiding any personal contact, even when he was instinctively drawn to a kindred spirit. Wilfrid Blunt describes meeting him for the first time on the Terrace of the House of Commons:

"Parnell was walking up and down at the far end in solitary gloom. George Howard introduced him. He was charming, with a sympathetic manner. His manner of gloom and reserve seemed unnatural to him, and every now and then there was a twinkle in his eye and a smile that seemed to show the real man. I should say he was a good fellow and I would get on well with him. At parting his manner was very *empressé*. . . . In appearance he is tall, good-looking, pale, with the least little touch of weakness about the mouth, such as one often sees in Irishmen— enough to show he is more Irish than English, and enough to lend charm to his countenance."

If Parnell had allowed himself to become really intimate with certain men of his own class, men like Wilfrid Blunt and Robert Cunninghame Graham, his life would have been a far happier one; if only he could have had one friend to confide in, one man to trust, in the same way as he trusted Katherine O'Shea, then maybe he would never have allowed himself to become so deeply involved in the intrigues of the Eltham household, till the spring of 1884 saw the curious spectacle of Mrs. O'Shea inviting both him and her husband to spend an amicable holiday in a furnished house at Brighton in order to discuss Mr. Chamberlain's proposal for a Local Government Bill.

CHAPTER THIRTY

No. 8 Medina Terrace is a high gray stucco house looking out over a bleak sea-front. It has none of the gaiety of the painted, bow-fronted Regency houses which give Brighton so much charm and atmosphere. It is grim, solid and Victorian, from its useful and ugly chimney-pots to the iron railings of its basement stairs, and no romantic aroma clings to the walls which once guarded the secret of a tragic love-affair.

When Captain and Mrs. O'Shea, accompanied by their children, came to take up residence at Medina Terrace, their neighbors had no more than a friendly interest in their doings. Mrs. O'Shea was considered to be a pleasant and agreeable person, though it did seem rather foolish of her to go on having children at her time of life. According to the standards of Medina Terrace, there was something slightly indecent about a woman producing babies when her eldest son was practically grown up. It was obvious that she was still suffering from the after-affects of her confinement, and it was rather odd that whenever she ventured abroad it was never with her own husband, but always leaning on the arm of a tall, bearded man who usually wore a heavy muffler, a cap drawn down over his eyes, and queer shapeless clothes. Brighton hotel-keepers already knew this curious figure under the name of Mr. Stewart, and the fishermen and coastguard people knew him as a harmless crank with a hobby for making model boats in the hopes of inventing a vessel which would cut through the water in such a way as to prevent it rolling in the heaviest sea; the railwaymen testified to another of his idiosyncrasies, for he was once found making an exact plan of the dimensions of the new station, and they would hardly have been gratified had they known that the roof of their handsome station, the pride of Brighton, was to be faithfully copied in an Irish cowshed.

No one questioned Mr. Stewart's identity till the neighbors of Medina Terrace noticed curious-looking individuals hanging round the door of No. 8. It was whispered that they were plain-clothes men, and the excitement increased when Press photographers took up prominent positions on the sea-front. Soon it transpired that this unknown Mr. Stewart, who went about in such strange disguises, was none other than the great Irish agitator who figured in the public imagination for all that was "sinister, treasonable, dark, mysterious and unholy." And from then onwards not even Mrs. O'Shea's golden-haired children could win more than a frigid smile from the respectable Brighton citizens.

In the interior of No. 8 the atmosphere was electric. Parnell was irritable and moody, O'Shea officious to the point of impertinence, and Katherine had to exercise all her tact in order to avoid an open rupture. With incredible complacence O'Shea allowed himself to dictate terms as the ambassador of Chamberlain, but unfortunately he lacked the courage to transmit Parnell's cold and reserved answers to the autocrat of Highbury. Mr. Garvin writes: "O'Shea luxuriated in his own sense of persuasiveness and address. He had put himself forward and had to sustain his rôle. He gloried in the notion that he was doing the great thing for Ireland and himself. That there was no man whom the Irish leader humored more, hated more and trusted less than the luckless self-complacent emissary, Chamberlain could not conceive."

But, though circumstances forced the Irish leader to humor O'Shea's political aspirations, he made no attempt to placate his feelings as an injured husband, and in his *Parnell Vindicated* Captain Harrison recounts an illuminating incident, showing what was the real state of affairs in the O'Shea *ménage*.

It was Katherine Parnell [1] who told him this story in the first year of her widowhood, and in spite of her grief she seemed to derive some satisfaction from the telling: "One evening when Captain O'Shea and Mr. Parnell had been discussing some important matter, the three of us dined together. As the night

[1] Mrs. O'Shea married Mr. Parnell in the summer of 1891.

drew on I retired before the others, and my door was still left standing open when Captain O'Shea, who was the second to retire, came upstairs. He spoke to me, and the discussion of the evening's debate began afresh, and in the course of it he entered my room and the door closed. Suddenly the door was banged violently open and Mr. Parnell stalked in, his head held high and his eyes snapping; he said not a word, but marched straight up to me, picked me up, threw me over his shoulder and turned on his heel; still without a word he marched out of the room across the landing and into his own room, where he threw me down on the bed and shut the door."

In such circumstances the domestic atmosphere of Medina Terrace must have been anything but pleasant, and, though his pecuniary interests forced O'Shea to keep up an attitude of bland, unquestioning tolerance, he was at times tempted to adopt a more menacing tone. In August 1884 one finds him writing to Parnell complaining of his causing a scandal by being seen too much at Eltham during his absence. A formal note giving him neither assurances nor explanations was the only reply. According to the Irish leader, "he could only suppose that the Captain had misunderstood the drift of some statements that had been made to him." It was not a very satisfactory answer to the complaints of an aggrieved husband, so Willie had to give vent to his feelings by picking a quarrel with his wife, who, being in a pregnant condition, was in an acrimonious mood. And she lost no time in reminding him of some rather sordid truths, as when she wrote:

"I am very sorry that you should have waited in on my account, but after our conversation on Tuesday I could not imagine that you would expect me. In any case I was feeling scarcely strong enough to travel again in the heat yesterday, and for the children's sake I should not like to die yet, as they would lose all chance of Aunt's money, and however good your appointment, they will scarcely have too much, I imagine, and certainly we have a better right to all she has than anyone else."

It was usually money which played the predominant part in

the O'Sheas' domestic differences, and, when more substantial promises failed to materialize, Willie would fall back on the chimeric possibilities of a political career. At such times he found it wiser to forget his marital grievances, and, shortly after his complaining to Parnell, he was once more his accredited envoy in negotiations with Chamberlain.

A week before Christmas, 1884, Mr. Chamberlain addressed a letter to a certain Mr. W. H. Duignan of Walsall, an old supporter of his, giving him an exact statement of his views on the subject of Irish local government. Home Rule he was opposed to, as it would infallibly lead to a demand for entire separation. On the other hand, he considered that Ireland had a right to a local government more complete, more popular, more thoroughly representative and more far-reaching than anything that had hitherto been proposed. He believed that there were questions not local in any narrow sense, but which required local and exceptional treatment in Ireland, and which could not be dealt with to the satisfaction of the Irish people by an Imperial Parliament. Chief among these were the education question and the land question, and he would not hesitate to transfer their consideration entirely to an Irish board, altogether independent of English Government influence. Such a board might also deal with railways and other communications, and would of course be invested with powers of taxation in Ireland for those strictly Irish purposes.

This was the extent of the concessions to which Mr. Chamberlain was willing to consent, and they formed part of the unauthorized program with which he was to galvanize the masses in the industrial areas, before which Mr. Gladstone's Midlothian addresses were to pale into insignificance, until the veteran Prime Minister was tempted to launch a policy more daring and more desperate than any that was ever contemplated by the radical "Jack Cade."

By the New Year the contents of "Mr. Duignan's" letter were known to the chief members of the Irish party, and the majority followed their leader's example in treating these friendly advances from Birmingham with coolness and circumspection. According to Mr. Garvin, "Parnell saw both the attractions and objections. First he suspected, quite wrongly, that Chamberlain was seeking to meddle and tamper with his own following and divide it; secondly, these very practical proposals might serve great intermediate uses in Ireland while the further future was still uncertain. But, thirdly, though welcoming the prospect of an Irish Central Board for administrative purposes, he did not wish it to have legislative powers such as Chamberlain designed, for this might weaken the full demand for an Irish Parliament and confuse the nationalist movement."

While allowing O'Shea to negotiate, with certain reservations, Parnell entrusted Katie with a secret document which she forwarded to Lord Richard Grosvenor, the chief Liberal Whip, on the understanding that it was to be shown to Mr. Gladstone. This was nothing less than a proposed constitution for Ireland, of which the main points were: an Irish Parliament with power to make enactments regarding all the domestic concerns of the country, but without power to interfere in any Imperial matter; with power to raise a revenue for any purpose over which it had jurisdiction by direct taxation upon property, by customs duties and by licenses; with power to create departments for the transaction of all business connected with the affairs over which it had jurisdiction, and to maintain a police force for the preservation of order and the enforcement of the law.

The office of Lord Lieutenant and the appointment of other Crown officials was to be abolished, and the Legislative Chamber was to include the constitution of courts of justice and the appointment or payment of all judges, magistrates and other officials, each appointment being subject to the assent of the Crown in the same way as no enactment of the Chamber was to have the force of law until it had received the royal approval.

A sum of one million pounds per annum was to be paid by the Chamber to the Imperial Treasury in lieu of the right of the Crown to levy taxes in Ireland for Imperial purposes; this sum was to contribute to the maintenance of any such naval and military force as the Crown thought necessary. Any excess in the cost of these forces was to be provided for out of the Imperial revenue, and no volunteer force was to be raised in Ireland without the consent of the Crown.

It is interesting to note that the thorny point as to whether the representation of Ireland in the Imperial Parliament was to be retained or given up was a matter of comparative indifference to Parnell, though this was the very question which roused so much anxiety and bitterness during the Home Rule debates.

The contents of this memorandum were kept strictly secret by Mr. Gladstone and Lord Richard Grosvenor, and, in his fear of committing himself before the time was ripe for action, the Prime Minister instructed his Whip to send no more than a terse and polite acknowledgment of Mr. Parnell's proposals.

It was a time of intrigues and plots within the very precincts of the Cabinet, a time of curious alliances and unscrupulous deals, of ominous rumors in the lobbies of Westminster and of nervous murmurings in the Reform Club. The triumphs of Midlothian, the overwhelming majority of 1880, had faded before the grim realities of Egyptian disaster and Irish coercion. In the Cabinet there were dissension and threatened resignations. Mr. Chamberlain and Sir Charles Dilke waved their revolutionary banners under the cold and hostile eyes of the scions of the great Whig families. No sense of party loyalty kept Whig and Radical from denouncing one another on the public platform. And it is small wonder that in such a stormy atmosphere Mr. Gladstone should have preferred to keep Mr. Parnell's memorandum a secret. When Chamberlain forwarded him a plan for local self-government which, according to O'Shea, had been approved by the Irish leader, the astute old parliamentarian replied that through Mrs. O'Shea he had received a similar scheme embodying Mr. Parnell's views. A fully fledged plan for a separate Parliament in College Green was hardly similar to a scheme for a local government board, but Mr. Gladstone had not the slightest intention of taking Mr. Chamberlain into his confidence.

When Parnell received no propitious reply from Downing

Street he allowed O'Shea to proceed with his negotiations, and the account of how the untrustworthy envoy deliberately misled both parties concerned is told in full detail by Mr. Garvin. While giving Parnell garbled versions of his interviews with Chamberlain, interpreting the Radical leader's views in his own cynical and flippant fashion, O'Shea did still more harm by deliberately suppressing two letters stating Parnell's real views on local government. He was concerned with one thing only—as to what personal advantage could be derived from the transaction. Chamberlain's fortunes were on the ascendant—there were rumors of Gladstone's retiring from public life, and, though Lord Hartington might try to form a ministry, he would be unable to proceed without the cooperation, or rather the domination, of the Radical element. So O'Shea hitched his wagon to Chamberlain's rising star, and in his anxiety to pull off a successful deal he concealed the two letters in which Parnell stated quite definitely that he did not consider Chamberlain's scheme to be a final settlement.

"In talking to your friend, you must give him quite clearly to understand that we do not propose this local self-government as a substitute for our Irish Parliament, but solely as an improvement of the present system of local government in Ireland. Our claim for restitution of Parliament would still remain."

And again: "The two questions of the reform of local government and the restitution of an Irish Parliament must, as I explained to you from the first, be kept absolutely separate."

Even though Chamberlain never saw these letters, he might have got a clear idea of Parnell's views from the famous *ne plus ultra* speech which the Irish leader delivered at Cork on January 21st, had not O'Shea been careful to point out that all this talk about recovering Grattan's Parliament was merely in order to placate the revolutionary section of the party.

Having dealt with the Radical leader in a perfectly fair and straightforward manner, Parnell concentrated all his forces on realizing his ultimate ambition. Moderate language and conciliatory policy were of the past. After two years of comparative inactivity he made a meteoric reappearance in the south of Ireland. From Arklow to Clonmel and from Clonmel to Cork the roads were lined with people cheering the uncrowned king, crying: "Down with Coercion!" "Down with Gladstone!" and "Down with the Red Earl!" In his own city of Cork, surrounded by priests and Fenians, Parnell delivered the speech which thrilled the heart of every Irish Nationalist, saying: "We cannot ask for less than the restitution of Grattan's Parliament, with its important privileges and wide-reaching constitution. We cannot under the British constitution ask for more than the restitution of Grattan's Parliament. But no man has the right to fix a boundary to the march of a nation, no man has a right to say, 'Thus far shalt thou go and no farther,' and we have never attempted to fix the *ne plus ultra* to the progress of Ireland's nationhood, and we never shall."

This was not only his answer to Mr. Chamberlain's proposals; it was also a hint to the Tories that if they wished to bargain for the Irish vote they would have to offer some substantial proposals. Lord Randolph Churchill had made the first advances by supporting the Parnellite motion for a fresh enquiry into the Maamtrasna trials [1]—a particularly sordid police case in which it had been suggested that a Crown official had induced an informer to give false evidence. Lord Spencer had already gone to the root of the matter, and had come to the conclusion that the verdict and sentence were just, but the Irish party had not forgiven the Viceroy for the way in which the loyal employees of Dublin Castle had tried to connect the Land League with the Phœnix Park murderers, and now they seized on the Maamtrasna trials as a useful weapon in showing up the malad-

[1] In the August of 1882 a whole family had been murdered at Maamtrasna. For this crime three men had been sentenced to death, and it was alleged that two of the men hanged had, in their dying depositions, declared the innocence of the third, while this man himself had protested to the last that he was not guilty. An informer then came forward and swore that he had been told by an official that his evidence would not be accepted by the Crown unless it applied to all the prisoners, and that from sheer terror of death he had been induced to swear away the life of the innocent man.

ministration and abuse of the Crimes Act. A sordid murder committed in an obscure corner of Connemara gradually developed into an important political issue, till it finally led to the so-called Maamtrasna "alliance" between the Conservatives and the Irish party.

While Lord Randolph flirted with the Parnellites, the Radicals made delicate advances to the princes of the Catholic Church, and, of all the curious alliances of that spring of 1885, none was more curious than the alliance between Cardinal Manning and the Nonconformist Joseph Chamberlain. Of the two, the former proved himself to be the more subtle and the more diplomatic, adhering to the opinion that confidential interchanges of points of view in no way involved him in "concordats" or "bargains," and he proved his goodwill by ascertaining the views of the Irish bishops on the subject of local government, the Catholic hierarchy showing themselves ready to accept "any real power of self-government, which should be effectual and not evasive." His Eminence went still further to secure the peace of Ireland by negotiating a private interview with Mr. Parnell, an interview which, had it been made public in the Press, would have had serious consequences for them both. The Holy Father would hardly have approved of one of his cardinals treating with the Irish agitator, and Parnell's Fenian supporters would have resented any suggestion of his being dictated to by an English cardinal. The meeting had no satisfactory results. Parnell was reserved and vague about his future plans, and his acceptance of Chamberlain's central council scheme was so guarded that Manning took it to mean little more than refraining from active opposition. When he gave Dilke and Chamberlain a confidential report of the interview, he never led them to believe that Parnell would regard their scheme as a final settlement.

But unfortunately there was O'Shea in the offing, playing the "rôle of Mercury" in carrying messages between Whitehall, archbishop's house, and Eltham, leading Chamberlain astray with false promises and faked documents, leading him to believe that he was the adviser and intimate friend who knew the inner workings of Parnell's mind. Never for a moment did Chamberlain question his sincerity, and in this respect the member for Birmingham showed himself to be far more ingenuous than either the cardinal or the Prime Minister. In spite of the Captain professing to be a good and loyal Catholic, Manning despised him both as a man and as a politician. As for Gladstone, he kept his own counsel and trusted no one. "He did not calculate upon Parnell and his friends, nor upon Manning and his bishops, nor was he under any obligation to follow or act with Chamberlain," but he gave his decisive approval to the Irish Council scheme, and when it was rejected by the majority of the ministers at a Cabinet meeting on the 9th of May, he said to one colleague: "Ah! they will rue the day!" and to another: "Within six years, if it please God to spare their lives, they will be repenting in sackcloth and ashes!" Undeterred by the defeat, he wrote to Lord Spencer that the scheme for the Central Board was dead, but for the moment only, adding significantly: "It will quickly rise again, I think, perhaps in larger dimensions." Meanwhile there was nothing to do but to announce the determination of the Cabinet to renew the Crimes Act in a modified form, a decision which brought fresh threats of resignation from Radical quarters.

It was during these weeks that Parnell paid a friendly visit to Lord Randolph Churchill at his home in Connaught Place, and, as they sat peacefully smoking their cigars, Lord Randolph gave his guest to understand that if the Tories took office, and if he were a member of the Government, he would not consent to renew the Crimes Act. Whereupon Parnell replied in his quiet, indifferent voice: "In that case you will have the Irish vote at the elections."

There was no compact or bargain of any kind; for the moment the Tories and Nationalists were useful to one another. Though Parnell still regarded Gladstone as the one man in England who had the strength to carry a Home Rule measure, it was to his advantage to support the weaker side, to equalize the two parties, so that both would be dependent on the Irish

vote. With a curious single-mindedness he was carrying out his
original policy—to prevent the English from ruling themselves
till they had given autonomy to Ireland. Only his tactics had
changed. With a following of seven he had been content to
obstruct the business of the House; now it lay in his power
to give the death-blow to a coercionist ministry.

On June 8th the second reading of the Finance Bill was moved
by Mr. Childers, the Chancellor of the Exchequer. Sir Michael
Hicks-Beach moved an amendment condemning the increase in
beer and spirit duties proposed by ministers. The House divided
on the question, the Irish vote was cast on the side of the Conservatives, and the Government were beaten by a majority of
fourteen. The scene was one of wild excitement. From the
Irish benches came the cry of "Remember coercion!" Lord
Randolph Churchill and his comrades of the fourth party stood
up on their bench, waving their silk hats, yelling like excited
schoolboys, and even the most cold-blooded Tory could not resist a shout of victory. Only two men remained calm. On the
Treasury Bench, Mr. Gladstone quietly continued his letter to
the Queen as if nothing unusual had happened, and in his seat
below the gangway Parnell sat pale and impassive, with that
gentle, remote look in his eyes as if he had played no part in the
evening's proceedings. The following day, in an interview,
when he was asked: "What advantage do you hope to reap from
last night's vote?" he answered very dryly and matter-of-fact:
"Well, in the first place, the pleasure and advantage of that vote
to us is increased by the fact that we have saved almost the
only remaining Irish industry from a permanent burden of
£500,000 a year." It was no mere pose on his part to ignore
the fall of a great ministry and the end of coercion, only, with
his strictly practical mind, he preferred to concentrate on immediate benefits, and, after all, the interests of the Irish distilleries
and breweries were not to be ignored.

By the end of the month Lord Salisbury had formed a ministry, though his chances of remaining in power seemed somewhat precarious. His ministry existed solely by virtue of the

Irish vote, and only Parnell's support could tide him over the next election. He had no choice but to trust to Lord Randolph's audacious guidance, to accept the young Tory democrat as a member of his Cabinet and to take the plunge into Parnellite waters. On the 6th of July the House of Lords heard with stupefaction a Conservative Viceroy plainly stating that the new Government proposed to rule Ireland by ordinary law.

CHAPTER THIRTY-ONE

WHEN the new Prime Minister appointed Lord Carnarvon as Viceroy of Ireland, he definitely committed his Government to a conciliatory policy. The statesman who had done so much towards cementing the ties between the colonies and the mother country, who had carried federation in Canada and tried to carry it in South Africa, was recognized both by his colleagues and by members of the Opposition to be that *rara avis,* a pure-minded and chivalrous politician who never let party considerations and election prospects interfere with the dictates of his conscience. For over ten years he had been studying the claims of Ireland to some form of federal Government, and he had exchanged a voluminous correspondence on the subject with Sir Charles Gavan Duffy, a veteran of the Young Ireland movement, who, after being proscribed in his own country, had risen to public eminence in Australia. Sir Charles had now returned to Ireland, and though he never professed to be a Parnellite, he was treated with respect and confidence by the leading members of the party, and it was at his instigation that Lord Carnarvon entered into communication with Mr. Justin McCarthy to enquire into the possibility of a private interview with Mr. Parnell. For a Tory Viceroy to open negotiations with a man whom a large proportion of the public considered to be little more than a murderer was an independent and courageous action, especially when one considers that up till now even Mr. Gladstone had never dared to have any personal contact with Parnell. Morley describes Lord Carnarvon's gesture as "one of the most sensible things that any Viceroy ever did," and whether the first overtures came from the Lord Lieutenant or from the Irish leader is not really important. Mr. McCarthy states that it was Howard Vincent who asked him on behalf of the Viceroy if an interview could be arranged, whereas Lord Carnarvon recounts that it was intimated to him that if he were willing Mr. Parnell would also be willing to meet him in conversation. As both Lord Carnarvon and Mr. McCarthy were scrupulously honest, these contradictory accounts were probably due to some mutual misunderstanding. Suffice it to say that the momentous interview took place on Saturday, August 1st, among "the dust sheets and rolled-up carpets" of a deserted Mayfair drawing-room, that no third person was present, and that as a result of the conversations Mr. Parnell definitely discarded Mr. Chamberlain's "national council" scheme as an implement for which he had no further use. In a previous meeting with Mc-Carthy, Carnarvon had been told of "the undoubted power of Parnell, of the fact that he really stood in front of the Irish people and that he wielded them, that he was cold, narrow and unimaginative, but ready to come to a compromise, to give and take, and that he stood between violence and law and had no real desire for confiscation or plunder." But the man whom he now met for the first time in the shrouded gloom of his sister's house in Hill Street was far more affable and more courtly than what he had been led to expect. The inaccessible, impenetrable Irishman showed himself perfectly willing for a free interchange of opinions on the understanding that there was to be "no sort of bond or engagement." He showed himself singularly moderate, perfectly fair, admitting every difficulty, and apparently anxious to find some common ground. The common ground was a proposed constitution for Ireland, for it soon transpired that Lord Carnarvon favored his views regarding a settlement that would give Ireland a free legislature on the colonial model. Naturally the Viceroy was careful to explain that he was acting for himself by himself, that the responsibility was on his own shoulders, and that he was not voicing the opinion of the Cabinet, also that he was there as the Queen's servant, and that he would neither hear nor say one word that was inconsistent with the union of the two countries. They then discussed more general topics—the protection of Irish industries, a system of migration for relieving the congested areas, and the importance of a Land Purchase Bill. The interview lasted for one hour and

a half, and Parnell left the room under the impression that, even
if Lord Salisbury and the majority of his Cabinet were not yet
ready to swallow the Home Rule pill, the very fact that he had
authorized his Viceroy to talk Home Rule was sufficient proof
that the Prime Minister was contemplating it as a possibility.
He was shrewd enough to realize that, in spite of Lord Carnarvon's taking upon himself the full responsibility in case of any
possible indiscretion, he would not have embarked upon this
interview without receiving his direction from headquarters.
Parnell never doubted that a detailed memorandum of the conversations would be despatched to Hatfield, and this, coupled
with the conciliatory speech with which Lord Salisbury had
opened his electioneering campaign, seemed to prognosticate that
the Tories were willing to pay a high price for Irish support.
Unlike Lord Carnarvon, Parnell was no idealist. In his eyes
there were no high-minded motives in politics, and it is not surprising that in this summer of 1885, when Liberals, Radicals and
Tories, prelates, journalists and Orangemen were all haggling
and bargaining for the Irish vote, his normally poor opinion
of his fellow-creatures should have sunk to a still lower level.
Unfortunately there was one man whom he underestimated,
and that was the honorable member for Birmingham, who,
owing to O'Shea's misrepresentations and the force of circumstances, saw himself thrown over by the Nationalist leader, after
being tricked and deceived into making overtures of friendship,
not only in words, but in courageous and decisive actions. After
splitting the Liberal Cabinet on the question of a practical Irish
settlement, he had opened his electioneering campaign with a
speech in which he had spoken of "our Irish Poland," denouncing "the absurd and irritating anachronism known as Dublin
Castle," and "the system founded on the bayonets of thirty
thousand soldiers encamped permanently in a hostile country."
He had given a still more definite proof of his friendship by
proposing with Dilke to visit Ireland, equipped with recommendations from Cardinal Manning to bishops who would put

him into personal contact with the leading men on the popular side.

Mr. Garvin has stressed the fact that neither Chamberlain nor Dilke ever exchanged one direct word with Parnell either in speech or in writing. Even after the fall of the Government, O'Shea was still the trusted intermediary, and he seems to have been sufficiently clever to delude Chamberlain into believing that, in spite of his uncompromising speeches, Parnell still favored the Radical program, and would give his whole-hearted support to the projected Irish tour. But all O'Shea's powers of deception were of no avail when two simultaneous rebuffs showed Chamberlain only too plainly that the Irish had definitely rejected his offers of friendship. The first blow fell when Cardinal Manning politely refused the promised introductions. However friendly he may have been in the early spring, his attitude had become noticeably cooler as soon as it was evident that a Conservative Viceroy was willing to seek the alliance of the Catholic prelates. As he himself said, how could he be "godfather to both Hengist and Horsa?" The second rebuff was both more formidable and more unforgivable. There appeared in Parnell's own newspaper a series of particularly virulent articles denouncing the Radical leaders as dangerous intriguers and warning them not to meddle with the affairs of Ireland, which refused to be used as a cat's-paw in furthering their interests. This was hardly a gracious reply to the Holloway speech, but O'Brien, who was responsible for the editorial column, was obsessed by the fear of an alliance between Davitt and the Radicals, an alliance which would endanger Parnell's leadership and confuse the Nationalist ideals with those of English social reform. However much Parnell may have deplored the articles, it was not in his interests to interfere with his editor's policy on the eve of a General Election. He was under no obligation to Chamberlain; from the very first he had instructed O'Shea to negotiate only with reservations, and, when the angry and disappointed negotiator tried to bludgeon him into making some kind of apology, he merely became cool and evasive, for neither out of consideration for Mr. Chamberlain, nor for the sake of the career of Captain O'Shea, was he willing to quarrel with a devoted follower who for the past two years had fought an almost single-handed battle against Lord Spencer's régime.

After forwarding O'Shea the cuttings from *United Ireland,* Chamberlain pressed for a plain statement of Parnell's views. He was no longer to be placated by plausible assurances, and the unfortunate envoy had to admit that in spite of his trying to "impress on Parnell the quackery of the Tories, and the folly of losing the substance and grasping the shadow," the majority of the party seemed inclined to be carried away by the tempting promises of the new Government. It can hardly have been pleasant for the Birmingham magnate to realize that he had been used merely as a bait to draw the Tories, and it must have been still more galling to feel that Lord Randolph had scored in the first electioneering round. In his Memorandum he made a terse note: "As a result of my conversations with O'Shea, and his statements, I came to the conclusion that Parnell was trying to negotiate a better bargain with the Tories. In fact O'Shea has said, 'He has had a better offer.' Under these circumstances it seemed unwise to pursue the matter any further, and accordingly I told O'Shea to let Parnell know that so far as I was concerned the matter was at an end." The break between Parnell and Chamberlain was complete, and though various efforts were made to bring about a reconciliation, though Labouchere and Healy expended their inexhaustible energies and resources in a maze of subterranean activities, the breach was never healed. As for poor O'Shea, he was worried "if not out of his wits, out of his hair." After a few sleepless nights he complained to his wife that he was "now balder than a coot," adding: "I wonder whether I shall die soon, or if the day will come. Would I had understood it had come when I was asked to go to Kilmainham."

But he still managed to keep on an intimate footing at Highbury, where his host was quite unaware that it was he and not Parnell who was the arch deceiver. In his study of *Parnell: the Last Five Years,* Sir Alfred Robbins recalls one night, in 1888, when the Irish leader told him how deeply he regretted "that the violent language of *United Ireland* and some of its adherents had assisted to prevent Chamberlain fulfilling his intention to make a political tour in Ireland in the autumn of 1885. He had good reason to know how favorable the English statesman at that time was to a very wide extension of local self-government in Ireland, and what at that moment might have been hoped from him—hopes checked by scurrilous attacks of a nature impossible to forget." By 1888 Parnell may have learned to regret his summary treatment of the Radical leader. In the force of Chamberlain's relentless antagonism he may have discerned those reserves of strength which would have made him such a valuable and trustworthy ally; one who with his superb gift of friendship would have preserved him from the very elements which he was now exploiting in order to encompass his ruin. It was not usual for Parnell to confide in journalists, and this frank confession to the correspondent of the *Birmingham Post* may have been a subtle hint thrown out in the hopes of a belated reconciliation with Chamberlain. But in 1885 he was too dazzled by the glamorous promises of Hatfield, the portentous whispers of Hawarden, even to consider the plain and prosaic proposals of Highbury.

The General Election was at hand, and behind the scenes the wire-pullers manipulated the tangled threads of party intrigues. The Conservatives tried to propitiate Ireland by a new Land Act, for, though Lord Randolph Churchill and Lord Carnarvon were both willing to take the final plunge, the Prime Minister betrayed a marked aversion towards "stewing in Parnellite juice"[1] while loyal Orangemen showed signs of growing restive under the irksome yoke of the Maamtrasna "alliance." Mr.

---

[1] "For my part I desire them for a few months to stew in their own Parnellite juice." Sir William Harcourt, at Lowestoft.

Chamberlain turned his back on Ireland and unfurled the banner of his "unauthorized program" to the delighted gaze of the enfranchised laborer, and Mr. Herbert Gladstone threw the Liberal camp into the wildest confusion by giving voice to a full-blooded Home Rule speech at Leeds, a speech which gave rise to the strangest rumors and the most embarrassing conjectures. Not all his father's enigmatical silences, nor his admirable attitude of fair play towards the present Government, could prevent the Liberal clubs from speculating on the future. The oak-trees of Hawarden told no secrets, but Mr. Gladstone's intimates found no difficulty in reading between the lines of his carefully worded letters. In August he wrote to Lord Granville apropos of the rejected Local Government scheme: "For my own part I have seen my way pretty well to the particulars of the minor and rejected plan, but the idea of the wider one puzzles me much. At the same time, if the election gives a return of a decisive character, the sooner the subject is dealt with the better." And a few weeks previously Lord Richard Grosvenor had been instructed to reopen the usual channels of communication with the Irish leader. Unfortunately for Mr. Gladstone, Lord Carnarvon had already secured his audience, and for the moment the replies from Eltham were as non-committal as those of Downing Street had been in the past.

To obtain a clear majority independent of the Parnellite vote was the only possibility of averting an Irish crisis, and when he retired to Northern waters to compose his Midlothian addresses, the Liberal leader gave not a thought to Mr. Chamberlain's social reforms, nor to England's foreign policy; he concentrated on— one might also say he was obsessed by one subject only—Ireland and the vital importance of a solid overwhelming majority in the next Parliament.

While the rival political parties laid their cards upon the electioneering table, Parnell surveyed the situation from the solitude of the Wicklow mountains. Living in the old military barrack which served him as a shooting-lodge he would go out to kill his grouse as happily as if there was no Home Rule hanging in the balance, no importunate politicians pressing him for terms, no Healys and Laboucheres intriguing in the background, no Willie O'Shea alternately nagging and cringing, insisting in his deadly obstinate way for an Irish constituency. For a few days he was at peace to wander over his own bog-lands, inspecting his turf and cattle, searching for tiny grains of gold in the river-beds. But the holiday was over all too soon. On August the 23rd he was back in Dublin meeting Justin McCarthy and Henry Campbell at dinner with his old friend Dr. Kenny, "the beloved Fenian apothecary," who had nursed him so faithfully in Kilmainham; strolling home through the moonlit streets, leading a great red setter on a chain, his tall form attracting the attention of some belated wanderer, who looked back and murmured: "Why, it's Mr. Parnell himself!"

On the 24th he was back on the round of public dinners, giving utterance to the thoughts which had been formulating in his mind ever since the interview with Lord Carnarvon, saying: "It is not now a question of self-government for Ireland, it is only a question as to how much of the self-government they will be able to cheat us out of. . . . I hope it may not be necessary for us in the new Parliament to devote our attention to subsidiary measures and that it may be possible for us to have a program and a platform with only one plank, and that one plank legislative independence." The following day, at a meeting of the National League, he was still more emphatic: "I believe that we will get a settlement of the national question from whichever Government or whichever party may be in power, whether it be Whig or whether it be Tory. . . . We are therefore in the position that, no matter which of the English sides loses or which of them wins, we are bound to win." On September 1st he attended a dinner at the Dublin Mansion House, and, in responding to the toast of "Ireland, a Nation!" he claimed for his country the complete right to rule herself. In all his speeches there was a ring of confidence and security, a quiet note of triumph, which inspired the farmer, the tradesman, and the poorest laborer to support him at the polls. What matter if Lord Hartington heaped coals of fire upon his head by protesting that all England would now unite in resisting so fatal and mischievous a proposal as an Irish Parliament? What matter if Mr. Chamberlain declared that "if these and these alone are the terms on which Mr. Parnell's support is to be obtained, I will not enter into competition for it"? There was now not only Lord Salisbury making a mild apology for boycotting in his speech at Newport; there was not only Lord Carnarvon touring Ireland in the spirit of friendship and goodwill, but there was Mr. Childers, the Liberal ex-Chancellor of the Exchequer, the friend and confidant of Gladstone, declaring himself willing to give Ireland her own legislature; there was Labby, running to and fro between Herbert Gladstone and Healy, bringing assurances that the G.O.M.[1] was disposed to grant the fullest Home Rule, but that he did not think it desirable to formulate a scheme before the elections; Labby, "who talked to everybody, wrote to everybody, and betrayed everybody," and whose early upbringing in diplomacy had fitted him to be the most consummate and the most genial of wire-pullers. And, most important of all, there was the famous Hawarden manifesto, issued on September the 18th, in which Mr. Gladstone, though still adhering to vague generalities, pleaded for a reconciliation between England and Ireland, insisting that "every grant to portions of the country of enlarged powers for the management of their own affairs is in my view not a source of danger, but a means of averting it, and is in the nature of a new guarantee for increased cohesion, happiness and strength"; adding, "I believe history and posterity will consign to disgrace the memory of every man, be he who he may, on whichever side of the Channel he may dwell, that, having the power to aid in all equitable

[1] Grand Old Man.

arrangements between Ireland and Great Britain, shall use the power, not to aid, but to prevent or retard it."

The shadow of Home Rule obscured the election prospects for both parties, and as yet neither of the leaders cared to grapple with the substance. In his Midlothian tours Mr. Gladstone adopted a magnanimous attitude towards the Government, which Mr. Chamberlain named so contemptuously "the Cabinet of Caretakers." In a solemn appeal to his electors, he said: "Apart from the terms of Whig and Tory there is one thing I will say and will endeavor to impress on you, and it is this: it will be a vital danger to the country and to the Empire if, at a time when a demand from Ireland for larger powers of self-government is to be dealt with, there is not in Parliament a party totally independent of the Irish vote."

Mr. Gladstone's refusal to be drawn by Parnell's flattering request "for him to approach the subject of Irish autonomy with that breadth of statesmanship for which he was renowned"; his declaration that it was impossible for him to intervene when the responsible Government was silent; his offer to the Tories to make the Irish question no longer a party issue, finally decided Parnell to throw his support on the weaker side. On November 21st, T. P. O'Connor, the President of the English branch of the National League, issued a flaming manifesto, calling on every Irishman to vote solid with the Conservatives, and Labouchere commented to Chamberlain in his cynical fashion: "My impression is that Parnell has been carried away with the idea of holding the balance, but that, if we beat the lot, he will be quite ready to treat!" From T. P. O'Connor himself one hears how unwillingly the Chief signed that manifesto which proved to be one of the few tactical errors of his career. There is no doubt that he was largely influenced by the fact that most of his followers were thirsting for revenge against the Gladstone Cabinet, who, after suspending their liberty of speech at Westminster, had imprisoned and humiliated them in their own country. At the same time he may have feared the effect of a large Liberal majority whether dominated by the Whigs or by the Radicals, and he probably felt a pardonable desire to outwit the tactics of the "Grand Old Spider," who, after instructing Lord Richard Grosvenor to reopen communications with him in July, now tactfully referred him to the present Government. But at the back of his mind he knew quite clearly that only Gladstone could carry through Home Rule, and a month later Katherine O'Shea wrote to the Liberal leader: "I know that Mr. Parnell never at any time expected the Conservatives to attempt any scheme of the kind I sent to you, for he has never at any time wavered from the belief that he has always felt that you alone could carry it, and even at the eleventh hour he asked me, on the eve of that decision which brought in the present Government, if I thought it possible to ascertain if you would consider a scheme for the settlement of the Irish question, as in that case, if any hope could have been held out by you, the Irish vote would not have been given to the Conservatives."

This manifesto decided the elections; the loss of the Irish vote cost the Liberals between twenty and forty seats—seats which a few months later played a great part in deciding the fate of Home Rule. From Liverpool, Parnell delivered a series of militant speeches prognosticating that until the Irish question was disposed of, it would be utterly impossible for any English question to proceed. The result on polling-day justified his prophecies, the Liberals securing 333 seats, the Conservatives 251, and the Nationalists 86. When the figures of the Irish election returns were made known, the immense power of Parnell began to dawn on the British public. Antrim was the only one out of thirty-two counties which had voted solid against Home Rule. Everywhere else the Parnellites were triumphant; they had routed the Liberals from the country, they had crossed the Boyne and invaded the sacred precincts of Belfast—the very priests had canvassed for them in the towns, and the "mud-cabin vote" had declared unanimously in their favor. Davitt, with his dreams of a Radical alliance, was overthrown; Dillon had returned to his native country, pledged to support his chief; O'Donnell, O'Connor, Power, all the old gang who had dared to question Parnell's supremacy, were wiped out. As the news of Parnell's victory traveled across St. George's Channel, Gladstone realized Home Rule to be inevitable, and on December 17th the "Hawarden Kite" fluttered on to the troubled political horizon.

CHAPTER THIRTY-TWO

THE so-called "Hawarden Kite" was in the form of a statement sent out by the National Press Agency and published simultaneously in the *Leeds Mercury* and in the *Standard,* alleging that Mr. Gladstone was prepared to take office with the view to the creation of an Irish Parliament to be entrusted with the entire management of all legislative and administrative affairs, securities being taken for the representation of minorities and an equitable partition of all Imperial charges. This momentous message was said to have been inspired by Herbert Gladstone who in his rôle of a dutiful son now committed his second indiscretion of the year—and, in spite of his father's protesting that this untimely disclosure was but a speculation on his views, the communal intimacy of family life at Hawarden, the reverent awe which Mr. Gladstone inspired in his children, was sufficient proof that "Master Herbert" would never have spoken without authorization from his father. The news caused equal consternation at Chatsworth and at Highbury, and in both camps it was regarded as a signal of war. At the age of seventy-six Mr. Gladstone was preparing to shed the powerful Whig connections which had been his main ballast in public life, merely for the sake of tilting a lance for Ireland against the impregnable walls of British prejudice. For the last time he made the tour of the stately mansions, many of which would be closed to him the following year, and on the terrace of Eaton Hall he had a private conversation with young Arthur Balfour, Lord Salisbury's kinsman. It was on this occasion that he expressed a desire to see Home Rule taken up by the Government, in which case they would have his loyal cooperation and support. But the "Hawarden Kite" showed the Conservatives quite plainly that such a coalition would be very far from idyllic. The paragraph in which Herbert Gladstone replied to the threats of Highbury, by stating that "Mr. Gladstone felt strong enough to carry the scheme through the House of Commons independent

287

of the support of the Radical Wing of the Party," made it quite clear that Mr. Gladstone also felt strong enough to carry the scheme through independent of Radicals, Whigs or Tories; independent, in fact, of all who dared to oppose him in the dominant obsession of his old age. So now Lord Salisbury declined to embark on perilous seas in the same frail craft as his great antagonist.

As for Parnell, he was furious at the Hawarden disclosure, regarding it as a deliberate move to damage him with the Tories, and he said to William O'Brien, "Master Herbert ought to be whipped. He will set Randolph on the look-out for some new deal, and start Chamberlain worrying the old man." At the same time he had his suspicions that both Labby and Healy were partly responsible; all that intriguing and bargaining with Herbert Gladstone, Chamberlain and Churchill was bound to lead to trouble. Labby was dangerous, and he was slowly drawing Healy into the enemy camp. The presumptuous follower boasted: "Parnell is half mad; we always act without him. He accepts the position; if he did not we should overlook him. Do not trouble yourself about him. Dillon, McCarthy, O'Brien, Harrington and I settle everything. When we agree, no one can disagree."

Only a few weeks later Parnell was to prove that he could still extort implicit obedience from his most refractory colleagues. There were bound to be times when men like Healy were tempted to rebel against his leadership. His mysterious disappearances, his abnormal reticence, the way in which he would allow them to manage the party in his absence, and then would suddenly reappear at a critical time, throw over their decisions as if they were of no account, take everything into his own hands, leaving them in ignorance of his views until he would state them in a public interview with the Press, afforded plenty of opportunity for criticism. On certain occasions he would appear at the House of Commons, make a speech, and leave without as much as exchanging a word with any of his colleagues. Up to the very last none of them had known what party he would support at the elections. Then, at the eleventh hour, he had gratified the wishes of the majority because it suited his purposes. By the middle of December he had realized his mistake, for the Irish vote had not been strong enough to secure a Conservative majority. Disappointed in their bargain, the Government refused to be his caretakers any longer, and, reckoning on a split in the Liberal ranks, they declared firmly against Home Rule. As Lord Randolph admitted with his frank cynicism: "I did my best for you, and now I'll do my best against you." There followed Lord Carnarvon's resignation, and in that twisted, scheming political world the Tory Viceroy stands out as the one integral and stainless figure ready to be sacrificed for the sake of his country.

Parnell played the game of cynical opportunity as well as, or better than, the English politicians. Not a month following the manifesto in which he had denounced the Liberals as "the men who coerced Ireland, deluged Egypt with blood, menaced religious liberty in the school and the freedom of speech in Parliament," he was once more negotiating with their leader. Whether allies, followers or opponents, they were all mere pawns in his skilful maneuvers. He had no consideration for British public opinion and he had no preference for either political party.

The "Hawarden Kite" had served its purpose in so far as it had forced Lord Salisbury to show his hand and Mr. Chamberlain to reconsider his position "as to whether it was better to be smashed with Mr. Gladstone and the Parnellites or without them," for in his opinion disruption was inevitable. Parnell admitted that "whatever chance there had been of a settlement with the Tories had disappeared when the seemingly authoritative statements of Mr. Gladstone's intention to deal with the question were published." But he refused to agree to an alliance without some very definite pledges. Warily he argued: "Suppose the Liberals came into power, and that they offered a settlement of so incomplete a character that we could not accept it, or that owing to defections they could not carry it, should we not, if any long interval occurred before the proposal of a fresh settlement, run considerable risk of further coercion?"

By the end of December Mr. Gladstone had committed himself to the extent of issuing a memorandum to the effect that if he were called upon to form a Government, the preparation of a scheme of duly guarded Home Rule would be an indispensable condition. A few days later Labouchere showed Parnell a document which was nothing less than a rough forecast of the Home Rule Bill of 1886, but even then the Irish leader displayed no undue haste about accepting Mr. Gladstone's terms. That anyone as indiscreet as Labby should have been entrusted with this delicate mission can only be accounted for by the fact that Mr. Gladstone may have wanted both Randolph Churchill and Chamberlain to be apprised of his action. Parnell, on the other hand, was in favor of keeping the negotiations as secret as possible, and he instructed Mrs. O'Shea to warn Mr. Gladstone that he had not "a very high opinion of Mr. Labouchere's discretion." When the momentous document was handed to him in the lobby of the House, he glanced hurriedly over it, coolly folded it, and put it in his pocket, in spite of Labouchere's protesting that he had been told not to part with it on any account. Then he disappeared, and it was only several days later that he consented to tell Labby that if Mr. Gladstone brought in a Bill upon the lines foreshadowed in the paper he would have the full support of the Irish party.

Parliament met on January 12th; on the 26th the Government announced a new Coercion Bill, and that very evening they were defeated by a combination of Liberals and Nationalists. The amendment in favor of "three acres and a cow" which brought about the downfall of the Cabinet of Caretakers was singularly inappropriate, as it formed part of Mr. Chamberlain's unauthorized program which had caused the first rift in the lute between Mr. Chamberlain and his chief. But any weapon is justifiable in times of stress, and that night Mr. Gladstone embarked on the greatest adventure of his career. By the 1st of February he was once more Prime Minister, his party split, his oldest friends estranged, and the gates of Chatsworth definitely closed against him.

As soon as Parliament had dissolved, Parnell crossed over to Ireland, and William O'Brien recalls one raw January night at Morrison's Hotel, when he and some of his colleagues were dining with the chief.

"With his characteristic indifference to personal discomfort, Parnell had neglected to order a fire, and his mutton cutlet was growing cold and his pint of Rhine wine unopened, while he doggedly made his way through bundle after bundle of letters awaiting his arrival. All of a sudden the very room lighted up for some of us like a bit of heaven, when, raising his head from some dull document concerning God knows what, in which he had been absorbed, he remarked casually and without emphasis: 'We are to have a Home Rule Bill. Will you, gentlemen, kindly turn it over and let me have your suggestions as to what we want—I mean what we can get.'" There was no bombast, no flourish of trumpets; with his old tenacity and caution he meant to bargain to the very end. He had secured the alliance of the greatest statesman of his age, a tactician whom he admitted ruefully knew more moves on the board than he did and who was still ready to outwit him at every turn. Gone was the joyous independence of the days when as a young guerilla leader he had won audacious victories against an insolent majority; when, allied with Biggar, he had trampled on the rules and regulations of the House; days when there was no need for gratitude or consideration towards any English party. Now he was a historical figure; men compared him to Bismarck and Cavour, and he was really so simple, so pathetically simple in the dim, lonely recesses of his soul.

Victory was within his grasp, but he seemed strangely apathetic. Maybe the strain of his dual life was already telling on his nerves; maybe Wilfrid Blunt judged rightly when he wrote that "his devotion to Mrs. O'Shea and the worry of his public life were too much for him."

As the curtain rose on the dawn of Home Rule the O'Sheas

once more occupied the center of the stage, the Captain baffled and disappointed in his status, his high hopes dissipated, his finances precarious, and the future threatened by the loss of his political position—for to Willie a seat in Parliament was not only a stepping-stone to higher spheres, it was also a valuable business asset. And, as he contemplated the situation, his temper of an "archangel" was rapidly giving way. As for Katie, she was nervous and overstrung, burdened by the responsibility of her secret negotiations with the Government, frightened not only of Willie's threats but of the ugly rumors and innuendoes that were being circulated about her relationship with Parnell. Circumstances forced the entanglements of the Eltham household into the very center of the political arena, while Home Rule hung in the balance.

To placate Willie by getting him nominated to a constituency, whether it be Nationalist or Liberal, was Katie's one obsession; to obtain her ends she was willing to supplicate Mr. Gladstone, bully Lord Richard Grosvenor, and nag her harassed lover, and the only one who failed to appreciate her determined efforts was the aggrieved husband, who loaded both her and Parnell with contumely and abuse. This time there were no covert attempts at blackmail; O'Shea openly demanded his dues, reminding his wife of Parnell's rash promise made in the first days of their friendship, when he had guaranteed him an Irish seat. And the autumn of 1885 found him at the Shelbourne Hotel in Dublin waiting to claim his pound of flesh. No Antonio brought to judgment before the Court of Venice could have been more sorely tried than the Irish leader. In the midst of his whirlwind electioneering campaign, while delivering clear, confident messages to his people, while framing the basis of the constitution which was to give freedom to his country, he was forced to turn a listening ear to the complaints and grievances of Captain O'Shea. Both O'Connor and O'Kelly told him quite plainly that there was not a constituency in the South that would accept a representative who refused to take the party pledge, and it was then that Katherine, "with her grim determination," forced

him to authorize her to buy Willie a Liberal seat in the North
with the help of the Irish vote. This was a month before he had
signed the manifesto of November 21st, and, though Gladstone
was willing to accept the bargain, the Orangemen of Armagh
showed Willie quite clearly that he was on a wild-goose chase.
After failing in his Northern venture, he gave full vent to his
bitterness, writing to his wife: "All I know is that I am not
going to lie in a ditch. I have been treated in blackguard
fashion, and I mean to get back a stunner. I have everything
ready. No drugs could make me sleep last night, and I packed
my shell with dynamite. It cannot hurt my friend,[1] and it will
send a blackguard's reputation with his deluded countrymen
into smithereens." But not all his threats to expose the negotiations with Chamberlain could alarm Parnell, now that he had
Home Rule within his grasp. He was probably dictated to by
other and more personal reasons. This was the year which saw
the fall of Dilke, when the world was witness as to how the
publicity of the Divorce Courts could ruin the career of one
who was already listed as a future Prime Minister. Even if
Parnell lacked the imagination to draw a parallel, Katie, with
her inward love of respectability, her outward regard of the
conventions, must have read in Dilke's fate a warning to the
effect that it would be wise to propitiate her husband even at
the risk of humiliating her lover. The connections she had established with Mr. Gladstone and Lord Richard Grosvenor now
stood her in good stead. By dint of her exertions her husband
was nominated as a Liberal candidate for the Exchange Division
of Liverpool, regardless of Lord Richard's confessing that "we
don't even know what his politics are." The candidate who
had already been chosen was induced to retire, and Nationalist
members were shocked and bewildered to see Mr. Parnell
"establishing himself for three weeks at Liverpool for no other
reason than to carry O'Shea for the Exchange Division."[2] No
practised wire-puller could have moved her puppets with a

[1] Chamberlain.
[2] *Dillon Papers.*

more consummate cleverness than Mrs. O'Shea, and her "strenuous determination" was worthy of a better cause. She prevailed on Parnell to make his headquarters at Liverpool, where he could "work quietly for Willie" at a time when he had hardly signed the manifesto denouncing the Liberals. T. P. O'Connor, who as President of the Irish National League of Great Britain had been nominated to stand for the one division where the Irish vote was strong enough to return a Nationalist, was surprised to find that his chief had not only decided to contest two other seats, but that he had actually chosen to stand himself for the Exchange Division. T. P. was still more bewildered when at the very last moment Parnell retired from the contest in favor of Captain O'Shea, who, as the Liberal candidate, had been incensing the Irishmen at Liverpool by talking of their leader's perfidy. One can understand the bitterness of those loyal Nationalists who saw the chief driving through the streets with set face and stony eyes, too proud and at the same time too ashamed to acknowledge the cheers of the excited crowds, who little knew that he was on his way to withdraw his candidature in order to support the one man whom he detested and despised. T. P. O'Connor writes: "Here, then, we had the extraordinary spectacle of Mr. Parnell denouncing the Liberal candidates throughout all England with the exception of a few men who had stood by us in our darkest hours . . . and yet supporting a candidate who was a Whig of Whigs, without the excuse of the English Whig in his nationality and his party ties. It was still more astonishing to see the perfectly frenzied efforts which Mr. Parnell made to return this candidate of all others. He spoke dozens of times, went to see everybody whom he could hope to influence and who was supposed to have any power of helping Captain O'Shea, was ubiquitous, persuasive, pathetically appealing to everybody to help in the return of Captain O'Shea. The Irishmen looked on in wonder, some in disgust, but loyal, affectionate, with blind faith in the patriotism and sagacity of their great leader; they obeyed his impulse and worked as hard for Captain O'Shea as if their confidence in him were as great as their distrust."

But all Parnell's efforts could not get Willie returned for Liverpool, and with each successive defeat the claimant, encouraged by the support of Joseph Chamberlain, became more arrogant in his demands. It was O'Shea who was primarily responsible for Chamberlain's enmity to the Irish leader, and now it was O'Shea who was to be used as a cat's-paw in the Radical intrigues for defeating a Home Rule Bill. It was in Chamberlain's interest to have the Captain returned for an Irish seat, and he had not lifted a finger to secure his nomination for Liverpool. This pliable and devoted agent could be extremely useful in stirring up trouble in a Nationalist constituency, and there was one Irish seat that was still available. At the General Election, T. P. O'Connor had been returned both for the Scotland Division of Liverpool and for the town of Galway. When he chose to represent the former, the party asked Parnell to nominate a candidate for Galway, whose inhabitants had been among the first to proclaim his leadership in the early days of the Land League. Nowhere did passions run so high as in this Western town; nowhere did the people display a more bitter antagonism towards all Whigs and place-hunters; and when Parnell, weary and disgusted by his Liverpool campaign, returned to Eltham, where he heard that nothing would satisfy O'Shea short of his nomination to Galway, he regarded the demand as frankly preposterous. But circumstances were to force his hand. Bitterly disappointed by Willie's defeat, overwrought by the strain and worry of the past months, Katie was in the throes of a nervous breakdown, and as she lay sobbing on a couch, full of unreasoning fears for the future, she was so pathetic and appealing that Parnell felt that any sacrifice was worth while that would entail her peace of mind. As Willie fumed and urged his point, with the deadly, nagging persistency which drove his wife to the verge of hysteria, the Irish leader gave way merely in the hope of securing a few weeks' peace for Katie's jangled nerves.

So while Mr. Gladstone's bombshell rent Society in twain,

with ominous reverberations at Windsor, while Lord Hartington wrote his historic letter severing a life-long tie, while the "Red Earl" announced his conversion to Home Rule, and Chamberlain and Morley came to the parting of the ways, the central figure of this great drama took his first step towards his downfall. Mrs. O'Shea relates how he sat one evening gazing into the fire, and said quietly: "It is no matter, Queenie. I was thinking this afternoon that we are giving ourselves much trouble about what really does not concern us. I'll run him for Galway." And, with sudden fierceness: "I'll get him returned. I'll force him down their throats, and he can never again claim that I have promised and not performed. It will cost me the confidence of the party, but that much he shall have and I shall be done with his talk of pledges. . . . We won't mind, Queenie, if it leads to worry and fuss. If it were not for the Bill I should be delighted, and, after all, if the country wants Home Rule it will get it sooner or later. Anyway, what shall be, shall be, and I told T. P. to-night that I meant to propose Willie." Then suddenly he laughed with his dry humor: "You ought to have seen his face, my Queen. He looked as if I had dropped him into an ice-pit."

T. P., genial, loyal and devoted, was dumbfounded at the news. His first instinct was to find Biggar, who expressed his indignation in no mincing terms. Between them they despatched a telegram to Dublin telling Healy to secure the services of the *Freeman* in helping them to oppose O'Shea's nomination. That very night they left for Ireland, and, by the time they got to Holyhead, T. P. had already regretted his hasty action. Perhaps it was the gentle, judicious counsel of young John Redmond, who happened to be traveling by the same train and who made him see that "if Mr. Parnell pinned himself publicly to the support of Captain O'Shea, then it became a question of his leadership; and as his leadership and the national and racial as well as party unity which it symbolized were then the chief hope of the coming proposals of Home Rule, everything was to be sacrificed to that, and even the lesser evil of Captain O'Shea's election was to be accepted."

But Biggar was of sterner stuff. He was not going to stomach that damned Whig as a Nationalist candidate just because he was the husband of Parnell's mistress, and he found a ready supporter in Tim Healy, who loathed the O'Sheas in the way one can only loathe what has helped to destroy one's ideal. Healy's love for his chief had been akin to hero-worship, and as long as he lived he would never forgive Kitty O'Shea for dragging his hero from his pedestal. Parnell the superman had the right to deny him his friendship and to keep him at arm's length, but, now that he had shown himself to be of common clay, Tim bitterly resented his supercilious reserve, his dictatorial attitude, and, as Parnell scented the germs of rebellion, his old kindliness and gentle tolerance changed to a harsh vigilance.

Though Healy's indignation was dictated by more personal motives than that of Joe Biggar, they were equally loud in their declarations of war, and regardless of the fact that O'Shea's candidature was already publicly announced in the *Freeman,* whose proprietor refused to disobey the mandate of his chief, regardless of the fact that O'Brien declined to join them in their revolt, saying, "I had rather blow out my brains than have any responsibility for interfering at the moment with the leadership of Mr. Parnell," and regardless of the fact that T. P., who had poured the first water into the simmering kettle, had announced his determination to await in Dublin the turn of events, Healy and Biggar left for Galway determined to fan a revolt. The town was already in a state of pandemonium, the people furious against O'Shea and clamoring for a local member. Dangerous passions were unloosed, and Parnell's candidate did not dare to make a speech without first ensuring his protection from the priests. In the narrow streets, blue-eyed fishermen from Aran jostled with American reporters; telegrams poured in from all over the world, for millions of Irishmen watched with apprehension the progress of this fatal election. Biggar and Healy kindled the flame, their speeches roused the town, and in his blunt, unpolished fashion the former told the electors of Galway quite plainly that Parnell had chosen O'Shea because he was the husband of his mistress, and, though the *Freeman's Journal* took care to suppress this paragraph in their report, the irremediable mischief had been done. The first blow at Parnell's leadership had been struck by his most loyal and devoted friend, a friend who in his rugged honesty did not hesitate to send him a telegram worded: "Mrs. O'Shea will be your ruin"—a sentence so frighteningly direct that Healy quickly changed it to "The O'Sheas will be your ruin." Public feeling was at fever heat. O'Shea sent supplicating messages begging Parnell to come to his aid. In Dublin there were frenzied meetings and consultations and despair at the aloofness and evasiveness of the chief. For two days he did not give a sign of life either to his candidate in Galway or to the members of the party who were waiting for his orders. It was not until O'Connor and O'Brien had decided to issue a public address of confidence in his leadership, a pledge of support such as would enable him to overcome all opposition, that he announced his intention of personally suppressing the revolt. He arrived in Dublin on the morning of February 9th, and he greeted his distracted colleagues as calmly and as gently as if the Galway election was of no account, apologizing for his delay by saying, "I am rather hard to start, but when I do, I keep on." Accompanied by O'Connor and a band of faithful supporters, he left immediately for Galway.

In the conflicting accounts of Healy and O'Connor one can recapture some of the passion and hysteria of those crowded nightmare days, during which the only two men who kept their nerve and self-possession were Biggar and Parnell. Their iron will and lack of imagination made them impervious to the emotions of the crowd, and it was characteristic of them both that all the hard and cruel words that were spoken never had the slightest effect on their personal relationship. What Parnell might resent in Healy he tolerated in Biggar, who, as T. P. O'Connor said, "was a strange mixture of love for his chief and hatred of such doings as this election and such companionship as that of Captain O'Shea." When he was asked as to how Mr. Parnell would be received, he did not hesitate one second before answering, "Mob him, of course."

At Galway station was gathered a seething, hostile crowd, armed with their blackthorns and spoiling for a fight, and, as Parnell stepped off the train, he was assailed by angry cries in place of the usual resounding cheers. Never had he borne himself more proudly, never had he shown himself more indifferent to public opinion. Smiling his casual pleasant smile, he seemed to be utterly unaware of their dark, threatening faces, and, cowed by his dominating personality, his undefinable magnetism, the crowds fell apart and let him pass in peace. But they had to have someone on whom to vent their fury, and the unfortunate victim was their late member, whom they now regarded as responsible for their troubles. T. P. would have been seriously injured had not Parnell fought his way back through the mob, seized him by the arm, and marched him off to the hotel, superbly contemptuous of the thousand blackthorns which still menaced their safety.

It was his courage and his pride which carried the election—the coolness with which he confronted Healy and Biggar in the sitting-room of the railway hotel, the smiling patience with which he listened to their arguments, the gentleness with which he responded to their taunts. Then he spoke in that quiet, unemotional voice, where every word was clear-cut and definite: "A rumor has been spread that if Captain O'Shea is withdrawn, I would retire from the party. I have no intention of resigning my position; I would not resign it if the people of Galway were to kick me through the streets to-day." An onlooker records that he "said this fateful sentence quietly, without brag, perhaps even with the suggestion of the sadness of the man tied by imperative duty to the stake." But these few words conquered Healy, who fell once more beneath the old spell, and Biggar was left to fight the struggle single-handed. The vital issue was now settled, and O'Shea was to be the Nationalist candidate for Galway, but the people had still to be pacified—those fierce young

Nationalists who were being forced against their will to accept their leader's nominee; those angry, dissatisfied crowds who now swarmed into the little tumbledown hall where he had promised to address them. As he stood on the narrow, swaying platform, he must have known for one moment the meaning of fear, their dark, sullen faces were so close to him, their shouts were so loud in his ears. As he had staked his leadership on this election, he would make them understand what his leadership entailed. Stretching forth one hand, he cried, "I have a Parliament for Ireland within the hollow of my hand. Destroy me, and you take away that Parliament." And the men of Galway, who knew nothing of the secrets of Whitehall, listened with bated breath. He had awed them into silence, and he brought his weapon home; "Reject Captain O'Shea, destroy me, and there will arise a shout from all the enemies of Ireland, 'Parnell is beaten, Ireland has no longer a leader.'" He paused; the crowd was subjugated, and in that serried mass of human beings there was only one man who dared to stand up to him— Biggar, the little humpbacked Ulsterman, who, elbowing his way to the front of the crowd, declared his determination to stand by the local candidate.

Captain O'Shea was accepted, but there were no cheers and no enthusiasm. With his ruthless will Parnell had forced him on the people of Galway; he had forced men like O'Brien to canvass in his favor; he had forced O'Connor to betray his old electors; and now they were to witness a strange scene. They were to participate at a dinner given by their chief, to which both Biggar and Healy were invited, but to which the Nationalist candidate for Galway was not requested. For, though Parnell spoke at O'Shea's meetings, and superintended all the arrangements at the polls, faithfully carrying out his bargain, he avoided him in private. The public charges of Biggar, the insinuations of Healy, had rendered friendly intercourse impossible, and from now onwards O'Shea was his avowed and open enemy.

O'Brien describes the end of that strange evening, when

Parnell drew him into his room, and, "with something more like a sob than ever before or after escaped his breath," confessed, "I know all that my friends' action to-day meant. They will never regret it for the country's sake. It was the first favor I ever asked from my countrymen, and it will be the last."

CHAPTER THIRTY-THREE

On April 8th, 1886, Mr. Gladstone moved the first reading of the Home Rule Bill among scenes of unparalleled excitement. Not even the Great Reform Bill of 1832, nor even the fight for Catholic Emancipation, had drawn such crowds to Westminster. There were members who waited outside the doors all night in order to secure their places; there were men who offered a thousand pounds for a seat in the Strangers' Gallery. Every available inch of the floor of the House was stacked with chairs; princes, ambassadors, peers and prelates jostled one another in the galleries; diplomats and journalists thronged the lobbies, and it is said that the very vaults beneath the chamber were crowded with members who had failed to obtain a seat. The country and the whole world waited for Mr. Gladstone's speech. For a short space the majesty of his presence, the glamor of his name and the magic of his voice, which enabled him to weave even the intricate details of finance into a spell of enchantment, subjugated his audience. For that short space men forgot the wranglings in the Cabinet, the ominous resignations, the pressure of Parnell and the bitterness of public feeling. As Morley commented, "Few are the heroic moments in our parliamentary politics but this was one."

Six weeks before one of his colleagues had asked Mr. Gladstone, "Will you really go on if you have not Hartington and Chamberlain with you?" And the old man had answered: "I shall go on if I have nobody with me." In this dauntless spirit he confronted his greatest adversary, an adversary whom with a little understanding and a little magnanimity he might still have kept as a supporter. When Joseph Chamberlain was offered a post in the Cabinet of 1886, he professed himself willing to give unprejudiced examination to the more extensive proposals of Irish self-government, on the condition that he should be left "unlimited liberty of judgment and rejection." Finding himself momentarily stranded between two parties, he preferred to join his old chief rather than enter into alliance with his arch-enemy Lord Hartington. It is maintained that if Mr. Gladstone had fairly recognized his talents by creating him a Secretary of State, a reconciliation might still have been effected, but once again his just claims were ignored. After declining the eminently unsuitable post of First Lord of the Admiralty, he was forced to content himself with the Presidency of the Local Government Board, while his old friend and ally, John Morley, was elevated to the post of Irish Secretary, with Lord Aberdeen as Viceroy. He soon realized that his hope of modifying the coming Home Rule Bill and of counteracting the influence of Parnell was vain, for Spencer and Morley were the only two members of the Cabinet whom the Prime Minister consulted on the Irish question. A rupture was inevitable, and the crisis came in the Cabinet meeting of March 26th. It was on this day that Mr. Gladstone first revealed the basis of his Home Rule scheme, by which he proposed to establish an Irish Parliament and Executive for the management and control of Irish affairs, reserving for the Imperial Parliament the following subjects: the army, navy, militia, defense, foreign and colonial relations, the endowment of religion, dignities, titles, trade, post office and coinage. Ireland's contribution to the imperial revenue was to be one-fifteenth of the whole, the Dublin police was to remain under imperial control for two years, and the Royal Irish Constabulary for an indefinite period, but eventually they were both to be handed over to the Irish Parliament. Then came the two controversial points: the Irish members were to be excluded from Westminster and the rights of customs and excise were to be given to their Parliament. Mr. Gladstone had barely laid his proposals on the table when both Chamberlain and Trevelyan announced their resignation, and it is recorded that the Prime Minister made not the slightest effort to detain them. But a few days later he was faced with opposition from other quarters; his old friend Hugh Childers proposed to throw up the post of Home Secretary if the rights of customs and excise were handed over to the Irish legislature, and this time he gave way rather than risk another resignation. It was his first sign of weakening, his first attempt to conciliate his party, and it brought him fresh trouble from the Irish camp, where Parnell, regardless of the mere ornamental details of the constitution, was grimly determined to save every penny for his country. As hard-fisted as an Irish peasant, no gratitude or consideration for Mr. Gladstone would prevent him from fighting for the best terms he could get. On one occasion he declared, "An Irish custom-house is really of more importance to Ireland than an Irish Parliament." And, in the crowded, breathless days before the introduction of the Bill, he would spend hours closeted with Morley, showing himself to be "acute, frank, patient, closely attentive, and possessed of striking, though not rapid, insight: never slurring over difficulties, nor trying to pretend that rough was smooth . . . measuring the ground with a slow and careful eye, and fixing tenaciously on the thing that was essential to the moment." What was the good of an Irish legislature stripped of its natural revenues? What was the point of talking of the restoration of Grattan's Parliament when the custom-houses of the Liffey were to be managed from Whitehall? Parnell never gave Mr. Gladstone any credit for the heroism of his venture; he was just a great parliamentary trickster whom one had to watch carefully all the time. What seems hardly credible is the fact that Gladstone and Parnell met only once during the weeks of the preparation of the Bill. The latter complained to William O'Brien: "I have time and again pressed that we should be better able to get to business by personal contact, and the old gentleman dodges the suggestion." Then he laughed incredulously: "Upon my word, I think he is afraid of me!" The Prime Minister, carefully guarded by his loving and anxious family, surrounded by an admiring group of faithful satellites, had a horror of conversations which might develop into arguments, arguments which might betray him into committing some tactical error. He preferred to rely on the accuracy and fidelity of his Irish Secretary, and failing Morley there was always Mrs. O'Shea.

But Parnell forced an interview three days before the introduction of the Bill, and Morley notes in his diary: "Mr. Parnell
came to my room at the House at 8.30 and we talked for two
hours. At 10.30 I went to Mr. Gladstone next door and told
him how things stood. He asked me to open the points of discussion, and into my room we went. He shook hands cordially
with Mr. Parnell and sat down between him and me. We at
once got to work, Parnell extraordinarily close, tenacious and
sharp. It was all finance. At midnight Mr. Gladstone rose in
his chair and said: 'I fear I must go. I cannot sit as late as I
used to do.' 'Very clever, very clever,' he muttered to me, as I
held open the door of his room for him. I returned to Parnell,
who went on repeating his points in his impenetrable way, until
the policeman mercifully came to say the House was up."

When, late at night, the Irish leader left John Morley's room
to find William O'Brien still working in the deserted library,
he was grave and almost awed by his encounter with the Grand
Old Man. With that sudden naïveté which was such a contrast
to his usual frigid composure, he said: "I never saw him closely
before. He is such an old, old man. His face is a bunch of
wrinkles. He had the wide, open eyes of a fine animal in a
fright. Once, when he yawned, I really thought he was dying,
but he flared up again. He will never live to see this through."

Three days later the veteran Prime Minister, inspired by some
superhuman force, delivered a speech lasting three and a half
hours to a rapt, attentive House, till it seemed as if the music
of his oratory could sway even the hard hearts of the dissentient
Liberals. But next morning, when the bourgeoisie of England
perused their *Times* over their bacon and eggs, they read Mr.
Gladstone's speech in more prosaic a mood. The average respectable taxpayer saw the Home Rule Bill as a threat to the
integrity of the Empire, an abject surrender to the Irish rebels,
and hitherto faithful followers of the Liberal patriarch now
firmly removed his portrait from their walls. In the upper
spheres of society, political passions ran high; families were di-

vided, old friends were estranged, ladies of the great Whig houses no longer called on Mrs. Gladstone, and frigid duchesses cut Lord Spencer in the street. The months which passed between the first and second readings of the Bill witnessed many a strange phenomenon. For the first time Lord Hartington and Lord Salisbury were to be seen on the same platform, and for the first time for many a year Mr. Chamberlain and Lord Hartington exchanged friendly communications. In this intermediate period vain attempts were made to patch up the differences, and once more Labouchere performed with zest the rôle of a "friendly broker." But then Mr. Gladstone committed his first great blunder by introducing a Land Purchase Bill for buying out the Irish landlords, a scheme which met with a cool reception from every quarter. His generous intention of creating a peasant proprietary in Ireland, of settling simultaneously the two chief planks of the Land League platform, was ruined in Parnellite eyes not only by the high terms he asked from the tenants, but by the fact that a Receiver General was to be appointed under British authority to receive the rents and revenues of Ireland while the scheme was in operation. But its death-blow came, not from Dublin, but from Birmingham. Gladstone was beginning to appreciate the strength of Chamberlain's antagonism, and, in order to placate him, he was ready to throw his Land Bill overboard. And Morley writes: "The Purchase Bill proved from the first to be an almost intolerable dose. Vivid pictures were drawn of a train of railway trucks, two miles long, loaded with millions of bright sovereigns, all traveling from the pocket of the British son of toil to the pocket of the Irish landlord."

The rights of customs and excise were now lost for Ireland, and behind the scenes at Westminster there were gloomy consultations following stern ultimatums from either Chamberlain or Parnell. If the Prime Minister yielded to the Radical leader, whose insistence on the retention of the Irish members in the British Parliament was merely an excuse for altering the whole structure of the Bill, then Parnell threatened to abstain from voting on the second reading. As Mr. Garvin writes: "He cared nothing for Liberalism; he only disliked it; he loved neither ministers nor their Bill. Its denial of tariff freedom, and nearly all its financial clauses, he detested. More than once he thought of throwing out the Gladstonians. Had they yielded to Chamberlain's terms he would have thrown them out. The Bill was his minimum."

On May 10th Mr. Gladstone moved the second reading of the Home Rule Bill. Lord Hartington proposed the amendment in the form of a simple rejection, and there followed a debate which lasted till June 7th; a debate during which ambitious orators ransacked the House of Commons library in search of quotations from Burke and Grattan, from Pitt and Castlereagh, and for the first time Englishmen heard from the lips of their own countrymen of the iniquities of the Union. Even now there were members in the Cabinet who urged on Mr. Gladstone the necessity of a compromise with Highbury, and the rumor spread that Mr. Chamberlain would assent to the second reading if the Bill was subsequently hung up.

The Prime Minister was wavering, and there was panic in the Irish camp, where certain members declared themselves willing to abide by the decision of the Cabinet. That was not Parnell's way. Through John Morley he sent a formal challenge to the Prime Minister, and the Irish Secretary records a second meeting with "Parnell, courteous enough, but depressed and gloomy, Mr. Gladstone worn and fagged." At the eleventh hour, the Irish leader firmly and deliberately proposed to kill the Bill rather than to see it being slowly destroyed by the Radical cabal.

No compromise could now satisfy the demands of Highbury. Embittered and disappointed, Chamberlain prepared for war, Labouchere retired discomforted, and at five o'clock on May 31st the Radical leader summoned a meeting of his followers in the ill-fated Committee Room 15, which four years later was to be the scene of a still more tragic upheaval. It was this meeting which doomed the Home Rule Bill. Fifty-five members were given the alternative either to abstain from voting or to veto the measure; pressure was put upon them in the form of a letter from John Bright, in which he announced his intention of voting against the second reading. There is no doubt that the decision of this venerable pundit, who in the past had always been the first to advocate justice for Ireland, now helped to turn the scales.

On June 7th the debate on the Home Rule Bill was brought to an end, and it was on this night that Parnell delivered one of the greatest speeches of his life. Up till now he had kept unobtrusively in the background, taking no part in the debate, slipping quietly into his seat wearing a rough tweed suit and shapeless hat, so that to the casual observer he might have been some obscure country member, centered in his local interests and oblivious of the tremendous issues at stake.

To-night he was a great statesman, pleading his country's cause, in a speech "which made even the able disputants on either side look little better than amateurs." In slow, vibrating tones he dealt with the loyal minority of Ulster, the settlement of education, the question of finance—all the thorny, controversial points brought forward by members of the Opposition—and he ended his speech with an impassioned appeal: "I am convinced there are a sufficient number of wise and just members in this House to cause it to disregard appeals made to passion, and to choose the better way of founding peace and goodwill among nations. And when the members of the division lobby come to be told, it will also be told for the admiration of all future generations that England and her Parliament in this nineteenth century were wise enough, brave enough, and generous enough to close the strife of centuries and to give peace and prosperity to suffering Ireland."

But, being a realist, he knew even as he spoke that the Bill was doomed. He had no belief in British generosity; of Mr. Gladstone and the English people he thought what he had always thought of them—they would do what he could make them do. The Irish vote was not omnipotent, and fifty-five dissentient Radicals had turned the scales. The Home Rule Bill was rejected in a full House by 343 to 313 votes, and, as Chamberlain returned from the lobby where he had voted against the Bill, Parnell commented audibly: "There goes the man who killed Home Rule!" Not all the angry cries of the Irish members directed against "Judas Chamberlain" were more charged with venom than those quiet words of their leader.

The fight was over, and once more the country was in the throes of a General Election, an election embittered by the hostility of old colleagues, the throwing overboard of old loyalties, the sundering of old ties. The Conservatives and the Liberal Unionists made strange bedfellows, and, when the results at the polls proved the country to be unfavorable to Home Rule, Lord Salisbury proposed that Lord Hartington should form a Cabinet rather than to undertake himself such an unenviable task. Mightier men than Lord Salisbury might quail at the prospect of resisting the formidable attacks of both Mr. Gladstone and his Irish allies. They were in a strong position, and he himself had helped to put many a useful weapon in their hands. Only eight months after he had authorized his Viceroy to discuss possible terms with Parnell, only six months after the Newport speech, where he had practically apologized for boycotting, he had declared on a public platform that Ireland was not one nation, but two nations; that there were races, like the Hottentots and even the Hindoos, incapable of self-government; and that it was impossible to place confidence in people who had acquired the habit of using knives and slugs. His policy for such a country was twenty years of firm and resolute government, adding: "At the end of that time you will find that Ireland will be fit to accept any gifts in the way of local government or repeal of coercion laws that you may wish to give her." Lord Salisbury's "Hottentot" speech was an invaluable weapon in Liberal hands, but, on the other hand, there was Joseph Chamberlain reminding Sir William Harcourt that he was now "stewing in his own

Parnellite juice," bitterly sarcastic about his old friend John Morley, who "told me some time ago that he did not want to be admiral of the fleet, but that he would not consent to be a powder-monkey. He has now changed his ship and his captain, but his position in the Service is much the same as before." In a brilliant speech, delivered at the Eighty Club on the morrow of defeat, the gentle, cultured scholar, who had been caught up in the turmoil of Irish affairs, hit back as hard as he had got. Comparing Gladstone's fall to the assassination of Cæsar, he quoted: "Look, in this place ran Cassius' dagger through. See what a rent the envious Casca made. Through this the well-beloved Brutus stabb'd." And from this day Chamberlain was "Casca" to his old colleagues.

Never had politics been more cynical on the one hand and more sincere on the other. While Lord Randolph Churchill traveled to Belfast, in order to incite the Orangemen to riot, fanning religious hatred and drenching the streets in blood for no other purpose than to oust the Nationalists from their Ulster seats, Mr. Gladstone toured the great cities of the North, preaching his new creed with all the fervor of a religious convert. In this bewildering state of party politics, Lord Hartington preferred to hold the balance rather than to control a Cabinet, and, when Parliament met on August 5th, Lord Salisbury was Prime Minister, with Lord Randolph Churchill as Chancellor of the Exchequer and Leader of the House and Sir Michael Hicks-Beach as Irish Secretary. It was not until some months later, when Sir Michael resigned owing to ill health, that the system of a firm and resolute government for Ireland was seriously enforced. At the beginning, the new Cabinet showed themselves disposed to rule the country by ordinary law; there were the usual Land Commissions and lengthy reports on the progress of Irish industries, but, unfortunately, the Agrarian question, which during the past year had been temporarily eclipsed in the excitement of the Home Rule struggle, once more came to the forefront. To the average Irish farmer the situation was more desperate than ever; the heavy fall of prices, combined with

the bad harvest, had brought them again to the brink of ruin,
and the Tory landlords, encouraged by the defeat of their opponents, once more threatened evictions. Though the Government
was willing to appoint the usual Royal Commission, it refused
to consider the Land Bill which the Irish Leader introduced at
the very beginning of the session. Owing to the serious fall in
prices, he advocated a reduction of rents, and the suspension of
evictions, but his Bill was thrown out in spite of his warning the
Government that, unless it made some attempt to meet the
Agrarian crisis, that winter would see the outbreak of another
Land war. He himself had no intention of fanning the revolt;
his one idea was to keep the country quiet, to run the movement
on strictly constitutional lines now that he had secured a Liberal
alliance. Though he had no great love for Mr. Gladstone, his
friendship was preferable to that of the Fords and Finertys who
ruled the Clan-na-Gael. Parnell was certainly no revolutionary,
and there were times when even his colleagues wondered what
were his politics. As a journalist once wrote of him: "His mind
was spacious, and his few ideas had room to take large root and
grow great." Political alliances, revolutionary methods, legal or
illegal agitations, were all just means to an end. At heart Parnell was probably a Separatist; at heart he probably dreamed of
an Irish Republic, for he had no sense of loyalty either to the
Crown or to the Empire, but his Parliament in Dublin would
have been run on Conservative lines, and the gentlemen of Ireland would have remained masters of their land. Just as in 1881
it had suited his purposes to tell one of his American audiences
that "we are obliged to make the situation a very hot one indeed.
It is impossible that the great cause can be won without shed-
ding a drop of blood," so now he disapproved of any action that
"would fetter the Old Man in his appeal to England." He even
managed to exercise control over the rival camps of the Clan-
na-Gael, and at the Chicago Convention of 1886 some of the
leading apostles of dynamite paid tribute to the success of his
policy.

Now comes the period of Parnell's life about which there have been so many suppositions, so many unfair rumors. For years he had been an invalid, suffering from kidney trouble, with severe gastric attacks which undermined his whole constitution. Only his tremendous will-power had enabled him to stand the strain of the past few months, and there followed the inevitable reaction. Men who had always been accustomed to think of him as an invalid were horrified to see the ghastly change that had suddenly come over him. His face was ashen, his body was flabby and emaciated at the same time, and in his eyes was the look of death. The tragic deterioration of his splendid physique had communicated itself to the smallest details of his personal appearance. He allowed his beard to grow ragged and untrimmed, and his hair to remain uncut until it grew almost to his shoulders; he who had always been so smart and trim now wandered about the House of Commons wearing clothes so peculiar and so shabby that they might almost have been a form of disguise. That satirical observer, Sir Henry Lucy, has left us a cruel description of the Parnell of this period:

"He would suddenly appear in a yellow-ocher rough suit, or with the crown of his head shaven, or with his hair brushed back behind his ears, almost to his shoulders. Sometimes he wears his yellow-ocher pantaloons crowned by a pot hat of rich brown hue. On the whole the dress is a triumph of laborious art, giving Mr. Parnell an appearance which is a cross between Mr. Oscar Wilde and a scarecrow."

Another peculiarity of these days was that, however neglected and careless he might be in his dress, he invariably wore a precious stone on his finger and a white flower in his button-hole. Both were worn for sentimental reasons, as they were the gifts of Mrs. O'Shea.

"Parnell is half mad. We always act without him." So wrote Tim Healy in 1885; but there was nothing mad about Parnell during the Galway election, or during the Home Rule fight. He was weak, perhaps, weak in giving way to the woman he loved, in risking his leadership for her sake, but it was the

normal weakness of the adoring lover. Still, there were strange
rumors and nervous whispers casting doubts on his sanity. All
during the previous session his manner towards his colleagues
had been harsh and overstrained. The slightest attempt at con-
tradiction had been sufficient to send him into a wild fury, and,
now that the struggle was over, it seemed as if he had been
drained of all life and vitality. A short stay at Aughavanagh, a
temporary holiday at Eastbourne, had not enabled him to re-
cuperate his health, and when he left the House of Commons
after the rejection of his Land Bill he looked a dying man.
There followed one of his mysterious disappearances, which the
Press accounted for in a hundred different ways. Some papers
said he was in America, others in Rome; there were reporters
who claimed to have seen him in Paris cafés, in company with
some leading Communists, and others who maintained that he
had gone to Switzerland for the sake of his health. Some said
he was taking a brief holiday, others that he had thrown up the
Home Rule sponge in despair, and among these idle, gossiping
paragraphs were a few launched with a deadly intent, and
charged with venom. Already on May 24th, 1886, the *Pall Mall
Gazette* had started on its campaign of defamation. In glaring
headlines it had published a notice on "Mr. Parnell's Suburban
Retreat," referring to an unfortunate episode when, driving home
to Eltham after midnight, Parnell's carriage had come into collision with a market-gardener's cart, an accident which led to
his recognition. Mr. Stead of the *Pall Mall Gazette* now com-
pleted the work begun at Galway; the Parnell-O'Shea liaison
was public property. The injured husband could no longer
feign indifference, he could no longer ignore the sneers of his
colleagues, and his position as a Nationalist member was un-
tenable. Not only did he abstain from voting on the second
reading of the Home Rule Bill, but the following day he applied
for the Chiltern Hundreds. Amicable relations between husband
and wife were no longer possible, and both Katie and her lover

must have realized that even the heaviest bribes would not keep Willie silent for ever.

Parnell's illness could not have come at a more unfortunate moment; he left his lieutenants without direction as to the policy of the coming winter. His secretary, who forwarded his post from the House of Commons, had orders to keep his whereabouts strictly secret, and it would have been far better had his followers known that he was lying at death's door rather than that they should have suspected him of frivoling at Eltham, for Michael Davitt voiced the opinion of the majority when he complained to Wilfrid Blunt: "It makes one's blood boil, at a time when every man of us should be working night and day, that he should be idling away at Captain O'Shea's. There are a hundred people at the moment in London waiting to see him on important business, and nobody can say where he is. When I see that old man, Gladstone, attending meetings night after night, in every part of the country, and think that our leader will not take the trouble to look in for half an hour at a single meeting here in London, I wonder our people are able to be patient. . . . It is the same about answering your letters, about deciding anything. People praise him and talk of him as if he were managing everything, and it is nothing of the sort. He is a mere *laissez-faire* leader." But at that very time Parnell was consulting an eminent specialist under an assumed name, and a few weeks later a Mr. Stewart, suffering from a severe nervous breakdown, accentuated by acute gastric trouble, was lying dangerously ill in a South London nursing-home. Weeks of insomnia, coupled with those strange nervous attacks from which he had suffered since childhood, the worry and strain both of his public and his private life, had proved too much for him. Some have said that he was mad; some have hinted that he suffered from that terrible malady which affects so many great men; parallels have been drawn between him and his tragic ancestors; but, though he had certain eccentricities and peculiarities, they were only those of the strong individualist; though at times he suffered from persecution mania, it was only the natural outcome of a life in which he was not allowed one moment's freedom. Even his morbid suspicions can be accounted for when one considers that he was constantly moving in an atmosphere of cabals and intrigues. Now a general debility had brought him to the verge of death, and when one judges the Parnell of the last five years, one must remember that he was a sick man, both in mind and body.

CHAPTER THIRTY-FOUR

In the late autumn Parnell's lieutenants took matters into their own hands, and the launching of "the plan of campaign" was a signal for another Land war. Though Tim Harrington, the secretary of the National League, was the official author of the plan, its chief instigators and abettors were John Dillon and William O'Brien, neither of whom had taken kindly to the more orthodox trend of Nationalist politics, resulting from the Liberal alliance. Both were men of transparent honesty and sincerity of purpose, both had the dangerous power of inflaming the mob by the very force and violence of their convictions, and it was these two men who all unwittingly came forward to challenge Parnell's dictatorship. Dillon had but lately returned to the country, but O'Brien was already firmly rooted in the hearts of the people. In 1886, while on an Irish visit, Wilfrid Blunt writes that "the two really popular men are O'Brien and Davitt." But, oddly enough, the latter would have nothing to do with the plan of campaign. It has been somewhat cruelly suggested that he resented it because it was not his own idea, and that he took advantage of Parnell's disapproval of the renewed Agrarian agitation in order to excuse himself from joining the movement. But Davitt was the last man to suffer any dictation or advice; on more than one occasion his independent views had been the cause of friction in the party; he had quarreled with most of his colleagues owing to his refusal to subordinate himself to the wishes of his chief and his insistence on remaining a free lance in Nationalist politics. They resented how he still kept up his old connections with the American secret societies, for, now that they were welcomed on Liberal platforms and lionized by society hostesses, men like Healy and Sexton would have liked to forget the fact that their parliamentary salaries were still paid out of funds which were largely supplied by American gunmen. In this respect their leader was more perspicacious than they, for, though he had had his differences with Davitt, though he had

316

denounced his policy of land nationalization, they had always kept up friendly relations, and the ex-Fenian was still the unofficial intermediary between him and the Clan-na-Gael.

As regards the Agrarian agitation, Davitt was both embittered and disappointed; he had seen his advice ignored and his schemes dismissed, and now he refused to identify himself with the new plan long before Parnell had made any definite statement on the question. The scheme which was first brought forward by Timothy Harrington in the columns of *United Ireland* proposed that on every estate where a reasonable abatement of rent had been refused, the tenants should join together in resisting their landlords by contributing the sum of what would be a fair rent to a common fund under the control of a managing committee. This committee would then be in a position either to prevail upon the proprietors to accept a reduced rent or otherwise to support the tenants in cases of ejectment and sale. This was the rough basis of the plan of campaign which spread like wildfire through the west and south of Ireland, where it met with an instantaneous success. Parnell's "Tenants' Relief Bill," which had been contemptuously dismissed by the Government, was now forced on some of the largest landowners. Before the plan had been two months in operation it had been accepted by Lord Dillon in Mayo, by Lord Dunsandle in Galway, and by Lord de Freyne in Roscommon, but unfortunately it was attended by the usual inflammatory speeches, followed by incidents of Agrarian crime, and before long the leaders of the movement were once more at daggers drawn with the Irish Executive. Mr. Dillon's speeches were those of a revolutionary agitator rather than those of a constitutional politician, and the fact that he spoke of Mr. Gladstone as an ally considerably embarrassed the Liberal leaders. It was impossible for them to approve of an illegal association based on a system of blackmail and intimidation, but they were not going to express any definite opinions until they had sounded Mr. Parnell's views on the subject.

Immediately after the General Election the Irish leader had been informed that in Mr. Gladstone's opinion "it would be a mistake for English and Irish to aim at uniform action in Parliament. Motives could not be at all points the same. Liberals were bound to keep in view (next to what the Irish question might require) the reunion of the Liberal party. The Irish were bound to have special regard to the opinion and circumstances of Ireland." The truth of this statement was soon proved, for the winter which saw the launching of the plan of campaign saw the ignominious failure of the Round Table Conference, started in the forlorn hopes of reuniting the Liberal party.

For two months Parnell had been lying dangerously ill, so ill that he "could not put pen to paper or even read a newspaper," and it was not until the beginning of December that he had sufficient strength to resume his political duties. By that time the new movement was well under way, and Mr. Dillon's violent speeches must have been unpleasant reading to a convalescent neurasthenic. He had never liked Dillon, and now all his old bitterness returned, but it was not only this personal distrust which made him disapprove of the plan. He regarded it as a tactical error which would have grave consequences by plunging the Nationalists into disrepute with their Liberal allies, by plunging Ireland once more into the horrors of Agrarian warfare which would inevitably lead to coercion. Parnell could see a mile where his followers could see a yard, and he was well aware what Lord Salisbury's "twenty years of firm and resolute government" might bring in the way of coercion. Then there was the financial question to be considered, for, as soon as the landlords were effectively supported by Dublin Castle, they were bound to rain evictions. Messrs. Dillon and O'Brien would then expect the League funds to subsidize the tenants whom they had incited to revolt, and Parnell had no intention of crippling the party by this needless expenditure.

On December the 7th he paid a visit to John Morley, who records: "Mr. Parnell called, looking very ill and worn. He wished to know what I thought of the effect of the plan of campaign on public opinion. 'If you mean in Ireland,' I said, 'of course I have no view, and it would be worth nothing if I had.

In England the effect is wholly bad; it offends almost more than the outrages.' He said he had been very ill and had taken no part, so he stands free and uncommitted; he was anxious to have it fully understood that the fixed point in his tactics is to maintain the alliance with the English Liberals. . . . He would send for one of his lieutenants and would press for an immediate cessation of the violent speeches."

Five days later Morley notes again: "Mr. Parnell came and we had a prolonged conversation. The lieutenant had come over and had defended the plan of campaign. Mr. Parnell persevered in his dissent and disapproval, and they parted with the understanding that the meetings should be dropped and the movement calmed as much as could be. I told him that I had heard from Mr. Gladstone, and that he could not possibly show any tolerance for illegalities."

The lieutenant was William O'Brien, who has left a curious, if somewhat melodramatic, account of an interview which took place on a foggy December morning in a secluded corner of Greenwich Park. His account differs considerably from the one given by Mrs. O'Shea, who states that Mr. O'Brien visited Mr. Parnell at her house at Eltham, and that Mr. Parnell was still lying ill in bed and had specially to get up in order to receive his "uninvited guest," but Mrs. O'Shea's book is neither accurate nor truthful, for she has the unfortunate predilection of making herself the center of every dramatic situation, and, however indiscreet Parnell may have been in his infatuation, he never went to the length of entertaining his colleagues in his mistress's drawing-room. It is true that O'Brien called at Eltham, but it was merely in order to verify an address which Parnell had omitted from the telegram, and his enquiries only brought him a frigid answer through the maidservant to the effect that the last time Mrs. O'Shea had heard from Mr. Parnell he was in some nursing-home in the Old Kent Road, the number of which she had forgotten. Katherine was not only resentful of any Irish member who had the slightest influence over her "King," but she also cherished a personal grudge against William

O'Brien, whom she had never forgiven for having once openly insulted her husband in the House of Commons. Before the bitter quarrels of that summer she had guarded Willie's reputation as jealously as her own.

In his search for the picturesque, Mr. O'Brien is also guilty of several inaccuracies and over-statements. Though Greenwich Park on a cold, foggy morning is not an ideal meeting-place, it was probably chosen not on account of some mad fancy emanating from a sick man's brain, but simply because it was both near Parnell's nursing-home, where he was still undergoing treatment, and within easy driving distance of London. O'Brien describes this rather dreary park as an "infernal place," and it seems to have inspired him to depict Parnell as one of those haunted figures in the drawings of Gustave Doré.

"I suddenly came upon Parnell's figure emerging from the gloom in a guise so strange and with a face so ghastly that the effect could have scarcely been more startling if it was his ghost I had met wandering in the eternal shades. He wore a gigantic fur cap, a shooting jacket of rough tweed, a knitted woolen vest of bright scarlet, and a pair of shooting- or wading-boots reaching to the thighs—a costume that could not well have looked more bizarre in a dreary London park, if the effect had been to attract and not to escape observation. But the overpowering fascination lay in the unearthly, half-extinguished eyes, flickering mournfully out of their deep caverns, the complexion of dead clay, the overgrown fair beard, and the locks rolling down behind almost to the shoulders. It was the apparition of a poet plunged in some divine anguish, or a mad scientist mourning over the fate of some forlorn invention."

When he heard that O'Brien was going around giving this description to his friends, Parnell complained bitterly: "All I got from getting up to see O'Brien was that he went about telling people that I was insane." But the imaginative journalist does not give a fanciful account of the interview itself, for he admits that "Parnell came straight to business" and before the day was out he was once more in admiration of his clear insight and cool logic. Every word the chief uttered was direct and to the point. He disapproved of the plan; he repeated the opinion of Gladstone's representative to show how it was damaging them with their new allies. He proposed that the authors of the plan should set bounds to their operations rather than that the party should be bankrupted and disowned by the Liberals, adding: "The farmers had the chance of their lives in the 'No Rent' days, and they left us in the lurch. So they will leave you when they hear the crack of a sharp Coercion Act in their ears. You won't get the Nonconformists to stomach the plan of fighting the landlords with their own rents, neither will you get the priests."

And when he heard that Archbishop Croke and the Bishop of Clonfert had already given their blessings to the campaign, he shook his head, and said in his quiet, prophetic way: "That's all very well until the day's going against you. The Irish priests individually are splendid fellows, but in a semi-revolutionary movement like ours, a time comes sooner or later when a priest has to choose between Rome and Ireland, and he will always choose Rome. I hear Norfolk is busy there already." A papal rescript denouncing the plan of campaign proved his prophecy to be correct. As a Protestant he declined to take any part in defying the Vatican or negotiating with the papal nuncio. On one occasion he calmly referred to the pontifical denunciation as "a document from a distant country, leaving his Catholic countrymen to justify their conscience in their own way."

During this interview he showed no bitterness except with regard to John Dillon and Tim Healy, whom he suspected of being at the back of the whole business. He had never forgiven Healy for the Galway election, and that spring they had had their first serious quarrel, when he had discovered that in the course of some negotiations with Labouchere his ambitious follower had accepted to dine with Joseph Chamberlain. Healy was still a useful tool and Parnell was the first to admit that he was the only one among his followers who had the head of a politician, but he no longer trusted him. As regards Dillon, the article in *The Times* which stated that "Mr. Dillon's energy was

to be accounted for by the fact that a section of a party of disorder had been always jealous of Mr. Parnell's ascendency," did
not tend to ease his suspicions. *The Times* was particularly
versed in the art of sowing dissension among the Nationalist
party, in planting cunning thrusts in the weak spots of their
armor, and in its implacable hostility to Ireland the great Government organ was about to risk its reputation and good name in a
desperate venture instigated by fools and swindlers.

It was during this winter that a certain Mr. Edward Caulfield
Houston, secretary of the Irish Loyal and Patriotic Union, called
for the third time on Mr. Buckle of *The Times,* bringing "a
black bag" containing incriminating documents and letters, in
which there was sufficient evidence to annihilate both Parnell
and Parnellism. Mr. Houston's previous visits had been in the
spring and in the summer, and each time the editor had declined
to make use of his loyal services; but now a new Government
was in power, a Government which was only too willing to believe Mr. Parnell to be guilty of crime or incitement to crime,
and the letters which were discovered in Paris in a black bag,
seemingly mislaid by one of the Phœnix Park assassins, and paid
for out of funds supplied by certain distinguished Unionists,
were now accepted as authentic by *The Times,* without the editor
or the manager as much as asking Mr. Houston from whom he
had procured these very interesting documents. It was all done
in a gentlemanly fashion, and each trusted the other's words;
unfortunately Mr. Houston trusted a wretched Irish journalist
called Dick Pigott, who has already figured in these pages, and
who was certainly no gentleman. Meanwhile the letters were
carefully docketed in the archives of Printing House Square,
pending a favorable moment for their disclosure.

The gloomy interview on the banks of the Thames, in which
Parnell and O'Brien discussed the pros and cons of the plan of
campaign, ended in a somewhat surprising fashion. Seemingly
oblivious of his strange accouterments, Parnell suggested to his
lieutenant that he should drive him back to town to dinner.
According to Mr. O'Brien, they seem to have paced the paths of

Greenwich Park from half past ten in the morning until evening, "too deeply engrossed in more absorbing concerns to notice
how the hours were flying and the frozen blast eating into our
bones." Whether they drove up to town for lunch or dinner is
immaterial to us; what is interesting is that the neurasthenic
recluse who had only just left the sick-room should choose to go
to the Criterion, one among the most crowded and fashionable
of London restaurants. It was one of Parnell's curious characteristics that whenever he went to a restaurant he always chose
some gay, cosmopolitan place, such as the Criterion, Romano's
or the Café Royal. He liked brightness and warmth in places
as well as in people: the very qualities that first attracted him to
Katherine O'Shea were her gaiety and spontaneity; the very
qualities which had made him pick on James O'Kelly as his one
intimate friend in the Irish party were his warmth and *joie de
vivre*. He was innately lonely, and one of the symptoms of the
disease which had such a lowering effect on his vitality was that
he could no longer bear to be alone. Pathetic stories are told of
how during the Irish tours he would persuade some colleague to
sit up half the night with him rather than be left to the horrors
of solitude. Perhaps it was a kindred feeling for their loneliness
which made him adopt any stray dog he found starving in the
gutter, which made him fly into a fury whenever he saw a
peasant ill-treating his donkey. He had a touching fondness for
all animals and children, and one can realize what it must have
meant for this proud, honorable man not to be able to acknowledge his own children before the world. No wonder he sometimes gave way to despairing loneliness, and it was probably in
one of these moods that he chose to dine that evening with
William O'Brien. Gradually he cast off his gloom. With that
peculiar gentleness, that almost womanly sweetness which only
showed in intimacy, he discoursed on his early life and the
growth of Fenianism, on science and religion. Bravely tragic in
the fact that he never complained of his ill health or of the hard-
ships of the political struggle, he let fall one telling sentence:
"Life is not supportable without the friendship of a woman, be

she good or bad. Take even the saints"; and, to the surprise of
his Catholic companion, he gave instances of great saints, like
St. Francis of Assisi, St. John of the Cross, and St. Francis of
Sales, who all owed so much to the collaboration of noble
women, adding with a slight smile: "You would never have got
young men to sacrifice themselves for so unlucky a country as
Ireland, only that they pictured her as a woman. That is what
makes the risks worth taking." That evening's conversation
showed that during the past two months the man of action had
been thrown back on himself. During his long illness he had
begun to speculate on the mysteries of science and religion—"that
something in life we don't understand and never will." He
still defended his childish superstitions, saying, "Don't you think
the apostles had just as lively a horror of the number 'thirteen'
the day after the Last Supper? I should never have burned the
witches of old. Macbeth's mistake was not in consulting the
witches, but in only believing the portion that pleased him in
their advice. You never know in what strange quarters knowledge may be hidden. The foolishness of the Cross was the
breath-of-life of Christianity."

They were only the simple, immature speculations of a man
who had neither the time nor the knowledge to study the prob-
lems of religion, but who desperately needed some channel of
escape from the hard world of facts.

Circumstances were hemming him in. Captain O'Shea was
on the war-path; the continual paragraphs in the *Pall Mall
Gazette* were galling to his self-esteem, and, somewhat late in
the day, he wrote accusing his wife of "tarnishing his honor."
She responded by losing her temper, telling him that the only
person who had ever tarnished his honor had been himself, and
that she refused to meet him while he used such disgusting and
ungrateful expressions about her. Nevertheless he appeared at
Eltham, and a sordid and revolting quarrel took place in front
of their children, who were already of an age to understand the
relations between mother and father. Katie held the prime card
in her hand: "Aunt Ben," aged ninety-six, was still alive, and in

her dotage she relied implicitly on her beloved niece. By her latest will she had left Katie her entire fortune, ignoring the claims of the other members of the Wood family; so if Willie dared to make a scandal he would only spite himself; for what would be his wife's and his children's money would then fall to the lot of the jealous relations. In spite of his grand talk, he had no intention of killing the goose which laid the golden eggs, but he went to the length of writing his wife's solicitor a stiff letter, advising him to tell his client "that reports being wide and strong as to her relations with Mr. Parnell it would for her children's sake be expedient that she should declare her renunciation of communication with him." This letter received no response, and, after failing to obtain satisfactory assurances of his wife's good conduct, he resorted to more devious ways of ruining Parnell. The dashing cavalry officer, the cynical man of the world, had sunk to the level of a common plotter, and Captain William O'Shea, late officer of the 18th Hussars, ex-M.P. for Galway, was now to be found consorting with spies and down-and-out Fenians in a certain dubious Irish public-house in Wardour Street, where the loyal agents of *The Times* gathered so much valuable material for their articles on "Parnellism and Crime."

Though Mrs. O'Shea's solicitor declined to carry out the Captain's orders, he seems to have advised his client to the effect that it might be wiser for her not to have Mr. Parnell so frequently staying at Eltham. This was not merely out of regard for her husband, but also on account of her relations, who would seize on any opportunity of making mischief with her aunt. So Katie found a charming house at Brockley, conveniently near to Eltham, where Parnell could take up residence under the pseudonym of Clement Preston. To live separated from the woman whom he not only regarded as his lawful wife, but whom he worshiped with a tender all-absorbing passion, must have been a terrible strain for the sick man. By March 1887 the house at Brockley was abandoned in favor of a *pied-à-terre* in town, which at least had the advantage of being nearer to the House of Commons. Mrs. O'Shea relates how "Parnell wearily said he did not want to live in London unless I would live there too, but, as I pointed out, that was impossible, and I took a house in York Terrace, Regent's Park, for him." After settling him in with his scientific instruments and engineering treatises she went home, "haunted by his grave, considering eyes, and his sad, 'You must not leave me here by myself. I don't want to be here without you,' hoping that he would settle down and feel the benefit of getting more quickly to bed."

He endured the solitude of his new home for three weeks, and every evening he sent a "good night" telegram to Eltham. Then the loneliness became unbearable, and early one morning, shortly before dawn, a cab drove up to the front of Wonersh Lodge. Half in a dream, Katie opened the window to see her lover coming up the garden-walk. And a moment later she was in his arms, as he whispered: "Oh, my love, you must not leave me alone again."

The winter of 1886-87 witnessed many eventful changes at Westminster. Lord Randolph Churchill's impetuous and disastrous resignation changed the whole face of party politics. At the very zenith of his power this darling of the gods staked his career on one reckless, ill-considered gamble and lost. He had issued his ultimatum just once too often, and Lord Salisbury, who was beginning to find that Tory democracy was "a carbuncle in the neck," accepted his resignation as blandly as Mr. Gladstone had accepted that of Joseph Chamberlain not even a year ago. It was Chamberlain who now found himself an Ishmael in the wilderness, for Churchill had been the only Conservative member with whom he had felt any sympathy, and the new Government was definitely damned in his eyes when his old enemy Goschen stepped into the breach as Chancellor of the Exchequer. Labeling the Whig Unionist as "the skeleton at the feast," he once more entered into negotiations with his old colleagues. But the history of the Round Table Conference is a history of failure; though the Radical offered to negotiate, he refused to compromise, and once more the Liberal leaders found that they had to choose between him and Parnell. Many of them would definitely have chosen him, but loyalty to Gladstone bound them to their Irish allies, and the conference broke up in disillusion, bitterness and wrath. In his antagonism to Parnell, whom he still firmly believed had deceived him during their negotiations, Chamberlain was led to support the Conservatives in a new Coercion Bill, to credit the atrocious accusations of *The Times* even to the length of believing in the authenticity of the famous forged letter, and to arouse public feeling against the Irish to the extent of publishing a letter in the Press on the subject of Welsh Disestablishment, saying: "Whether the process occupies a generation or a century, poor little Wales must wait until Mr. Parnell is satisfied and Mr. Gladstone's policy adopted. They will not wait alone: the crofters of Scotland and the agricultural laborers of England will keep them company. Thirty-two millions of people must go without much-needed legislation because three million are disloyal." This bitterness against Ireland was reflected in all his speeches; in many ways it was not unjustified, for the Nationalist members were overwhelming him with vituperation and abuse, and the loudest of them all was Mr. Healy, who not so long ago had been anxious to be his friend. But he was chiefly influenced by his personal enmity to one man, and, in order to bring about that one man's downfall, he was ready to encourage Captain O'Shea in his seemingly devoted zeal, even though by this time he had no very high opinion of his friend's character. For one finds him writing to his American *fiancée*, "He is a great supporter of mine, and has been very useful to me occasionally in all Irish matters, but like all Irish politicians he is, I am afraid, unscrupulous and cynical."

The beginning of March saw the resignation of Sir Michael Hicks-Beach, and the elevation of Arthur James Balfour to the office of Irish Secretary. At first it was a source of wonderment and amazement that Lord Salisbury should have chosen his young kinsman to fill a post where many a more experienced Minister had failed. But events were to prove that the Prime Minister had been right in judging his man. The languid young philosopher, the "Prince Arthur" of Uncle Toby's Diary, who

till now had been known as the most academic and the most
ornamental of the fourth party, was to rule Ireland with an iron
hand, till even the coercion of "Buckshot" Forster and the
régime of the "Red Earl" paled before the exploits of "Bloody
Balfour." Before he had been a month in power, Parnell's
prophecy proved true; the peasant-demagogues of the West heard
the crack of a sharp Coercion Act in their ears, and by the end
of the session a new Crimes Act had been added to the statute
book, an Act which not only reenacted all the worst features of
the previous Coercion Bills, but which was a supposedly permanent measure not restricted to one or a limited number of years.
Lord Salisbury's twenty years of firm and resolute government
were only enforced through the Ministry summoning to its aid
the historic rights of closure. It was on this memorable occasion,
in protest against the injustice of the Speaker's action, that Mr.
Gladstone and all the members of the Opposition, whether English or Irish, walked out of the House, leaving behind only the
Tories and the Unionists. A Liberal eye-witness recalls that in
passing out of the House he cast a glance at Joseph Chamberlain,
who still sat in his place, looking pale and dazed. Surely at this
moment the member for Birmingham must have felt all the
pangs of a deserter.

In Printing House Square the difficulties of the new Government were both appreciated and condoned, and, in order to
lighten Mr. Balfour's task in dealing with the public—who, however prejudiced they might be against the Irish, were still honest
and fair-minded enough to dislike the idea of a perpetual Coercion Act—*The Times* now published a series of articles entitled:
"Parnellism and Crime," the purpose of which was to show that
the Parnellite party were hand in glove with the physical-force
movement, and that the men whom Mr. Gladstone upheld as his
allies were the friends and abettors of assassins and dynamiters.
On April 18th, the very day of the second reading of the Crimes
Bill, the famous forged letter flashed upon the world; a letter
which had been found among a pile of incriminating documents,
left in a black bag in an unknown Paris hotel; a letter signed

with Parnell's signature, and supposedly addressed to Patrick Egan after the Phœnix Park murders, of which the contents were the following:

"Dear Sir,—I am not surprised at your friend's anger, but he and you should know that to denounce the murders was the only course open to us. To do that promptly was plainly our best policy. But you can tell him and all others concerned that though I regret the accident of Lord Frederick Cavendish's death, I cannot refuse to admit that Burke got no more than his deserts. You are at liberty to show him this and others whom you can trust also, but let not my address be known. He can write to the House of Commons.

"Yours very truly,
"Charles S. Parnell."

No wonder that the vast majority of the English reading-public, who regarded *The Times* as something sacrosanct, should have thought, on reading this letter, "There goes Home Rule and the Liberal party too!"

CHAPTER THIRTY-FIVE

THE story of the forged letters and of the Parnell Commission is all too familiar. Varying accounts are to be found in the biographies and journals of every statesman of the day. The letter reproduced in facsimile in the decorous pages of *The Times* was at first hailed with delight by the Conservatives and consternation by the Liberals; for in the ranks of the Opposition there were many whose conversion to Home Rule was still of too recent a date to dissipate their distrust and uneasy suspicions of the man whom their leaders claimed as an ally. Mr. Parnell was still regarded as a sinister, somewhat mysterious figure; the reserve with which he treated their friendly advances at a time when most of his colleagues preened themselves like delighted children in the unfamiliar atmosphere of Mayfair drawing-rooms, his obvious reluctance to appear on Liberal platforms, did little to mitigate the dislike that he still inspired in some of the most fervent Home Rulers. It was not so long before that Mr. Forster had risen in their midst denouncing him as an instigator and abettor of crime, and men still remembered the frigid indifference with which he had treated those accusations.

It was with the same frigid indifference that he stood up in the House at one o'clock on the morning of April 19th to denounce the letter as an audacious and unblushing fabrication, adding that "politics are come to a pretty pass in this country, when the leader of a party of eighty-six members has to stand up at ten minutes past one in the House of Commons in order to defend himself from an anonymous fabrication such as that which is contained in *The Times* of this morning." But his statement disappointed his supporters, for it was too calm and reasoned for their tastes; they expected a display of righteous wrath in place of a contemptuous denial. There are many varying accounts given of Parnell's first reaction to the forged letter. Mrs. O'Shea relates a dramatic and plausible story of how he saw *The Times* at breakfast, and looked up to her with a smile, saying: "Wouldn't you hide your head with shame if your King were so stupid as that, my Queen?" Unfortunately, she spoils her story by several flagrant untruths, as when she writes that he returned home early that evening in order to finish some experiment in gold assaying, in which he was so absorbed that he never even mentioned *The Times* article until she called his attention to the matter, whereupon he said wearily: "They want me to fight it, but it will be a terrible nuisance, my Queenie." Parnell spent the night of April 18th at Westminster waiting for an opportunity to make his official statement to the House, when he definitely asserted that "I heard of this precious concoction before I saw it, because I do not take in or even read *The Times* usually." That this was true is substantiated by Tim Harrington's account of how the chief never saw *The Times* until the evening, when he strolled casually into the House to find the whole place in a ferment of excitement. When he was handed the facsimile of what purported to be his signature, he never showed the slightest sign of indignation; he merely put his finger on the "s" of the signature, saying quite calmly: "I did not make an 's' like that since 1878." But this tranquil demeanor was merely a mask put on for the benefit of both his colleagues and his opponents. He was far from indifferent in his attitude to *The Times* articles, which he recognized as a deliberate attempt to discredit him with the Liberals and to alienate public sympathy from Home Rule. Though he had always been, and still was, supremely contemptuous of the personal regard of Englishmen, now that he had made an alliance for the good of his country he was not going to see it destroyed by his own private enemies, for Parnell believed this forgery to be inspired out of a personal vendetta rather than out of purely political motives. He did not suspect *The Times* staff of anything worse than crass stupidity in putting themselves in the hands of the men who wished his downfall. As he said: "I cannot understand how the managers of a responsible and what used to be a respectable journal could have been so hoodwinked, so hoaxed, so bamboozled." But he had his suspicions—suspicions which gradually developed into an obsession, and which dictated his course of action during the following year. IIis adherents, supported by the Liberal leaders, who from the very first had denounced the facsimile letter as a barefaced forgery, now demanded the appointment of a select committee of the House of Commons to enquire into the serious assertions which had been cast on a fellow-member. The Government refused this demand, telling Mr. Parnell that his remedy was an action for libel, brought either in London or in Dublin, for Mr. Smith, the leader of the House, had direct assurances from Mr. Walter of *The Times* to the effect that if Parnell gave them the chance they would go into the whole history of the movement, and have commissions to take evidence in America and Australia which would be sure to prove that the Nationalists were closely associated with the worst revolutionary elements. Maybe Mr. Walter was right in banking on the fact that Parnell would never bring an action which would entail not only a cross-examination, but a general prying into his private life, for no steps were taken to prosecute *The Times,* which was allowed to continue its libelous articles until they failed any more to arouse the public interest. Meanwhile Mr. Chamberlain traveled round the country interspersing his speeches with pithy extracts from that favored journal; Lord Salisbury publicly accused Mr. Parnell "as one tainted with a strong presumption of conniving at assassination," and Mr. Balfour's Coercion Act became the law of the land.

Many conflicting reasons have been given for Parnell's obvious disinclination to appear in court. Some are just fantastic suppositions, such as the one which tried to prove that the forged letter was the copy of an original one written by Henry Campbell at Parnell's dictation, and that the Irish leader did not dare to take any definite steps until he had verified that the original letter was no longer in existence. At one time this was a fairly popular theory, and Justin McCarthy recounts a curious little incident of how, when he asked the chief what he was going to do about the forgery, adding, "Of course it is a forgery," Parnell looked at him in a kind of wondering way and said: "Well, I

shouldn't think you had much doubt in your mind about that?"
There was no indignation in his tone, just a wonderment that if
his old and trusted colleague had any doubts, what, then, would
be the opinion of the majority? Gladstone and Morley upheld
him strenuously; even Sir William Harcourt, who bore him no
great love, denounced *The Times* letter as "a malignant fabrication"; but one finds even that ardent Home Ruler, Wilfrid Blunt,
writing that he had compared the signature of the facsimile letter with Parnell's and was quite certain that it was not his,
"though of course just such a letter might have been written,
for, though the Phœnix Park assassinations were in no sort of
way due to the Parnellites . . . yet there is no question that Irish
feeling in America was with the assassins, and Parnell may well
have found it necessary privately to qualify his public condemnation of it." There was hardly an Englishman living who did
not suspect Parnell of some underhand dealings with the Fenians, and Morley probably had this at the back of his mind when
he discouraged him from taking an action "where not only the
plaintiff's own character, but the whole movement that he represented, would have been submitted to a Middlesex jury with all
the national and political prejudices inevitable in such a body,
and with all the twelve chances of a disagreement that would be
almost as disastrous to him as an active verdict for his assailants."

Morley feared that the secrets of a semi-revolutionary movement like the Land League might prove damaging both to
Gladstone and to Home Rule, and to bring a libel action in
Dublin was useless, for what did England care if a favorable
verdict was given in the Four Courts? Not only Morley, but
many of his old friends, such as Justin McCarthy, urged Parnell
to do no more; "that, having given his full and manly denunciation of the forgery, he ought to rest there. Those who will not
believe him now would not believe him although one rose from
the dead."

But Parnell did not allow himself to be influenced either by
Morley or by his colleagues. His conduct was dictated by a far
more personal motive: the man whom he suspected of being

responsible for the forged letter, the man who had had the fullest opportunity of studying his handwriting, and who had the strongest motives for revenge, was William O'Shea, working under the ægis of his old friend and patron, Joseph Chamberlain. So dominant was this obsession that Parnell refused to listen to reason. The day following the publication of the facsimile letter, Tim Healy told Labouchere that he suspected the forger to be Richard Pigott, who was an old hand at the game. Maybe Tim knew of the letter which the wretched blackmailer had written to the Archbishop of Dublin asking for a loan in order to help him in averting a tragedy which was about to befall the Nationalist party. Labouchere took Healy at his word, and in the columns of *Truth* he boldly published the fact that the letter looked like the handiwork of Richard Pigott. Meanwhile Patrick Egan, writing in the *New York Herald,* alleged the letter to be a forgery, adding that he held certain documents proving Pigott to be the forger. But Parnell was still a sick man, with all a sick man's notions and illusions, and he refused to believe what all his colleagues knew to be true, namely, that "O'Shea was incapable of playing the heavy villain."

No doubt the Captain regarded the appearance of the facsimile letter as a heaven-sent blessing "which would blow a blackguard's reputation into smithereens" without entailing a scandal at Eltham. He was on friendly terms both with Sir Rowland Blennerhassett, a well-meaning Unionist who contributed to the funds of the Irish Loyal and Patriotic Union without enquiring too deeply into what use was being made of his money, and with the down-and-out Fenians whom he met at the Irish public-house in Wardour Street. It was here that he heard the fantastic tales of how Parnell had supplied the Invincibles with funds, and of how he was in constant communication with the Paris agents of the American Dynamiters. It was here that he fraternized with the spies and casual informers and discredited journalists, who were all ready to blacken Mr. Parnell's reputation for some small consideration. Among them was an able and venomous paragraphist called Philip Callan, whom Parnell had kicked out of the party when he discovered him to be spying on his private life. Here, too, came Frank Hugh O'Donnell, embittered and impoverished, still cherishing his dreams of fallen greatness. All these fertile imaginations were put at the disposal of Mr. Houston's well-filled purse, and the cynic in O'Shea must have rejoiced to see how avidly the respectable Unionists were swallowing their doses of Parnellism and crime; but when his turn came to lend a helping hand he showed himself an able apprentice of their methods.

Even his friend Joseph Chamberlain was willing to rely on the accuracy of Printing House Square, for it was not until the summer of 1888 that he discovered that Parnell had always been straightforward in his dealings, and that he had allowed himself to be misled by the misrepresentations of O'Shea. Meanwhile he wrote to Miss Endicott in America: "People in England are greatly interested in *The Times* against Parnell and Co., and there is no doubt that they have additional evidence and that they entirely believe it to be true. Such a journal as *The Times* has a great reputation to keep up, and would never bring accusations lightly. . . . He [Parnell] contents himself with a blank denial which carries no conviction. It is almost certain that Parnell would go to a court of law if he were not afraid of the cross-examination."

So the months passed without any definite steps being taken, and even the vituperations of *The Times* could not stay the Liberal triumphs at the by-elections. In Ireland the Agrarian War had begun in grim earnest. Dillon and O'Brien were arrested under the new Crimes Act, and it soon transpired that, under Mr. Balfour's régime, prison was no mere detention camp for troublesome gentlemen, but entailed hard labor, plank beds, and all the rigors of penal servitude. The martyrdom of Tullamore Jail made O'Brien the hero of the hour, and the tale of how he resisted the authorities by lying naked in bed rather than submit to the indignity of convict clothes was the subject of many a popular ballad. In England there were mass demonstrations in Hyde Park protesting against the tyranny of the new Government; prominent Liberals visited Ireland in order to bear witness to Mr. Balfour's iniquities; the days of "the union of hearts" were at hand, and on Irish platforms Gladstone's name was as loudly acclaimed as that of Parnell. Then came the disgrace of Mitchelstown, where, at a crowded meeting following O'Brien's prosecution, the police came into collision with a hostile crowd. Driven into their barracks, they lost their heads and fired at random, killing three men and mortally wounding two others. These excesses on the part of the authorities were exploited by the Liberals with as much avidity as when the enquiry into the Maamtrasna murders was made a rallying-cry for the Conservatives. For the second time the happenings in an obscure part of Ireland developed into a great political issue. Morley remarks that "the slaughter of three men was finally left just as if it had been the slaughter of three dogs. No other incident of Irish administration stirred deeper feelings of disgust in Ireland or of misgiving and indignation in England." For a short while "Remember Mitchelstown!" was Mr. Gladstone's favorite slogan in counteracting the effects of "Parnellism and Crime." Mr. Balfour conducted the whole affair with an air of gentle disdain, coupled with an iron intransigence which led Sir William Harcourt to describe him as "a philosopher who has got hold of a Coercion Bill. And a philosopher is a very dangerous person to trust with such a terrible implement as that. Now, emperors and tyrants and even heroes are susceptible to human weaknesses, but a philosopher has none. He carries on the most excruciating experiments in vivisection in the interests of science; the palpitations of the victims only add a zest to the experiments."

So strong was the public reaction in favor of Ireland that Harcourt and Morley actually discussed the feasibility of making a political tour in that country, but in their private correspondence one can see that this sudden enthusiasm for their Hibernian friends was only skin-deep. Home Rule was first and foremost a party issue, and even Morley "wished to heaven our allies were Englishmen, with English habits of business." As for Harcourt, he had always been quite frank in his poor opinion of the Irish, though now he was tolerant enough to crack kindly jokes at their expense, saying: "Patriotism does not seem to be a healthy occupation. What a lot they are! Parnell, Dillon; O'Brien, Sexton; all interesting gentlemen in the last stages of debility." With regard to the projected tour, he was anxious to know what the old "Serpent of Avondale" said on the subject. Parnell had always resented the idea of Englishmen appearing on Irish platforms, and even the union of hearts had not converted him. But at this time he was probably too ill to be held responsible for vetoing a project which anyway never materialized. All during the year of 1887 he was in such a poor state of health that he could only make fitful appearances at Westminster. There was no longer any question of his shirking his duties as a leader, or of his "shamming to be ill," as *The Times* so genially suggested, for he was in such a desperate condition that within the party rumors were rife as to who would succeed to the leadership. Wilfrid Blunt writes: "In 1887 Parnell was in wretched health, and against the plan of campaign. He said in a foreboding spirit: 'I don't care who leads when I am gone, but I am anxious that the old country should get some kind of Parliament as a result of our troubles, and, unless Mr. Gladstone can do this for us, no other living Englishman can.'" Because he believed in Gladstone's power he was willing to subordinate his personal dislike and resentment of the man who had once dared to put him into prison. He never shared in his colleagues' emotional enthusiasm for the Grand Old Man, and it must have been galling for him to find that even in his own constituency of Cork the people cheered for Mr. Gladstone and the Liberal party. Three years later, when he was deserted and discredited by his old allies, he confessed to one of his faithful followers: "I gained nothing by meeting Mr. Gladstone. I was no match for him. He got more out of me than I ever got out of him. . . . I did not want a close alliance. I did not make a close alliance. I kept away from the Liberals as much as I could. You do not know how much they tried to get at me, how much I was wor-

ried. But I tried to keep away from them, as I had ever done.
I knew the danger of getting mixed up with English statesmen.
They only make you give way, and I gave way a great deal too
much. . . . They call me a dictator. I was not dictator enough."

He knew that Mr. Morley was only acting in the interests of
his party when he dissuaded him from prosecuting *The Times*.
Had he not been haunted by the obsession that O'Shea was responsible for the forgery there is no doubt that he would have
taken action. But he did not dare to risk a glaring exposure of
his private life. So firmly rooted was his delusion that there
were times when in some strange disguise he could be seen
loitering round Soho and the Seven Dials, the quarters frequented by certain Fenians, in order to trace some connection
between O'Shea and the extremists. This search was not altogether fruitless, for it was here that he came into contact with
the spies and agents, who, however ready they may have been
to help *The Times* in fabricating their articles and in supplying
Richard Pigott with original material, were equally ready to help
Parnell on the same terms.

The continual strain and worry were driving him to the verge
of another breakdown. One day the London Stock Exchange
posted a telegram announcing his death, and that same evening
he appeared at the House looking so ghastly that, when Mc-
Carthy and Morley met one another in the Lobby, they "both
could only say in one breath 'Good God! Have you seen Parnell?'" There were times when he would disappear for days;
then one evening he would be seen passing hurriedly through
the lobby on his way to the post office, where he would collect
his huge bundle of letters—probably the accumulation of a week
or fortnight. From there he would disappear towards the library, speaking to no one on the way, passing out by the back
staircase, which he always used for the simple reason that he was
certain thereby to avoid meeting anyone who might speak to
him or would expect to be spoken to. His silent unobtrusiveness,
his sudden appearances and disappearances, enveloped him in an

atmosphere of mystery, and, unfortunately for him, he aroused
the greatest interest of any member in the House. Everything
about him whetted the appetite of the curious; the fact that he
was reputed to be living in a London suburb under an assumed
name, that no one knew his address, that he never went out in
society, and that he was rumored to be entangled in a romantic
love-affair, made him into the "mystery man" of politics. His
simplest actions gave rise to the wildest speculations. Even the
black bag which he always brought to Westminster aroused intense curiosity until one day it was lost, and Scotland Yard
found it to contain nothing more interesting than a change of
socks and boots, thoughtfully provided by Mrs. O'Shea, owing
to the doctor having told her that nothing was worse for "Mr.
Stewart's" health than that he should get his feet wet.

The Times charges were sinking into oblivion, and the ardent
Unionists, who in their loyalty to the Crown had financed Mr.
Houston in his patriotic efforts, were beginning to feel that they
had wasted their money, when, in the autumn of 1887, Frank
Hugh O'Donnell, believing himself to be libeled by certain statements in "Parnellism and Crime," brought an action against *The
Times,* claiming damages to the amount of fifty thousand
pounds. As Sir Alfred Robbins writes: "The matter would have
been a farce if *The Times* had not leaped with alacrity at the
chance thus given to bring out its whole case in an English court
of law in circumstances most favorable to itself."

The first outward sign of an understanding between the Government and *The Times* was when the newspaper briefed as
leading counsel the Attorney-General, Sir Richard Webster, and
though, when the case came on in the summer of 1888, the plaintiff did not go into the witness-box, though his counsel called no
witnesses nor tendered any evidence save *The Times* publications,
Sir Richard, disregarding the usual rule of procedure, opened the
case in full, and read in court not only the facsimile letter, but a
whole new batch of Mr. Pigott's concoctions, including several
letters of Egan and Parnell. Among them was the famous docu-

ment supposedly written by the Irish chief, in which the mis-spelling of one word gave a clue to the forger:

"DEAR E.,—What are these fellows waiting for? This in-action is inexcusable, our best men are in prison and nothing is being done. Let there be an end of this *hesitency.*"

For three days the Attorney-General hurled a list of unproved charges not only against Parnell, but against all the men who were identified with the Parnellite movement. The aggrieved plaintiff was ignored, and, when it was known that Philip Callan had counseled O'Donnell to bring the action, the rumor went round that he had acted on the instigation of *The Times* in order to provoke Parnell to take a definite line of action.

Healy writes in his *Letters and Leaders of My Day:* "To bring a libel action against *The Times* required means, and O'Donnell had none. The reader must therefore make up his mind as to whether, in provoking the bogus trial under the pretense that he had been attacked, O'Donnell was merely spiteful or was an agent or in collusion with an undisclosed principal." The allegations brought forward by Sir Richard Webster forced matters to a crisis. Through the careful examination of certain documents in Printing House Square, Mr. George Lewis, Parnell's solicitor, was able to convince his client that O'Shea was not the forger. At the same time Patrick Egan despatched to Europe a batch of original documents which proved some of the letters produced by the Attorney-General to be pure fabrications. Immediately following the collapse of the O'Donnell action, Parnell once more asked the House of Commons to appoint a select committee to enquire into the matter, and again the Government refused. But now they had to deal with a man who, no longer afraid of exposure, was ready to fight with his back to the wall. His patience was at an end, and he boldly informed Morley that he was not afraid of cross-examination. The new batch of letters had strengthened his position, for not only were they palpable forgeries, but they also mentioned the absurd story that he had given a hundred pounds to assist Frank Byrne in his flight from justice, a story which even the most credulous Tory found hard to believe. The Liberal leaders were still of an opinion that "Parnell ought to have lain low," but this time their advice was ignored, and Morley wrote somewhat bitterly to Harcourt: "I told Mr. P. our views yesterday afternoon, with the usual effect that we might as well have saved our breath to cool our porridge."

When the Government countered Parnell's demand by proposing a special commission "of three judges to investigate, not the letters specifically, but all the allegations and charges made against members of Parliament by defendants in the recent action," the Opposition benches voiced their indignation, but Parnell was now determined to have the affair thoroughly investigated, whether by fair means or foul. As Morley said: "He was burning to get any expedient, committee, or commission which would enable him to unmask and smite his hidden foes." The only thing he stipulated was that the first duty of the Commission should be to test the authenticity of the letters. The Government's answer to this request was to introduce a bill appointing a special commission to enquire not only into the charges brought against certain members of Parliament, but *also against other persons."* Without consulting the Irish Solicitor-General, without asking *The Times* what evidence could be produced, the ministry, encouraged by the Liberal Unionists, decided to put the whole Nationalist party on trial, deprived of a jury and accused of unspecified offenses. Healy might well write that "what Burke declared impossible a century earlier, 'an indictment against a nation,' had begun."

Joseph Chamberlain played a prominent part in encouraging the Government to adopt this course. Mr. Garvin states that he took his "effective part in defeating the Irish leader's demand for a parliamentary committee to deal specifically with the forgeries, and in substituting a legal tribunal to judge an insurrectionary movement," and that "as never before the Nationalist chief was roused against the Radical Unionist." Neither the Attorney-General nor the Solicitor-General was in favor of a special commission. Maybe they both realized that a thorough investigation into the origins of "Parnellism and Crime" was bound to bring discredit on their party, and in the late summer one finds Sir Richard Webster writing to Sir Edward Clarke: "Every day I curse Chamberlain and the Liberal Unionists for their obstinacy, but perhaps they are wiser than I am."

The struggle between Parnell and Chamberlain was now staged in public. Inspired by a blind and relentless hatred, both men were ready to resort to any weapon to effect one another's downfall. On the night of July 30th, during the debate on the Parnell Commission Bill, the Nationalist leader made a bitter attack on Mr. Chamberlain, accusing him of having used Irish members to do his dirty work, and of having betrayed the secrets of the Cabinet of which he had been a member. Lord Haldane, who was an eye-witness to the scene, writes that Parnell's speech, delivered in slow, deliberate tones, "made me feel as if he were dropping vitriol down Chamberlain's neck. The House was pained and yet overcome by the power and incisiveness of Parnell's words." As the debate adjourned, the cries of "Judas Chamberlain," rising from the Irish benches, once more shocked the House, and, when Parnell resumed his attack the following evening, the aggressive eyeglass and exotic buttonhole of the member for Birmingham were seen to flourish in the embarrassing vicinity of that arch-Whig, Lord Hartington. Once more the disturbing skeleton of the Kilmainham negotiations stalked across the floor of the House; once more the name of O'Shea was introduced as that of the luckless go-between. As Sir Henry Lucy writes: "Here was Mr. Parnell in the dock, as it were, upon a charge of complicity with murder. Instead of pleading 'Not Guilty' and endeavoring to prove his innocence, he suddenly turned upon one of the principal supporters of the indictment and forced him into the position of the accused. It was not business as business was set down upon the orders. But it was a development of bold and unexpected tactics which left the House in a state of profound excitement." When Chamberlain rose to address the House, "in a manner the studious calm of which excelled even Mr. Parnell's," his speech came somewhat as an anticlimax. "At first he showed a disposition to deny everything. He had not, he said, the remotest idea of the special circumstances Mr. Parnell had alluded to; but, as he went along, Mr. Parnell, by various interjections, helped his memory, and in the end Mr. Chamberlain admitted that he had from time to time between 1880 and 1885 held communication direct and indirect with Mr. Parnell. But—and here was the gist of his defense— he declared that every one of those communications he had made known to Mr. Gladstone, Lord Hartington, Mr. Forster, and other colleagues in the Cabinet directly concerned." That same evening Mr. Chamberlain wrote to America: "My answer was, in a sentence, that my colleagues were informed of everything I was doing, and Mr. Gladstone, to whom I appealed, was obliged to confirm me, though I must say he appeared to do so very unwillingly. . . . The atmosphere is most hostile and the situation most interesting."

As a result of this passage at arms, O'Shea, at the advice of his patron, incautiously committed himself to print, and, as the crowning irony, the duel that had begun in the House of Commons was continued in the pages of *The Times,* which published Parnell's answer to O'Shea in the firm belief that Chamberlain would be able to annihilate his statements. It was then that the member for Birmingham discovered to his cost that his trusted intermediary was but a man of straw. Brought to bay, O'Shea was forced to admit that he had been guilty of deliberate misrepresentations, and, to the disappointment of *The Times,* Mr. Chamberlain's letter was couched in mild and respectful terms, which, in view of the impending events, must have made them wonder whether the Radical Unionist was already regretting his zeal in forcing the Government's hand.

One would imagine that after this rude awakening Chamberlain would refuse to have any more dealings with O'Shea, but he was already too deeply involved. On August 3rd, the day following the publication of the Captain's letter to *The Times,* the editor, Mr. Buckle, wrote to the Radical leader asking whether his friend, Captain O'Shea, would be willing to appear in court as a witness on their behalf. At first the satellite refused to expose himself to cross-examination, but later in the month, when he was subpœna'd by Parnell, he professed his readiness to give evidence for *The Times* "in order to have the opportunity of refuting the slanders circulated about me by Mr. Parnell and his friends in regard to these letters."

Even though Chamberlain now regarded him as "an indiscreet and therefore a dangerous person," he was still too useful to be ignominiously dismissed. But there was a slight *contretemps* when O'Shea not only wished "to exchange views as to old events before going into the box," but also to have use "of all letters, memoranda, and telegrams of mine between 1882 and 1886"—a demand which Chamberlain felt obliged to refuse. Unfortunately, there was nothing to prevent O'Shea from making free use of his name in the witness-box, and the Captain's hints and innuendoes helped to circulate the rumor that the Radical Unionist was the Government's evil genius.

Meanwhile the stage was set for a mammoth trial. Stormy scenes marked the progress of the Parnell Commission Bill; unpleasant questions were asked to which evasive answers were given; but by now the Government was so lost to any sense of fairness or of shame, and political passions ran so high, that the measure was rushed through in the end by the ruthless exercise of the guillotine. By September 17th the Commission, composed of three judges, Hannen, Day, and Smith, had commenced its preliminary sittings. As Morley has said: "Three judges were trying a social and political revolution. The leading actors in it were virtually in the dock. The tribunal had been specially set up by their political opponents, without giving them any effective voice, either in its composition, or upon the character and scope of its powers." Close on a hundred Irishmen were indicted in this trial. At vast expense and personal inconvenience these men had to throw up their jobs in order to appear in the witness-box of the London Law Courts. Sir Charles Russell, the most famous advocate at the English Bar, was briefed as their leading counsel; out of patriotism for his country this great Irishman had sacrificed a substantial retaining-fee from *The Times* in order to appear in the defense of Mr. Parnell, and it was during this trial that his comparatively unknown junior, Mr. Asquith, scored his first legal triumphs. But the Irish party had to fight not only *The Times* but the Government. Before the Commission had begun to sit, the staff of Printing House Square must have been aware that, with regard to the facsimile letter, everything pointed to the fact of its being a forgery. During the O'Donnell trial the Attorney-General had declared that not for any consideration would he reveal the names of the parties from whom *The Times* had obtained the letters, and the manager, Mr. Macdonald, had repeated this statement to Mr. Houston in writing, for the misguided secretary of the Irish Loyal and Patriotic Union had already been warned by Richard Pigott that on no account should he be brought into the witness-box. The day had come when *The Times* had learned that it was Richard Pigott who had procured the letters, and after their solicitor, Mr. Soames, had examined his record, the situation did not look encouraging. But, even though Mr. Macdonald and Mr. Houston had allowed themselves to be hoodwinked by a scurrilous little journalist, they still had the alliance of the Government, and the whole machinery of Dublin Castle was put at their disposal in order to smash Parnell and Parnellism. Spies, informers, and *agents provocateurs* were summoned as the witnesses of England's most respectable newspaper; even convicts, enduring lifelong sentences, were brought in custody from the Irish jails. Men of the Royal Irish Constabulary camped in Lincoln's Inn; peasants from Kerry and Connemara were to be seen wandering down the Strand. Priests, detectives, land-grabbers, and widows of murdered landlords told their pathetic tale in Probate Court No. 1. It was no longer a question of Mr. Walter and *The Times versus* Mr. Parnell and other members of Parliament; the Irish party was in the dock, and the prosecutor was Her Majesty's Government.

CHAPTER THIRTY-SIX

When the Special Commission adjourned for the Christmas Vacation, the question of the letters had not yet been discussed in court. For two months the proceedings had taken their slow and ponderous course; interminable witnesses had been called; squalid incidents of Agrarian crime, many of them dating nearly ten years back, had been brought up by way of proving the iniquities of the Land League. Dreary police reports, unintelligible evidence given by Irish-speaking peasants, the wearisome reiteration of out-of-date speeches soon killed the public interest, and no one was more weary or more irritated by this intolerable waste of time and money than Parnell. At times his attendance at the Law Courts was so irregular as to arouse the indignation of his leading counsel, who complained that he was a "very selfish fellow who thought only of himself, for he took no trouble about any part of the case but the forged letter." In Parnell's opinion the general charges against the Land League were ancient history not worth the lawyers' fees which had to be paid for dealing with them, and he told Barry O'Brien, "If we can prove the letter to be a forgery, everything else will go by the board. If we cannot prove it to be a forgery, then no matter what may be the finding of the Commission on the general issue we shall stand condemned. We must put the man who forged that letter into the box and wring the truth from him. Our victory will then be complete." As early as September his solicitors had served a subpœna on Richard Pigott, and by the end of October both he and *The Times* suspected this wretched journalist to be the forger. With the help of Labouchere and his sleuth-hounds of *Truth,* Pigott had been forced into a situation from which he could no longer extricate himself. Among the melodramatic incidents of the trial none is so melodramatic as when Parnell and George Lewis came face to face with Pigott in the library of Labouchere's house in Grosvenor Gardens. It was here that the solicitor charged him point-blank with forgery, and after making a poor attempt to brazen it out, the hardened blackmailer, who in his day had duped both Dublin Castle and the Fenians, collapsed and confessed to his guilt. But his oral confession was not sufficient, for at that very moment *The Times* agents were shadowing the house, and the interview which had been arranged by Labouchere with a view to purchasing the originals of the Egan letters, from which Pigott had concocted his forgeries, was known not only to *The Times* detectives, but to their solicitor, Mr. Soames, who fully approved of the plan that might compromise both Parnell and Labouchere. As has been said before, they were no longer under any illusion as to Mr. Pigott and their one idea was to keep him out of the witness-box for as long as possible; to incriminate the Parnellite movement so deeply in the murders of the Clan-na-Gael and the more sordid details of Agrarian outrage till the forged letters would be regarded merely as a subsidiary issue. Nothing would have suited *The Times* better than that Labouchere should advance sufficient money for the Egan letters to enable Pigott to fly the country. They would then have had a convincing case, proving Mr. Parnell to have bribed the most important witness to disappear rather than to have the truth come out. This was what Davitt feared when Parnell told him triumphantly that Pigott had confessed his guilt, for years of close contact with the inner workings of the secret societies had made him more watchful and more wary in these matters than even his cautious chief. But, unfortunately for *The Times,* Mr. George Lewis was present at the interview, and however much Mr. Labouchere may have allowed himself to be carried away by his enthusiasm for the hunt and his natural indiscretion, the astute lawyer was not going to commit his client. No money exchanged hands that evening, and an appointment was made for Mr. Pigott to visit Mr. Lewis' office the following morning, where he could make his confession in writing. But by the following day Pigott had changed his mind. Failing the necessary money to go to Australia, he was forced to brave it out; he knew that he was undone—that one of his own confederates had sold him to Parnell.

Distraught and penniless, he still played for high stakes, demanding £5,000 as the price of committing perjury on behalf of *The Times*. And in a letter to Mr. Houston, written on November 11th, a copy of which he forwarded to Mr. Soames, he writes: "If *The Times* compel me to come forward, I can only repeat that I will do so unwillingly and with the feeling strong within me that I have been unfairly dealt with. And I would also again warn them of the grave consequences to myself, which I have already indicated to you, that are certain to follow my appearance in the witness-box. But, above and before all, I would impress upon you that it is my settled conviction that, should I have to appear, the cross-examination would most certainly tend to discredit my evidence in chief. It must of necessity do so, as I feel utterly unable, from defect of memory and other causes, to refute satisfactorily the many allegations founded on remote events of my career as a Nationalist journalist that are now certain to be brought up in judgment against me. May I venture to suggest as an alternative that I should not be asked to come forward but be provided with means to leave the country, if not for good, at least for a prolonged period?" Unhappily for him the fact that he had already told Mr. Soames an elaborate story of how Labouchere had offered him £1,000 to swear that he had forged the letters made it impossible for *The Times* to lay themselves open to the charge of bribery, and, however glad they would have been to see him on his way to Australia, they were forced to rely on him as one of their principal witnesses, though they did not bring him into court until the fifty-fourth day of the Commission's sittings.

Up till then the proceedings dragged slowly and monotonously, interspersed by some short dramatic interludes, such as on the last day of October when Captain O'Shea stepped into the witness-box. To the uninstructed his presence was both curious and inexplicable, unless, as Sir Alfred Robbins states, "it was to do a good service to Chamberlain and an ill turn to Parnell, which seemed the only points likely to emerge from what he testified." Neither did the uninitiated know why he was so delicately handled by both Webster and Russell, nor why, when Tim Healy rose to ask him a question regarding the Galway election, Parnell should have whispered nervously: "What are you going to ask him?" Whereupon the lieutenant, who had not forgiven his chief for the fact that his name had been deliberately canceled from the list of counsels representing the Irish party, answered somewhat acidly: "Don't be afraid." That day the court beheld the unusual spectacle of Parnell sitting grimly attentive in his seat, fixing the witness with his dark, inscrutable eyes, now and then contradicting his assertions in a short, fierce undertone. All the elements of great drama were in that scene. O'Shea, smooth-faced and shifty-eyed, glib in his answers but nervous in his manner, not quite able to forget his school-days at Oscott when he had been taught that perjury was a cardinal crime. Well might Pat Egan say that "he was incapable of playing the heavy villain," for when the Attorney-General asked him to identify the handwriting of the facsimile letter, he faltered, saying, "I am not an expert," adding, "It appears to be Parnell's signature," and the most to which he would commit himself was that he believed it to be his signature. Even that required all his courage, so unnerved was he by that white, haggard face, and those dark eyes which watched him so intently from across the room. When it came to his cross-examination, he gave his evidence cleverly and carefully, and afterwards he boasted to Chamberlain, "Once it came to fighting Russell, however, all went well, and I had him down round after round," ignoring the fact that in the interest of his client the great advocate had deliberately desisted from giving him a grilling. The story of his attempted negotiations, of his friendship and subsequent quarrel with Parnell, was carefully reconstructed, with here and there a little twist, a plausible explanation or extra emphasis laid on some particular point. And Parnell had to sit through it all, nursing a bitter and impotent hatred against a man who he knew would now stop at nothing to bring about his ruin. When O'Shea left for Spain, following his brief and mysterious appearance in the witness-box, he still believed in the invincibility of *The Times,* but two months later he was beginning to have his doubts, and in the last dying agonies of an old lady at Eltham he saw his opportunity.

For Parnell the rest of the proceedings in Probate Court No. 1 were interminably dreary. Even the appearance of that master-spy, Henri Le Caron, alias Beach, who had been summoned from across the Altantic in order to identify the leaders of the Nationalist movement with the blackest crimes of the American Dynamiters, failed to rouse him from his apathy. Cynically he said that if Ireland wanted him to cudgel a clean bill of health out of England she would find work for all the blackthorns she grew. And while Le Caron, with perfect poise and collected manner, thrilled his audience with the tale of his adventurous career, of how after serving in the Federal Armies he had joined the Fenian Society as a spy in the British Secret Service, finally leading up to Parnell's American mission, which was alternately financed, supported and suspected by the leaders of the Clan, Parnell himself would stroll late into the court exasperating his leading counsel by his air of lordly indifference. On one occasion Sir Charles Russell was so irritated by his behavior that he complained to Davitt: "Tell Parnell straight from me that if he doesn't turn up in good time to-morrow, I shall throw up my brief." When this was repeated to Parnell he just smiled: "Oh, Russell is a bully, you know, and you have to tame him a little." But the following morning he was punctual in his attendance, and he was even willing to humor his legal advisers to the length of ordering a new frock-coat from Poole's when they remonstrated that his Irish homespuns did not look well in court.

For his highly strung, nervous temperament, the hours of tedium were intolerable, and Davitt recounts how on one occasion, when he was supposed to be listening to an important witness, he saw him undoing a small paper parcel containing a piece of gold, about the size of a pin's head. With real joy and enthusiasm he then turned towards him, saying, "After fourteen years' search for gold at Avondale, this much has at last been found. I got it out of a parcel of stone sent to me two days ago by my agent." Then he carefully wrapped it up in a piece of tissue paper, put it into his cigar-case and turned a leisurely attention to what was going on around him.

Gradually the stream of witnesses thinned. So much had been said and nothing had been proved, even the victims of the "Kerry Moonlighters," even the boycotted agents and the murdered police-officers had not uttered a word to blacken the reputation of either Mr. Parnell or his party, and at last the principal protagonists had to be called into the box. From the lips of Mr. Houston, the scandalized public heard on what slender evidence these weighty allegations had been hurled against one of the most eminent politicians of the day. They heard how, financed by distinguished Unionists, a needy Dublin journalist with an unsavory reputation had scoured the underworlds of Paris, London and New York in order to collect sufficient evidence with which to send the leader of a country into penal servitude. They heard the miserable tale of the "Black Bag" left by some runaway criminal in a Paris lodging-house, and of how not only Houston, but a respectable professor of Trinity College had been willing to hand out hundreds of pounds in payment to men they had never seen. And, worst of all, they heard how these letters had been hawked round London and refused by several Unionist journals, until they were finally taken by *The Times,* whose legal adviser had accepted Mr. Houston's guarantee without asking any further questions.

When Richard Pigott was called as witness, on February 20th, 1889, the public were already expectant of some tremendous revelations. Every available seat in the court was taken by the time the shortish, stoutish, white-bearded man, looking, as an eye-witness records, "rather like a coarsely composed and rather cheapened Father Christmas," stepped into the witness-box. As Parnell said: "The rat is caught in the trap at last." And yet in answer to Webster's questions he gave his evidence so calmly and so consecutively that there were moments when the Nationalist members despaired of being able to prove the forgeries. It was only when Sir Charles Russell rose for the cross-examination that he was seen to falter, and a feeling of tension ran through the court as in a clear, stern voice the barrister ordered him to write at his dictation the following words: "Livelihood," "likelihood," his own name, "proselytism," "Patrick Egan," "Egan," "hesitancy." When the scrap of paper was handed to Sir Charles, who passed it on to his junior counsel, it was obvious that he had played into their hands. The rat was caught and the trap was closed, and from now onwards every word the miserable culprit uttered only involved him deeper in a maze of crime. All the details of his discreditable past, his attempts at blackmail, his swindling enterprises, were ruthlessly exposed, and for two agonizing days he stood the test, held in the merciless grip of the greatest cross-examiner of the day, while the somber Law Courts reechoed with peals of sardonic laughter. How could those present desist from laughing when they thought that this poor wretch, who confessed himself a swindler and a blackmailer, and who pathetically asked for mercy, saying: "I don't pretend to be very virtuous," this illiterate penny-a-liner who couldn't even spell the words he had forged with such an adept hand, should have managed to fool the greatest English newspaper? What must have been the feelings of the respectable Unionists and the directors of Printing House Square, to be confronted with this product of the Dublin back-streets, this vendor of obscene literature, knowing that in this broken reed had centered all their hopes of a sensational victory over their political opponents? Well might Parnell accuse the Government a few days later in the House of Commons, saying: "You wanted to use this question of the forged letters as a political engine. You did not care whether they were forged or not. . . . It was a very good question for you to win elections with. . . . It was also a suitable engine to enable you to obtain an enquiry into a much wider field and very different matters, an enquiry which you never would have got apart from these infamous productions."

On Friday afternoon of the 22nd February the court adjourned till the following Tuesday, and when Pigott left the witness-box Parnell turned to his lawyer and said: "That man will not come into the box again. Let him be watched. If you don't keep your eyes on him you will find that he will leave the country." Whereupon Lewis replied: "It's little matter to us now, Mr. Parnell, whether he stays or goes." The last days of Richard Pigott make pathetic reading. Pinning his ultimate hopes on Labouchere he called at his house and made a valueless confession in the presence of the well-known journalist, George Augustus Sala. Then he fled the country, only to blow out his brains a fortnight later in a hotel bedroom in Madrid, while the police were waiting outside with a warrant for his arrest. There are many unexplained mysteries surrounding his flight. How and why was he allowed to evade the vigilance of the detectives? Who supplied him with funds? And why, once he had got to Spain, a country where no extradition law existed, did he commit suicide? All are questions which have never been cleared up. Curiously enough, the last Englishman who saw him alive was William O'Shea, who caught sight of him in a Madrid café the day before he shot himself, a coincidence which confirmed Parnell in his belief that there was an understanding between them.

When the court met on Tuesday the 26th to find that the principal witness had flown, leaving behind a full confession of his guilt, *The Times* had no choice but to withdraw the letters and to proffer an apology which the general public felt to be but poor amends for a grievous wrong, while an action for libel, brought against them by Parnell, was settled out of court by a payment of £5,000, *The Times* publishing an acknowledgment that it had no legal defense for the action, and "no alternative but to come to terms with our opponent, or to abide by such a verdict as the jury might think proper to award." Though the sittings of the Special Commission were to drag on for several months, while the judges exhausted themselves in the perusal of bluebooks and musty memoranda, though Sir Charles Russell was to deliver his historic speech in defense not so much of his clients as of a nation, a speech so eloquent in its descriptions of the sufferings of the Irish peasantry that it drew tears even to the eyes of Parnell, who confessed, half-ashamed, to Davitt: "I don't remember ever crying before, not even when I was a child, but I really couldn't help it." And though Parnell, Davitt and Biggar were all to appear in the witness-box, the public interest died the day when Pigott left the Law Courts.

The Irish leader was vindicated, and every fair-minded Englishman felt that he had been the victim of a political conspiracy. The dramatic revelations in Probate Court No. 1 had turned the tide in favor of Home Rule, and even the most hidebound Tory squire was now willing to shake hands with the man he would gladly have found to be a traitor. When Parnell entered the House of Commons on the night of March 1st he received an ovation such as is but rarely given even to a Prime Minister. Every Nationalist and Liberal in the House—not to omit a few generous-hearted Tories—rose to acclaim him with enthusiastic cheers. Mr. Gladstone bowed low in homage to him, and the whole Opposition front bench, with the exception of Lord Hartington, followed his example. In his autobiography the Solicitor-General, Sir Edward Clarke, who eighteen months later was to play an unwitting part in bringing about his downfall, testifies to his greatness at that hour.

Quoting from a speech delivered at Plymouth two years later, he writes: "I saw Mr. Parnell standing erect among the whole standing crowd. He took no notice of it whatever. He had not asked them to get up. When they had finished standing up they sat down, and he took no notice of their rising up or of their sitting down. And when they had resumed their places he proceeded to make a perfectly calm and quiet speech in which he made not the smallest reference, direct or indirect, to the incident—extraordinary as it was—which had just happened. I thought as I looked at him that night that that man was a born leader of men—calm, self-confident and powerful."

Only Parnell's nearest neighbors could see that while he spoke his hands were nervously twitching behind his back, and when he sat down he whispered to a colleague: "Why did you fellows

stand up? It almost frightened me." He was unnerved and
taken aback by this tremendous reception, but he was not moved
by it, for as he told Katie afterwards: "They would all be at
my throat in a week if they could," adding, "You see, my dear,
these people are not really pleased with me. They thought I
had written those letters, and now they are extolling their own
sense of justice in cheering me because I did not write them.
I might as wisely shout myself hoarse if a court of law decided
that Gladstone had not told somebody to rob a bank! They
only howl with joy because I have been found within the law.
The English make a law and bow down and worship it, till they
find it obsolete, long after this is obvious to other nations. Then
they bravely make another, and start afresh in the opposite direction. That's why I am glad Ireland has a religion; there is so
little hope for a nation that worships law." And when the
woman who was so proud of him, so ambitious for his sake,
said: "But don't you feel a little excited and proud when they
all cheer you, really you?" he answered: "Yes, when it is really
me, when I am in the midst of a peasant crowd in Ireland, then
I feel a little as I do when I see you smile across the street at
me before we meet, but for these others, it is then I know how
I hate the English, and it is then, if I begin to feel a bit elated,
I remember the howling of a mob I once saw chasing a man
to lynch him years ago. Don't be too pleased with the clapping
of these law-lovers, Queenie. I have a presentiment that you
will hear them another way before long." With his clear, far-
reaching mind he foresaw the unavoidable dangers ahead of him.
At the hour of his greatest triumph, while Katie was tied to the
bedside of her dying aunt, whose death would finally enable
O'Shea to come out into the open as the injured husband, he
foresaw all the squalor of the divorce court. But there was one
thing he never foresaw, one thing he never contemplated, which
was that his own people would throw him over at the bidding
of the English Liberals. Wearily he submitted to the lionizing
of London hostesses and the acclamations of enthusiastic Home
Rulers; cynically he listened to Mr. Gladstone and his colleagues

defending the Plan of Campaign which but a year ago "had offended almost more than the outrages." He himself had never wavered in his disapproval of the Agrarian agitation, and at a dinner at the Eighty Club he had not hesitated to voice that disapproval in public. It was all very well for a Don Quixote, like Wilfrid Blunt, to court martyrdom in Galway Jail, but it was not he who was going to be landed with thousands of evicted tenants on his hands; it was not he who would have to supply the funds for Mr. Dillon's "New Tipperary." And when people asked Parnell why he did not cross to Ireland and join in the campaign, he answered: "My head is of far more use to the party, unbroken here than broken there." It might suit Mr. Gladstone's purpose to play the agitator, and to inspire his party by his fiery denunciations of Mr. Balfour's Irish rule, but then Mr. Gladstone did not have to hold the Fenians in leash in order to earn the approval of Maynooth, and it was Parnell's moderation and statesmanlike qualities which won him the admiration of the greatest of all colonists. In 1888 Mr. Cecil Rhodes sent him as a mark of his estimation, £10,000 for the Home Rule cause, and a friendly meeting took place in the summer at the Westminster Palace Hotel. During this interview the two men exchanged their views as to how Irish Home Rule would ultimately affect Imperial Home Rule, and an active correspondence resulted from this meeting. It was said that Rhodes was responsible for the message sent to Parnell following the proceedings of the Divorce Courts, telling him to "resign, marry, return." But, however much Parnell professed to be an admirer of the great Empire builder, he never had the slightest intention of taking his advice. It is interesting to note that, in spite of his discouragement of the Plan of Campaign, Parnell handed the whole of the Rhodes' Tribute over to Dillon and O'Brien, an isolated action of goodwill prompted by his personal sympathy for O'Brien, for on no other occasion could he be brought to identify himself with the Agrarian war.

Mrs. Benjamin Wood died at Eltham, and, while Katherine mourned her aunt, Parnell was the unwilling guest of honor at

political receptions and Liberal dinner-parties. It was no longer
considered wise tactics to keep him at arm's length; on the contrary he was now fêted and courted as the hero of the hour.
At the end of March one finds him dining with the Sydney
Buxtons to meet Mr. and Mrs. Gladstone, and the hostess notes
that "after dinner Mr. Gladstone and Mr. Parnell had a long
talk. Mr. Gladstone, of course, assumed that Mr. Parnell knew
all about the ancient history of Ireland, and when he said, 'That
occurred, you will remember, in '41,' Mr. Parnell looked as if he
didn't know what century and didn't in the least care." But
she, like all the other society women who fluttered round him
in this year of triumph, was fascinated by his grave, quiet manner, his illuminating smile and dry, subtle humor. He was so
mysterious, so intangible, and it was "breathlessly exciting"
merely to shake hands with him, merely to receive a kindly look
from what Gladstone's daughter called "his fire-darting eyes."
It was probably to this dinner that Lord Oxford refers in his
memoirs, when he writes that, on the occasion when Gladstone
and Parnell met in private for the first time, "I can still remember the pained and troubled look which came over Gladstone's
face when Parnell betrayed complete ignorance of the date and
purpose of Lord Fitzwilliam's mission to Dublin." Mrs. Sydney
Buxton must have prided herself on having arranged a memorable meeting, but when the Irish leader left the house with
Augustine Birrell his only comment on Gladstone was: "The old
gentleman is very talkative." And when he rejoined Katie
later in the evening he said, with a sigh of relief, "That's over,
thank goodness!" But it was only one of a long sequence of
dreary parties, among which a soirée given by Sir Charles Russell
was a pleasant exception, for it was here that he met Katherine
Tynan, the friendly little Irish poetess "who looked as shy as I
felt." At a dinner at the Eighty Club, held in his honor, attended by most of the Liberal leaders, he leaned across the chairman to shake hands with Lord Spencer, a handshake which
Lord Rosebery described as "historic," but his greatest triumph
was when he appeared for the first time on a Liberal platform

at a great meeting at St. James's Hall. Morley himself was regarded as little more than a Master of Ceremonies when the
"Uncrowned King of Ireland" passed cold and impassive through
the cheering throng. "He'll soon set the English as mad as the
Irish" was the opinion of a casual bystander in the crowd. And
he was seemingly so indifferent, so regardless of his audience,
saying what he had to say without any dramatic effects, without
any attempt to come into personal contact with these Englishmen who were cheering themselves hoarse at every sentence.
When he left the hall the people hemmed him in just as they did
after those rough-and-tumble meetings in the Irish villages, calling out his name, struggling to clasp his hands, so as to be
able to boast that they had shaken hands with Parnell.

Though his appearance as a witness before the Special Commission two months after Pigott's flight did not attract the general attention of the public, it drew vast crowds of his sympathizers to the purlieus of the Law Courts, and in Mary Gladstone's Diary one finds an echo of the almost hysterical hero-
worship which he inspired at the time. On Thursday, the 2nd
May, she notes, "Straight off to Commission at the Law Courts.
Immediately Parnell stepped forward as witness so close to us
that we could whisper to him. The most absorbing, exciting
thing I ever remember. . . . The Attorney-General's manner
odious in cross-examination. Parnell's coolness wonderful. He
really exhibited all the fruits of the spirit, love, peace, patience,
gentleness, forbearance, long-suffering, meekness. His personality takes hold of one. The refined, delicate face, illuminating
smile, fire-darting eyes, slight, tall figure, so done he seemed
almost fainting. At four we shook hands with Mr. Parnell."
The quality the Irish leader possessed of rousing that most dangerous of all feminine instincts, the maternal feeling, is evident
when Gladstone's daughter confides in her Diary: "Love Parnell's
spiritual face. Only one's heart aches over his awfully delicate
frame and look." But the following day her hero did not acquit
himself so well in the witness-box. Worn-out with weariness
and boredom, suffering in health, he gave way to one of those

waves of inertia which came over him at times, making him unable to think clearly or to concentrate on the matter in hand. Casually and quietly he informed the scandalized court that when, during the debate on the Coercion Bill in 1881, he had said that secret societies had ceased to exist in Ireland, it was possible that he had made that statement with the deliberate intention of misleading the House of Commons. Naturally the Unionists tried to make capital out of this unfortunate remark, but, as Mrs. Sydney Buxton said, "I should like to see the Unionists cross-examined on oath as to their intentions when they say that the power of the agitator is at an end in Ireland, and things of that description. Moreover when one remembers the tremendous accusations brought against Mr. Parnell, a single instance of an attempt to mislead the House of Commons does not seem much to be proved." Nevertheless his mental aberrations and general vagueness must have been exasperating for his legal advisers, and Asquith recounts how when they left the courts together Parnell said, with unruffled complacency, "Didn't you think Webster's bowling very wide to-day?" Whereupon his young counsel growled in reply, "The bowling was wide enough if you hadn't hit the wicket."

This "gaffe" was as bad as the occasion when, during an important phase of the Commission, Parnell was called upon to produce some important document. Nonchalantly he pulled a paper out of his pocket, gave it one look, and said, without the slightest trace of embarrassment, "Forgive me, it's the wrong one. This is my subscription to the Meath Hunt." Yet in spite of all these maddening vagaries he had won through, and after all the mud-slinging there was not the slightest stain on his political integrity or on his reputation.

The year 1889 was one of royal homage, culminating in a visit to Hawarden, that most exclusive of all Liberal temples. In July he received the freedom of the City of Edinburgh, and Lady Aberdeen, whose husband presided at the banquet given in his honor, recalls that, though the proposal to make him a freeman was carried by a large majority in the municipal council, it was opposed by the bulk of the townspeople, who expressed their disapproval by drawing down their blinds when he drove through the streets. But even the churlishness of these rigid Covenanters did not impede Parnell's triumphal progress. In London the National Liberal Club elected him as an honorary member, a privilege he did not even deign to acknowledge. He was literally mobbed at a soirée held by the Women's Liberal Association, and even in the House of Commons he had only to make some short statement on the Irish Land question, and the benches were immediately crowded with attentive listening members. On one occasion he surprised the Radical Home Rulers by following Mr. Gladstone's lead in voting in favor of the Royal Grants, a courteous gesture which brought him an invitation to lunch with the Prince of Wales. It would be interesting to know what were the topics of conversation between the genial heir-apparent and the silent Irish leader. In Liberal eyes the political horizon had never seemed more unclouded, no one doubted that the next elections would see the Home Rulers in power: "The flowing tide is with us," cried Mr. Gladstone, ignoring the fact that one man's hand could stem that tide, and when Mr. Parnell accepted the invitation to stay at Hawarden in the late autumn it was in order to discuss the main features of the next Home Rule Bill. As he traveled north the storm-clouds were already gathering over Brighton, where he and Mrs. O'Shea had made their home ever since the death of her aunt.

Mr. Gladstone's record of Parnell's visit is short and to the point. On December 18th he writes: "Reviewed and threw into form all the points of possible amendment and change in the plan of Irish government, etc., for my meeting with Mr. Parnell. He arrived at 5.30 and we had two hours of satisfactory conversation, but he put off the 'gros' of it. December 19th: Two hours more with Mr. Parnell, on points in Irish Government Plan. He is certainly one of the very best people to deal with that I have ever known. Took him to the Old Castle. He seemed to notice and appreciate everything." A more human note is struck by his daughter, who talks of the excitement in the atmosphere, the thrill of sitting next to Mr. Parnell at dinner, the calmness with which he discussed burning points, "his cool indifferent manner, in sharp contrast to the deep piercing gaze of his eyes, which look bang through, not at yours, and his compelling, undefinable power."

That the two leaders were not in complete accord over the amendments for a coming Home Rule Bill was only made public a year later by Parnell. At the time he did not take a single one of his colleagues into his confidence, for, regarding himself as the spokesman of Ireland, he considered that it was for him alone to make the decisions. There were two characteristics he shared with the majority of his countrymen: he never forgot and he never forgave; and when he asked Miss Gladstone, with a smile, where her father kept his dungeons, he showed that he still remembered Kilmainham. He firmly believed that his hatred of Gladstone was reciprocal, and when the day came for the Liberals to turn against him, he said quite calmly to Katherine O'Shea, "You know as well as I do that Gladstone always loathed me." But who could presume to guess the innermost sentiments of the man whom he himself called the greatest actor of his time, and never by a word or deed did Gladstone show that he resented the agitator who had forced him to accept his alliance on his own terms.

While Parnell admired the sylvan beauties of Hawarden, a "dreadful scene" occurred at No. 10 Walsingham Terrace, Brighton, a scene which resulted in Captain O'Shea filing a petition for divorce on the grounds of his wife's adultery with Mr. Charles Stewart Parnell. Whether the scene itself was premeditated, whether Captain O'Shea went deliberately to Brighton in order to produce a convincing frame-up for the Divorce Court, or whether, as he wrote to Chamberlain, his son called unexpectedly at his mother's house and found a lot of Mr. Parnell's things, some of which he chucked out of the window, is immaterial. Already in the early autumn the Captain had decided to take definite action, and the circumstances which led the acquiescent, worldly O'Shea to expose himself to the publicity of a divorce, where the briefest cross-examination would prove him to be guilty of connivance, have been given in detail by Captain Harrison. There can be no doubt that Mrs. Benjamin Wood's will played a prominent part in the tragedy of Parnell's downfall, for when the old lady died, leaving her vast fortune to her niece Katherine, unhampered by any binding clauses, tying it down to the O'Shea marriage settlement, the aggrieved husband may well have felt cheated of his highest hopes. It had been bitter enough on his return from Spain to find that instead of exulting over Parnell's ruin he had to bear witness to his triumphs, but this was the crowning irony. He had sacrificed so much in his pursuit of the Wood fortune, and now he had no other alternative but to make common cause with his brothers and sisters-in-law who were contesting the validity of the will. But there were other means of retrieving his fortunes, coupled with all the sweetness of revenge. As early as September, Sir Alfred Robbins, the correspondent of the *Birmingham Post,* was asked by one on the inside of the Liberal Unionist *Machine,* "whether Parnell would be politically ruined by a divorce, the then recent Dilke instance being given as a promising precedent, and Captain O'Shea, it was added, being willing to take proceedings." Though the Unionist wire-puller got no encouragement from a man who was not only one of the most trusted members of his profession, but also a personal admirer of Parnell's, one finds O'Shea writing to Chamberlain on October 13th, "Owing to some recent circumstances it is under consideration whether some strong action should not be taken by me, and I am anxious that you (and a few others) should be rightly informed." Chamberlain's biographer, who publishes the carefully worded note in which the Radical leader replies to this communication by sympathizing with the Captain's difficulties, saying, "I am not sure that the boldest course is not always the wisest," is emphatic in declaring that Chamberlain was not in any way connected with the divorce proceedings. And it is certainly hard to believe that this clear-headed politician, who in the past had been so tricked and misled by O'Shea, should have let himself be involved in an unsavory affair which in all probability would miss fire. There were other agencies more directly interested in Parnell's downfall, and it is curious that the first solicitor consulted by O'Shea should have been Mr. Soames, the hard-worked legal adviser of *The Times*.

The path of the betrayed husband was not a smooth one. As a good Catholic he besought the aid of Cardinal Manning, in order to obtain a dispensation from Rome, but for political and religious reasons His Eminence did not see his way towards countenancing a "separation" which he shrewdly suspected to have been prompted by ulterior motives. Discarding his religious scruples, O'Shea then consulted the Conservative Solicitor-General, and events took their inevitable course. As Winston Churchill wrote in the biography of his father: "Her Majesty's Government regained in the Divorce Court the credit they had lost before the Special Commission."

CHAPTER THIRTY-SEVEN

At a convivial dinner-party at Brooks's Club, held in honor of the Prince of Wales, Morley heard from the lips of George Lewis some unpleasant details as regards the coming O'Shea divorce case. It was February 3rd, 1890, the very day that *The Times* announced the settlement of the Parnell libel case by an agreed verdict of £5,000; but Mr. Lewis was far from jubilant, and the following morning Morley communicated the bad news to Harcourt, saying: "He told me much else which cannot well be written down. I can only say that, when the time comes, Walter will have his £5,000 worth of revenge. It will be a horrid exposure, and must, I think, lead to the disappearance of our friend." But the Liberal rank and file were inclined to take the Nationalist view in believing that this fresh menace to Parnell's career was but another political conspiracy directed against a powerful leader. That this was the general opinion of the Irish party is only natural, considering that they knew of certain personal assurances given to William O'Brien. As early as January 1890, Parnell had written to his faithful colleague: "If this case is ever fully gone into (a matter which is exceedingly doubtful), you may rest assured that it will be shown that the dishonor and the discredit have not been on my side." Similar assurances were given to Davitt, but, apart from these brief confidences, Parnell took no further notice of the coming storm. At Westminster his attendance was as irregular as usual. He now lived permanently at Brighton, which, though beneficent to his health, estranged him more than ever from his colleagues. Nevertheless, he was the undisputed dictator of his party, and on the rare occasions when he consented to lead a debate he still showed himself to be the stern disciplinarian and exacting commander. In Wilfrid Blunt's *The Land War in Ireland* one is given a pleasant glimpse of one of his last appearances as the leader of the United Irish party. It was on the occasion of William O'Brien's wedding in London, where

"Parnell made an excellent speech, dignified and graceful and delivered in the best parliamentary manner. It raised my opinion of him immensely, for hitherto I have rather underrated his intellectual qualities. Dillon's was less good, rough-hewn, and in part awkward, like the speech of one unaccustomed to public speaking. By far the best, however, was Dr. Croke's. This was astonishingly outspoken, and full of wit and tenderness. . . . He paid compliments to Parnell, who, he said, had made him a Land Leaguer. . . . Parnell's speech, everyone said, was the best they ever heard him make, as it showed some heart, which is generally absent from his speeches. Certainly all he said of O'Brien was graceful and even affectionate, besides being extremely well delivered. Altogether this wedding festivity has done me good and put me back once more on the higher lines of thought a noble cause inspires." So great was Parnell's prestige that William O'Brien regarded it as the highest honor when his chief expressed a wish to attend his wedding, and yet in reality he was the simplest of men, happy in any informal family gathering. Besides, he was genuinely fond of O'Brien, who writes: "His refined face, so brilliantly handsome in its pallor, his shy gentleness and words of affection are remembrances never to be dimmed. We often, by the light of later days, recalled the emotion with which, in the little church crowded with happy faces, he remarked to Archbishop Croke, who performed the marriage ceremony, 'How happy I should be to be married like that!'" As he said those words Parnell never realized the price he would have to pay for that happiness, for how could he know that the colleagues who gathered round him at this wedding would be among the first to desert him? He realized that "there would be a howl, but it would be the howling of hypocrites." The Nonconformists would do their best to ruin him, but surely the people of Ireland, who were so slow to give a man their confidence, would be still more slow to withdraw it? Thus argued Parnell, ignoring the fact that there was one man who exercised a greater spell and a greater magnetism than he did. So unconcerned did he seem regarding the impending proceedings that the general public began to doubt whether the O'Shea case would ever come on. They regarded it as just another attempt to frighten Parnell, though, as Justin McCarthy remarked: "Who on earth could believe in frightening Parnell?" But gradually as the summer turned to autumn the rumors grew more ominous; uneasy Parnellites exchanged nervous confidences; the Liberal leaders were seized with panic. "Edward Clarke has some terribly odious material in his hands," wrote Morley to Harcourt, and from Hawarden Mr. Gladstone sent an alarming message to his Chief Whip: "I fear a thundercloud is about to burst over Parnell's head, and I suppose it will end the career of a man in many respects invaluable."

All eyes turned to Brighton, to that bleak exposed house at the far end of Walsingham Terrace which Parnell and Mrs. O'Shea had made their home, and it was the happenings in this house which influenced the events of the following months. The news which Parnell had received with a serene equanimity, almost with joy, bringing, as it did, an end to all the subterfuges and deceit, finally entitling him to claim his wife before the world, was received in a very different fashion by Katherine O'Shea. More worldly wise than her lover, she foresaw the inevitable consequences, and she recognized herself as the cause of his ruin. If only Willie had waited a few months she would have been in command of unlimited wealth, able to comply to his most exacting demands, to hand him over the large share of her fortune which he demanded as the price of his silence, and to buy off the custody of Parnell's children. But the will was still in probate, challenged by her own brothers and sisters, with whom Willie had made common cause, and Parnell was unable to come to her assistance owing to severe financial difficulties of his own. Over a year later, Captain Harrison heard from her own lips the following confession: "From the moment that my name was publicly mentioned—from the moment that the divorce petition incriminating my name was presented—Mr. Parnell insisted that there must be a divorce so that he could marry me. It was a matter that touched his pride. Apart altogether from our love, he could not bear that my name should be compromised through him. He would do nothing—assist in nothing—consent to nothing that would prevent the divorce taking place, and he would have nothing to do with any discussions as to a settlement, with any negotiations as to a way out except on the basis of there being a divorce. Yet with all this he left me to act as I thought best for myself and my children." That was the pity of it! If only Parnell had not placed his destiny quite so unreservedly in the hands of the woman who now allowed herself to be dominated by her fury and resentment, not only against her husband, but against her sister, Anne Steele, who till now had been the recognized mediator in the O'Sheas' matrimonial complications! At first Katie regarded the divorce petition merely as another move in Willie's game, and she shrewdly suspected that it was all just a question of cash. Soon it transpired that £20,000 was the figure he demanded for the renunciation of his conjugal rights, and, as she told Captain Harrison: "If I could have got £20,000 to give Captain O'Shea, his charges against me would have failed, and my countercharges against him would have succeeded. Mr. Parnell and I would have been cleared by the Divorce Court, and I should have been a free woman, free to marry Mr. Parnell without a slur or a reproach to either of us. I had got it all arranged in spite of the cross-currents—in spite of the others who were egging on Captain O'Shea for their own purposes. But I could not get the money, and nothing except the actual money itself was any use. You see, it would have been the final surrender of everything for Captain O'Shea, and he could not be expected to make it unless the price of it was in his hands."

The only counter-charge she contemplated at the beginning was a simple denial of the adultery, coupled with a charge of misconduct brought against the petitioner, a charge which she would have no difficulty in proving. It was only later, in a moment of madness, that she brought the terrible accusations against her husband and her sister which tended more than anything else to alienate public sympathy from her side.

Failing to obtain the £20,000, O'Shea proceeded to tell his legal advisers that he had been offered this sum in order to abandon the suit. Maybe he had hopes that this would come to the ears of the influential agencies who were showing such a benevolent interest in his personal affairs. At first he was singularly unlucky in his choice of legal advisers, for, when he was informed that the fact of his having secured the services of *The Times* solicitor would prejudice him with the jury, his next choice fell on the young son of Mr. Justice Day of the Special Commission, but finally Sir Edward Clarke persuaded him to employ a lawyer who had no public connection with Probate Court No. 1. If O'Shea was unwise in the management of his affairs, his wife was doubly so. After having secured the invaluable services of Parnell's solicitor, Mr. Lewis, she promptly quarreled with him, and, though Parnell still retained him as his legal adviser, she placed her own case in the charge of a pliant family solicitor who would never dare to contradict her. Over-confident in what she considered to be her infallible instinct, she was deaf to all reasoning and advice, and, after her failure to obtain the necessary guarantees for the £20,000, she completely lost her head. Her rancor was largely directed against the relations whom she held responsible for the circumstances which prevented her from drawing on her aunt's money. They were "those others who were egging on Captain O'Shea for their own purposes," and in a moment of blind rage she launched her counter-charges. To accuse her husband of connivance was foolish, in so much as it did not appreciably better the situation, but to accuse him of adultery with her own sister was not only foolish but wicked, even if the charges had not been, as Sir Edward Clarke says, "utterly base and wanton." If Mr. Lewis had been acting in her interests, he would never have allowed her to bring these counter-charges into court. But, unfortunately, she was a woman with whom it was impossible to argue, for she was quick-tempered and sharp-tongued, and capable of losing all control in a moment of anger. When she saw her lover attacked and all her hopes and ambitions dashed to the ground, she became the primitive female fighting with her claws, but her claws only hurt herself and the man she loved. How and why Parnell ever allowed her to launch these accusations has never been explained. The most obvious reason was that she was in such a hysterical, overwrought state at the time that he did not dare to aggravate her condition. There was only one matter he was definite about: he was not going to fight the case, and his colleagues were wrong when, in a natural hatred of Mrs. O'Shea, they asserted that it was she who would not allow him to defend himself, as she wanted a divorce so as to marry him. To the very last moment both Katherine and her counsel, Sir Frank Lockwood, begged him to fight it out. "But what's the use?" he said. "We want a divorce, and, divorce or not, I shall always come where you are." He dreaded a verdict of collusion, the appearance of the King's Proctor, and a decree which would leave Katie tied to the man whom he now regarded with an almost abnormal loathing, and he dreaded still more the fact that his two children would be the hostages of O'Shea. Only a few weeks before the case came on he consulted a leading barrister as to whether there was any European country in which Mrs. O'Shea, in spite of the orders of an English court, would be able to retain the custody of the younger children.

Yet all during this nerve-racking time he gave the impression of being serene and confident in the future. Asquith recounts how he met him one day in the Temple looking far more alert and debonair than was his wont, and how, when he asked him, "Well, is it going to be all right?" he smiled almost genially and replied, "Of course it is. You needn't worry about that." Strangely enough, his very appearance had improved for the better, and people were struck not only by his *insouciance* but by his trim, youthful look, for in the last months he had thrown off the inertia and sickly lassitude of the chronic invalid; even his strange, shapeless clothes had been discarded, and he once more appeared at Westminster immaculately dressed, with the inevitable white rose in his buttonhole. This seeming indifference and almost unnatural calm were no mere pose on his part. In many ways the news of the impending divorce had been a tremendous relief, for at last he was free, free of all the secrecy and lying, the endless bargaining and constant humiliations; and, even if the Liberals should throw him over, Ireland was now united and far stronger than when he had fought her battles almost single-handed in a hostile Parliament. Maybe the conversations at Hawarden had shown him that there was not so much to be got out of Mr. Gladstone after all, that Irish liberty would always remain emasculated as long as it was an English party cry. When Morley came down to visit him at Brighton a week before the final crash, he was still the haughty dictator, stating his terms and refusing to be bribed by a seat on the Treasury Bench.

It never struck the late Chief Secretary as impertinent of Parnell to keep him waiting two hours at the Metropole Hotel when he writes: "I had fixed the time from 6 to 8, and therefore it was a virtuous degree of punctuality when he came walking cheerfully into the room at 8.20. He has certainly as fine and pleasing a carriage as any man in the House of Commons, free, erect, lithe, and with every mark of unaffected dignity. He was more than usually cordial and gracious." And when they dined together in a private sitting-room, Morley observed that, whenever the waiter came into the room, Parnell would half unconsciously turn his chair away, "so as to have an inverted face from the invader." Their talk was amicable and confidential; they discussed the question of land purchase, the underhand intrigues of the priests, and the chances of a future Liberal Government, with Morley enquiring as to whether Parnell could see his way to taking the post of Irish Secretary. But on this point the Nationalist leader stood firm; neither he nor any member of his party would join a Government, and a fortnight later, in his counter-attack to Gladstone's denunciation, he made a ruthless exposure of Morley's well-meant confidences. In spite of the friendly atmosphere and pleasant discursions, when for a few moments Parnell discarded his habitual reserve and talked of his love for the Wicklow hills, and of the happy days he spent at his small shooting-lodge at Aughavanagh, Morley could not help noticing the callous neutral tone of his voice whenever he mentioned Gladstone's name. And only at the end of dinner did he dare to question him on the matter which for the past months had been hanging like a black cloud over the Liberal camp. Tentatively he said: "There is one point on which I have no right to speak to you—and if you don't like it you can say so. But it is important we should know whether certain legal proceedings about to come on are likely to end in your disappearance from the lead for a time." Parnell smiled all over his face, playing with his fork. "My disappearance! Oh, no, no chance of it. Nothing in the least leading to disappearance, so far as I am concerned, will come out of the legal proceedings. The other side don't know what a broken-kneed horse they are riding!" By these words Morley inferred that there would be no adverse decree, and he lost no time in assuring Mr. Gladstone that Parnell would once again emerge triumphantly from his difficulties. When the Irish leader spoke of "the other side," he meant his political opponents, and the "broken-kneed horse" was obviously O'Shea; but did he really believe, even at the eleventh hour, that O'Shea would accept Katherine's promises of future payment as sufficient guarantee, and allow the tables to be turned on him in court, and did he really believe that the Unionist wire-pullers who had been so active of late would once more consent to see their plans miss fire?

On November 15th the O'Shea divorce suit came before the court, and the petitioner's counsel found to their surprise that not only had the corespondent briefed no counsel at all, but Sir Frank Lockwood, in representing the respondent, informed the court that he proposed to take no part in the proceedings. The hearing might then have been limited to the production of necessary evidence had it not been for the counter-charges which, besides prejudicing the respondent in the eyes of the jury, gave Sir Edward Clarke the opportunity of making a full disclosure of the relations between her and the corespondent. The Irish leader was presented to the world as the guilty home-breaker trespassing on the hospitality of his unsuspecting friend. His various devices for avoiding Government spies and importunate reporters, the houses rented under assumed names, the strange disguises, the secrecy attached to his movements, were all laid down to the promptings of a guilty conscience. Once again Captain O'Shea gave his evidence carefully and glibly, slurring over any incidents that might arouse the suspicion of the jury. Letters were read in court which left the public under no illusion as to the character of either husband or wife, but the most damaging of all was the famous "fire-escape" episode, where, on the evidence of a temporary servant, Parnell was labeled as a furtive, deceitful coward. Not only the vulgar-minded, but also serious and influential politicians, who had known the Irish leader personally, were ready to believe that on a certain occasion, at Medina Terrace, Brighton, he had escaped from the balcony by a rope fire-escape in order to avoid Captain O'Shea finding him in the house. So eloquent was Sir Edward Clarke on this subject that both judge and jury credited this fantastic tale, while the popular Press seized on it with avidity, delighting a vast public with comic sketches and scurrilous details of "Mr. Stewart and Kitty O'Shea." The mud-slinging had begun, and in the coming pantomime season no character was to be more popular than that of the bearded Irish leader climbing down a fire-escape. Well might O'Shea say with his usual cynicism: "The joke of it all was that there was no fire-escape." But, having decided on the policy of silence, Parnell was powerless to intervene. Mr. Macdonagh relates how, on the first day of the proceedings, he strolled into the London office of the *Freeman's Journal* "wearing a heavy ulster coat, its high collar turned up about his ears, a thick woolen muffler covering his beard and the lower part of his face, and on his head a cloth traveling-cap, with the peak pulled low down over his forehead and the flaps tied under his chin." In this disguise, he fondly believed that he escaped the attention of the crowd, but he betrayed no nervousness or anger when he read the report of the proceedings as it arrived in copy from the courts. Only when it came to the "fire-escape" episode did he vehemently cry: "What a blackguard invention!" As he left the office, the *Freeman* correspondent, Mr. Tuohy, who for the last ten years had made a faithful record of his parliamentary victories, questioned him uneasily: "Now that it is clear that a verdict will be given against you, might I ask whether you intend the verdict to affect your public position?" Whereupon he replied in his haughtiest manner, "No, I shall not permit the result to affect my public position in any way whatsoever." And the next day he dictated the usual letter to his parliamentary followers, summoning them to appear at Westminster for the opening of the session on November 25th.

During the following week it almost seemed as if his powerful personality and tremendous prestige would triumph over the storm of indignation fostered by the English Press, the howling of the righteous Mr. Stead, the vituperation of the Nonconformists, and the cheap jokes of embittered journalists, one of whom wrote: "Can any sane man believe that the Home Rule cause will benefit during the next six months by the hero of the many aliases being retained as one of the twin commanders-in-chief, or that the 'fire-escape' will be the golden bridge to conduct the waverers back to Liberal fealty?" There was a strange silence both from the Liberal camp and from the Catholic hierarchy, but the Nationalist Press and the Nationalist party rallied enthusiastically to their leader. Only one man in Ireland spoke out against him, and that was honest Michael Davitt, who threw him over purely on moral grounds. Such being his views, he had every right to complain of the conduct of the bishops, "who should have been before the Nonconformists in expressing their condemnation," but the Irish bishops took their lead from the English Cardinal Manning, and His Eminence took his lead from Mr. Gladstone, who, strangely enough, expected Rome to extricate him from the unenviable position of acting as schoolmaster to the Irish party.

In England, the effect of the divorce had been shattering, but Mr. Gladstone allowed a whole week to elapse before he launched his thunders. His first reactions were voiced to Morley in calm and measured terms: "I think it plain that we have nothing to say and nothing to do in the matter. The party is as distinct from us as that of Smith or Hartington. I own to some surprise at the apparent facility with which the Roman Catholic bishops and clergy appear to take the continued leadership. But they may have tried the ground and found it would not bear. It is the Irish parliamentary party, and that alone, to which we have to look." On the following day he again repeated that "we, the Liberal party as a whole, and especially we its leaders, have for the moment nothing to say to it, that we must be passive, must wait and watch." But in this letter he added, "I again and again say to myself, 'I say I mean in the interior and silent Forum, It'll na dee!'" Whatever may have been Gladstone's doubts, he kept a rigid silence till the day before the opening of Parliament, when the Nonconformist conscience had already spoken from a hundred chapels, when Harcourt and Morley had reported from the annual meeting of the National Liberal Federation at Sheffield "that the opinion was absolutely and unanimously strong that if Parnell is allowed to remain as a leader of the Irish party, all further cooperation between them and the English Liberals must be at an end." It was only then that Mr. Gladstone decided to discard the alliance of a man "in many respects invaluable."

In Dublin the parliamentary party stood firm by their chief. At a meeting of the National League presided over by John Redmond, a resolution pledging the members to stand by Parnell was carried with acclamation. Two days later, on November 20th, a popular demonstration, presided over by the Lord Mayor, took place at Leinster Hall. The proceedings opened with the reading aloud of a message of confidence, signed by the members of the Nationalist party who were at that moment in America. John Dillon and William O'Brien had escaped there following their arrest in Tipperary, and, assisted by T. P. O'Connor, T. Harrington, and T. D. Sullivan, they were raising vast sums of money in aid of the evicted tenants. Only four of these men signed the cable announcing that they stood firm "to the leadership of the man who had brought the Irish people through unparalleled difficulties and dangers, from servitude and despair, to the very threshold of emancipation, with a genius, courage, and success unequaled in our history." The delegate who abstained from adding his signature was that famous writer of ballads, T. D. Sullivan, who refused to champion the man whom he now regarded as a moral delinquent.

What matter to repeat all the hysterical professions of loyalty and affection, the chorus of indignation roused by the verdict of the English Press, that were uttered that day in Leinster Hall by the men who not a week later denied their leader. Justin McCarthy, that amiable lion of literary drawing-rooms, came especially to Dublin in order to inform his colleagues of the chivalrous and generous motives which had dictated their leader's silence in the divorce court; Tim Healy rose from a bed of sickness to assert in his high, passionate voice his unswerving devotion to his chief; but there was many a man present who knew that Tim's loyalty was but skin deep, and that only Gladstone's silence led him to declare that "Mr. Parnell was less a man than an institution." The bitter hostility that he was to show in Committee Room 15 was charged with the accumulated envy and resentment of years. Even the brave words of the Lord Mayor "that they had no more right to question Mr. Parnell's private actions and motives than they had to interfere with him as a Protestant if he chose not to go to church on Sunday or eat meat on Friday" were of no avail before the judgment of Hawarden.

The scene shifts back to England, where during the week-end the Liberal leaders were led to believe that, out of consideration for Mr. Gladstone, Parnell was contemplating a temporary retirement. After many fruitless attempts to force a meeting with "the errant chief," Morley had finally to be satisfied with the assurances of his secretary, Mr. Campbell, who promised to procure him an interview before Tuesday's opening of Parliament. The rumor of Parnell's retirement was utterly unfounded. In his proud, lonely way the Irish leader took no one into his confidence, and not even his old friend and colleague, McCarthy, dared to penetrate the precincts of Walsingham Terrace. The only advice he sought was that of an overwrought, unbalanced woman, who, in an obviously feminine reaction, told him to fight to the end. Maybe the rumor is true which says that it was due to the tantrums of Mrs. O'Shea that Parnell never received Gladstone's famous ultimatum.

On Monday afternoon the Liberal leaders met at a house in Carlton Gardens. In reviewing the situation, Harcourt had come round to the opinion that Parnell should be told to go without any *égards* and without waiting for any spontaneous action on his part. He particularly stressed the fact that Gladstone should express his condemnation on moral rather than on political grounds, but here the old leader contradicted him with flashing eyes. "What! Because a man is what is called leader of a party, does that constitute him a censor and a judge of faith and morals? I will not accept it. It would make life intolerable." Morley was inclined to be conciliatory; he realized that Parnell would have to be sacrificed for the sake of Home Rule, but he wanted it to be done as gently and as tactfully as possible. While the English politicians were calmly deposing the Irish leader, McCarthy was waiting for their verdict. As the vice-chairman of the party he had been forced into the center of the conflict. Labouchere, that indefatigable wire-puller who only a few days before had defended Parnell in the columns of his paper, had approached him over the week-end with a message from Morley and Harcourt as to whether a letter from Gladstone advising Parnell to renounce his leadership would make any impression. This had been followed by a request from Mr. Gladstone bidding him to meet him on his return to town.

The "momentous interview" was at hand, and there was nothing harsh or dictatorial about the way in which the Liberal leader gave McCarthy to understand that, in spite of Parnell's splendid and unrivaled services, his remaining at the head of his party would mean the loss of the next elections and the indefinite postponement of Home Rule. On the contrary, he spoke sadly, as if he realized the pain he was inflicting on Parnell's old and trusted friend, and he left this friend the thankless task of conveying his views to the Irish leader. At least, that is what McCarthy understood. He was never told of the letter that Gladstone had decided to write to Morley on the understanding that it was to be shown to Parnell, and he certainly was never told that his friend should be asked to resign. When Morley, meeting McCarthy a little later, said, "I suppose you are acquainted with Mr. Gladstone's views," the latter never realized that he was referring to an ultimatum. That Gladstone himself had not yet decided on that ultimatum has been proved in Morley's *Recollections,* when he recounts the story of how, that same evening, his chief handed him the draft of the famous letter in the middle of a dinner-party attended by the members of the Cabinet of 1886, a letter in which there was no mention of "the very thing that would be most likely of all things to move Parnell." It was only at the dictation of his followers that Mr. Gladstone went to the writing-table and inserted the all-important phrase to the effect that the continuance of Parnell's leadership "would not only place many hearty and effective friends of the Irish cause in a position of great embarrassment, but would render my retention of the leadership of the Liberal party, based, as it has been, mainly upon the prosecution of the Irish cause, almost a nullity"—a phrase which he himself thought should only be added as a postscript, until Morley remarked, "Just imagine! 'P.S. By the way, I forgot to mention that, if he does not go, my leadership of the Liberal party is reduced to a nullity.' What a postscript to be sure." And what in Mr. Gladstone's eyes was merely an afterthought was transformed into an edict of excommunication. Such was the beginning of what William O'Brien has called "the Parnell tragedy of errors." Neither McCarthy nor Morley succeeded in finding the Irish leader, though there is good reason to believe that Mr. Gladstone's letter was received at Brighton and destroyed by a woman indignant at the hypocrisy of the men who for the last ten years had known of the relations between her and Parnell.

At two o'clock of November 25th the Irish members met in Committee Room 15 to reelect Parnell as chairman of the party. Up to the very last moment the chief had remained invisible— an art in which he was a past master. Well aware that Justin McCarthy, and in all probability John Morley, were both waiting for him in the lobbies, he came into the House of Commons by a back entrance and went straight to the committee room accompanied by his private secretary. Poor McCarthy, flustered and perturbed and quite unfitted to cope with the situation, was now only able to give him the briefest outline of Mr. Gladstone's message; a message of which he did not take the slightest notice. Cool and unembarrassed, gracious and condescending, he took his place as leader of the party, and in the midst of a stirring ovation he was reelected by men who, with the exception of McCarthy, knew nothing of the Liberal thunders gathering in the background. Only one obscure member, a blunt-spoken Ulsterman, begged him to retire for the sake of his cause, much in the same way as Biggar might have spoken if he had not died six months before. Prompted by a warm feeling of gratitude towards these men who had so spontaneously given him their confidence, Parnell for the first and last time spoke in his own defense. "With regard to the divorce proceedings," he said, "I am accused of breaking up a happy home and of shattering a scene of domestic bliss and felicity. If the case had been gone into, and a calculation had been made, it would have been proved that in the twenty-three years of Mr. O'Shea's married life he spent only four hundred days in his own home. This was the happy home which I am alleged to have destroyed. I am also accused of betraying a friend. Mr. O'Shea was never my friend. Since I first met him in Ennis in 1880 he was always my enemy—my bitter and relentless enemy. There is a further charge against me that I abused this man's hospitality, but I never partook at any time of Mr. O'Shea's hospitality, for I never had bite or sup—never had a glass of wine at his expense. . . . Now that I have lifted a corner of the curtain, I will ask you gentlemen to keep your lips sealed, as mine are, on what you have heard until the brief period of time will have elapsed when I can vindicate myself and when you will find that your trust in me has not been misplaced."

But Parnell forgot that he was addressing himself to men the majority of whom were austere and intensely religious Catholics, living in humble circumstances, with very little sympathy or understanding for human weakness. His defense of his conduct only reminded these men that in supporting his leadership they were acting against the dictates of their conscience. Silently and gloomily they filed out of Committee Room 15, only to be greeted by dismayed Liberals crying out, "You have done a nice thing to have reelected Parnell after Gladstone's letter," when not one of them knew what Gladstone's letter was.

It was then that the pandemonium began. Some of the very men who had been chiefly responsible for Parnell's reelection now declared that they had only voted for him on the understanding that he would abdicate of his own accord, so frightened were they at the prospect of being cast out into the wilderness by their Liberal allies. As for the Liberals, they were almost worse than the Irish. "Our men were mad, frantic, cursing, crying, the whole place in an uproar. A terrible scene which I could not stand," wrote Lewis Harcourt to his mother. His father was foremost in the fray, bludgeoning the unfortunate Nationalists who all unwittingly had disobeyed Mr. Gladstone's decree, which was now being rushed into print, to be published in the evening papers for all the world to read. It was a day of misunderstanding, with tragic consequences. Parnell met Morley in the lobby, graciously excusing himself for having been prevented from making a previous appointment, and, as they strolled along the corridors towards Mr. Gladstone's room, he told him quite casually that he had just been reelected as chairman of the party. In Gladstone's untenanted room Morley now read to him the famous letter, only to find that it made not the slightest impression on him. The days of the "Union of Hearts" were numbered, and the Irish leader was once more icily indif-

ferent to the opinion of his English allies. Loftily he asserted
that the feeling against him "was but a storm in a tea-cup, and
would soon pass," drily adding that he had to look to the future;
that if he once let the leadership go it was all over. When he
left the room he gave one "wintry smile," saying, "Of course,
Mr. Gladstone will have to attack me. I shall expect that. He
will have a right to do that." And later, when he heard that in
a moment of unreasoning anger the Liberal leader had decided
to publish the letter in the Press, he said, "I think Mr. Gladstone
will be quite right to do that. It will put him straight with his
party." Then he went quietly off to enjoy a cigar and cup of
tea with Henry Campbell, seemingly oblivious of the very circumstances which were distracting his unfortunate colleagues,
for the lobbies and corridors were crowded with frantic, gesticulating Irishmen who for the first time were unable to seek the
advice of the chief on whom they had always depended. To
men like Sexton and McCarthy, who formed the solid backbone
of the party, Gladstone's ultimatum left them no choice but to
choose between Ireland and Parnell, for in their eyes a rupture
with the Liberals spelt irremediable disaster for their country.
Unfortunately, their opinion was echoed by those who were
ready to seize on any pretext in order to dethrone a hitherto in-
vincible leader. On the other side were the men who refused to
submit to English dictation, who, having condoned Parnell's
moral offense, saw no reason why they should throw him over
on political grounds, and among them were those who worshiped
him both as man and as the leader essential to their cause. But
they were not the majority, and the majority now clamored for
another meeting where Parnell would be given the chance to
abdicate in favor of McCarthy. Thus started the proceedings of
Committee Room 15, which began on a note of impassioned
appeal gradually degenerating into a series of squalid wrangles,
while the Liberals looked on and sneered "at the Irishmen upstairs fighting like Kilkenny cats and coming out at intervals to
have drinks all round."

Healy, who was to play a fatal rôle in the discussions of Committee Room 15, was too ill to attend the first meeting, to which Parnell arrived looking so disdainful and aloof that a wit remarked "he looked as if it was we who had committed adultery with his wife." Not a word did he utter while his supporters and opponents delivered eloquent speeches for and against the retention of his leadership, and when the meeting was adjourned till the following Monday, so that time might be given for obtaining the views of the absent members, he closed the proceedings by simply leaving the chair. When he returned to Brighton that evening, he took Katie in his arms, saying, "I think we shall have to fight, Queenie. Can you bear it? I am afraid it is going to be tough work. . . . I am feeling very ill, but I think I shall win through. I shall never give in unless you make me, and I want you to promise me that you will never make me less than the man you have known."

It was in this mood that he composed the manifesto to the people of Ireland which proved to be the death-warrant to his political career, a manifesto which led Cardinal Manning to write to Gladstone: "Mr. Parnell's conduct is that of an unsound mind. It has recalled to me Sir Henry Parnell, who made an end of himself when we were very young. If Parnell goes to Ireland, the issue will be between dangerous politics and the faith of Ireland." It meant a return to the old struggle between the Fenians and the priests, when, at the instigation of the English cardinal, the Irish hierarchy launched a proclamation against the Protestant "adulterer" three weeks after the verdict of the divorce courts. In all fairness one must admit that Parnell's manifesto gave them every opportunity to declare against him. When the Irish leader read it aloud at a meeting of his most trusted colleagues on that memorable evening of November 28th, Justin McCarthy, his voice broken with emotion, made only one comment: "I disapprove of every word of it"; for it was not the manifesto of a calm, reasoned politician, it was that of a man fighting for his life against overwhelming odds, regardless of scruples, regardless of pledges, exposing the tactics of the Liberal leaders in order to show his people that they were to be cheated out of a full measure of Home Rule by those English politicians whom during the last four years they had been taught to regard as their liberators; exposing the secrets of Hawarden, the confidences of Morley, exposing "the measure of the loss with which you are threatened unless you consent to throw me to the English wolves now howling for my destruction." How could he hope to reconcile the most wavering opponent when he wrote, "The integrity and independence of a section of the Irish party having been sapped and destroyed by the wire-pullers of the English Liberal party, it has become necessary for me, as the leader of the Irish nation, to take counsel with you, and, having given you the knowledge which is in my possession, to ask your judgment upon a matter which now solely devolves upon you to decide"? It was with a heavy heart that McCarthy parted from his beloved chief, who in one of his rare moments of tenderness now said to him, "Well, happen what will, you and I are always friends. God bless you, my dear old friend." And, after all the bitterness of Committee Room 15, in the midst of the horrors of the civil war, McCarthy and Parnell were still to cling to the tattered remnants of their old friendship.

It was with a heavy heart that O'Brien and Dillon now signed a public manifesto throwing over their old leader, and, though they ranged themselves on the side of the seceders, it was they who were to be responsible for the good intentions of the Boulogne negotiations which ended in such lamentable failure. Of the delegates in America, Harrington was the only one who remained true to his chief, and he tells of how, when he was leaving his hotel in New York to rejoin Parnell in Ireland, "the servants, almost all Irish boys and girls, gathered in the hall, or on the stairs, or in the passages, and as I came away all cried out in voices broken with emotion, 'Mr. Harrington, don't desert him. Don't give him up.'" For the Parnellite split had not

only brought chaos to Ireland; it had spread gloom and dismay
in the hearts of all the Irish exiles scattered through America
and Australia. The proceedings of Committee Room 15 flashed
across a thousand wires to the four corners of the world, where
men took sides as fiercely as if they were participating in the
struggle at St. Stephen's.

Parnell had voiced his defiance of Gladstone, and the Parnellite
split threatened the disintegration of Liberal hopes. A Tory
victory at a by-election was an ominous forecast of how the
winds might blow at the next General Election. Small wonder
if the Unionists stood by and smiled, while Lord Salisbury said
in his jeering way, "Kitty O'Shea deserves to have a monument
raised to her in every town in England." Chamberlain may well
have thought that O'Shea had served his purpose after all when
Sir Edward Clarke confessed to David Plunkett, "I knew I was
throwing a bombshell into the Irish camp, but I did not know
it would do quite so much mischief," whereupon the Irish Tory
replied, "Oh, you did not know that when it burst they would
pick up the pieces and cut each other's throats with them." It
was imperative for the Liberal party to get rid of Parnell as
quickly as possible. Gladstone enlisted all his forces. From
Labouchere to Cardinal Manning they were all working for the
destruction of the Irish leader, and yet at certain moments in
Committee Room 15 it almost seemed as if Parnell would triumph after all, in spite of the bitterness of Healy, in spite of the
antagonism of John Barry, "the leader-killer who sharpens his
poignard to stab me as he stabbed the old lion Isaac Butt in the
days gone by."

His self-control was almost superhuman. There he sat presiding over a gathering of men, the majority of whom were in
favor of his deposition, and yet he could still put the questions
in a calm, unemotional voice, he could still exchange a friendly
joke with Sexton or McCarthy. It was only when Healy rose to
speak in favor of his resignation that his face contracted in
anger; Healy, who dared to say that for the last years he had

been maintained by his parliamentary colleagues, who dared to assert that his power was gone, that he was like an iron bar bereft of its magnetism and electric action! Proudly Parnell turned to answer the little Bantry clerk whom he "had raised from the gutter" and said, "Mr. Healy has been trained in this warfare, and who trained him? Who saw his genius? Who telegraphed to him from America to come to him? Who gave him his first opportunity and chance? . . . That Mr. Healy is here to destroy me is due to myself." He was now at bay, challenging these men whose careers he had made, whose qualities he had been the first to recognize, whom with patience and with foresight he had molded into a first-class fighting team, a team which would be lost without a leader. Bitterly he asked, "Why did you encourage me to come forward and maintain my leadership in the face of the world if you were not going to stand by me?" But there was a note of genuine sorrow in his voice when he added, "I want to ask you, before you vote my deposition, to be sure that you are getting value for it, for if I am to leave you, I should like to leave you in security."

Well might John Redmond say, "We are asked to sell our leader to preserve the English alliance. It seems to me that we are bound to enquire what we are getting for the price we are paying." And in these words Parnell saw his great opportunity. To maneuver the debate so as to center it round Gladstone's position instead of his own, to force the seceders to obtain definite assurances from the Liberal leaders, assurances which he well knew would never be forthcoming, and thus to estrange the Irish party from their English allies, to gain time and strengthen his position in Ireland, were all the tactics of a brilliant strategist. "Don't sell me for nothing," he cried. "If you get my value you may change me to-morrow"; for he promised that if Gladstone, Morley, and Harcourt committed themselves to some definite information on the vital questions of the constabulary and the land, then he himself would be perfectly willing to retire. It sounded a fair enough proposal, and the majority of the party were just children in his hands. On December 3rd the Liberals heard with indignation that even Healy and Sexton had consented to the idea of an Irish delegation to be sent to Mr. Gladstone. As if Mr. Gladstone would allow himself to be caught in Parnell's rat-trap, as if he would disclose the secrets of the next Home Rule Bill to men who had not yet had the courage to depose the man who in his manifesto had violated every trust and confidence! "It is a very dangerous thing to approach an expiring cat," wrote Harcourt in a moment of panic. But the Grand Old Man had no intention of running any risk. He received the delegation frigidly, telling them with firm politeness that he would only renew relations once they had settled the question of the leadership. Secure in the alliance of Cardinal Manning, he declined to make the slightest concession, and it was the bishop's manifesto of December 3rd which sealed Parnell's doom.

Gradually it dawned on the seceders that Parnell was only playing for time; that every resolution put forward by his followers was merely another attempt to confuse the issues, to carry the battle from Westminster to Dublin, where the people were Parnellite to the core. And the last hours of Committee Room 15 were seared by bitter words and unforgivable insults. All decency and restraint were thrown to the wind, and so coarse and violent was the vituperation of Barry and Healy that some of the younger Liberals such as Asquith, Haldane, Grey, and Buxton felt very genuine compassion at "the spectacle of a man of infinite boldness, determination, astuteness, and resource, with the will and pride of Lucifer, at bay with fortune and challenging a malignant star."

Could any Irishmen present in that room ever forget the moment when, in defense of his chief, John Redmond declared that the seceders had chosen Gladstone as the master of the party, only to be interrupted by the snarling voice of Tim Healy, "And who is to be the mistress of the party?" It was then that Parnell lost all control. With a face contracted in fury and a demoniacal look in his eyes, he turned to Healy as if he were about to strike. So obvious was his intention that a few of Healy's friends clustered round to defend him, and, in the hopes of relieving the tension, one man stood up to speak. "I appeal to my friend the chairman," he began, when the chief cried out in a voice vibrating from the quivering of his nerves: "Better appeal to your own friends, better appeal to that cowardly little scoundrel there who dares in an assembly of Irishmen to insult a woman"; and as he spoke there was hardly a man in the room who would not gladly have struck Tim Healy down. It was then that McCarthy rose, and, with tears in his eyes, declared that he saw no further use in carrying on a discussion which must be barren of all but reproach, ill temper, controversy, and indignity. He therefore suggested that all who thought with him at this grave crisis should withdraw with him from the room, and forty-four men silently arose and followed their new leader. Twenty-six men remained in their seats—twenty-six men who had pledged themselves to fight under Parnell's standard in defiance of outraged morality and the dictation of English politicians. And now of one accord they turned to cheer their leader, who sat staring straight in front of him with wide, fixed, unseeing eyes— eyes that saw only the ruin of a great party. Bravely he rose to answer the cheers and bravely he spoke: "Gentlemen, we have won the day. Although our ranks are reduced in number, I hold this chair still. Although many of those who were our comrades have left us, Ireland has power to fill our ranks again, Ireland has power to send us a good man and a true for every one of those who have left us, and I little know our gallant country if I am mistaken in the opinion that when she gets the opportunity she will freely exercise that power."

Three days later he was in Dublin, acclaimed by the multitudes, driving through the streets at the head of a torchlight procession, addressing a great meeting in the Rotunda, speaking simply and directly to a "sea of passionate faces, loving, admiring, almost worshiping him"—so wrote Katherine Tynan, who was among the worshipers, and Parnell may well have thought that evening that victory was still within his grasp. He relied on Dublin. "Dublin is true. What Dublin says to-day Ireland will say to-morrow."

EPILOGUE

It was nine months later, on a wild autumn day at Creggs, with the rain drifting in swollen clouds over the bogs and stone walls of Roscommon, drifting over the gray slate roofs of the town, pouring down the gutters in the market-place, where a wooden platform had been erected in the open in preparation for Parnell. They came crowding to hear him speak, the young men and stalwart Fenians—the "hillside men," as Healy so sneeringly called them, all wearing an ivy-leaf as symbol of their adherence to the chief. They came regardless of their parents' wrath and of the denunciation of the priests; regardless of the mob of Healyites and Davittites screaming their obscene songs of Kitty O'Shea through the length and breadth of the country; regardless that they were fighting for a losing cause.

Ireland was seamed and torn with all the corroding bitterness of civil war. It was the Fenians against the priests, and how could the God-fearing Irish peasants defy the dictums of their Church? Parnell was the last to blame them; he never felt any bitterness against those people who, after worshiping him as a superman, now hounded him down. The woman who in the streets of Ennis had turned on him with tears, crying, "May God forgive you, Mr. Parnell; you've broken my heart," was only one of the thousands who still expected their leaders to be as pure in mind and body as were their kings of old. He bore all the indignities and insults with a patience that was terrible to behold; in the streets of Arklow, an old fishwife had spat upon him as an "adulterer"; at Castlecomer the miners had bespattered him with lime; and at the hustings of Kilkenny they had flaunted a woman's shift as "the banner of Kitty O'Shea." That is what hurt him most, this filthy abuse which they hurled at the woman he loved.

At the beginning there had been a certain fierce exultation in the fray. Free of all considerations and bereft of caution, he had set out to fight his own battle backed by the Fenians, who had always been the first to rally to his standard. That day in Dublin when he had stormed the offices of *United Ireland*— which had gone over to the enemy—thrown the editor out of doors, and established his rule by force, had been among the first glorious days of the campaign. But then came the by-election of Kilkenny and the defeat of his candidate at the polls, where the priests themselves acted as personation agents while Healy stung him with his poisoned barbs. And after Kilkenny came Sligo and Carlow, a series of humiliating failures, while he battled with unflagging energy, so determined to win that his exhausted frame seemed to gather a superhuman strength. The whole countryside was against him, and even the support of the townspeople was of no avail before the verdict of the "mud-cabin vote."

Week after week he traveled from Brighton to Ireland, week after week he addressed vast, clamorous crowds, who in their mad excitement dragged him down to their level. That was the worst—to see Parnell, the proud, the fastidious, who till now had always been so sublimely indifferent of his audiences, indulging in vituperation, shouting himself hoarse with passion in order to gain the applause of a mob of corner-boys and village blades. "Who is against me?" he cried. "That jackdaw Davitt; Dillon, that melancholy humbug; and Healy, the man I raised from the gutter." But never a word did he utter against the priests, who in the name of chastity encouraged his opponents to strike him the foulest blows.

There was a time when it almost seemed as if his star would rise again. Dillon and O'Brien had returned from America disgusted at the way in which their colleagues were conducting the campaign. Still liable to arrest if he set foot in Ireland, O'Brien now asked Parnell to meet him at Boulogne in order to discuss the possibilities of peace. Certain incidents at Kilkenny were hard to forget, and Parnell was in no mood to negotiate. It was only at the urging of his colleagues that he consented to travel to France, though, once there, he conducted the maneuvers in such a masterly way as to divide the ranks of the anti-Parnellites and to involve the Liberals in fresh difficulties with their Irish allies. He almost succeeded; he had almost captured O'Brien if Dillon had not arrived on the scene and with a few thoughtless words banished all hopes of compromise. Parnell's nerves were still too sensitive and raw, the insults of the hustings were too recent for him to remember that these men were acting in his interests. The negotiations were broken off and the Liberals breathed again, for, as McCarthy wrote: "Gladstone had taken fright at the shadow of Parnell in the background."

His presence still haunted the House of Commons, where Parnellites and anti-Parnellites sat side by side hardly exchanging a friendly word. He who had so rarely visited Westminster when he was the leader of a powerful party now took part in debates at times when he had not a single colleague to support him. Small wonder if his adherents avoided the hostile atmosphere of the House, where, possessed by some driving fury, Tim Healy and his brother were determined to hunt their quarry down. "Let him resign from his constituency of Cork, let him come up for reelection and prove that he represents the feeling of the people." Such was their challenge, delivered to the accompaniment of Liberal cheers, while the object of their loathing and derision sat still with folded arms and hat drawn low over his eyes, appearing, as an eye-witness records, "to be beyond the provocation of hate."

It was only in Dublin that Parnell still commanded the adoration of the masses, in Dublin where Healy hardly dared to walk through the streets for fear of being lynched by the angry mob. After the humiliating defeats in the country, the lukewarm demonstrations by the roadside, Parnell would seek refuge in the capital. Haunted and obsessed by the fear of ultimate failure, worn out in health and nerves, he clung to the company of the few men whom he still could call his friends, dragging them the round of music-halls and oyster-shops, keeping them up till the early hours of the morning, talking as he had never done before merely in order to escape from his own gloomy thoughts.

Yet even in these last months he had his hours of happiness. There was that lovely day in June when he married Katherine O'Shea in a little Sussex registry office, a marriage which brought him the defection of the *Freeman's Journal,* which redoubled the prosecution of the priests and which cost him the friendship of O'Kelly, the one member of his party to whom he was genuinely devoted. Now he knew how bitter was the hatred of his friends against the woman who had brought about his ruin. Did he still believe that he could bring her back to Avondale as his bride, to live in a country where the passing of nearly fifty years has not yet removed the stigma from her name, or were his plans of the future just hopeless day-dreams which he knew would never materialize?

The end was near. When he mounted the platform at Creggs to speak bareheaded in the pouring rain, he was already in the last stages of exhaustion. Crippled with rheumatism, he carried his right arm in a sling and he was in such obvious pain that at the beginning he found the greatest difficulty in enunciating his words. Gradually he seemed to gather strength from the lusty cheering of his audience. "If I had taken the advice of my doctor," he told them, "I should have gone to bed when I arrived in Dublin, but if I had done that my enemies would be throwing up their hats and announcing that I was dead before I was buried." They never knew of the loneliness of his campaign, of his pathetic message to John Redmond begging him to accompany him to the West, a message which his chief lieutenant chose to ignore. Redmond was still faithful; it was only his caution and his prudence which made him unwilling to defy the priests on the open platform. Time after time he had advised his chief not to flout public opinion, to wait quietly till the storm had blown over and then to consolidate his position. But this was not a moment for clear-headed logic; he was dealing with a sick and desperate man, and how could he have allowed him to make that long, dreary journey utterly alone except for the company of two friendly reporters of Opposition newspapers —a journey where, owing to some casual oversight, he was forced to remain for hours in his rain-sodden clothes patiently listening to the endless orations of village patriots?

When Parnell returned to Dublin, he was a dying man suffering from acute rheumatism. For three days he stayed at Dr. Kenny's house, obsessed by the idea that there was still work to be done, matters to be settled with regard to his new paper, the *Irish Independent*. He refused to retire to bed, and even at night he would lie on the drawing-room sofa, talking in hopeful terms about the future, trying to derive some confidence from his own words. He was still at bay, refusing to admit defeat even in this struggle for a life where he had known so little peace.

On the evening of September 30th, he left Ireland for the last time. It was useless of Dr. Kenny to insist that he was still too ill to travel, for now he had only one longing—to return to Katie, who was always so comforting and reassuring about his health, and who might still be able to cure him of this terrible pain.

An hour before sailing he appeared on the balcony of the doctor's house in Rutland Square to address a small crowd gathered below, and it was only Dr. Kenny and this straggling group of casual passers-by who heard him promise to come back "next Saturday week"—a promise he was to keep even in death. A week later he fell asleep for the last time in the arms of the woman for whose sake he had sacrificed both himself and his cause. Early on the morning of October 7th, 1891, the world learnt that Parnell was dead.

They brought him back to Ireland on a stormy, raging sea, and the fury of the elements was reflected in the wild grief of the people who gathered round his bier. They came in tens of thousands from every corner of the country to pluck an ivy-leaf from his coffin as it lay in state in City Hall and to whisper one last prayer beside his grave. To the sound of muffled drums and the wailing of old Gaelic laments they bore him to rest at Glasnevin, and for an hour the voice of controversy was hushed, the demons of civil war stood by as United Ireland mourned her chief.

BIBLIOGRAPHY

ANDERSON, DAVID. *Scenes in the Commons.*

BLUNT, WILFRID SCAWEN. *My Diaries.*

BLUNT, WILFRID SCAWEN. *The Land War in Ireland.*

BRYCE, Rt. Hon. JAMES. *Studies in Contemporary Biography.*

BUTLER, Sir WILLIAM. *The Light of the West.*

CAREW, JAMES. "My Captain and my Friend" (*Irish Weekly Independent,* October 7th, 1893).

CHURCHILL, Rt. Hon. WINSTON. *Lord Randolph Churchill* (2 vols.).

CLARKE, Sir EDWARD. *Story of My Life.*

Daily Graphic. "A Sketch-Biography of Parnell."

Dana, The. 1905.

DAVITT, MICHAEL. *The Fall of Feudalism in Ireland.*

DICKINSON, EMILY. *A Patriot's Mistake.*

Dictionary of National Biography.

Dillon Papers.

DUFFY, Sir CHARLES GAVAN. *Young Ireland.*

ERVINE, ST. JOHN. *Parnell.*

EVERSLEY, Lord. *Gladstone and Ireland.*

FILON, AUGUSTIN. *Profiles Anglais.*

Freeman's Journal. January 1880; February 1880; November 1890; December, 1890.

GARDINER, A. G. *The Life of Sir William Harcourt* (Vols. I and II).

GARVIN, J. L. *Joseph Chamberlain* (Vols. I and II).

GARVIN, J. L. "Parnell and his Power" (*Fortnightly Review,* December 1898).

GLADSTONE, MARY. *Diaries.*

Gladstone Papers.

GWYNN, DENIS. *The Life of John Redmond.*

GWYNN, DENIS. *The O'Gorman Mahon.*

GWYNN, STEPHEN, in collaboration with Miss TUCKWELL. *The Life of Sir Charles Dilke.*

Hansard. February 1881; January 1881; May 1882; February 1883; May 1886; April 1887; July 1888.

HARDINGE, Rt. Hon. Sir ARTHUR. *The Fourth Earl of Carnarvon.*

HARRISON, HENRY. *Parnell Vindicated.*

HEALY, T. M. *Letters and Leaders of My Day* (2 vols.).

JOHNSTON, R. *Parnell and the Parnells.*

LECKY. *History of Ireland in the Eighteenth Century* (5 vols.).

LESLIE, SHANE. *Henry Edward Manning.*

LESLIE, SHANE. *Studies in Sublime Failure.*

LOCKER-LAMPSON, The Rt. Hon. GODFREY. *A Consideration of the State of Ireland in the Nineteenth Century.*

LUCY, Sir HENRY. *Diary of Two Parliaments.*

LUCY, Sir HENRY. *Diary of the Salisbury Parliament.*

LUCY, Sir HENRY. *Sixty Years in the Wilderness.*

McCARTHY, JUSTIN. *History of Our Own Times.*

McCARTHY, JUSTIN. *Our Book of Memories* (in collaboration with Mrs. CAMPBELL PRAED).

McCARTHY, JUSTIN. *Reminiscences.*

McCARTHY, JUSTIN. *The Story of an Irishman.*

MACDONAGH, MICHAEL. *The Home Rule Movement.*

MORLEY, VISCOUNT. *Life of Gladstone.*

MORLEY, VISCOUNT. *Recollections.*

MOORE, GEORGE. *Parnell and his Island.*

O'BRIEN, BARRY. *Life of Lord Russell of Killowen.*

O'BRIEN, BARRY. *Life of Parnell* (2 vols.).

O'BRIEN, WILLIAM. *An Olive Branch in Ireland, and its History.*

O'BRIEN, WILLIAM. *Evening Memories.*

O'BRIEN, WILLIAM. *Recollections.*

O'BRIEN, WILLIAM. *The Parnell of Real Life.*

O'CONNOR, T. P. *Parnell.*

O'CONNOR, T. P. *The Parnell Movement.*

O'DONNELL, FRANK HUGH. *The Irish Parliamentary Party* (2 vols.).

O'DONNELL, FRANK HUGH. *The Lost Hat, the Fallen Idol, or the Fate of the Uncrowned King.*

O'FLAHERTY, LIAM. *Tim Healy.*

O'HARA, M. *Chief and Tribune, Parnell and Davitt.*

O'ROURKE, The Rev. J. *History of the Great Irish Famine.*

O'SHEA, KATHERINE. *Charles Stewart Parnell* (2 vols.). (His love story and political life.)

OXFORD AND ASQUITH, The Earl of. *Fifty Years of Parliament.*

Pall Mall Budget. Extra "Home Rule" number, 1886; extra "O'Shea Divorce" number, 1891; ordinary number, November 20th, 1890.

PARNELL, JOHN HOWARD. *Life of Parnell.*

Parnellite Split, The, reprinted from *The Times.*

Punch. April-May 1886; November-December 1890.

REID, WEMYSS. *Life of the Rt. Hon. W. E. Forster* (Vol. II).

RHODES, JAMES FORD. *History of the United States* (Vol. VI).

ROBBINS, Sir ALFRED. *Parnell, the Last Five Years.*

SALA, GEORGE AUGUSTUS. *His Life and Adventures.*

SHERLOCK, THOMAS. *The Life of Charles Stewart Parnell, with some account of his Ancestry.*

SULLIVAN, A. M. *New Ireland.*

SULLIVAN, T. D. *Troubled Times in Irish Politics.*

The Times. "Parnellism and Crime," Special Commission Reports.

THOROLD, ALGAR. *The Life of Labouchere.*

TYNAN, P. J. *The Irish National Invincibles and their Times.*

WEST, Sir ALGERNON. *Private Diaries of.*

WYSE POWER, Senator. *Words of the Dead Chief.*

YEATS, W. B. *Autobiographies.*

INDEX

ABERDEEN, LORD, 303, 360
ADDISON, JOSEPH, 1
Agrarian question, 80-1, 85, 93-4, 99-100, 266, 311
Agriculture, Irish, landlords and tenants, 4-5, 39-40
American Land League, 113
Amnesty Movement, 39
ARGYLL, DUKE OF, 148
Arms Bill, 1881, 184-5
Army Regulation Bill, 91
Arrears Bill, 234, 238
ASQUITH, H. H. (EARL OF OXFORD AND ASQUITH), 345, 358-60, 370, 386
Australia, convict settlements, 8
Avondale, 1, 31, 69-70, 157-8, 200, 225, 252

BALFOUR, ARTHUR JAMES (LORD BALFOUR), 148, 287, 328, 332, 336, 357
BALMECEDA, dictator of Chile, 182
BARRY, JOHN (M.P.), 52, 53, 62, 68, 72, 77, 79, 120, 122, 203, 384
BEACH, alias LE CARON, q.v.
BEACONSFIELD, LORD (BENJAMIN DISRAELI), 37, 45, 49, 52, 58, 63, 65, 81, 91, 115-16, 138, 148
BENNETT, GORDON, 106-7, 110
BESSBOROUGH, LORD, 162
BIGGAR, JOSEPH GILLES (M.P.), 48, 51, 58 et seq., 61-2, 66, 77, 91, 100, 112, 117-18, 123, 139, 147, 155, 165, 182-4, 187-8, 196, 210, 230, 242, 291, 296 et seq., 355, 379
BIRRELL, AUGUSTINE, 358
BISMARCK, PRINCE, 42, 291
BLENNERHASSETT, SIR ROWLAND, 42, 334
BLUNT, WILFRID SCAWEN, 193, 261, 291, 314, 316, 333, 337, 357, 365-6
BOYCOTT, CAPT., 141-2
BRADFORD, LADY, 58
BRADLAUGH, CHARLES, 149, 164

BRENNAN, THOMAS, 99-102, 119, 147, 188, 209, 237
BRIGHT, JOHN, 28, 91, 148, 161, 164, 185, 247, 308
BROWN, GEORGE, 119
BUCKLE, of The Times, 322, 344
BURKE, MR., Permanent Under-Secretary for Ireland, murdered, 1882, 228, 230, 329
BUTT, ISAAC (M.P.), 23 et seq., 40, 42, 46, 49, 51-2, 58 et seq., 65, 67, 71-2, 84-5, 90, 155, 186, 190, 204, 253, 384
BUXTON, SYDNEY (LORD BUXTON), 358-60, 386
BYRNE, FRANK, 219-20, 246, 341

CALLAN, PHILIP, 335, 340
CALLIGY, MICKY, 219, 219 n
CAMPBELL, HENRY, 254, 282, 332, 376, 381
"Captain Moonlight," 87, 87 n, 100, 205, 208, 215
CAREY, JAMES, 245
CARLISLE, LORD, 20
CARNARVON, LORD, 275-89
CARROLL, DR., 78 et seq., 81, 118, 139
CASHEL, ARCHBISHOP OF, see Croke
CASTLEREAGH, LORD, 29, 54
Catholic emancipation, 1, 63, 302
CAVENDISH, LORD FREDERICK, 227-34, 245, 329
CAVOUR, CAMILLO, 291
CHAMBERLAIN, JOSEPH, 91-3, 148, 161, 185, 202, 216-18, 221, 224, 226-7, 231-6, 246-7, 259-60, 266-72, 276-84, 289-95, 302-10, 321, 327-8, 334-5, 342-50, 363, 384
CHAMBERS, CORPORAL, 71
CHARLEMONT, EARL OF, 88
Chester Castle, 27, 32
Chicago Convention, 1886, 311
CHILDERS, HUGH, 273
Chipping Norton, 17-18

399